"*Washington State Politics and Government* is more than just informative and illuminating: it's a flat-out good read. Even if you consider yourself well versed in Washington politics, government, and history, you'll likely learn something new and undoubtedly be entertained. Meticulously researched and engagingly presented, this should be on the bookshelf of every Washington student, politician, and voter."
—**Cheryl Reid-Simons**, Fife School Board director

"If you are seeking to restore your faith in the power of government to build a better society in these dark times of division, look no further than T. M. Sell's *Washington State Politics and Government*, an engaging, colorful, and hopeful illumination of the mechanics of Washington State's political world. For all of the state's tax and geographic tensions, T. M. Sell reinforces how lucky we are to live here."
—**Vicente Omar Barraza**, attorney for the First Homeowners Association

"*Washington State Politics and Government* provides detailed information every Washingtonian who wants to understand state politics and policy would benefit from. It delivers an entertaining and readable summary of how Washington State government was established, how it developed, and the nuances of our political culture, with a rich understanding of the state constitution and how law is created in Washington. Every person seeking to gain expertise in how Washington State government works needs to read it."
—**Paul Berendt**, former chair of the Washington State Democratic Party

"T. M. Sell provides an incredibly comprehensive description of the systems, structures, and people of Washington State government. *Washington State Politics and Government* includes aspects and details often missing from textbooks and overlooked by academics. Sell uses his wealth of experience to provide us with a thorough and complete accounting of how the wheels of democracy turn in Washington State. He brings the subject to life with personal stories, profiles, and an infectious passion for democracy."
—**Dave Upthegrove**, King County councilman

"At a time when the worst elected officials get the most attention, *Washington State Politics and Government* will educate and inspire the reader to believe that our collective ambitions for our community can be achieved through participation in government at every one of the many levels that exist. . . . What a refreshing and enlightening work."
—**Dan Satterberg**, King County prosecuting attorney (2007–22)

"I've known T. M. Sell my entire political career. This book is such a wonderful gift to all of us in Washington State and beyond at a time when we need to put partisan bickering and rhetoric-filled nonsense away. It's such a good reminder of how much great work can be done when we bring diverse ideas and voices together for the common good."
—**Mia Su-Ling Gregerson**, Washington State representative (D-SeaTac)

"This is a story about government, your government. It's also why access, ownership, and voice matter. It's why it's called the 'people's house' doing the 'people's business'—trying to make things better for everyone. The goal may be simple, but the process is not, which is why this book is such a great read and a great teaching tool."
—**Claire Wilson**, Washington State senator (D–Federal Way)

"T. M. Sell has written the consummate book on political life in Washington State. Though the book is based on empirical research and written by an academic, it is also the perfect book for those who are not experts on government but have a desire to be better informed. . . . Sell's voice is avuncular and reassuring though steeped in knowledge and research. Whether you are a college student, a member of government, or a just curious citizen, you should read this book and become a more knowledgeable and better citizen."
—**Jasper M. LiCalzi**, professor emeritus of political economy at the College of Idaho and author of *Idaho Politics and Government*

"This delightful text is a nod to some of the best of classic political science. . . . This text is useful to instructors beyond the Palouse and Columbia River, as it serves as a deep examination of Washington State politics as a case study nestled in the broader context of a federal United States. I'll happily assign it in my final year class on U.S. politics at my British university."
—**David Brockington**, lecturer in politics and social science methods at the University of Plymouth, UK

WASHINGTON STATE POLITICS AND GOVERNMENT

*Politics and Governments
of the American States*

Founding Editor
DANIEL J. ELAZAR

Published by the University of
Nebraska Press in association with the
Center for the Study of Federalism at
the Robert B. and Helen S. Meyner
Center for the Study of State and
Local Government, Lafayette College

Washington State Politics and Government

T. M. SELL

UNIVERSITY OF NEBRASKA PRESS

LINCOLN

© 2023 by T. M. Sell

All rights reserved

The University of Nebraska Press is part of a land-grant institution with campuses and programs on the past, present, and future homelands of the Pawnee, Ponca, Otoe-Missouria, Omaha, Dakota, Lakota, Kaw, Cheyenne, and Arapaho Peoples, as well as those of the relocated Ho-Chunk, Sac and Fox, and Iowa Peoples.

Library of Congress Cataloging-in-Publication Data
Names: Sell, T. M., author.
Title: Washington state politics and government / T. M. Sell.
Description: Lincoln: University of Nebraska Press, [2023] | Series: Politics and governments of the American states | Includes bibliographical references and index.
Identifiers: LCCN 2023003670
ISBN 9781496230669 (paperback)
ISBN 9781496237880 (epub)
ISBN 9781496237897 (pdf)
Subjects: LCSH: Local government—Washington (State) | Washington (State)—Politics and government. | BISAC: HISTORY / United States / State & Local / Pacific Northwest (OR, WA) | POLITICAL SCIENCE / History & Theory
Classification: LCC JK9216 .S45 2023 | DDC 320.809797—dc23/eng/20230520
LC record available at https://lccn.loc.gov/2023003670

Set in Minion Pro

For Sharon

CONTENTS

Preface, xi

Part I. The View from Above

ONE
Not-So-Mobile Homes: The Story of a Bill, 3

TWO
Overview: The Playing Field, 19

THREE
Federalism: States within the State, 29

FOUR
Rules of the Road: The Constitution, 37

Part II. Choosing Leaders, Chasing Policy

FIVE
How We Choose: Elections and Voting, 55

SIX
Initiatives and Referenda: Government by (Some of) the People, 69

SEVEN

Let's Party! Political Parties in
Washington State, 74

EIGHT

Interest Groups: The Politics of Power, 89

PART III. **State Government: Olympia and Beyond**

NINE

Where It Happens: The Legislature, 105

TEN

The Gang of Nine: The Executive Branch, 135

ELEVEN

All Rise: The Courts Are in Session, 154

TWELVE

Turning Policy into Practice: State Agencies
and What They Do, 169

THIRTEEN

Where It Comes from and Where It Goes:
The Budget and Taxes, 185

PART IV. **In Your Neighborhood: Local Governments**

FOURTEEN

County Government: Regions within
the State, 207

FIFTEEN

Cities: Police, Planning, Parks,
and Potholes, 240

SIXTEEN

Special Purpose Districts: Services
Where You Live, 253

SEVENTEEN

Tribal Governments: Nations within
the Nation, 282

EIGHTEEN

Jobs and Money: Economic
Development, 298

Epilogue: The People's Business, 336

Notes, 339

Bibliography, 353

Index, 355

Preface

This book has a point of view. That point is that government, while decidedly imperfect, is not a bad thing. And Washington State government, though not beyond criticism, actually works pretty well. You don't have to agree with this premise, but if I'm wrong—and I often am—try to figure out why.

I stress this because for the last forty years, candidates of all stripes have campaigned against the government while running for office. For some, this was a way of getting elected, but it poisoned the idea of government in the minds of many people. And many Americans, with only the dimmest notion of how anything works, don't take much prodding to believe any number of outlandish things. Granted, the Vietnam War, Watergate, and the odd scandal have tested people's faith in government, but that doesn't have to mean that the institution at its core is wrong. To me, it makes no sense to say, "The legislature is corrupt, except for our guy." If your guy or gal is okay, how is it that the other voters across the state are sending people to the state capital who are corrupt, inefficient, and ineffective? ("Corruption" has become the catch-all word for what we disagree with, much in the way that "socialism" was for an earlier generation.)

What seems more likely is that people from other parts of the state may have different priorities. We should remember that nearly everyone who ventures to work in government at any level goes there with the intent of trying to make things better. We may disagree with their priorities, but that doesn't make them bad people.

Many Americans appear to make questionable assumptions about their government. For example, twenty-first-century Americans seem to want all the services government can provide, and they want them for free. That simply isn't going to happen. None of us really like paying taxes, but taxes are the price of civilization. Washington's tax system has its strengths and weaknesses, and what it should or could be is a topic worthy of debate and about which reasonable people can disagree. If nothing else, it underscores one of the key elements to understanding government: everything involves trade-offs. Every policy choice represents choices foregone, and sometimes there's no perfect answer, just one we can live with. Maybe.

Meanwhile, too many people don't seem to know what their government does. In a survey in the late 2000s, 60 percent of the people who were getting assistance from the government didn't know it was coming from the government. It is this level of ignorance that gave us, during the debate over the Affordable Care Act, people at rallies holding signs that read, "Keep the government out of my Medicare!" In case you missed it, Medicare is a government program.

But that isn't all. Big chunks of the population can't identify all (or any) of the three branches of government, let alone how they work.[1] Other research appears to show that Americans don't trust their government but often think it's doing a good job.[2] Americans apparently know even less about their state governments, which, it can be argued, impact more of their lives.[3]

Unfortunately we're at a time when state and local government are rarely reported on, if at all. If you're lucky enough to live in a community with a local newspaper, you're getting something. Local TV news rarely covers politics on a meaningful level, and no local TV station has a full-time reporter in Olympia during sessions of the state legislature anymore. And even when they did, it wasn't usually someone who understood much about how government works.

It's not that Washington doesn't have problems—it does. We have too many homeless. Growth in the central Puget Sound region has made housing prices prohibitively high. And while the greater Seattle area is often booming, rural parts of the state often struggle with a lack of good jobs and resources. People of color suffer substantially higher rates of poverty, arrest and conviction than do other groups. Our overall strong economy, coupled with a nineteenth-century tax system, means that government typically fails to naturally capture its share of the growth in the state's wealth. And frequently, rather than taking action, we just study a problem until a crisis forces us to do something.

So this is a story about government—what it is, what it does, how it works, and how it could be better. You will meet a lot of people in this story. Ordinary people with a little spark and a belief that they could make things work better for their fellow citizens. Not everybody in government is a saint, but they aren't all devils either. I worked in the state legislature for nearly three years, and I met people in government of all persuasions—the good, the not as good, the bright, and the kind of slow. The great majority thought they were acting for the greater good.

It's important to keep in mind: they're just folks, with all the possibilities and problems that can involve. One of the officials I interviewed did a good job of making sure their office did what it was supposed to do but then came under fire for bullying their staff and making racist and sexist remarks. A former staffer in that office confirmed to me that this person was awful to work for. This poses a question for every voter: How much weight do you give an elected official's performance and how much to how they conduct themselves in office?

Whatever your decision, there's room for you in all this. The dozens of elected and appointed officials I interviewed for this project have a common story: they saw an opportunity to get involved and thought they could do some good. But most also understand that it's about serving citizens, not advancing their careers.

"It's important that we do that [govern] to serve the people. That's what we're there for," said one state legislator.

"The most important job in government is citizen," said another elected official. "I'm not in charge. I work for you. . . . Part of it is just this whole thing of owning the system. You own the system. You're inheriting it."

"You have an office," said another. "The office of citizen. The person who pays attention, who asks questions, who says, 'You said what?' . . . When there's a little too much bluster, ask what they're embarrassed about."

"Your silence does not bring fair government," said one Washington mayor.

Meanwhile, state and local government are more important than people may suspect. Never was this made clearer than during the 2020 COVID-19 pandemic. With the federal government under Donald Trump unwilling to act, it was left to states to take the lead on containing the virus and keeping the public safe. Governors—who can issue executive orders for a variety of reasons, including public health and safety—were left to take action. Some did, some didn't, and states with less action tended to have more cases of COVID-19 and consequently more deaths.

The people represented in this work are largely those who responded to my questions. Not everyone had time to respond, so if some stories are not represented here, it's only because we didn't manage to connect, not because I was trying to exclude any viewpoint. As for my viewpoint, I urge the reader to do what I tell my students to do: doubt, ask questions, be skeptical (but not cynical), and see if you think I'm right. I tell my students they don't have to agree with me, but that they should have reasons for what they believe. Even then, our opinions should lead us to more questions, not necessarily to more conclusions.

I have lots of people to thank for their help in this effort (in no particular order). Dozens of current and former officials shared their experiences in the course of researching and writing this book. There would be no book without them. John Hughes, historian with the secretary of state's office, was tireless in helping me find nuggets of information about the state and its history, as was Highline College reference librarian Jack Harton. Thanks to my friend and colleague Bruce Lamb for explaining some finer points of court procedure. Thanks to my friend Megan Davis, who read quite a bit of this and provided some needed perspective about state agencies. Thanks also to the staff at the University of Nebraska Press, including Sara Springsteen, Tish Fobben, Ann Baker, Taylor Gilreath, Tom Swanson, Robert Taylor, and especially Abigail Kwambamba, whose careful copyediting saved me from myriad embarrassments.

And special thanks to Sharon, who suggested I get to work writing when I was stuck in Shanghai, China, without enough to do. Good idea!

To all these people and more, much credit is due. The mistakes are mine.

WASHINGTON STATE POLITICS AND GOVERNMENT

PART I

The View from Above

State and local government should be understood in context. Because our system of government is federal in nature, states have the ability to do some things on their own, while in other areas they defer to the federal government. Every state is a little bit different, so one might consider the history, geography, and demographics of a state in trying to understand its politics and government. In this section we will learn about those areas, so that we understand that no government operates in a vacuum, independent of the other governments that make up the United States.

The other idea we should keep in mind is that in large part, government is about deciding who gets what. The political scientist David Easton described this as "the authoritative allocation of values." Government is authority; values are the things we want. That makes government an arena for competition among groups, each of which wants something—policy, privilege, and power.

CHAPTER ONE

Not-So-Mobile Homes

THE STORY OF A BILL

The extension of Sound Transit's light rail line to the north and south of Seattle is in many ways a good thing. Although some people will always oppose such projects, for others it had long been clear that there are few options to build more roads in the Puget Sound corridor. Seattle traffic has been rated anywhere from the second to the ninth worst in the country. The construction of light rail gives commuters more choices and tends to spur development along the rail line, boosting property values and raising tax revenues for nearby local governments. From its start, Sound Transit has enjoyed heavy ridership, growing with the addition of each new station along its routes.

The Puget Sound region once had a rail transit line, the Interurban, which ran via train and bus from Tacoma to Bellingham. Quite popular in its time, it was shut down in 1928, done in by the automobile and a lack of maintenance. Voters later turned down several transit proposals, beginning in 1969, when it would have been a lot cheaper to build. But traffic got worse over the years as the population grew. Interstate 5 northbound, built in the 1960s, inexplicably goes from six lanes to two in the space of a few miles heading toward downtown Seattle, producing a bottleneck of epic proportions (and the reversible express lanes north of downtown were not replicated south of downtown).

When voters finally approved what became Sound Transit in 1996, it meant that the agency would have to overlay an entirely new transit system in a region that was already largely developed. Nonetheless, despite several serious hiccups along the way, Sound Transit started operation of the first piece of the light rail network in Tacoma in 2003. The first piece of the Seattle portion began operation in 2009, reaching to Seattle-Tacoma International Airport later that year and to Angle Lake, in the city of SeaTac, in 2016. This was no surprise; Sound Transit was very clear about where it was going, and its board conducted numerous hearings about where the line should run and where substations would be built. So, like a train in a tunnel, you could see it coming from a long way away.

And that's when things started to get complicated, at least for the owner of a nearby mobile home park and his tenants. Across the street and a little south from the Angle Lake Station sits The Firs Mobile Home Park, 6.7 acres, with 72 spaces and 170 people living in a community described by many as "a family." Some residents had lived there for nearly two decades. Ninety of the residents were children; for many, this was the only home they had ever known. Mostly Latinx, many were immigrants, employed at various jobs in the SeaTac area.

Businessman Jong Soo Park bought the park in 2007 for a little less than $5 million. As late as 2016, the land had been appraised at $4.1 million, its value depressed by the bursting of the real estate bubble in the 2007–8 Great Recession.

And then the light rail started glimmering in the distance. Park decided he could redevelop his land and make a lot more money with it as a hotel and apartment complex, than he could if it remained a mobile home park. At The Firs, residents owned the homes they lived in but not the land underneath. They paid Park $500 a month to rent the spaces, much less than the cost of an apartment. In October 2016 he told the residents that he was closing down the park and they would have to leave. With the number of mobile home parks declining, and some of the homes too old to be moved, residents reacted with fear and surprise. Where would they go? Park offered $2,000 per family to help them move, but even when you can move a mobile home, it generally costs $5,000 and up to do so. Residents organized and created a homeowners association; they lobbied the City of SeaTac for help and tried to get Park to sell to them. They got legal help from several organizations. And they managed to get their plight splashed across local media. But the city said no, and Park wasn't selling. Park responded by putting eviction notices on the doors of the organizers of the homeowners group.

It's a story that gets at the heart of the kinds of decisions that government must make. On the one hand, Park had the right to sell or develop his land. On the other hand, many of the residents faced the prospect of being thrown out on the street, and rising homelessness is a widespread and serious problem. As more people become renters, landlord-tenant rights and disputes have become a thorny issue at multiple levels of government.

Some said the City of SeaTac's hands were tied. Park had filed the paperwork he needed, and the land was zoned for commercial use. If Park followed procedure, the city had to let him use his land as he saw fit. Others said the mostly white city council just didn't care about a bunch of brown people in a small development that could produce more jobs and revenue if it became something else. Earlier in the decade, a very conservative group had taken over the city council. Their first city manager—later fired—had instructed city staff to compile a list of all the Muslims living in SeaTac.

The Firs residents filed suit, claiming that established procedure wasn't being followed. In June 2018 a King County superior court judge ruled that key data was missing from Park and the city's paperwork and required that it be redone. That gave the residents an extra three months. Meanwhile, with friendly state legislators working on the issue, the state came up with $2.5 million to help the residents buy The Firs. But by then the land had been appraised at more than $10 million, and Park still didn't want to sell his park.

This is how legislation gets started. Something happens; citizens get concerned and involved; government at various levels attempts to address the issue; and sometimes the law changes. This is what state and local governments do: they make rules that affect you where you live.

But this is just a small piece of what happens in state and local government in Washington State. These are the levels of government closest to you and perhaps the ones about which people know the least. State and local government includes states, counties, cities, and special purpose governments such as school, water, sewer, hospital and transportation districts. It also includes state and local court systems. State and local governments are the chief providers of government services, even though $500 billion in state and local funds come from the federal government.

States are responsible for roads, welfare, taxes, schools, health care, and public safety. Some 95 percent of the nation's prison inmates are in state and local jails. States also often take the lead on consumer protection and business and environmental regulation.

Most of the growth in government in the last fifty years has been at the state and local level. State and local governments employ just under 20 million people and spend $3.2 trillion (versus 2.8 million federal employees and around $4.5 trillion in federal spending). In addition to the 50 states, the country has 87,000 local governments, including more than 3,000 counties, 19,000 cities, 16,000 towns, 14,000 school districts, and 31,000 other special purpose districts. On the whole, however, state and local taxes are less than one-third of the nation's total tax burden.

You should care about state and local government because it affects you where you live. Traffic tickets, education, and local roads are all part of state and local government. For example, if you attend a public college, it is an agency of state government. It is governed by a board of trustees who are appointed by the governor and confirmed by the state senate. Your tuition pays for no more than half of the cost of your education; the rest comes from state tax dollars apportioned by the state legislature. When you pay sales tax on anything you buy in Washington State, some fraction of that money goes to pay for part of your college education. The legislature's level of funding determines how many students the college will be able to admit. The legislature also helps set tuition by allowing colleges the authority to charge up to a certain percentage more. By limiting how much money they give colleges, legislators will virtually ensure that colleges will raise tuition close to the limit. However, you get to vote for legislators and the governor, who will frequently campaign on the basis of what they're going to do to and for education.

Your local public high school is part of a local government—a school district—that is governed by an elected board of directors and funded through state and local taxes. The city council and mayor hire people in the building department who will help decide how much you pay in permit fees to build a garage or add a room to your house. Cities will set speed limits for various roads, address local traffic problems, and hire police who may give you a ticket if you drive too fast—or decide to install a speed camera at a tricky intersection.

All these things involve public policy—choices made by elected officials whose job it is to sort out a host of different demands and desires. The entire system has evolved in a certain way for reasons that should become clear and that involve a vast series of trade-offs: every choice we make in government is a series of choices we forgo. We could do things differently, but one must always ask: What will we get in return? What will we give up? Is the new solution better than the old one?

Meanwhile, The Firs hadn't been completely logged over. Some people might look down at folks who live in mobile homes, but we should remember: That's their home. They worked to buy that place and it puts a roof over their heads. For many people, it's an affordable way to own a home. There's no shame in that. An estimated 7.5 percent of Washington's residents live in manufactured housing, about 540,000 people, of whom 75,000 to 80,000 live in about 1,700 mobile home parks. Mobile home park closures in Washington in 2017 displaced 203 families. Four to five more park closures were expected in the next couple of years. Another park in SeaTac sold for $51.2 million in May 2019.

One local legislator took up the cause. State Rep. Mia Gregerson is from SeaTac. She previously served on the city council, including a stint as mayor. When she heard about the plight of the people at The Firs, she decided to try to help. In the 2018 legislative session, Gregerson was able to get the $2.5 million added to the state capital budget in the form of a direct grant to the state's housing trust fund. Park didn't want to sell the land for less than its $10.7 million assessed value. The next session, Representative Gregerson went back to work.

Gregerson became the prime sponsor of House Bill 1582, which would change some terms of the state's laws regarding mobile home parks and tenants' rights. After being comfortably reelected in the heavily Democratic Thirty-Third District, Gregerson was beginning her fourth term in the state house of representatives. She had risen to become chair of the State Government and Tribal Relations Committee, as well as serving on the Labor Relations & Workplace Standards Committee and the Transportation Committee. Gregerson managed to get thirteen cosponsors to sign onto the bill, which indicated some support for the measure. It doesn't take much to be a cosponsor—you sign on the dotted line. All the cosponsors were Democrats, less of an issue for the bill as the Democrats had a 57–

41 edge in seats in the state house. That was up from 50–48 in 2016–17, when a single defection could scuttle a bill. Three of the cosponsors of Gregerson's bill served on the House Civil Rights and Judiciary Committee, including the committee chair, State Rep. Laurie Jinkins (D-Tacoma). After its introduction on the house floor, that's where the bill was sent.

Jinkins was already supportive of the bill. "One of my top priorities for the 2019 legislative session was to attempt to address the homelessness crisis," she said after the end of session. "For that reason, my committee heard several bills designed to reduce the loss of stable housing, including House Bill 1582. The American dream of homeownership can quickly change into a nightmare for those who own mobile homes. It is a misnomer that these homes are 'mobile'; moving them is often not an option, and when a mobile home park is sold, this literally sells the land out from underneath someone's home. Mobile home ownership is one of the most affordable options for low-income families and seniors."

The bill intended to make a number of changes to the state's Manufactured/Mobile Home Landlord-Tenant Act, which hadn't been revised in more than twenty years. This law "governs the legal rights, remedies, and obligations arising from any rental agreement between a landlord and a tenant regarding a mobile home lot within a mobile home park where the tenant has no ownership interest in the property or in the association which owns the property."[1] Mobile home park tenants typically own their homes but pay rent to the park owner to use the land the home sits on. The bill would have increased the minimum lease from one to two years; extended the "pay or vacate time" from five to fifteen days; required closure notices in multiple languages; and extended notification of rent increases from three to six months. It also would have extended closure notices from twelve months to three years. Basically, all of this would give tenants more time to make other plans if their park was going to close.

PEOPLE IN POLITICS: MIA GREGERSON

As an infant, Mia Gregerson was left on the doorstep of a police station in Taiwan. Now she's left in charge of important state issues.

Gregerson was adopted by an American family and grew up in South King County. Along the way she went to college, had a daughter, and bought a house. "I'm an accidental politician. It really was by chance," she said of her introduction to politics. "I had recently moved and was busy doing a lot of volunteerism in my community. I had the extra time to get more involved, and my new neighbor was [King County] Councilwoman Julia Patterson. She was the one who got me interested and helped me with my first campaign. I ran unopposed, and there really was no opposition in our little city [SeaTac] at that time."

That decision to run was driven by Gregerson's awareness of everyone's role in society.

"I realized I was supposed to give back more than I take," she said.

But in retrospect, she said, not having an opponent wasn't a good thing. "I had no platform, no stump speech."

She was elected to the SeaTac City Council and eventually became mayor. On the city council, she helped lead the fight for a $15 minimum wage, which citizens approved in 2013. And then the legislature beckoned.

"This is nearly the same story," she said. "I was pretty happy doing work at the city level. I was busy with a full-time job in West Seattle running a small business and raising my teenage daughter. Councilwoman Patterson was retiring (from the King County Council), and the state representative who was moving into her position was vacating this spot. When I saw who was going for the appointment no one had the same interests that I did, so I worked to be appointed by the King County Council and was successful."

To fill a vacant legislative seat, precinct committee members in a legislative district vote and send three names to the nearest county council. Every legislative district is divided into precincts, each with its own elected precinct committee member. These are elected positions; if you look carefully at your ballot, you see this office pop up from time to time. When the Thirty-Third District Republicans or Democrats meet, it is the precinct committee members who are supposed to show up. After the precinct vote, the council then chooses one of the three names submitted. Gregerson's was one of those names and she was appointed. The appointee must run for election at the next available opportunity. Gregerson was elected in her own right in 2014, and then reelected in 2016, 2018, 2020, and 2022.

Of course, helping run a state is a bigger job than helping run a city. "I am constantly challenged by my role as a state representative because the issues are so diverse and complex," she said. "It forces you to get outside of your comfort zone. I'm very much a suburban South King County gal, but the needs are quite different (and the same) in the different parts of the state. That provides a natural challenge when you are trying to do good work for all 7.7 million Washington residents and businesses."

Despite the challenges, Gregerson said, there are rewards. "I feel rewarded all of the time. People in general are appreciative of the work we are trying to do. There is always a 'complicated truth' to our work, but when you feel like you are building community or bridging issues, that's really rewarding."

In her fifth term in Olympia, she has seen some changes. Although her party, the Democrats, have the majority, longtime Speaker of the House Frank Chopp stepped down from that role in July 2019. "My party and my chamber are facing the first Speaker of the House election in over twenty years. This will be a new experience for everyone but two representatives," Gregerson said before the election that saw State Rep. Laurie Jinkins chosen as Washington's first female Speaker of the House.

Gregerson also became chair of the State Government and Tribal Relations Committee in 2019. "I really enjoyed my first year and am excited to continue to challenge myself and others to push on how we govern," she said.

She would also like to see better civic education throughout society. "If we did a better job at it, then our children and new Americans would know how to find us and how to get more involved," Gregerson said. "With all this in mind, I hope that people learn about what it is we do and understand why we do it. This will help better inform their interactions with us and we will in turn be more involved and accountable."

Hundreds of bills get introduced every legislative session. Some get hearings in committees and subcommittees; most simply die without a vote. "It's true that a committee may sometimes have too many bills to give all of them a public hearing, and the chair will thus need to make choices," said Representative Jinkins, chair of the Civil Rights & Judiciary Committee before she became Speaker. A bill can pass the house and die in the senate, or it can live and die the other way around. A bill can be rewritten, amended, and finally founder because the two chambers can't agree on the amendments. And the governor can decide, in the end, to veto the bill. The legislature can override a veto with a two-thirds vote of the house and the senate. In recent times a veto is nearly a death sentence since the legislature would be hard-pressed to get a two-thirds vote to agree that a blue sky is a nice thing on a sunny day. The system is designed not to make law but to keep law from happening. The idea is that only the best bills will survive to become laws.

Gregerson's bill, HB 1582, was referred to the Civil Rights & Judiciary Committee on January 24, 2019. And for a couple of weeks, there it sat. Committee chairs are under no obligation to hear a bill or to bring it up for a vote. Leadership in the majority caucus can put pressure on a committee chair to move a bill forward, but as with anything in legislative politics, you want to spend your chips wisely. Finally, on February 12, the committee held a public hearing on the bill. Having been publicized ahead of time, the open hearing invited advocates and opponents to line up, sign up, and say why they thought this bill was a good idea or a bad one.

Representative Gregerson spoke on behalf of her bill, citing seventy-five thousand families in mobile home parks across the state. "If you raise the rent $100 in the suburbs, we know that's the difference between people going homeless" or having a roof over their heads, she said.

"Is it reasonable to allow people to purchase their homes, improve them and then tell them they have to move out and lose all that equity in just twelve months?" asked Ishbel Dickens, speaking on behalf of The Firs homeowners group. "This is not a radical bill as some of the park owners have suggested. It's a bill that provides stability for low-income families, seniors, veterans and people with disabilities."

Owners of mobile home parks spoke against the bill. They opposed extending eviction notices from fifteen to thirty days, saying that would make everyone suffer from disruptive neighbors. They objected to tying rent increases to the consumer price index, a measure of inflation. One owner said this kind of measure would make it harder to operate mobile home parks, making them disappear even sooner.

"Sadly, HB 1582 provides no input from housing providers," said park owner Christy Mays.

"I was monitoring this bill for a couple of clients, who were going to issue closure notices immediately if the three-year [closure] notice went into effect," said one local attorney. "In the short term, the bill could well have had a negative impact on the people it was trying to help."

Despite the objections of park owners, the bill was scheduled for executive session on February 20. Executive session means different things at different levels of government, but at the legislative level it means the legislators are done taking testimony and will vote. Or might. On February 20 no action was taken. The bill was then "substituted," meaning that it was replaced by a new version and became Substitute House Bill (SHB) 1582. This happens to most bills; changing measures to improve them is at the heart of the legislative process. A "perfect bill," which sails through the whole process without any changes, is a pretty rare thing. A committee vote was rescheduled for February 22, and then it passed 9–5 with one "no recommendation." The vote was strictly along party lines: Democrats voted yes, Republicans voted no.

Despite the vote, there was discussion. "Rep. Morgan Irwin deserves a lot of credit for being willing to stay at the table with me, even if he didn't agree with the bill," Gregerson said of the ranking Republican on the Civil Rights & Judiciary Committee. "I as a Democrat really appreciate a Republican who's willing to sit down and learn."

Having passed its original committee, the bill went to the Rules Committee. The Rules Committee again decides which bills live or die because they determine which bills go on to the full house for amendments and final passage. For that to happen, someone on the committee has to "pull" the bill—formally sending it to the house floor for action.

"For those of us who are not on Rules, we have to have somebody pull it," Representative Gregerson said. Fortunately for Gregerson, cosponsor Sharon Wylie (D-Vancouver) served on the Rules Committee, as did Gregerson's Thirty-Third District seatmate, Rep. Tina Orwall (D–Des Moines). Orwall was already familiar with the bill since she also sat on Civil Rights & Judiciary. Most importantly, Speaker of the House Frank Chopp (D-Seattle) was supportive. "I want to give him a lot of credit on this," Gregerson said. "It's thanks to him that all this ended up happening."

On March 1 the Rules Committee pulled the bill, and it was sent to the house floor for consideration by the entire chamber. This is called second reading, in which amendments to the bill can be offered from the floor. Legislators will offer amendments to both hurt and help a bill. The only amendment on the house floor in this case was from Gregerson herself, which was adopted. Gregerson said her amendment made changes called for by some "stakeholders"—people with an interest in the bill.

"There were several stakeholder meetings. These meetings were well attended, very productive, and had both landlords—they had their own spectrum of willingness to agree—and the community," she said. "With that, we kept bringing forward strikers [amendments] in order to show a good faith effort in the process and to keep building a bill that more and more could support." A striker simply eliminates some part of the bill, leaving the original law otherwise unchanged.

That accomplished, the bill was advanced to third reading—final passage—and passed 53–42, largely along party lines. From there the bill, now labeled ESHB 1582, was sent to the senate. The "E" stands for "engrossed," which has an added, somewhat archaic meaning of "amended." On March 14 it was assigned to the Senate Committee on Housing Stability & Affordability. The Democrats had a majority in the senate, 28–20, which meant they would have a majority on every committee.

Patty Kuderer (D-Bellevue) was the chair of the committee. In that role she got to decide whether a bill got a hearing. "I get pretty much absolute leeway" in deciding what bills get considered, Kuderer said. "That's the function of a committee chair. But I don't do that in a vacuum. I consult with other members of the committee. Committee members will come and ask if a bill can have a public hearing."

By the time a bill gets to the opposite chamber, in this case the senate, half the session is over and bills increasingly face do-or-die deadlines. There's a shrinking window through which to move a bill ahead. Two factors worked in favor of ESHB 1582, however.

"It was a new committee so there were fewer bills," Kuderer said. She was able to give a hearing to every bill that came before them. An established committee, such as Law & Justice, "traditionally has an overflow of bills."

Kuderer also was familiar with the underlying issues. She has two mobile home parks in her district and had visited them between legislative sessions. "I thought that it was addressing some changes that needed to be made with the Mobile Home Landlord-Tenant Act," she said. "I thought the bill was quite timely given the crisis of housing affordability and homelessness in our state."

Kuderer's committee conducted a hearing on March 25, which again drew a busload of testimony for and against the legislation. This was Kuderer's first time as a committee chair, but observers said she did well in moving the bill forward despite determined opposition. "She worked magic," said State Sen. Karen Keiser (D–Des Moines). "I think Patty laid down the law to the mobile home association."

"I was actively involved in bringing those groups [stakeholders] together in the discussions on the bill and making recommendations for certain changes as a result of those conversations," Kuderer said. "One of the things that the landlords talked about, when a park is in closure [it's going to close at some future date], they're not allowed to take tenants, and that's lost revenue." Upkeep of the park usually suffers for lack of funds. A change to the bill allowed landlords to engage in short-term leases to people with RVs.

On the other side, Kuderer added, "tenants said one of the leading causes of eviction is rule violations," essentially a three-strikes-and-you're-out provision. "There were times that they [tenants] didn't even know the rules had changed," she said. The bill added a three-month grace period for rule changes. "The rules are in effect, but you get a warning."

The bill also extended the grace period for non-payment of rent from five to fourteen days. Kuderer pointed out that fourteen days is the standard for apartment rentals and gives people enough time to either collect another paycheck or tap into public assistance for rent. "A three- or five-day period was not workable from the tenants' standpoint, to even allow them to get the help that was out there," she said. "When you cut down on evictions, you keep people housed."

"In the end, not all the landlords were on the same page with the changes that were made," said Kuderer. "Nor were the tenant advocates. They were happy with some, but none of them were happy with all of the changes."

The bill passed on April 3 on a straight party line vote, 4–3. From there the bill went to the Senate Ways & Means Committee. Ways & Means is a longstanding name for committees that write budgets, and if a bill has any financial impact in terms of state spending, it must go through a budget committee. After an April 5 hearing, Ways & Means voted 13–9, with two "no recommendations," to advance the bill on April 9.

Gregerson said the actual financial impact was a matter of some debate; the bill had not gone to the House Appropriations Committee. "We argued the fiscal note [a statement of a bill's financial impact] with the Department of Commerce," she said. "At first they said it would cost a bunch of money to help community members who would have two years to relocate versus one year (current law). We argued that it was the same work just spread out over two years versus one. The senate eventually put a task force on to the bill and that added cost. The last component of the bill that the Department of Commerce stated was to translate the document into ten languages. We saw this as a one-time cost."

Having cleared that hurdle, ESHB 1582 went to the Senate Rules Committee. The vice chair of the Rules Committee was another of Gregerson's Thirty-Third District allies, State Sen. Karen Keiser, flanked by Senator Kuderer, who already supported the bill. On April 11 the Rules Committee advanced the bill to second reading. Second reading saw some action. Ten amendments were proposed, nine of which were withdrawn by their sponsors. The one that passed came from State Sen. Hans Zeiger (R-Puyallup), who, as the ranking Republican on the Housing Committee, had voted against the bill.

"[ESHB] 1582 was in my opinion fairly on the side of the tenants, and I acknowledge that there are major issues," said Zeiger. "There could be some unintended consequences. We certainly heard that from a lot of the landlords." After most of a decade serving in the house and senate, "I kind of know what a good stakeholder process looks like, and I didn't feel like there had been one," he said. "If you look at the house vote, you'll see that there were Democrats who were opposed to the bill when it left the house."

On second reading on the senate floor, Zeiger proposed an amendment, a striker, that removed the language extending the lease-notice terms to two years from one. That left current law unchanged.

"There was an issue with getting enough votes in the senate [off the floor] and so Zeiger's striker was the only way we could get enough votes to send it back to the house," Representative Gregerson said. She added that it's a "painful reality to how legislation becomes law."

Zeiger's amendment also included a study group to look further into the issue, "a work group that's going to get together and that will include representatives of tenants and landlords and other stakeholders," he said. "I think that's going to be an important opportunity because these are issues that have been going on for years. My hope is that this will be an opportunity to resolve these things in a thoughtful and deliberative way.

"It's hard to do this in the heat of a session," Zeiger said, noting that they were facing a deadline to move house bills through the senate. "Tenants are facing some real challenges, and we want to make sure they have a voice in this process. But also you don't want to chase owners out of this business.

"I think that was the good way to resolve the thing," Zeiger added. "I just want to make sure we're making policy in a way that values the perspective of everyone involved with this."

After his amendment passed, Zeiger joined several other Republicans to vote in favor of the bill, which passed 36–12. But now the bill was different than the one that had passed the house. Before a bill can be sent on for the governor's signature, making it law, it must pass both chambers in exactly the same version. On April 23 the house voted to accept the senate amendments, 60–36, which meant some Republicans who had voted against the bill before now voted for it. It went to the governor on April 25; he signed it into law on May 9. The governor tends to have a lot of things to sign at the end of a session.

"When a park closes, an entire community risks falling into homelessness. When we talk about affordable housing solutions, we cannot leave mobile/manufactured homes out of the conversation," Representative Gregerson said after the bill signing. "We will be working hard over the interim to enact even stronger protections for these communities next session."

In the end, Gregerson's bill didn't directly impact the residents of The Firs. In March 2019 they reached a deal with Jong Park, getting to stay rent-free until June 2020 and receiving $10,000 in relocation assistance. Of course, many of the homes were too old and beat up to be moved, and several residents expressed sadness that they had to move at all. The community they had built would be no more. "I think it's very little money in exchange for our homes," said park resident Guadalupe Rodriguez. "They didn't offer us another place where we can move."[2]

Park said he thought the settlement was fair. A related bill, SHB 1033, would have provided more money for relocation. Although it passed overwhelmingly in the house, it died in the Senate Ways & Means Committee after passing in the Housing Stability & Affordability Committee. But as a bill is never really dead, it was part of a package of mobile home–related bills added to SB 5183, sponsored by Senator Kuderer, which passed both chambers. Meanwhile, The Firs residents subsequently sued the City of SeaTac for, in part, shutting them out of the process by which closure of The Firs was approved.[3] In 2022 they lost the suit, and everyone was forced to move out.

The story of The Firs involved nearly every part of state and local government, from citizens and business owners, to a city council, the court system, and finally the legislature. A decision by a super-regional government on where a light rail transit station would be located affected nearby property values and the homes of people living in a nearby mobile home park. A local government approved the park owner's plan; courts ruled on whether they were right. A local school district even weighed in, concerned what the loss of ninety students would do to a nearby elementary school. Finally, the state legislature stepped in to try to help the families affected by all this change.

For those of you keeping score, this is also an example of one of the big questions in political science: Who's really in charge? One school of thought, pluralism, suggests that different groups compete for policy, power, and privilege. Another flavor of theory says that in fact the system is often dominated by elites—people with money, power, and influence—who get what they want for all kinds of reasons. We should be able to see both theories demonstrated here: multiple groups and interests competed over the future of The Firs, and the elites—the city and the business owner—appear to have gotten their way in the end.

We could also look at this as an example of Sell's Second Law of Political Economy: the decision will be made in the direction of the greatest value, which usually means money.[4] This is not to say that the mobile home park had no value—it certainly had lots of value to the residents. But for the city, which had to decide, a hotel complex generates more tax revenue and jobs than a mobile home park does. This doesn't make it the right decision, just a predictable one.

Also playing a role was Sound Transit, the regional government that pushed the light rail line through less-wealthy neighborhoods, whose residents were less likely to have the resources to oppose the intrusion.

Even forces with resources didn't agree on where the line should go: the city of Des Moines, just south of SeaTac, didn't want it to run along Pacific Highway South, since that would disrupt businesses within city limits, and businesses represent the jobs and taxes that cities want more of. Nearby Highline College, however, preferred the line come down the highway because if the transit station ended up on campus, it would be easier to attract students to enroll. Enrollment figures impact state funding. Ultimately, Sound Transit's board decided the line should cut east of The Firs to Interstate 5, helping the city but not the college. If nothing else, the city would be in a better position to sue to change the route, delaying the project and raising its costs. In the end, everybody wanted something, but not everyone got what they wanted. That happens a lot in government too.

You may side with the residents or with the owner; you may think that the new mobile home law is an improvement or an infringement. Either way, this is what state and local governments do: they make and enforce laws that impact people's lives. In what follows, we will try to sort out how all these pieces fit together and how politics and government work in Washington State.

CHAPTER TWO

Overview

THE PLAYING FIELD

To understand government and politics in Washington State, we should understand a little about the history of the state.

Washington became the forty-second state on November 11, 1889, part of the Enabling Act of that same year, which also admitted Montana and gave us two Dakotas (North and South). Washington was part of what became the Oregon Territory in 1848, and a separate Washington Territory was officially established in 1853. Often called North Oregon, its name was to be Columbia, but a congressman from Kentucky managed to get it changed to Washington in honor of the president, since we already had a District of Columbia. Some people pointed out that having two Washingtons was no less perplexing, and there was a small push for "Washingtonia." Nonetheless, Washington it became, leading to more than 150 years of confusion.

Washington's Euro-American founders wanted statehood much sooner than 1889. Oregon had become a state in 1859, but it had a lot more people. In the 1860 Census, Washington Territory had fewer than twelve thousand people while Oregon had more than fifty thousand.

Of course, there were people in what is now Washington State long before statehood. It was home to rich and diverse Native American societies, occupying both sides of the Cascade curtain. A smallpox epidemic in the 1770s greatly reduced the population,[1] and eventually Euro-Americans bought or stole most of the land from the original inhabitants. The treatment of Native people is not a high point of U.S. history, and unfortunately, Washington was no different.

The Europeans started showing up a century before statehood. Beginning in the 1770s, Spanish and British sailors explored the coast of what became Washington. The territory was first claimed by Spain, then by Russia. The Spanish and Russians agreed to divide the land at latitude 54°40′, which became important later on. The British also laid claim to the northwestern reaches of the continent, eventually reaching a deal with Spain for possession of the land north of California. Nobody asked the people who were already living there what they thought, of course.

Then the Americans arrived, beginning with Capt. Robert Gray in 1792 (for whom Grays Harbor County is named), followed by Lewis and Clark in 1805. The Americans extended their claim to the land via the Adams-Onis Treaty of 1819, by which the Spanish again relinquished land claims north of California (and also sold Florida to the United States). This treaty led the Americans to claim everything up to 54°40′, although the Anglo-American Convention of 1818 called for joint occupancy of the region with Britain. It was known as the Columbia District to the British and the Oregon Country to the Americans.

While the two sides settled on the forty-ninth parallel from the Great Lakes to the Rocky Mountains as the border, everybody wanted all that they could get of everything west of the Rockies. The Americans were rapidly filling up Oregon, and while there were more British than Americans north of the Columbia River, the British realized that the Americans would eventually push north as well. Although James Polk got elected president in 1844 with the campaign slogan of "54°40′ or fight!" the Oregon Treaty of 1846 extended the border along the forty-ninth parallel all the way to the sea.

Even then, there were the San Juan and Gulf Islands to resolve. Although the treaty with the British said the border extended through the main channel, leaving the British with Vancouver Island, apparently nobody noticed that there are in fact two channels, running north and south of the San Juan Islands. The available maps were incomplete—the Euro-Americans were still sorting out just exactly where everything was. By 1856 the British and the Americans were in serious discussion over who had title to what. And then, on June 15, 1859, American farmer Lyman Cutlar found a pig rooting in his potatoes on his farm on San Juan Island, so he shot it. The pig was owned by an employee of the British Hudson's

Bay Company, Charles Griffin. Cutlar offered him $10; Griffin wanted $100. The British threatened to arrest Cutlar, and the Americans called for backup. The two sides built camps down the road from each other (now a small but lovely national historical park) and waited. Although the governor of Vancouver Island ordered British forces to attack, cooler heads prevailed and no shots were fired. The only casualty of the Pig War was the pig. The dispute was finally resolved via the Treaty of Washington in 1871. The final division left the United States with Point Roberts, a part of Washington State that is only accessible through Canada. Consequently, western Canada's southernmost city, Victoria, is south of Washington's northernmost city, Blaine.

Washington residents wanted statehood, but amid the Civil War, adding another distant, underpopulated state was probably not a high priority. Even after the war, it took time. A measure to call a state constitutional convention was on the territorial ballot in 1869, but with so few people in the territory, Congress was less likely to act on a statehood measure for Washington and the measure failed. The 1860 census counted fewer than 12,000 people in Washington Territory, which then included Idaho as well as parts of Montana and Wyoming. The 1870 census found fewer than 24,000 in what was to become Washington State, Idaho having been split off in 1863. By 1876 only 3,500 people called Seattle home, and there were only 50,000 in the whole of Washington, but those folks voted for a constitutional convention that year. Statehood was delayed as Republicans and Democrats in Congress fought over the issue, with each side afraid that the other would get some advantage. Democrats feared that Washington would vote Republican, tipping the balance of power in Congress, while Republicans delayed admitting potentially Democrat-leaning states. (This same issue keeps both Washington DC and Puerto Rico from achieving statehood today. Republicans fear the new states would vote Democrat.) The statehood bill that included Washington didn't go forward until Republicans got full control of Congress in 1888.[2] Backers of the territorial legislation, and eventually the statehood bill, promised that there were plenty of people in the soon-to-be state. After statehood, there soon were. The 1890 census showed that the newly minted state had 357,000 people, up from 75,000 only ten years before. Washington was on its way.

PEOPLE IN POLITICS: ISAAC STEVENS AND ELISHA P. FERRY

Two of Washington's first governors are united by the fact that they are the only two governors after whom counties are named. Otherwise, they're quite different from each other. Then again, they confronted different situations as they took office.

Washington had eighteen territorial governors before it became a state, all appointed by the federal government. Washington's first governor was Isaac Stevens (1818–62), appointed territorial governor in 1853 and serving until 1857. Stevens graduated first in his class at West Point and saw action in the Mexican War. A supporter of President Franklin Pierce (who also got a county named after him), Stevens was appointed by the president to be territorial governor and also superintendent of Indian Affairs.

Stevens had his ups and downs. He chose Olympia as the territorial capital. He negotiated treaties with the Native American tribes, which cost them most of their land, but Stevens thought he was preventing war. When miners in the Yakima area assaulted some Native women, violence broke out and Stevens pursued that with as much vigor as he had pursued the treaties. He declared martial law and jailed people who disagreed with him, including a judge who was calling for his replacement. Stevens waged war on the Yakamas, and approved the execution of Nisqually leader Leschi, who was by all other accounts a good and decent man. (Leschi was exonerated by a court of historical inquiry in 2004.) Nonetheless, Stevens was elected the state's delegate to Congress in 1857 and 1858. He was killed while serving in the Union Army at the Battle of Chantilly in 1862.

Territorial governors had some power but couldn't veto acts of the territorial legislature until 1864. Then again, the legislatures couldn't make a law binding unless it mirrored an act of Congress. The legislature voted to move the capital to Vancouver, but territorial governor Henry McGill stalled for time until citizens overturned the decision by referendum in 1861.[3]

Elisha P. Ferry was one of Washington's last territorial governors and its first elected governor. Although many territorial governors served only a year or two (we had fourteen governors in thirty-six years), Ferry served the longest, eight years. Ferry (1825–95) was an attorney, a Republican, a Mason, and a devout Episcopalian. He was born in Michigan Territory near Detroit, and he practiced law in Illinois for twenty-three years and was elected mayor of Waukegan, Illinois, in 1859. He joined the Union Army during the Civil War, where he made friends with both Abraham Lincoln and Ulysses S. Grant. President Grant appointed him surveyor general of the territory in 1869, whereupon the Ferry family moved to Olympia. Grant appointed him territorial governor in 1872.

As territorial governor, Ferry was noted for tidying up state finances, in part by getting counties to pay their taxes. Prior to Ferry's tenure, tax collections were uneven and unreliable, and folks with connections tended to pay less.[4] He helped with the development of the Northern Pacific Railroad. He got the territorial legislature to create San Juan County. He also called out the militia more than once to help break strikes by railroad workers and miners.

After two terms as territorial governor, Ferry returned to private life, working in law and banking, before being elected Washington's first governor in 1889. As governor Ferry had to find a balance between pro-business and pro-farmer interests within the state, at which he was not always successful. Failing health led him to resign from office before the end of his first term, and he died two years later in Seattle.

WASHINGTON NOW

Today Washington has more than 7.5 million people, making it the thirteenth most populous state in the country but only twenty-fifth in population density (people per square mile). With a population gain of more than 14 percent over the last ten years, it's the sixth fastest growing state in the country. It has 71,362 square miles of territory, ranking eighteenth. It is the smallest state in the West except Hawaii but bigger than any state east of the Mississippi. It is the second most populous state in the West after California. About 75 percent of the state's population lives on the west side, with the greatest number in the Central Puget Sound region. The median age is 37.6; the population is slightly more female (50.1 percent) than male. Washington's population is 68.7 percent white, 12.7 percent Latinx, 7.8 percent Asian, 5.3 percent multiethnic, 3.6 percent Black, and 1.9 percent Native American. Ten percent of the population is foreign born, and 1 percent are estimated to be undocumented immigrants. Washington has fewer Black residents but more Asian and Native Americans than the country as a whole. The state now ranks twelfth for Latinx citizens. Washington residents also are wealthier, more educated, and slightly younger than the nation at large.

Washington ranks eighth in the country for per capita personal income, at $57,896, and fifth in per capita GDP (gross domestic product, a standard measure of the size of an economy) at $70,799. Even so, in 2022, at 3.7 percent it had the thirty-second worst unemployment rate in the country. Eleven percent of its citizens were living in poverty, thirty-seventh in the country but still nothing to be proud of. Washington ranks thirty-second in per capita federal grants, $1,848, and twenty-ninth in per capita state expenditures, $6,034. The state ranks sixth in the country for per capita state and local debt at $11,686, but as we'll see later, that tends to just mean that government is building and fixing more things. The state's average bond rating is 9 out of 10, tied for eighteenth, which is good, or residents would be paying more for all that debt. Washington has 1.7 full-time state employees for every 100 people in the state, ranking eighteenth. It ranks nineteenth for per pupil school expenditures at $12,691, which is up quite a bit since the state supreme court told the legislature it had to follow the state constitution and fund public schools. If you just count state money, Washington rises to twelfth. Washington is twenty-sixth in the country for average annual in-state college tuition, $9,760 a year, and twenty-fourth for average annual per pupil support for higher education, $6,982. Think taxes are too high? Washington ranks twenty-first in per capita state revenue, $7,018, but sixth in per capita local revenue at $6,469. State and local taxes consume 21 percent of personal income, ranking twenty-sixth. Washington spends 23.9 percent of its budget on all forms of public assistance, ranking thirty-fifth. Washington's state and local governments spend $575 per person on transportation infrastructure, ranking twenty-first, while spending $252 per person on public safety, putting the state at seventeenth.[5]

Despite the state being largely white, areas such as South King County are among the most diverse in the country. Seattle elected Wing Luke, one of the country's first Asian American office holders, to its city council in 1962. Seattle is the biggest city with the smallest number of Black citizens to elect a Black mayor, Norm Rice in 1989. Gary Locke, in 1996, became the first Asian American to be elected governor of any state not named Hawaii.

Washington has, among other things, a higher juvenile suicide rate, fewer minorities (although the non-white population is growing), fewer churchgoers, more unionized workers, a younger population, and higher voter turnout than many other states. Some 90.8 percent of Washington adults are high school graduates, ranking sixteenth nationally; 34.5 percent have college degrees (eleventh) and 12.7 percent have advanced degrees (thirteenth). Seattle has the highest percentage of college graduates of any city in the country. Washington and Seattle frequently end up highly ranked on various lists of the best places to live.

Economic rankings of the states are a little dicey because the people compiling them usually have an agenda. However, in 2017 Businessinsider.com said Washington had the second best economy in the country, with the second highest average weekly wage ($1,107.20), the fourth highest growth rate, and seventh highest job growth rate.[6] A year later, in the same source, the wage growth rate had fallen to fifth. At $506 billion, Washington has the thirteenth largest economy among the states, rising to fifth if you standardize by population. Trade, transportation, and utilities is the largest employment sector, while government is the single largest sector of the economy (at about 14 percent of GDP). Manufacturing, health care, and information are other large sectors. One should not overlook agriculture, where the state leads the nation (and sometimes the world) in production of everything from apples and asparagus to peppermint and spearmint oil and pea seed. Yes, that minty-fresh taste of your toothpaste likely started as a small, leafy green plant on a farm in Washington. And it's good to be born here: Washington ranks forty-fifth in infant mortality, with 4.3 deaths per 1,000 live births.

As others have noted, it's an interesting state to be in.

In terms of political culture, Washington citizens display two common strains: moralistic, in which citizens tend to believe government can be a force for good; and individualistic, in which citizens believe government is there to encourage private activity and facilitate markets.[7] These are defined in part by geography. Eastern Washington is more conservative; western Washington is more liberal, particularly in the Puget Sound area. Eastern Washington is more agricultural, and although many farmers depend on government support for their crops, people there may tend to say that less government is better. People from the eastside also sometimes refer to Puget Sound as "the coast"; Puget Sounders tend to think of the coast as Aberdeen and Ocean Shores. The west side, being more diverse and sometimes wealthier, tends to see government as a potentially positive influence, even as people there often overlook and misunderstand the role business plays in society. So while Seattle can elect Kshama Sawant, an avowed socialist, to the city council, Spokane can elect a state legislator such as Matt Shea, who has said eastern Washington should form its own state (an old and frequent refrain) and has basically called for a holy war against people who disagree with him.[8]

But these patterns can change. Following the Great Depression, eastern Washington, like a lot of the country, was solidly Democratic. Over time Seattle became a stronghold of liberal Republicans (an endangered species of late). As the east side of Lake Washington grew, it became redoubtably Republican. But the arrival of Microsoft, Nintendo, and other tech firms attracted folks with different priorities, and the area now is strongly Democrat. Thurston County, home of Olympia and state government, is determinedly Democrat, whereas next-door Lewis County is reliably Republican. As they have grown, Vancouver and Spokane have started to lean Democrat. As generations of farmworkers have begun to put down roots, parts of eastern Washington have begun to become more liberal. One must suspect that former president Trump's anti-immigrant tirades may motivate those voters even more.

So much of the state's population is located in the Central Puget Sound region—more than a quarter in King County alone—that it is possible for a statewide candidate to win all of eastern Washington and still lose an election. King, Pierce, Snohomish, and Kitsap Counties make up about 46 percent of Washington's headcount; throw in Skagit and Whatcom and you've got half the people in the state. Those counties are largely Democratic (though rural Whatcom elects some Republicans). This seems to produce a certain amount of resentment east of the mountains, and "We don't want to become like Seattle" is a frequent refrain in recent Washington politics. It makes me want to respond, "What don't you like? The wealth or the cultural opportunities?" It is a fact that King County basically subsidizes the rest of the state, given that it pays out more in taxes than it receives in government services.

But even that wealth provokes political disagreement. Successful businesses mean jobs which generally means immigration, more traffic, and higher housing prices. So if the economy is booming, many people bemoan the costs of growth. Most recently that's taken the form of strident protests that "Amazon has ruined Seattle!" At other times, when the economy is hurting and jobs are scarce, we witness a chorus of Newtonian wailing—an equal and opposite reaction—that Washington is too dependent on Boeing or whomever residents would like to blame at that moment. This management-by-crisis approach to government tends to discourage a more prudent, long-term approach to policy. Washington is not alone in this pendular view of policy, but it's very common here.

Washington politics, with notable exceptions here and there, has long enjoyed a fairly clean reputation. Police and city halls aren't for sale; state legislators and executives aren't feathering their own beds at public expense. On the other hand, Washington politics sometimes has an obsession with process—everyone must participate, and any problem must be studied to death before it can be resolved. As a top state official once said, "Back east, they know this as the land of process."

Consider the Alaskan Way Viaduct, which cut across Seattle's waterfront for more than seventy years. At least since the 2001 Nisqually earthquake, it was very clear the viaduct was a disaster waiting to happen. Another serious earthquake would probably have pancaked the whole structure. This could have involved considerable loss of life if it happened at rush hour. Others argued that the viaduct was somehow forestalling development of the waterfront and preventing the city from reaching some nebulous but glorious destiny. And so the debate began, with arguments for just removing it and letting traffic waddle through on city surface streets; repairing it; and replacing it with a tunnel. There was even a fringe movement for building a bridge. All of the options had their costs and virtues, though replacing the viaduct with nothing would have provoked a traffic nightmare for anyone driving through town. But whereas in other parts of the country they probably would have concluded "unsafe road, must be replaced" and done so, local folks spent more than a decade debating the issue to the point where one state legislator confided, "I sometimes hope it just collapses in the middle of the night, when there's nobody on it." Eventually they settled on a tunnel, which was built. You won't have to wait long to begin hearing what's wrong with it and how it was a mistake.

While I imagine that this kind of harangue happens in other parts of the country, it is a distinct feature of Washington politics. When the West Seattle Bridge got hit by a freighter heading up the Duwamish River in 1978, half the bridge was knocked out of service. It took until 1984 to build a new bridge, which naturally led to a chorus of complainers declaring that Washington spent way too much money on a bridge that had more capacity than would ever be needed. Of course, within a few years it became clear that a second span was necessary. The lower-level Spokane Street Bridge was finished in 1991. (And then, in 2020, the bridge had to be closed again when potentially catastrophic cracks were found. Fixing it in two years was something of a record.)

And yet government in Washington doesn't work too badly. It's often slow and burdened by an antiquated tax system and governors and legislators who can fritter away opportunities until there's a crisis. But it's not a bad place to live, things largely work the way they're supposed to, and the overwhelming majority of public servants—appointed and elected, Republicans and Democrats—are there because they think they can make a difference for somebody. And for all the times partisans bicker, especially in the state legislature, over one policy choice or another, at many other times people of different backgrounds come together to craft laws that really do help people lead slightly better lives. This is another example of pluralism in action—different groups competing for policy outcomes, which can end in compromise and maybe even a little progress. Either way, this is a story about how all that works.

CHAPTER THREE

Federalism

STATES WITHIN THE STATE

One of the first things to understand about state and local government is how it fits into the bigger picture of American government as a whole. And to understand anything about American government at any level, you have to understand federalism. It is one of the defining features of U.S. government and it has huge implications for state and local government.

It's also important to understand that we live in a republic, not a democracy. People wave the term "democracy" around without really understanding what it means. The precise definition, which is the one you might care about, is direct rule by the people. In Washington State and some others, citizens exercise direct rule via initiatives and referenda. More on that later.

In a republic people elect officials to make decisions. This may seem like a questionable choice, but when the Founding Fathers created the republic in 1787, they understood that people can get carried away. Putting the power of government in hands once removed from those of the mass public puts a check on the power and passions of the people. Historically, direct democracies such as ancient Athens made rash decisions and persecuted unpopular people, ultimately putting tyrants and demagogues in charge. Demagogues tell people what they want to hear but tend to do the very things they criticized others for. In a republic, people maintain power through elections, and the people throw the rascals out more than you might think. It's not incorrect to call this a representative democracy, since people vote to select representatives. But we probably shouldn't call it a democratic republic since that was the name applied to many communist states in the Cold War era. And they were neither democratic nor republican.

Our republic employs what has been called the congressional system of government. In the congressional system, power is divided between different branches: the president, Congress, and the court system at the federal level, mirrored by the governor, legislatures, and the courts at the state level. Congress and nearly all state legislatures are further divided into two chambers, in Washington's case the house and senate. This is the essence of the oft-mentioned checks and balances: the different branches are supposed to keep the other branches from getting carried away. As the United States has such a broad conception of liberty, we often seem capable of justifying any sort of policy or behavior to the point where we sometimes need to put the brakes on our desires.

Meanwhile, effective government does not require a two-chambered legislature or even division into different branches: Nebraska has a unicameral, nonpartisan legislature, and folks there say it works just fine. Nor is Nebraska alone. The usual alternative to congressional-style government is the parliamentary system, in which the legislative body holds power, largely undivided. Half the countries in the world have parliamentary governments, far more than have congressional governments. British Columbia, Washington's neighbor to the north, has a parliament featuring the Legislative Assembly and the king's representative, the lieutenant governor. Neither the king nor the lieutenant governor tries to tell the Legislative Assembly what to do, so both legislative and executive power rest with the assembly. The assembly elects a premier from its ranks, typically the leader of the majority party. That person is the executive of provincial government and a member of the Legislative Assembly.

STATES OF THE NATION

Our republic is also a federal republic. Federalism is a system of government that divides and shares power between different levels of government. Nearly 90 percent of the world's governments are unitary, in which power is largely in the hands of the national government and only lent to local or subnational governments.

There are different degrees of federalism; Canada has strong federalism because the Canadian provinces have slightly more power relative to the national government. They are not more powerful than the national government, they just have a little more independence than do U.S. states. Mexico has weak federalism because the Mexican states don't have a lot of power relative to that of the national government.

The United States is somewhere in between Mexico and Canada (geographically and politically). The federal government and the states share and divide power, and we've been arguing for almost 250 years about just what that power-sharing arrangement should look like. At various times the states and the federal government have had largely separate spheres of influence; at other times the federal government has somewhat dominated the states, providing money and dictating policy. Two scholars have referred to the current situation as "ad hoc federalism," "ad hoc" being a Latin expression meaning "for that purpose." The authors' point was that people increasingly want the states to have more leeway on some issues such as gay marriage and marijuana but prefer the federal government to be supreme when it comes to things such as civil and voting rights and vice versa. "Conservatives, at least rhetorically, still were the strongest states' rights advocates. Yet when states' rights conflicted with key portions of the conservative political agenda, conservative groups still fought tenaciously for federal supremacy over the states," they wrote. "Ad hoc federalism makes everyone an equal opportunity hypocrite."[1] This presumes that a rigid but consistent ideology is somehow better, but the authors have a point. People tend to be selective about what they believe if it supports what they want to see happen.

The roots of federalism are found in the U.S. Constitution. The document says a few things about state-federal power sharing, but in its typically vague way, it leaves a lot of room for interpretation. In some few places, it's quite clear. The Constitution defines relations between states—state laws can't favor citizens of one state over another. Only Congress may admit new states; only Congress has the power to regulate interstate commerce.

The Constitution was intended, among other things, to prevent the federal government from overwhelming the states. The Tenth Amendment seems to suggest as much: "The power not delegated to the United States by the Constitution, nor prohibited by it to the states, are reserved to the states respectively, or to the people."

This could mean almost anything, and it has. States do have some separate powers—states must ratify amendments to the Constitution—as well as concurrent powers: they can do within their own spheres what the federal government can do in the national arena, such as raise taxes and regulate commerce. We should note that local governments are not an explicit part of the federalist equation. States have a lot of ability to set the rules for local governments, and they sometimes do.

In our time some state leaders have argued that the states should be able to unilaterally nullify laws coming from Congress because that would somehow make things better. A related argument is that the way to fix the federal government is to take away its power to tax. Americans, who sometimes have frighteningly little understanding of their own history, tend to forget that the inability to tax was the thing that most doomed the feeble government that existed under the Articles of Confederation and prompted the writing of the Constitution. Moreover, if states can just say no, we're a confederation, not a republic, and history tells us confederations just don't work. A government that requires the agreement of all the member states will eventually be unable to act. In fact, the Constitution seems to make clear that the federal government is above the states, at least in some key areas. This is spelled out in several places:

> The necessary and proper clause of the Constitution (found in Article 2, section 8): Congress shall have the power "to make all Laws which shall be necessary and proper for carrying into Execution the foregoing Powers, and all other Powers vested by this Constitution in the Government of the United States, or any Department or Officer thereof." Sometimes also called the elastic clause, it appears to grant Congress the power it needs to do what it is supposed to do.
>
> The supremacy clause (Article 6): "This Constitution, and the laws of the United States which shall be made in pursuance thereof; and all treaties made, or which shall be made, under the authority of the United States, shall be the supreme law of the land; and the judges in every state shall be bound thereby, anything in the Constitution or laws of any State to the contrary notwithstanding."

This means that the Constitution and federal law supersede state laws and constitutions.

The commerce clause (Article 1, section 8, clause 3): It allows Congress "To regulate Commerce with foreign Nations, and among the several States, and with the Indian Tribes." This means only Congress can regulate interstate commerce; Idaho can't put a tariff on Washington potatoes. It also means states can't cut their own trade deals with foreign countries.

The spending clause (Article 1, section 8, clause 1): "The Congress shall have Power To lay and collect Taxes, Duties, Imposts and Excises, to pay the Debts and provide for the common Defence and general Welfare of the United States; but all Duties, Imposts and Excises shall be uniform throughout the United States." This gives Congress the power to raise and spend money. Because the national economy is so much bigger than any state's economy, this gives the federal government a bit of leverage with the states. Money talks.

Altogether, this gives the federal government some ability to tell the states what they should do. The national government also has power because of the overall power of the president and because of its greater ability to raise revenue.

One of the things that people tend to misunderstand is who does what in the various levels of government. The federal government handles issues at the national level—things related to defense, foreign policy, monetary policy, and interstate commerce. States do much more with education, criminal law and local transportation, as well as matters occurring purely within state boundaries. Beyond that, state and federal (national) powers tend to overlap, creating both conflict and cooperation. The two levels tend to share responsibility for social services, and there is overlap in regulation and environmental protection.

The federal system has advantages and disadvantages and is a perfect example of the trade-offs inherent in any system of government. For example, it provides for a multiplicity of programs and regulations, which allows specialization but impedes the adoption of national standards.

Among federalism's advantages:

- It allows experimentation and specialization at the state and local level. In theory, at least, states and local governments can try different policies out, test driving them for everyone else.
- It allows flexibility and diversity in making policy. Different parts of the country may have different priorities, so that state governments can tailor their policies to meet local needs and expectations.
- It brings government closer to the people, ensuring responsiveness. If we had to rely on Washington DC for decisions close to home, we might be waiting a while.
- It splits up power between different levels of government, making it harder for any single interest group to dominate the government. In the age of Donald Trump, for example, many states and larger cities pushed back against several of the president's policies.
- It helps to protect liberty, by providing a strong national government that can prevent states from usurping liberty, but also making it harder for the federal government to do the same. This has been important. The federal government forced the southern states to finally accept and enforce civil rights, while states have led the way in normalizing gay marriage, medical marijuana, and, to a lesser extent, immigrant rights.
- It increases opportunities for citizen participation. There are, in fact, many opportunities to get involved in government at all levels.
- It helps to manage conflict by providing arenas for its articulation. This is another important feature, as long as you believe that talking about and trying to resolve problems peacefully is better than throwing things at each other.

It also has its weaknesses:

- It can make government seem more remote. We have so many levels and branches and pieces of government, we sometimes can't see the beach for the sand, leaving many Americans confused about who does what.
- It makes elections more complex. Especially in Washington, particularly in presidential years, we have some of the longest ballots of any country on earth.

- It impedes adoption of national standards, and thereby predictability and uniformity. Ever been to Oregon? Don't try to pump your own gas.
- It can lead to duplication and confusion. (See remote government, above.)
- Local biases can damage the national interest. What's good for Washington might not be good for Iowa, and vice versa, and any such disagreement begs the question of whether it's good for the country.

What's most true about federalism is that states constantly argue that they should 1) get more autonomy from the federal government but 2) not lose any funding as a result. States often have a legitimate complaint that the Congress and president sometimes order states to engage in one program or another without providing the money to make it work. Congress and President Bush, for example, provided little funding to implement No Child Left Behind, while at the same time threatening school districts with loss of funds if they didn't meet the program's goals. The fact that the federal government provides relatively little money for education at any level should underscore how tight most school district budgets are.

Advocates for greater state control range from those who simply want more leeway to engage in policy initiatives to those who hope to use the states to do away with programs such as welfare and to limit some groups' right to vote. A more conservative U.S. Supreme Court has provided help to advocates of "states' rights" by limiting the power of the federal government to tell states what to do. It should be noted that until recently states' rights was pretty much a code phrase for legalized discrimination against non-white people. Originally, national leaders believed—and the courts ruled—that the Bill of Rights of the Constitution only applied to the federal government because it was believed that the states would not discriminate against their own citizens. They did, however, and it took until the 1950s before a more progressive Supreme Court began to enforce observation of basic liberties on the states.

As long as the dollars keep flowing from the other Washington, states tend to play along. Like all states, Washington has benefitted greatly from federal investment. Federal dollars helped pay for the Hanford Nuclear Reservation (a mixed blessing, but a lot of jobs); the Columbia River dam system; and irrigation projects in the Columbia Basin. These projects helped make eastern Washington the agricultural powerhouse that it is, to the benefit of the entire state.[2] (As always, there are tradeoffs: dams mean more water for people and agriculture but are very bad for salmon runs, another important part of the local economy.)

Washington and all the states exist within the context of a federal republic. They are not entirely free to do whatever they want, but they still have a great ability to organize and try to improve society in a way that benefits their citizens. You will have to decide whether your state is living up to that ideal.

CHAPTER FOUR

Rules of the Road

THE CONSTITUTION

In addition to the U.S. Constitution, every state has its own constitution, including Washington. The idea of constitutions grew in part out of the royal charters granted to the original thirteen colonies; Congress ordered the states to write new charters soon after independence was declared. Massachusetts's constitution, largely written by John Adams in 1780, is the oldest constitution in continuous use in the world (the U.S. Constitution wasn't written until 1788). If you remember how federalism divides and shares power between the states and the federal government, it should be easy to see that states need constitutions because they have their own spheres of authority.

Constitutions are supposed to establish basic principles of government, and also define the roles of government and citizens within that government. Constitutions compel citizens and governments to adhere to the laws as written. They restrain government from infringing on citizens' rights and they outline citizens' responsibilities and duties as part of society. While most Americans are probably aware that we have a constitution and that it says things about rights and government, the majority of U.S. citizens are apparently unaware that their states have their own constitutions. Which is too bad because they really can have an impact on your life.

"They should know it exists, and it really makes a huge difference," said Hugh Spitzer, a University of Washington (UW) law professor. "It makes a difference not only at the state level but at the national level, because the states have so much ability to counteract the national government."

The usual rap on state constitutions is that they're too long, too detailed, and sometimes contradictory. And indeed, some of them are. Alabama's constitution is 310,000 words long, making it the longest (and most amended) constitution on earth. The average state constitution is 27,000 words long, though that number falls a bit if you throw out Alabama's. The U.S. Constitution, including twenty-seven amendments, is 7,591 words long.

Constitutions are supposed to limit themselves to fundamental law, but most state constitutions don't. State constitutions spend too much time trying to account for every event. The constitution of the state of Georgia, for example, includes a clause about how to tax mobile homes. This is actually an important issue; it affects both homeowners and state revenues. But by putting it in the constitution, it's much more difficult for the Georgia General Assembly to amend the law as circumstances change. In Georgia, as in Washington, a constitutional amendment requires a two-thirds vote by both the state house and the senate, plus a majority vote by the citizens of the state. To this day, state constitutions include clauses about how to dispose of dead animals; the treatment of pregnant pigs; whether to teach home economics in schools; and regulating steamboats.[1]

Some have viewed Washington's constitution in a similar light. "Washington's state constitution is a contorted combination of basic law with dozens of specific provisions that are the functional equivalents of legislative enactments at the constitutional level," wrote one observer. She said it is a "check on legislative authority and . . . a practical obstacle to flexible, modern government."[2] Of course, she didn't really say why she thought this, and there are some potentially good features of Washington's constitution, depending on your point of view. More on that in a moment.

The U.S. Constitution is only 4,543 words long if you exclude the amendments. Such brevity is uncommon in the world of constitutions. Only the Vatican's constitution is shorter than ours. At least one study noted that longer constitutions tend to require more amendments because they're so specific they end up hurting people. Those authors also found a correlation between longer constitutions and weaker economies, though that could be because countries with weaker economies are more likely to write bad constitutions.[3]

Given the relative singularity of the U.S. Constitution, it's possible that our expectations are unrealistic.

"Our expectations of what a constitution should look like is driven by the U.S. Constitution, which is clean and spare and has very few words," said UW professor Spitzer. "If you look comparatively around the world, suddenly our state constitutions look normal. Many, many countries have long constitutions with a lot of detail.

"The issue is what kinds of things do you want to entrench, what kinds of things do you want to strengthen?" he added. "You can debate that. Look at Article XII [in the Washington constitution]: railroad tracks of the same gauge have to have an interchange switch. What was important to people at the time may not be to us."

As noted above, the challenge of this is that it's much more difficult to change a constitution than it is to amend a law. Most legislative changes to the law require a simple majority vote; amending a constitution typically requires legislative super-majority votes (three-fifths or, as in Washington, two-thirds), plus a majority popular vote. So while it may be wise to make bedrock principles of government harder to change, setting everyday matters in political concrete may make less sense.

Then again, brevity tends to invite differing conclusions on what something means. The U.S. Constitution is precise in a few places and vague in many others. That has made it open to frequent and divergent interpretation. Despite their length and specificity, state constitutions frequently run into the same challenge. That leads to different ways of trying to interpret what our constitutions say. For example, originalists ask, what was the intent of the authors? Strict constructionists argue that the constitution should be interpreted exactly as written. A third school, "the living constitution," says that the document needs to be reinterpreted in light of current conditions.

There's a logic to all three approaches. What the Founding Fathers thought shouldn't be dismissed out of hand; some pretty bright people worked on the document and we might still learn from them. On other hand, they lived in a different world, and the one thing that they really have in common is that they're all gone.

Strict constructionism can be appealing because if words don't have specific meanings, there is no way for us to agree on anything. If words mean whatever we want them to mean, do they really mean anything? On the other hand, the First Amendment to the U.S. Constitution says, in part, "Congress shall make no law . . . abridging the freedom of speech, or of the press; or the right of the people peaceably to assemble." And yet there is an entire body of law that restricts freedom of speech, such as the idea that you can't yell, "Fire!" in a crowded room (unless there is one). Moreover, in many places you may need a permit to have a parade or a protest. So "no law" doesn't always mean no law.

Finally, the idea of a living constitution is somewhat compelling because it can allow us to reinterpret and apply the document as needed. For example, the Second Amendment guarantees the right to bear arms, but it's at least worth asking if the Founding Fathers would have felt the same way had they dealt with AK-47s instead of flintlock muskets. Then again, if it means whatever we want it to mean, does it really mean anything?

In practice, people tend to be very uneven in their application of constitutional principles, choosing one interpretation over another depending on their desires. As our critic of Washington's constitution, the late Linda Louise Blackwelder Pall noted, "Many have offered arguments advocating adherence to the text of a constitution and the framers' intent in the guise of getting back to the real foundations of the constitutional document. More often than not, these arguments seek to constrain more liberal, progressive, and modern interpretations of constitutional provisions."[4]

PEOPLE IN POLITICS: SHERYL GORDON MCCLOUD

Sheryl Gordon McCloud kept wanting something bigger. Eventually, that led to her becoming one of the people responsible for interpreting and applying the Washington State constitution.

After college, she got a factory job, then did some office work. That led to working as a legal secretary, during which time she thought, "I could do that."

Her law firm supported her journey through law school. "When I got out of law school I went to a large firm in LA and decided that was not for me," she said. She ended up working in the public defender's office in Seattle.

Eventually, she moved her specialty to appellate cases—appeals of lower court decisions. "It's a way to have more of an impact than just one particular case," McCloud said.

"I had clerked for a Ninth Circuit Court of Appeals judge," she said. "Working on appellate cases gave me the opportunity to really reflect on the law and have an impact on more than one person. Because if it's a published decision, that can really have an impact."

That led to a distinguished, thirty-year career as an appellate attorney until she decided to try for something bigger. In 2012 she was elected to the Washington Supreme Court.

"In a way it's a big jump, but in a way I was running for what I really knew how to do the best," she said of going from being an attorney to serving on the highest court in the state. As an appellate attorney, she had seen how the state supreme court worked. "So I think I really knew the business of the court, far better than most attorneys."

Others on the court have more judicial experience or experience in different kinds of legal practice. Justice McCloud said she thinks that variety of experience is good for the court.

Nonetheless, when she became a justice, there were still surprises.

"Pretty much everything surprised me," she said. "I have to get a robe? How do I sign my name? I get two clerks and the law library is at my disposal?

"In terms of the cases, though, I had been litigating appellate cases for almost thirty years, so I was pretty familiar with some of the subject matter, unfamiliar with others," she said.

The state supreme court hears appeals from lower courts.

"We're a court of discretionary review," Justice McCloud said. "We end up taking about 10 percent of the cases that are presented to us."

Five justices must agree to hear an appeal. "We generally sit in a department of five to consider all the cases that are presented to us. If the five are unanimous, that's that. If the five are split, it goes to all nine to make a decision."

The court hears a variety of cases, not all of which involve substantial constitutional questions (unlike the U.S. Supreme Court). "Maybe a statute that affects people all over the state," Justice McCloud said. "We'll take it if there's a conflict in the courts below, a conflict in one of our decisions, or with the U.S. Supreme Court."

While most appeals go through the court of appeals first, they can go from a trial court to the state supreme court if the issue is pressing, she said.

Writing decisions that affect people's lives, such as *State v. Arlene's Flowers* (2017), in which the court ruled that a florist couldn't refuse service to a gay couple for their wedding, is a big responsibility, Justice McCloud said.

"It's a lot of responsibility," she said. "It's a privilege, in that people voted for me to trust me with that responsibility to do what the law requires, even if I don't agree with that, or it's not my personal position."

Her usual approach is to focus on the job at hand.

"I love my job," Justice McCloud said. "I loved being an advocate also, I just loved it. I was able to be involved with such important issues."

While acknowledging that it worked for her, McCloud said she thinks electing judges is a workable system. Some states appoint judges; others use elections.

"It's a valid question whether electing or appointing judges is the best way to go," she said. "Being elected is going to skew my viewpoint. There's plusses and minuses to both of them [electing vs. appointing judges]. I think you can make a mess of either system, or you can get the best out of either system."

Elections do pose a challenge, however, since they are decided by majorities. "The job of the judge is to not be influenced by the majority but to protect the rights of the minority," Justice McCloud said.

Either way, courts give citizens a way to resolve disagreements among people.

"The courts do one thing and that is resolve disputes peacefully," Justice McCloud said. "It's the thing that holds society together, because conflicts are going to arise, in business, personal life, in crime, due to greed or to power. Having courts that people have confidence in means that they'll turn to the courts and won't take to the streets. We resolve disputes as best we can and settle them peacefully."

And the courts aren't just for lawyers and judges, she said.

"They [people] should know that we're open to the public in every sense of the word," Justice McCloud said. "Our hearings are all televised on TVW [the public channel that broadcasts much of what happens in Olympia]. You can go online, they're all archived. Our doors are open to all our hearings. We produce opinions and our name goes on those opinions, we're out there for everyone to see, yell at, get involved with, watch—we are an open branch of government. We welcome the public and we welcome public supervision. Washington has a special constitutional provision to have open courtrooms. I'm pretty proud of that and I want people to know."

DIFFERENCES: THE U.S. VS. STATE CONSTITUTIONS

Although they touch on many similar subjects, there is one fundamental difference between the U.S. and Washington constitutions. The U.S. Constitution is largely aimed at restraining the power of government. It spells out what government can do and makes clear that it's not supposed to do more than that. It was a product of its time and was written by people who came from thirteen separate states who thought of themselves as sovereign and thereby grudgingly surrendered some spoonfuls of power to a new national government. The general tenor of the document is that the states and the people have ceded certain powers to the national government, which it would not otherwise have. The original states, which started as British colonies, predated the national government and took a different view of government power. Under state constitutions, including Washington's, states are presumed to have power and constitutions spell that out. So the absence of something in a state constitution doesn't preclude a state being able to take that action. This is sometimes called "plenary power," power that is not open to interpretation.

Consider the differences in how the two documents treat the question of freedom of speech. In the First Amendment, the U.S. Constitution says, "Congress shall make no law respecting an establishment of religion, or prohibiting the free exercise thereof; or abridging the freedom of speech, or of the press; or the right of the people peaceably to assemble, and to petition the Government for a redress of grievances." Aside from lumping a lot into one amendment, the federal document simply restrains the ability of government to circumscribe citizens' right to say what they want.

Contrast this with how Washington's constitution addresses the same subject. First, Article I, section 1 immediately sets a slightly different direction from the U.S. version: "All political power is inherent in the people, and governments derive their just powers from the consent of the governed, and are established to protect and maintain individual rights." As we just noted, the intent of the U.S. Constitution is to restrain the power of government. But the Washington State constitution immediately establishes that it is the duty of the state to protect people's rights. Whereas the

U.S. Constitution is a limit on power, the Washington constitution begins with a call to action. This leads us, a few lines later, to Article I, section 7: "Every person may freely speak, write and publish on all subjects, being responsible for the abuse of that right." This is a far cry from "no law"; in Washington's constitution, you have the right to free speech and you are responsible for how you use it. So while contemporary interpretation of the First Amendment has generally left room for some restrictions on freedom of speech, Article I, section 7 clearly implies that government has the power to regulate speech.

That idea can be applied differently by state and federal courts. Whereas the U.S. Supreme Court said a shopping mall could bar people who were only there to protest the Vietnam War (*Lloyd Corporation v. Tanner*, 1972), the Washington Supreme Court said that a mall owner had to show that its private property interests outweighed a reasonable exercise of free speech (*Alderwood Associates v. Washington Environmental Council*, 1981). Washington courts have often used the state constitution to go further in preserving individual rights and liberty, treating federal constitutional rights as "a floor, not the ceiling."[5]

ORIGINS

Washington's constitution got its start with statehood. Washington citizens wrestled with the idea of becoming a state almost as soon as it became a territory, finally agreeing to pursue statehood in 1876, when it appeared that Walla Walla might be lost to Oregon. The 1878 Walla Walla Convention drafted a constitution, as submitting such a document was one of the requirements of joining the club. State voters approved it by a 4–1 margin, but it was never officially adopted as Washington didn't immediately achieve statehood.

The constitution in use today was drafted at a convention in 1889, with the 1878 constitution as one of its stepparents. The convention featured seventy-five elected delegates, two-thirds Republicans and one-third Democrats, elected from twenty-five districts scattered across the territory. The voting arrangement ensured that some Democrats, then the minority party, would be at the convention. It was a mix of people, including lawyers, farmers, business owners, doctors, editors, loggers, bankers, and at least one fisherman.[6]

Their task, as has been the task of every group of people trying to create a new government, was to craft a government that was strong enough to do something but not so strong that it could oppress its own citizens. They feared power but knew it was necessary; they greatly distrusted corporations, including railroads, and wrestled with how much power to give each office. Some thought the new state's legislature should be so large it would be difficult to bribe, while others thought it should be small since a larger body would be more expensive. "The fear of an overly powerful Legislature was so great that a delegate was quoted in a Tacoma newspaper as saying that if a foreigner were suddenly dropped into the convention, he would think that the delegates were fighting a great enemy—the Legislature."[7] For some reason they trusted a governor more than a legislature, but not much. They created eight statewide elected offices but granted the governor more veto power than that held by any other elected official in the country (at that time). The governor only got veto power because the framers so distrusted the legislature.

Like most people who find themselves in the position of writing a constitution, Washington's founders had to face what we now call the legitimation crisis: How do we keep the state (government) legitimate in the eyes of groups of people whose interests don't always coincide? The founders had to balance the interests of small and large groups, individuals and businesses, and all sorts of interests within the commercial sphere. Later, the constitution was amended to limit the governor's line-item veto power to appropriations (spending) bills. This meant the governor could still veto other kinds of legislation, but she or he has to veto entire sections, not just eliminate words or sentences to change the intent of the measure.

The document got its start as did other western constitutions, by borrowing from existing documents. Washington's constitution is largely borrowed from that of other states, with big chunks of it lifted wholesale from the constitutions of the United States, California, Oregon, Wisconsin, and Indiana. As two scholars noted, "Indeed, few of the provisions in Washington's constitution can claim originality."[8] Voters approved of the document in a special election in October 1889, again by a 4–1 margin. It was sent to the other Washington, along with another request for statehood. This time it worked.

WHAT IT SAYS

The constitution as adopted sets up the structure of government and provides a rather expansive guarantee of individual rights and liberties. As one of its stepparents is the U.S. Constitution, and that document guarantees U.S. citizens a republican form of government—electing officials to make decisions on citizens' behalf—so the congressional Enabling Act directed the territory to create the same. It also required religious freedom and civil and political rights regardless of race or color.

Washington's constitution has thirty-two articles comprising 230 sections, covering everything from citizens' basic rights to the composition of the state militia. Along the way it touches on the branches of government; the nature of local governments; and what shall be the official state seal. It includes a germaneness rule, which means you can't amend a legislative measure with an addition that has nothing to do with the original bill. Public officials are subject to recall: if enough signatures are gathered, citizens can vote to remove someone from office. All three branches of government (executive, legislative, and judicial) are subject to democratic control via direct elections. Many states don't elect judges.

As noted earlier, Washington's voters, like so many before and after, had a fundamental distrust of power, living at a time of concentrated wealth, corporate power, and a fair amount of government corruption. (As with so many other terms, this word has a meaning that people often stretch. Corruption means people in government taking money in exchange for decisions and not just anything we happen to disagree with.) The authors of Washington's founding document responded to the conditions they experienced, and so executive authority was fragmented between the governor, lieutenant governor, secretary of state, treasurer, superintendent of public instruction, commissioner of public lands, attorney general, and auditor. Not content with that, the state's political ancestors later added the insurance commissioner. This disperses executive authority: the governor can't just tell a group of executives—who are elected separately rather than appointed by her or him—what to do. Separately elected officials don't owe their power or position to anyone but the people who elected them.

The founders of Washington's government especially distrusted corporate power. They lived at a time when railroads dominated the economic and social fabric of the nation, and other giant industrial organizations were beginning to exert a lot of influence on governments large and small. Nearly half the country still lived on farms in the 1880s, and likely more than that in Washington. Amid the industrial revolution, farmers were becoming more productive, which meant bigger harvests but lower crop prices. Railroads, meanwhile, provided the only efficient way of moving goods east and west. Without any real competition, they could charge higher prices, and so farmers tended to blame all their problems on the railroads. And railroads, because they were so economically dominant, had a lot of political power, and successfully resisted efforts to regulate their business.

We see here the fundamental competition between groups that defines both pluralism and elitism. In this case, power of the elites—railroad interests—was opposed by other groups—farmers and non-railroad commercial interests. As a consequence, Washington State's founders sought to spread power into the hands of the voters and away from the powerful interests. There are a lot of trade-offs here. On the one hand, a new governor is limited in changing policy in state government because there's so much of the government he or she doesn't control. On the other hand, it makes it more difficult for a bad governor (there have been a couple) to run roughshod over the people.

"That was the original intent of having so many elected officials," said UW professor Spitzer. "In some states you elect the governor and that's about it. The theory is that state government is more responsive because you've got one person to look to and that's the governor. The people who wrote the [Washington] constitution didn't believe that."

And yet power is granted to the government. As we noted earlier, whereas the U.S. Constitution limits government to the things expressly outlined in the document, under Washington's constitution, government can do anything not expressly forbidden.[9]

Washington's constitution lists twenty-seven separate individual liberties, placing them in Article I and not, as in the U.S. Constitution, as an afterthought in the Bill of Rights. Washington's constitution addresses them as a "positive affirmation of liberties . . . and therefore can be interpreted against both the government and private power."[10] It is particularly clear about freedom of religion, and it bars giving public money to support any religion.

Article XII specifically addresses corporate power. Among other proscriptions, it restricts legislation that would only benefit certain parties (under Washington's constitution, if your business gets a tax break, every business in the same field also gets that tax break). It specifically bans monopolies and trusts. Finally, it bars the lending of public credit to private enterprise. The state couldn't just make a loan to Boeing or Microsoft (unlike a lot of states). Stronger restraints on corporate power were considered but did not pass.

DETAILS, DETAILS

At thirty-two thousand words, the Washington constitution is not as unwieldy as some, but it's still probably got too much detail. Too-precise constitutions hamstring states when it comes to making policy. For example, in the early 1980s, amid a deep recession, the legislature tried to help out the timber industry by giving it a break on the fees it paid to harvest timber on state lands. But because those fees go to help fund school construction, and the state constitution makes clear that school funding is a priority, the measure was thrown out by the courts.

This one issue—school funding—has been echoing down the halls of the Capitol since the 1970s. Article IX of the state constitution, "Education," specifies what the state must do with regard to "common schools," essentially the public K–12 school system. Section 1, the preamble, says, "It is the paramount duty of the state to make ample provision for the education of all children residing within its borders, without distinction or preference on account of race, color, caste, or sex." No other state constitution has a provision like that, and those are the words from 1889. The key word in that passage is "ample," because in a series of lawsuits brought by parents, the state courts have consistently ruled that the state legislature was not adequately funding public schools. Early decisions required the state to spend more on local school districts, which previously had been largely funded by local property tax levies. That led to wildly uneven funding, since a district with a strong property tax base could collect a lot more money than a district with a weak one. In the most recent case, *McCleary v. Washington* (2012), the state supreme court ruled for the plaintiffs and ordered the legislature to come up with more money for schools. In 2013, for example, Washington ranked thirty-ninth in the country in per pupil spending and spent less than the national average. Thereupon commenced six years of wrangling, including, at one point, the court holding the legislature in contempt for its failure to act. Finally, in 2018 the court ruled that the legislators had done enough and the case was settled. While this may raise questions about the balance of power in the state, the bottom line is that the constitution compelled judges and lawmakers to act. Several Republican legislators complained that the court had overstepped its bounds, but the court's 7–2 vote and the rather clear language of the constitution might indicate otherwise.

AMENDMENTS

If you don't like what the constitution says, you can amend it. Amending Washington's constitution requires a two-thirds vote in both the house and the senate, plus a majority vote of the people. It could also be amended by a constitutional convention. Voters have twice rejected such conventions. Washington's constitution has been amended 106 times, which isn't bad by state-level standards. Some states have rewritten their entire constitutions wholesale, multiple times. Georgia has written ten constitutions; Louisiana is on its eleventh.

Many more amendments are proposed than actually become law. Among the changes to the constitution have been direct primary elections in 1907; women's suffrage in 1910; the creation of port districts, 1911; and initiatives, referenda, and recall in 1912. All totaled, 180 amendments have been proposed and made the ballot, with 106 adopted.

There have been many calls to rewrite the state constitution over the years. Voters turned down a constitutional convention in 1918. Constitutional reform commissions got nowhere in the 1930s and the 1960s. Gov. Dan Evans tried three times to push for constitutional reform between 1965 and 1972, including a convention in '72. Given the somewhat scary things people say today about rights and liberties, the idea of opening up the whole thing might sound a bit iffy. But at that time, there was still something of a broad civic consensus in Washington politics.

"When Gov. Dan Evans was in his last term of office, he decided to advocate some major reform of the state government," said Sam Reed, who was involved in the effort. "Among other steps he took, he created the Commission for Constitutional Alternatives. He recruited me to be its executive director. It was a blue ribbon, bipartisan, diverse commission. It was a two-year project. I was authorized to hire a small staff.

"After some initial research, we concluded that our state constitution is antiquated, too prescriptive, contained too much micro-managing and was characterized as having too much statutory rather than constitutional language," said Reed, who later became secretary of state. "Consequently, the commission proposed that a state constitutional convention be called to start over—so to speak. At that point in history, a number of states had done that."

It's not entirely clear how this would work. If a convention is called for by two-thirds of the legislature, the idea goes to the ballot. Or it could happen via initiative. Presuming the voters say yes to the convention, in its next session the legislature passes enabling legislation to call the convention. And then, in a maddening bit of vagueness, Article XXXIII, section 2 says, "Such convention shall consist of a number of members, not less than that of the most numerous branch of the legislature." This could mean that in enabling the convention, the legislature must determine the details of the affair and how delegates are to be chosen, knowing that there must be at least ninety-eight members of the convention. Or not.

"We assumed that the legislature would decide the terms and that delegates would be publicly elected," Reed said. Governor Evans submitted an "executive request" bill to the legislature, calling for the state constitutional convention. It passed in the Republican-controlled house of representatives. "But the Democrats controlled the state senate and stopped it in committee. Our 'nose count' indicated that we had the votes if it got to the floor, but that didn't happen," Reed said.

"So, a group of us who believed in this filed an initiative to call for a state constitutional convention," he said. "Volunteers were very successful in getting signatures, but we didn't have money to pay for signature gatherers. So, we fell short of qualifying for the ballot. Based on polling, it looked like the public would have voted for it, but they didn't get a chance.

"Interestingly enough, most of the major reforms that we specifically addressed have subsequently been corrected via individual constitutional amendments," Reed added.

Whether you like Washington's constitution or think it's a bit clunky, it's the defining document of the state's government. Within that framework, government and citizens must figure out who can do what, how it gets paid for, and try to make it all work.

PART II

Choosing Leaders, Chasing Policy

Politics and governance involve some common building blocks: parties, interest groups, and elections. Parties organize to win elections and make policy. Interest groups try to make sure the policy benefits them, trying to influence both elections and the legislative politics that follow. Once again different groups compete to get what they want out of government or to keep government from doing things they don't like. This competition is partially decided via elections, where Washington State has a less common electoral system but a national reputation for clean and secure election systems. As we'll see in part III, this policy competition gets played out in the legislature and the governor's office. But it all begins with elections.

CHAPTER FIVE

How We Choose

ELECTIONS AND VOTING

Elections are how we choose the people who represent us. In Washington and some other states, people also vote to decide on various ballot measures. Remember that Washington residents live in a republic, not a democracy, so generally we elect people to make decisions on our behalf.

Washington State has elections every year. Not just the four-year cycle of presidential elections; not just the two-year cycle of congressional elections. In odd-numbered years, citizens vote for local offices—cities, counties, school boards, public utility districts. And all of these elections matter. In fact, local elections might matter more. In many counties in the state, county elections are held in even-numbered years, which means higher turnout but confronts voters with even longer ballots. King County elected county officials in odd-numbered years until 2022, when voters there approved moving those races to even-numbered years. (This was pushed by majority Democrats on the county council, who hoped to increase voter turnout. Ironically, this should help Republicans since Republican voters are more likely to keep voting all the way to the end of the ballot, where you'll find the county races.)

Elections in Washington State occur annually in a two-part cycle. First come primary elections in August, in which the number of candidates is narrowed to two. The two candidates who get the most votes in the primary advance to the general election in November. Having primary elections in August is a relatively recent change, made to help elections officials do a better job of managing the electoral process. For most of the state's history, primaries were in September, which helped legislative incumbents by giving them more time to seek reelection after the legislative session ends sometime in the spring.

Washington's primary elections have changed several times in recent years. Candidates were chosen via party convention in Washington until 1907, when the state switched to primary elections. Washington adopted the blanket primary, via initiative, in 1934. The goal was to encourage the election of more centrist candidates.[1] Under this system you could show up at the polls and vote for a Republican in one primary contest and a Democrat in the other. Before states adopted primary elections, candidates were chosen by the parties alone, and if you weren't in good standing with the party, you couldn't get your name on the ballot. Primaries in general, and the blanket primary in particular, were a reaction to parties' power and the frustrations of many voters and potential candidates.

In a blanket primary, the primary election whittled down the field to one Democrat, one Republican, and any third-party candidate who managed to get more than 1 percent of the vote. Turnout is usually lower in primaries, so that the party faithful—people who strongly identify with Republicans or Democrats—were the ones who determined who got the party's nomination. This sometimes meant that the party's nominee was to the right or the left of most voters.

The parties didn't like the blanket primary. They argued that voters from the other party could "cross over" and nominate someone who was less electable in the general election. There isn't much evidence that this has ever happened, although some voters probably did cross over and vote against unpopular incumbent Gov. Dixie Lee Ray in the 1980 primary. Moreover, parties would prefer that all voters have to register to vote by party (the norm in many states), meaning only real Republicans or definite Democrats could choose the party's nominee. This system also gives parties easy access to a large database of potential supporters and contributors.

California adopted a blanket primary in 1996; California parties sued, and the U.S. Supreme Court ruled in 2004 that it violated the U.S. Constitution's right of free association, forcing the parties to represent candidates with whom they had no real association. Washington State's parties, despite Washington voters' overwhelming preference for the blanket primary, said they would challenge the state's law. They filed suit and eventually the courts also threw Washington's primary law out. The state legislature then passed a new primary law, featuring a Louisiana-style primary. In Louisiana the top two candidates in terms of primary votes advance to the general election, regardless of party.

Then-governor Gary Locke vetoed this law, leaving only the part of the bill that was the back-up plan, which was called the Montana plan or the pick-a-party primary. The Montana plan said you had to choose which party you would vote for in the primary election only. If you decide that day you are a Republican, you can only vote in the Republican primary, and so on. This could have further depressed primary election turnout, as many primary elections are not contested. This would put the parties further in the hands of the extreme section of each party, the rock-ribbed Republicans and die-hard Democrats who vote almost no matter what. Those folks tend to be further to the right or left of where most voters are, so they aren't necessarily indicative of what the majority thinks.

The Washington State Grange, the farm-based organization that originally sponsored the initiative that created the blanket primary way back in 1934, sponsored an initiative to restore the Louisiana-style primary in 2005. But in July of that year a federal court overturned the initiative, bringing the state back to the Montana-style primary, in which you vote by party in the primary election only. Then in 2007 the U.S. Supreme Court ruled that we could in fact have a Louisiana-style primary, so the state was back to square one. The Grange pushed through an initiative for the top-two primary, which the U.S. Supreme Court found constitutional in 2008. The system, they said, had to make clear that names on the ballot weren't necessarily endorsed by a particular party. For that reason, primary election candidates list "prefers Democratic Party" or "prefers Republican Party" in the state voters' pamphlet. The candidates sometimes get a bit creative with their party identification, including the not uncommon "GOP Party." GOP stands for Grand Old Party, a post–Civil War nickname for the Republicans. So, such candidates are saying they prefer the Grand Old Party Party. Party on, dudes!

Parties still don't like this system, despite the fact that 76 percent of Washington voters continue to favor the top-two primary.[2] Parties continue to claim that voters could cross over and choose the worst candidate for the other party. Aside from the 1980 election, there is no evidence that this has ever happened. They also say it robs voters of choice because in some districts, as there may not be a Republican or a Democrat on the November ballot. While that could be true, in those districts in the past the choice has not been meaningful—voters could choose between the candidate from the dominant party in that district or the underfunded Democrats and Republicans who had no chance of winning. The parties' final complaint, that candidates could run as Republicans or Democrats when they really weren't, has always been true. The top-two primary changes nothing in that regard. However, it's very hard on third parties, such as the Libertarians, who find it difficult to survive the primary vote and make it to the general election ballot. The only time you see a Libertarian on the general election ballot is when either a Republican or a Democrat didn't file for the office. Despite worries that the blanket primary could have some negative impact on the kinds of candidates seeking office, research shows that the type of primary appears to have little effect on who runs.[3] It may have meant, however, that fewer legislative contests are contested by both major parties.[4]

General elections are the first Tuesday in November, the same as the rest of the country. Special elections, such as school levies and parks bonds, can come any time of year (although elections always fall on a Tuesday). State and federal candidates typically run for office in even-numbered years, while odd-numbered years feature local elections, such as city councils and special purpose districts.

Any losing candidate can call for a recount if she or he is willing to pay for it. Parties and groups of at least five voters have the same right. If the difference in an election is less than one-half of 1 percent, and less than two thousand votes, a recount is mandatory. The state reimburses county elections departments for mandatory recounts.

VOTING

Another important feature of Washington elections is that voting is done entirely by mail. This makes it easy to vote as all you need is a pen. In 2018, after experiments by King County found that postage-paid mailing envelopes increased turnout, the state came up with the money so that no one would have to use a stamp. All counties in the state have ballot drop boxes in addition to prepaid postage. Despite prepaid postage, nearly half of voters statewide used a drop box in the 2018 election.

The ballots hit the mail eighteen days before the election and must be postmarked (or in a drop box) by election night. Consequently, you can vote at your leisure as long as you get it in on time. This fact alters the practice of campaigns, since a last-minute campaign push won't affect the people who have already voted. Meanwhile, it seems to be working: voter turnout has been up slightly, and 99 percent of the ballots in the 2016 election were able to be counted. Less than 1 percent were invalidated, which can happen, for example, if your signature doesn't match the signature on file from your driver's license or official state ID.

In order to vote, you have to register. Thanks to recent changes to state law, you can now register to vote up to eight days before an election. If you have a valid state ID, such as a driver's license, you can register to vote online. You can also use that service to change your address so that your ballot finds you wherever you might have moved. As of 2019 Washington residents who are citizens are automatically registered to vote when they renew their driver's licenses (although you can opt out—before, you had to opt in). You can register to vote in person at your county elections office up to election day. In addition, sixteen- and seventeen-year-olds can preregister to vote, although they still won't be eligible to vote until they turn eighteen. Of course, you must be a citizen to vote, and contrary to a number of assertions by one side of the political spectrum, voter fraud is extremely rare anywhere in the United States, including Washington. Legions of non-citizens are not lining up to cast ballots; party operatives are not "harvesting" ballots and changing people's votes. In fact, Washington's voting system would be very difficult to hack since it is not tied to the internet. This is one of the reasons why internet voting hasn't been adopted—it's not entirely clear how you would ensure that the people voting are in fact who they say they are.

You also need to be a legal resident of the state to be able to vote; that means being in the state for at least thirty days before election day. You must be eighteen by election day, not disqualified by a court order, and not currently under Department of Corrections supervision for a felony. Ex-felons can get their voting rights restored, but it's not a simple process.

WHO VOTES AND WHY

Despite candidates' money, time, and effort, Americans don't vote in high numbers, and they vote in local elections least of all. Turnout can be under 30 percent in some elections, and that's only turnout of registered voters—it doesn't even count eligible but unregistered non-voters. This is somewhat surprising given how much Americans complain about government.

Turnout patterns are predictable: the greatest number vote in presidential years, followed by even-numbered non-presidential years (which feature congressional and state legislative races in Washington), followed by odd-numbered years (local elections), which have the lowest turnout. Turnout tends to be higher if the economy is doing poorly, and lower if it's doing well. Turnout for primary and special elections tend to be the lowest of all. For example, statewide turnout was 78 percent in the 2016 general election, but just under 27 percent for the 2017 primary. That only rose to 37 percent in the 2017 general election. General election turnout in 2020 (84.1 percent) was almost double the turnout in 2019 (45.2 percent). It's difficult to say why people pay less attention to elections that are much closer to home. They may not understand the impact of local government. The decline of newspapers amid the age of social media means that local government can get very little media attention, but local elections have nearly always had low turnout, even before the internet. And the overall complexity of American government—branches, levels, and overlapping jurisdictions—may mean that people may not recognize exactly who does what.

The demographics of Washington voters speak to this. Older, better educated people tend to vote more often than do other groups. People sixty-five and over are the largest group of registered voters in the state and those eighteen to twenty-four are the smallest. Ironically, people ages eighteen to forty-four are 47 percent of the population, 34 percent for forty-five to sixty-four and 18 percent for ages sixty-five and up. Women are more likely to be registered than men and more likely to vote if registered. Ironically, perhaps, in Washington men are more likely to file for office. Nationally, voting correlates strongly with education and income. The more you have of either, the more likely you are to vote. White and Black Americans are more likely to vote than either Asian or Latinx Americans. It's also not clear why either of those things is true; it may have something to do with more of the latter groups coming from places where voting was either discouraged or effectively didn't matter. Then again, people of color are less likely to be registered to vote, with fewer than 50 percent of Blacks registered for the 2008 election.[5] By 2020 that number had risen to 69 percent, still less than whites but more than Asian and Hispanic/Latinx Americans.[6] In Washington that year, 78.2 percent of whites were registered versus 64.7 percent of Blacks, 63.1 of Asian Americans, and 61 percent of Hispanic Americans.[7]

Overall, 5.3 million of Washington's more than 7 million citizens are eligible to vote, but only 4.3 million have registered. When 3.3 million voted in the 2016 election, that was the most ever. In 2020, however, that number rose to 4.1 million out of just under 4.9 million registered voters.[8] Most elections don't draw that kind of interest.

"In real life, people [elected officials] are chosen by a minority," said former secretary of state Kim Wyman, the state's top elections official. People vote for a variety of reasons. They like or dislike certain candidates; they want to be patriotic; they want to make a statement; or they want to see or stop change. The reasons eligible citizens don't vote—lack of time, lack of information, fear, dissatisfaction with the candidates, the issues, or the system—are somewhat harder to defend. Some economists have argued that one's vote makes such a small impact on any election that it simply doesn't matter if you vote. Of course, that presumes that others are voting. If more people chose that logic, it would further empower those who still voted.

The objections to voting are not difficult to answer. It doesn't take much time to vote. Information, via the voters' pamphlet (if not the internet) is easy to come by. Dissatisfaction with candidates represents an unrealistic view of the world: don't let the perfect be the enemy of the good. If you're expecting perfection in anything, you're likely to be disappointed. And there are some good reasons to vote. It is the one time in your life when you really are the equal of everyone else. Bill Gates and Jeff Bezos have no more votes than you do. And it matters. First, some elections are very tight. Some elections in Washington State have been decided by only a few dozen voters—the elections were that close.

Moreover, an important but often overlooked feature of elections is margin of victory, and this is why your vote always counts. It's important to vote even if your candidate doesn't win. Margin of victory is crucial to results down the road. Let's say Candidate X is challenging Senator Y for a seat in the state legislature. X is a Republican and Y is a Democrat. If X doesn't get more than 40 percent of the vote in the primary, no one's going to give her any money for the general, and you're likely stuck with Y for another four years. But in the general election, the closer the loser is to the winner in terms of the final vote, the more likely the winner will face a serious challenger next time. The other party concludes that the winner is vulnerable and tries to find a better candidate to run in the future. So if you don't like the winner, you vote against him or her to encourage more challenges down the road. If you do like the winner, you vote even when you know he or she is going to win in order to discourage serious challengers next time around. The more Y wins by, the less likely it is that she will face a serious challenger the next time around. The closer X gets, however, the more likely Y is going to get determined opposition in his next election. So your vote counts almost no matter the immediate outcome.

Finally, voting gives you the right to complain. One honest legislator who visits my classes regularly tells the students that he really doesn't have to listen to their concerns because eighteen- to twenty-one-year-olds vote less than any group in the country. Senior citizens have a better voting average than anybody. Who does the legislator listen to? Do the math. "You have the power every election to have your voice heard," said Kim Wyman. "Every time you choose not to participate, you give your power to them"—the people who do vote.

RUNNING FOR OFFICE

It's not difficult to run for office, though there are a few hoops to jump through. To run for most state offices you need to be eighteen and a citizen. People that young, or nearly that young, have been elected. Some offices, such as seats on the King County Council, require you to be twenty-one or older. You don't even have to be registered to vote, a fact that has hurt more than one candidate's campaign when people find out that the person who wants to represent you has, in fact, rarely voted. The filing deadline for offices is in May, and you can withdraw up to about a week later (or your name ends up on the ballot). There's usually a filing fee of 1 percent of the first year's salary for the office. Alternatively, you can submit a petition with the signatures of registered voters, one per dollar of the filing fee. (In 2020, amid all the restrictions because of COVID-19, the governor waived the filing requirements. As a consequence, the state had thirty-five people running for governor, all of whom appeared on the primary ballot.)

For statewide offices and for federal and state legislative districts that cross county boundaries, you must file with the secretary of state's office. For local offices and offices that fall within a single county, you file with your county elections department. You're supposed to be a resident of the area you hope to represent, which is sometimes a point of contention in campaigns when rumors start to circulate that candidate X does not in fact live in that district (which is not usually true).

Filing for office is just the start. You've got a campaign to run and that's going to take a number of things, most of which involve money. It takes money to get elected at any level. Research shows fairly consistently that candidates who get more money tend to do better. They can buy ads, hire consultants, and engage in social media campaigns. It gives them a chance to get their message out to potential voters. Asking for money is many candidates' least favorite part of the whole experience, but without it it's hard to get elected. On top of that, in Washington State, campaign contributions—except to political party committees—are limited. Interest groups such as businesses or unions (and individual donors) can give no more than $1,000 per election to a state legislative candidate, and no more than $2,000 to statewide or judicial candidates. This tends to encourage groups to spend money on behalf of or against a candidate on their own.

It helps to have a profile in the community you're trying to represent. If you're serious about politics, your first step should be to volunteer at the food bank, join the Rotary or the Kiwanis (or both), or get appointed to a citizen advisory board. If you just moved there, or you haven't been involved in the community in some meaningful way, your opponents will try to use that against you. Word of mouth matters. If Candidate X is a good person whom folks are always able to count on when something needs to be done, word gets around. And if Candidate Y isn't that person, word doesn't get around. That's not good when it comes time to fill in the ballot because people are more likely to vote for someone they've heard of. By the same token, the number of candidates who attempt to start at the top is surprising. Unless you're already well known, run for something smaller—school board, city council—before you attempt to run for Congress or governor.

Campaign finance in Washington State is regulated by the Public Disclosure Commission (PDC), a small, underfunded but feisty agency created via initiative in 1974. Candidates must report both contributions and expenditures. Candidates have a short-form reporting option that doesn't require them to divulge much information but also greatly limits how much they can spend. The PDC is generally underfunded, and some evidence indicates that limits on contribution size is encouraging people to just not report contributions. Both parties in the state have been slapped for unreported contributions. Limits on contributions may also have resulted in fewer contested legislative races, as parties channel scarce resources to the races they think they have the best chance of winning.

As noted above, serious candidates need serious money. In 2016 $144 million was spent on state and local elections in Washington State. Legislative campaigns average $70,000 a pop, with a handful of hotly contested state senate races topping the $1 million mark.[9]

The concern over money in elections is two-fold: first, candidates who spend more money tend to win more often (though not always), and second, big money flowing into campaigns from wealthy interest groups calls into question who elected officials are representing. The fear is always that interest groups with money will get their way, and not always to the benefit of ordinary citizens.

The city of Seattle, trying to get big money out of politics, adopted a program called Democracy Vouchers in 2015. In this program every qualifying Seattle resident gets four $25 democracy vouchers, which they can distribute to the city candidates of their choice. The 2019 election was to be the first big test of the program, funded by a voter-approved $3 million property tax levy. This is designed to limit the influence of big donors on candidates while helping to fund candidates' campaigns. It also limits how much candidates can spend. Seattle's plan immediately ran into a problem that has occurred elsewhere in the country with publicly financed campaigns, something I call the political prisoner's dilemma. The prisoner's dilemma is a classic logic game in which two prisoners must decide whether to cooperate or defect. If they cooperate, they both go free. But if one defects and the other cooperates, the defector goes free by ratting out the other prisoner.

Given those conditions, it's safer to defect. Applied to publicly financed campaigns, candidates will be tempted to skip the democracy vouchers, raise all the money they can, outspend their opponents, and win. The top money-raising candidates in the 2019 Seattle City Council elections did just that. Meanwhile, with limits on campaign contributions, interest groups were mounting their own campaigns for and against various candidates. Money, like electricity, seeks the path of least resistance.

Regardless of where they get their money, the ideal candidate would be bright, educated, experienced, well-connected in the community, and with an ability to understand and talk about important issues of the day. Money can help make up for so many candidates' general lack of these qualities. Money can hire consultants; pay for surveys; send out mailings to potential voters; print brochures, signs, and bumper stickers; or buy advertising. The preferred method of advertising has become direct mail, those cards and letters that fill up your mailbox every election cycle. Why? You can target mailings strictly to your district or city, or even to certain voters within your area. Media advertising, especially radio and TV, doesn't make sense for most local candidates because too much of that advertising dollar will go to contact people who don't live in your district—you're paying for eyes and ears that belong to people who couldn't vote for you if they wanted to. Ditto for billboards—are the people driving by residents of your district or your city? If not, you're paying for eyeballs that belong to people who can't vote for you.

Yard signs remain a staple of campaigning at the state and local level—simple, brightly colored, with the candidate's name prominently featured and some hint at what office she or he is running for. Candidates and their campaigns look for good spots in which to put them, especially if there's a way to anchor the sign, because the other side will steal signs whenever possible. Candidates may also grab a few signs and find a busy corner during commute hours, waving and smiling and attempting to attract attention. This has become particularly common in Federal Way. One candidate did it a lot and won, and now every race in that city, state and local, features candidates jockeying for position at South 320th Street and Pacific Highway South (a very busy intersection), waving their signs like a bunch of mattress store bird-dogs. It's hard to say whether this works, but the candidates think it does, so there they go.

Perhaps the most effective method of campaigning at the local level is doorbelling. Candidates can purchase maps of neighborhoods showing who's a likely voter and who's not, and they knock on the doors of the people they think they have a shot of convincing. Generally speaking, they're hitting up single-family neighborhoods, where you're more likely to find registered voters, and they're avoiding apartment complexes, where the residents may be more transient and less politically involved. Nothing is more effective in getting out the vote than pounding the pavement, shaking hands, answering questions, and passing out brochures. Most candidates report fairly positive interactions with voters. They also report some angry souls who answer the door in a bad mood as well as the occasional naked person. Knocking on doors is not for the faint of heart.

And in the age of Trump, people aren't always friendly. One candidate reported people in his district were a bit hostile at the door if they disagreed with him. That's even more true on social media.

"People can get extremely upset on social media," said the candidate, a longtime legislator. "There are no filters, and you can be as brutal and uncivil as you want."

Buttons and bumper stickers, once staples of campaigning, have faded in importance. Candidates used to also give away knickknacks, doodads, gimcracks, and gewgaws with their names on them—emery boards, keychains, combs—something vaguely usable to remind the voter of the candidate every time they pull it out.

Local newspapers, where they still exist, will interview candidates, and sometimes do endorsements, and once again it's not clear how much difference they make. Candidates don't buy as many newspaper ads as they once did, which seems questionable, since the people who still read newspapers are much more likely to be voters. Any serious candidate now has a social media presence, and candidates across the country have used social media to their advantage. Candidates have built up legions of twitter followers, Facebook pages, and even old-school dodges such as email lists to woo and keep in touch with supporters. (Be warned: make one tiny campaign contribution and you're going to hear from everybody and their sister for years to come.) On the other hand, the unfortunate part of politics and social media is that people say things online that they wouldn't dream of saying to someone in person, and online communication, lacking context and personal nuance, can greatly exaggerate someone's intent.

THE GREAT AMERICAN MYTH

Some people's answer to electoral disappointment is term limits. Term limits state the length of time someone can serve in office. Term limits were adopted at the federal level for the presidency in 1951, after Franklin Roosevelt was elected four times to office. Fifteen states have term limits for legislative seats, and thirty-seven states have term limits for governors.

Washington isn't one of them. State voters adopted term limits in 1992 via initiative; the state supreme court threw that out in 1998 so they never took effect. The purported logic behind them is that people become so entrenched in office that they can't be dislodged, which is somehow derailing the course of progress. This may or may not be true, but it basically argues that the voters who put that person in office again and again had no idea what they were doing. One thing that is certain about term limits is that they limit the amount of experience among elected officials. This serves to make lobbyists and agency officials—the other important players in legislative politics—more powerful, because there are fewer people who've been around long enough to know when someone is trying to pull a fast one. And you don't get to vote for lobbyists or agency officials. Most legislators, as well as city and county councilmembers, generally need to be there a little while before they learn how things actually work. And we already have term limits. They're called elections.

It's true that some elected officials stick around too long. When I worked in Olympia I saw some legislators who had served for decades and should have stepped down (though some were still effective—when they weren't asleep). But that's up to the voters in their districts. Considering how low voter turnout is in most places, the enemy is not long-term legislators. It's us.

This speaks to a great American myth. If we had to give it a name, it could be Dave. *Dave* was a lovely little film starring Kevin Kline, in which Kline's character is a dead ringer for the president. As it turns out, the president is in fact nearly dead. Members of the president's inner circle draft Dave to fill in for the president, after which his folksy charm and decent good nature make the country a better place. In perhaps the most memorable scene, at least in terms of the myth, Dave sits down over sandwiches with his accountant and they balance the federal budget. Seriously, if it were that easy, wouldn't we have done this by now?

But that's the myth: if only good, honest people could get elected, all of our problems would go away like the happy ending of a Hollywood movie. (And there are more films like *Dave*.) Unfortunately, political problems tend to be much stickier since everyone wants something and people aren't always willing to compromise. In fact most of the people in government, whatever their stripe, think they're doing the right thing. Moreover, politics is the only line of work where one can argue with a straight face that an utter lack of experience is somehow a virtue. If you want a plumber, do you look for the person who says, "I've never done this before, but I kind of like pipes"? Someday you may run for office, and your opponent may very well say at some point, "I'm not a politician." The correct response should always be, "That's too bad. Last time I checked, this job was all about politics." But I've moderated candidate debates where nearly every candidate, regardless of their experience, attempted to paint themselves as outsiders. The myth probably won't go away any time soon.

The other mistake folks sometimes make is trying to start at the top. I've seen many potentially attractive candidates fail because they decided to run for Congress or governor without any experience. "Generally, you're going to have someone who has served in lower offices," one longtime elected official said of successful candidates. "Start out more humbly to really understand how the political system works, so you have an appreciation for what you need to do and how to do it. And so you have a better understanding of the people who you are going to represent and what they want. There are some real advantages to having that kind of background.

"I tell future candidates who are interested in running, particularly for higher office, it's crazy to think you can just walk in and just establish yourself," he said. "People do really look at your background. What have you done? It really does come down to how can I count on you to represent my interests if you've never been there before?"

CHAPTER SIX

Initiatives and Referenda

GOVERNMENT BY (SOME OF) THE PEOPLE

Initiatives and referenda are two ways citizens can participate directly in lawmaking. An initiative allows citizens to directly propose and vote on a law; a referendum allows legislatures to refer a measure to the voters, or for the citizens to call for a vote on something the legislature has passed. As with everything else in government, there are distinct trade-offs in allowing this to happen.

Washington is one of twenty-one states that allow direct initiatives. Direct initiatives go straight to the ballot. Washington and seven other states also allow indirect initiatives. An indirect initiative goes first to the legislature, which can pass the law as written. Or they can ignore it, in which case it goes to the ballot. Or the legislature can pass an alternative, in which case both the original and the legislative alternative go to the ballot. An initiative in Washington can change any law except the state constitution.

Washington also is one of twenty-six states allowing citizen-initiated referenda, which lets citizens invalidate a law just passed by the legislature. Another twenty-four states, including Washington, allow their legislatures to refer measures to the citizens for a vote. The state constitution protects legislation "necessary for the immediate preservation of public peace, health or safety," or "support of the state government and its existing public institutions" from referenda. This can be challenged in court, and the courts sometimes side with the legislature.[1]

In Washington State a direct initiative is called an Initiative to the People, and an indirect measure is called an Initiative to the Legislature. Any resident citizen can propose a measure, with filing deadlines each year to make the next ballot (December for direct initiatives, March for indirect). Several hurdles must be cleared—the full text of the proposal, a ballot title, a brief description, a $5 filing fee, and registering the campaign with the Public Disclosure Commission.

Those aren't the big barriers, however. To get an initiative or referendum on the ballot, you need the valid signatures of registered Washington voters equal to 8 percent of the total vote for governor in the most recent election. Other than the presidential election, the governor's race attracts the largest number of votes on the ballot. In the 2016 election, just over 3.2 million people cast a vote for governor, making the magic number for initiative signatures 258,949. Typically a large number of signatures are invalidated, so you will probably need more than 300,000 to be safe.

The Washington secretary of state's office checks the signatures, throwing out duplicates, signatures that don't match those on file, and people who simply aren't registered to vote. Most of the time they check a random sample of the signatures, which is generally a fairly accurate gauge of whether the campaign gathered enough valid autographs to make the ballot.

Washington voters adopted initiatives and referenda in 1912 because they didn't trust "legislatures or legislators."[2] This was a time when the legislature met every other year for sixty days, had no staff or resources, and may not have known more than the average citizen. As tempting as it might be, it would be incorrect to argue that the same is true now. The legislature now meets every year for at least sixty days, has full-time professional staff, and has access to a lot more information than the average citizen does.

Nonetheless, almost from the start, citizens' exercise of direct political power must appear quixotic. In the first two initiatives on the ballot in 1914 they said yes to prohibition but no to an eight-hour work day.[3] Since then initiatives have been used to make some big changes in Washington State. For example, voters approved the formation of public utility districts in 1930, eventually saving many people a lot of money on electricity, water, and sewer bills.

Until the 1990s an initiative campaign generally had to capture the public's interest to have a chance. More than a dozen were filed every year, but most didn't make the ballot. But then interest groups began to recognize the virtues of the system, and they employed paid signature gatherers, which made it much easier to get something on the ballot. The U.S. Supreme Court said that paid signature gathering was legal in 1988; previously it was illegal in Washington. So whereas initiatives were once used to roll back legislative salaries (actually a questionable idea) and create the Public Disclosure Commission (and with it campaign finance transparency), they now are regularly used by powerful (wealthy) interest groups to amend the law as they see fit. So initiatives still come from citizens, but they are most often the ones with money.

The late Paul Allen used the initiative process to get funding for a new stadium for the Seattle Seahawks. Costco used an initiative to end the state liquor monopoly and be able to sell Jack Daniels along with jumbo jars of mayonnaise. The beverage industry used a referendum to overturn a tax on bottled water by convincing people that this was a tax on groceries.

As one writer noted, "A process conceived and begun as a way to circumvent the political power of concentrated capital became a tool of concentrated capital."[4] Then there's always the question of how much the voters are paying attention. Like voters in a lot of states, in the 1993 election Washington voters said yes to a "three strikes and you're out law," which meant three felonies put you in jail for life. This greatly increased the prison population, as well as the expense of maintaining it, and reduced the discretion of judges, who we presumably elect to exercise discretion. As it turns out, the for-profit private prison industry was one of the groups supporting this change. Many states, now overwhelmed with lifers, turned to privately run, for-profit prisons to handle the overload. Washington doesn't have any private prisons, but taxpayers still get the cost.

In 2000 voters overwhelmingly approved Initiative 728, which commanded school districts to reduce class sizes, and Initiative 732, which called for increased teacher pay. Please note that no funding mechanism was included with either measure. The very next year, voters approved Initiative 747, which limited property tax increases to 1 percent a year without voter approval. Property taxes are a major source of revenue for the state and for local governments, including school districts. One can debate the relative merits of all three of these measures, but the bottom line is that Washington citizens voted to increase spending and limit revenue. This is like buying a new car and then quitting your job. It's not sensible.

Washington voters have said no to restricting abortion rights; have said both yes and no to term limits; no and yes to permitting charter schools; consistently said no to a state income tax, in any form; yes to medical marijuana; no to GMO labeling; said yes to same-sex marriage (via referendum); and no to a tax on carbon emissions. A dozen initiatives are filed every year, and there's nearly always a couple on the ballot.

Anti-tax, anti-government activist Tim Eyman has been responsible for several initiatives, with mixed results. Eyman broke into the limelight in 1999 with an initiative to reduce car tab fees, which were high in Washington State and largely not being used for transportation improvements. A lot of the money was going to a sales-tax equalization fund, which was being used to bail out cities without strong retail bases. Eyman proceeded to sponsor a series of anti-tax measures. Some made the ballot; some didn't. A number were thrown out by the courts, either because they contained more than one subject (a state constitutional limit on initiatives is that they stick to one thing) or because they effectively altered the state constitution. Most notably the courts ruled that nothing in the state constitution says you can require a two-thirds vote on any tax increase without changing the constitution first. Eyman did manage to get approval for an initiative requiring advisory votes on any revenue increase passed by the legislature, no matter how small, blessing every state election with a series of meaningless votes on those measures. Most recently the state has hauled Eyman into court for a series of alleged campaign finance violations, and his success rate with initiatives has declined. He ran for governor as a Republican in 2020 but did not make it through the primary.

One more trade-off for initiatives is the fact that they circumvent the legislative process. As with everything else in politics, this is both good and bad. Sometimes the legislature just won't budge on something people say they want, such as campaign finance reform or the easing of marijuana laws. On the other hand, an initiative is just an up-or-down vote. A bill before the legislature gets debated, discussed, reviewed, and revised, allowing for improvements or, often, outright rejection if it's not such a good idea. Initiatives can't be amended except by two-thirds vote in the house and senate for the first two years of their existence. So they tend to obscure the actual virtues of a republican form of government, wherein people have to talk about things first and then take action based on those discussions.

Referenda (the plural of "referendum") are more rarely on the ballot, both referendum bills (from the legislature) and referendum measures (from the people). But they have had an impact. For example, in 2002, after much work, the legislature crafted a reform to the state's workers' compensation program. This is basically a state insurance fund that helps people who are injured on the job. Research had shown that like any insurance fund, they should be charging more to the people who use it more. In this case it turned out the construction industry had more on-the-job injuries than anybody else. So it was determined that this industry would pay more because its workers needed to use workers' comp more often. The largest group representing the industry, the Building Industry Association of Washington, got its overalls in a twist over this idea, got a referendum on the ballot, and convinced people to vote down the law.

Initiatives and referenda have had a big if uneven impact on the practice of government in Washington State. Depending on your point of view, they have done both good and bad. What seems most clear is that rather than just being a tool for citizens to goad stubborn legislatures into action, they have also become a tool for powerful interests to get their own way. You'll have to decide whether that's a good thing.

CHAPTER SEVEN

Let's Party!

POLITICAL PARTIES IN WASHINGTON STATE

Although the Founding Fathers of the United States warned against them, we have always had political parties. Political parties are in effect broad-based interest groups. They organize around mutual goals; they pursue political outcomes. Parties take root and evolve wherever elected legislatures are present. Parties are yet another example of the competition between groups to get what they want out of government. Parties are also a perfect example of how elites attempt to make the system work for them. At their best they can push for needed changes; at their worst they can lose sight of what matters to ordinary folks.

The United States has a two-party system because of the way our elections are structured. With winner-take-all elections, voters take great risks in voting for a third-party candidate. The payoff for voting for a third-party candidate is tiny, and consequently the costs are high. You are more likely to vote for someone who has a chance of winning instead of for someone who, though you may like his or her positions, does not have a real chance of victory. Serious candidates therefore gravitate toward parties that have a chance. (That's why Bernie Sanders ran as a Democrat for president instead of as a Socialist.) As a consequence, in systems that use winner-take-all elections, parties tend to be more internally diverse. Democrats and Republicans don't always march in lockstep when it comes to how they feel about various issues.

Some countries have some form of proportional representation, where if your party gets 5 percent of the vote, you get 5 percent of the seats in the legislative body. Parties tend to be smaller under this arrangement and more narrowly focused on their issues. A number of different voting schemes have been suggested to try to improve the whole affair, but it's not clear that they would actually improve on anything, and they'd certainly add new costs to the system.

The dominant parties in American politics, at least since the Civil War, have been the Republicans and Democrats. At various times in the country's history one party has been in power, though in more recent times different parties have controlled different parts of government. Democrats in Washington have often been in power since the Great Depression of the 1930s. Eastern Washington has been dominated by Republicans since the 1980s, and Republicans on occasion have managed to get control of the state legislature or at least the state senate. Whatever labels the parties choose, we've always had a party that purported to represent business interests (generally the Republicans and their predecessors) and a party that claimed to represent working people (the Democrats). The Democrats have been around from the start, originally calling themselves Republicans (and never, like it says in some texts, "Democratic-Republicans"). They began to adopt the Democrat label in the 1820s.

The party we know as Republicans started out as an anti-slavery third party in the years before the Civil War. Politicians in general seem to migrate to wherever the power is at the moment. After the North won the Civil War, the Republicans went from being an upstart party to being the party of power and influence, at least in the North. Democrats, who had often opposed the war, took power in the South after Blacks were effectively (and often forcefully) excluded from meaningful participation in politics. After the Great Depression swept Republicans from power nationwide, people who wanted electoral success joined the Democrats, eventually producing a conservative class of Democrats from rural areas such as eastern Washington. After Ronald Reagan was elected in 1980, conservative Democrats jumped ship to become Republicans, and liberal Republicans fled their Grand Old Party to become Democrats.

Parties once were very powerful in American politics, including at the state and local level. Parties controlled who ran for office and who got money to finance election campaigns, and people frequently voted on a straight party line. Political party machines relied on large numbers of recent immigrants for their power bases. Local politics was unforgiving back then; machine politics was not terribly democratic or inclusive. You toed the party line or you were out. The Progressives, led by business people who didn't think city contracts should be awarded on the basis of who kicked back the most money to party bosses, got local elections changed to nonpartisan balloting so that candidates couldn't be identified by party. They also got rid of district-based elections, replacing them with at-large elections, meaning neighborhoods couldn't unite around one candidate. Candidates generally don't have to declare a party when they run for city council or other local races, especially in the western United States. Progressives also pushed for primary elections so parties couldn't dictate who was on the ballot. This curbed the power of the machines, but it also gave us situations where parts of cities went unrepresented. At one point in the 1990s, eight out of nine Seattle City Council members came from the same (wealthy, white) neighborhood. In 2015 voters agreed to switch to a system featuring seven districts and two at-large seats. Similarly, until Yakima was forced by a 2015 court order to adopt districts a city that was 50 percent Latinx had never elected a Latinx council member.

Parties aren't as powerful as they once were. Nonetheless, parties still perform some important functions: *Parties organize elections.* Party identification still provides voters with potentially useful information about how a candidate might perform in office. Except in nonpartisan elections, candidates run under one party banner or another. Because of the top-two primary election system, candidates in Washington have to say "prefers Democrat Party" or "prefers Republican Party," so as to not imply that a particular candidate is endorsed by that party. But generally speaking, it's not hard to tell which party any candidate leans toward. Read and listen to what they say. Are they avowedly pro-business? Probably Republican. Concerned with social services and climate change? Likely Democrat.

They recruit, train, and fund candidates. Especially in legislative elections, parties want to contest as many races as they can. Even when they have no chance of winning, they want candidates in place in as many districts as possible. Why? Both major parties have essentially one overarching goal: getting a majority in the legislature, both the state house and state senate. If you don't run, you can't win. In fact, control of the legislature comes down to a relatively small number of districts called swing districts because they can swing either way—Republicans and Democrats have roughly equal chances of winning. So why bother to find a Republican to run in devotedly Democratic Seattle or a Democrat to run in reliably Republican eastern Washington?

Here's what happens: interest groups will give money to candidates, oftentimes candidates from both parties (sometimes even in the same race). They want access to legislators, ears that are willing to listen to their points of view. Campaign contributions help with that. But resources are finite, even for big interest groups, and the size of contributions is limited. Groups tend to be a little bit picky about who they give money to. Some of that money is thus going to go to candidates from "safe" districts, where either Republicans or Democrats generally win. Candidates from those districts, once elected, tend to be in office for a while, which usually means they move up the food chain and get elected by their caucuses to positions of leadership, such as committee chairs or caucus officials. Interest groups prefer to be connected to candidates who win, especially to candidates who rise to leadership positions. This means that people who don't really need all that money are getting it anyway, which further means they can give money to candidates in swing districts on whose races control of the legislature rides. The fact that they can dole out money also helps them get elected to leadership roles. So if these incumbents from safe districts face actual opponents, they will have to spend some money to get reelected, meaning they have less to give to candidates in swing districts. That increases the other party's chances of taking control of the house and senate.

The legislative party organizations have some sense of who has a chance and who doesn't, so they will signal friendly interest groups about who needs help and who's not worth it. Also, if a candidate does relatively better than expected in the primary election, they may get more help in the general election. But if they do poorly—say, south of 40 percent of the vote—the money tends to dry up. So while the parties can't control who runs, they do have something to say about who has a chance of winning. Serious opposition candidates do try to win when challenging incumbents in safe districts, but they rarely succeed.

A change in Washington law has made parties even more important. In 1992 Washington voters approved Initiative 134, which limited the size of direct campaign contributions except to party organizations. Consequently, state, local, and legislative party organizations have become the leading funders of legislative campaigns, spending more than $30 million a year in recent elections. As one scholar notes, this money is hard to track; the Olympia-based Republican Leadership Council gets its money from national Republicans and large corporations, while Democrats get lots of money from unions.[1]

Former legislator and legislative staffer Chris Vance, who worked on the initiative, said Republicans pushed the measure to head off publicly financed campaigns, which they thought would hurt them. "The big danger we have in our political finance system is that only incumbents can be competitive. This addresses that. If a challenger convinces the party that they can win, the caucus can get them the funding so they can be competitive," he said. "We put some stuff in it that is good, but it also was cynically designed to help Republicans" by giving big donors an outlet for their contributions without restrictions.

Parties organize grassroots politics. Within each legislative district in Washington State is a party organization—the Fifth District Democrats or the Thirty-Third District Republicans. The districts are divided up into dozens of precincts, which are about like neighborhoods. Precinct committee officers are either elected or appointed (in the case of vacancies), and they are in effect the party governing committee for that district. PCOs vote to recommend people to fill vacant legislative seats and also vote on party platforms and convention delegates. If a legislator leaves office mid-term for any reason, PCOs vote for three names that are relayed to the nearest county council, which picks someone from that list to fill out the rest of the term. If you want to get involved in state and local politics, this is the grass roots. Be forewarned: the people who get truly involved in party politics tend to have pretty strong beliefs one way or the other. That's part of why they get involved.

Parties provide a framework for organizing legislative politics. This is an especially important task. Party organization within the legislature, for example, provides coherent approaches to policy and a way to bargain and reach compromise. Legislators meet by party caucus—house Republicans and Democrats and senate Republicans and Democrats. Each of the four caucuses meets regularly to discuss legislative strategy: Do they have the votes? Who's going to speak on amendments or for or against a bill? The leadership of the caucus makes committee assignments and chooses committee chairs and vice chairs (or "ranking members" if your party is in the minority). If things aren't going well, they meet to choose new leadership.[2] Caucuses can run smoothly or they can run ragged; a large majority can be unruly because everyone doesn't have to toe the line, but a minority caucus can be just as unhappy because they're not in the majority and not getting their bills through.

"Since I've been chair, the caucus has been fairly good about remaining focused," State Sen. John McCoy (D-Tulalip), the caucus chair of majority Democrats in the state senate, said in 2019. "We get a hiccup here and there but resolve it quickly." Still, he described his job as "cat herder."

On the other side, another senator said being in the minority did not build cohesion for senate Republicans. "I was under the impression that the Republicans worked pretty well together because there was only seventeen of them—they didn't have much choice," one legislator recalled from when he first got to Olympia. "Later I learned there were two reasons"—two senators who didn't get along with anybody.

Most of all, parties work on elections. As noted above, organizations within parties are created with the task of gaining legislative majorities and thus controlling policy making at the state level. They try to educate voters about their point of view; they recruit candidates and try to train them to be better candidates; and they provide direct financial support to the candidates who might actually win. Ultimately, citizens go to the polls and decide who's right.

Washington is not a strong party state. Voters do not register by party for elections, and Washington voters have tended toward the moderate for most of the state's history. The legislature tried to impose party registration in 1921, but voters overturned that move via referendum in 1922. In recent years, between 37 and 42 percent of the state's voters have identified as independents.[3]

Politics and parties are a bit different in the Age of Trump, although one could argue that the changes happening now have been coming for some time. Liberal Republicans and conservative Democrats were often successful in Washington State, but that has changed in the last few decades with more conservative Republicans and liberal Democrats finding favor with voters.

Former state Republican Party chairman Chris Vance said that really began to change with the 2000 election. "For the first time we had lost a seat in the suburbs," he said. They did a lot of research, leading them to conclude that they needed more moderate candidates. "We'd be okay if we nominated moderates in suburban districts and statewide candidates, and that's how we'd win," Vance said. "It didn't work. It worked less and less as years went by. We stopped nominating the Ellen Crasswells and the John Carlsons [conservative candidates for governor in the 1996 and 2000, respectively], but it didn't work." The problem was that voters were associating all Republicans with very conservative national Republicans, he said. "You can't distance yourself from the national brand. Political parties define you and you can't break away from that." Vance said the contemporary Republican party has been overtaken by radicals, and that the same thing could happen to Democrats. "A political party has three layers," he said. "At the top are the elites, candidates, strategists, big donors. And then the activists, the people who go to all the meetings. And then there's the base, and they vote in the primaries.

"The parties used to be run by the elites and the activists, but now it's been taken over by the base, and they are the radicals." Normally, he said, "the professionals persuade the base even when the base doesn't want to be persuaded. In 2016 the base overwhelmed the professionals and the base now runs the party. A lot of the old-line consultants and professionals are scared to death of the base.... Really now the mob has taken over on the R side and is on the verge on the D side."

So who are these people? Think for a minute what those terms mean—liberal and conservative. In an American context, liberal has often meant more willing to change while conservative has implied more willing to preserve. In recent years, these terms have become harder to pin down as different political factions have adopted positions that at one time would have been antithetical to each other. For example, at present, liberals tend to favor more government involvement in the economy, while conservatives rely on the functioning of markets to decide society's big questions. Liberals also have taken to calling themselves "Progressives," even though they have little in common with the Progressives of an earlier age.

On the other hand, while conservatives used to be for less government, period, contemporary conservatives tend to want to dictate social standards in areas of private life, such as gay marriage, abortion, and decriminalization of marijuana. In these areas liberals tend to be more hands off. The presidency of Donald Trump has polarized these camps even more, with Republicans ignoring actions such as running up big budget deficits, which if committed by a Democrat would have driven conservative Republicans to rage and scorn. Meanwhile, many Democrats say government should stay out of people's private lives, except for their economic lives. Washington Republicans, to their credit, have not campaigned for disenfranchising groups of voters through restrictive voter laws, and the most recent Republican secretary of state (an office held by Republicans continuously since the 1960s) was aggressive in working to get more people registered and voting.[4]

There are logical arguments for both conservatism and liberalism, which neither side is particularly good at explaining. The basic conservative argument is that people will do what they learn how to do, and so they'll do better if they understand that they won't be bailed out if they mess up. In recent times this has been taken to an absurd conclusion, with national Republican leaders saying that catastrophic illnesses, for example, are just poor planning on the part of the people who suffer them. The liberal response, which is even less coherently articulated, is that there is a social cost to people's suffering, and sometimes people just need help. The danger is often taking either of these ideas too far. On the one hand, it's hard to lift yourself by your own bootstraps if you don't have any boots. On the other hand, the assumption that the economy can simply be resliced to give everyone an equal share represents a fundamental misunderstanding of how markets work. One might conclude that markets are in fact very good for some things but won't solve every problem by themselves.

To understand the differences between these two groups we must understand the concept of markets. We live in a society that is essentially capitalist, meaning that the means of production are largely in private hands and that people vote with their feet and their dollars about where they want to work, what they want to buy, and how much they're willing to pay. Meanwhile, we do have publicly owned enterprises in Washington State, such as public utility districts that supply water, sewer services, and electricity. They are democratically managed, overseen by elected boards of commissioners, and historically very efficient. Many other states have similar entities. So the best description is to say that the United States has a mixed economy, which is in fact true of almost every country on earth.

Critics of public enterprises refer to things like public utility districts as socialism, and in this one instance they're right. Calling things such as the Affordable Care Act (Obamacare) socialism is fundamentally incorrect. Socialism is an economic system that involves large-scale public ownership of productive resources. Doubtless there are Democrats in Washington State who think this is a good idea (one recent-vintage Seattle City Council member, Kshama Sawant, certainly does). And reliably there are state Republicans who think the government should be as small and feeble as possible. Neither of those positions seems to be where the majority of either party—or the voters—makes its philosophical home.

Republicans, including some in Washington State, tend to believe that markets are the best way of solving many if not all problems. Markets are efficient and productive. They produce more wealth and encourage people to work hard and be thrifty. Republicans also thereby tend to favor lower taxes and less regulation, as these make private enterprise less efficient. Democrats, on the other hand, are somewhat skeptical of markets and favor more support for the poor, public education, and social services. They appreciate the importance of taxes in paying for services that people say they want and the necessity of regulation in ameliorating the excesses that markets can create. They also tend to underestimate the impact of taxes and regulations on businesses and consumers in the state. Washington Republicans have been slightly less agitated about social issues than are their national counterparts. Some legislative Republicans even voted to approve same-sex marriage legislation in 2012.

The differences in the parties are made plain on their webpages. The first line of "Our Party" in the "about us" section on the King County Democrats website says, "The King County Democrats work across Martin Luther King Jr. County to promote Democratic values, principles, and policy directions by electing Democrats to office and championing sound public policies."[5] Meanwhile, in contrast, the preamble to the Pierce County Republican platform says, "Republicans in Pierce County, Washington affirm that it is the proper role of government to protect our unalienable rights and principles of individual liberty and responsibility on which our state and our country were founded. We seek policies that empower individuals, families, and businesses to pursue prosperity with freedom from government intervention."[6]

In a similar vein, the state Republican Party platform spells out the party's general direction when it comes to politics: "The Washington State Republican Party is dedicated to preserving a constitutional republic through active participation by citizens for the protection and preservation of conservative values including: the sanctity and dignity of human life; religious freedom; personal rights and responsibility; preserving a free society, free markets, and free trade; limited government; low taxes; minimal bureaucracy; national security and sovereignty; and private property rights. We believe that good citizenship begins with protected rights and ends with accompanying responsibilities. We believe that government should be the last resort for individuals and do only those necessary things that they cannot do for themselves."[7]

The state Democrats' platform moves in a different direction: "Washington State Democrats, as citizens of the planet, place the well-being of the people as our highest priority. We believe in the values of community, empathy, equality, tolerance, opportunity, and the common good of the interdependent world we share."[8]

So it's easy to see that within the broad framework of American government, the two parties have different approaches. The Republicans emphasize individual choice; the Democrats tend more toward community (but not, as some of my students have claimed, communism). The Republican approach is somewhat about the responsibility of the individual to the community, whereas the Democrats' approach leans toward the responsibility of the community to the individual. There are virtues to both philosophies and inconsistencies in each party's stated creed. Contemporary Republicans tend to favor such liberties when it comes to economics but not in people's private lives. Democrats, meanwhile, support more choice for people's conduct of their private lives but in recent years don't always extend those liberties to people's economic choices.

Most voters are less wound up about orthodoxy of one kind or another and may very well vote for Democrats one time and Republicans the next. But sometimes people are determined to vote by party no matter what.

Or they're just not paying attention. In a state senate race in 1998, the incumbent in the Thirty-Third District seat, Julia Patterson, was challenged by a Republican, Wayne Ericksen. Ericksen, as it turned out, lived in my neighborhood. He was a quiet but not unfriendly man who could be seen walking into town to get a coffee and then walking home. People who knew him reported he was a pleasant and peaceful fellow. One of my students interviewed him for the campaign, apparently the only interview he was ever asked for. In the course of that interview, Ericksen said that the Russians had tried to shoot him with a laser rifle (and he knew who it was because only the Russians had such a weapon), because they could not stand the thought of the son of God becoming president of the United States. The shot, Ericksen said, bounced off his belt buckle. Ericksen, sadly, was mentally ill. Other media somewhat made light of this situation, but mental illness is a serious disease and nobody asks for it. But what's interesting about this campaign is that Ericksen, who at that point, if elected, might have faced some challenges in being an effective legislator, got 34 percent of the vote in the primary. That number fell to 24 percent with higher turnout in the general election, but some folks were determined to vote Republican regardless of who was on the ballot. There have been similar—if not quite as stark—situations involving unqualified Democrats in state elections as well.

THIRD PARTIES

There have been and are other political parties in Washington State. The short-lived Populist Party took control of the legislature and the governorship in 1896 before fading away and being absorbed by the Democrats. John Rogers, Washington's third governor, was elected the first time in 1896 as a Populist but the second time as a Democrat. In the early years of statehood, and continuing until around World War I, Washington voters sent quite a number of other party candidates to the legislature: the People's Party; the Citizens Party; Silver Republicans, who favored free coinage of silver instead of just the gold standard; Progressives (the real ones); the Farmer Labor Party; and one Socialist in 1913. The last third-party candidate was a Progressive, Knute Hill of Yakima, elected to the house in 1926.

In recent times the third party most often seen on the ballot are the Libertarians. Libertarians believe in the least amount of government possible.

Unlike contemporary conservatives, true Libertarians really do believe in less government, not just less government when it suits them. Libertarians believe that government should not intervene in the economy, and they also believe government should not dictate how people live their private lives. So, for example, at a time when people and some governments are pushing for an end to plastic garbage bags and incandescent light bulbs because of their environmental impacts, Libertarians argue that people should be allowed to make their own choices. They assert that markets are best at solving most issues since people will be rewarded for good decisions and punished for bad ones—like using bad products. The classic Libertarian joke is that Ayn Rand, Rand Paul, and Paul Ryan walk into a bar. The bartender serves them tainted alcohol because there are no regulations, and they die. A former student and sometime Libertarian remarked that the bar would lose business because it sold bad alcohol, so that was okay. Apparently the deaths of three people is a small but necessary price to pay to prove an ideological point. Libertarians run a fair number of candidates for state office, but none have survived the primary unless there was only one major party candidate on the ballot.

As of 2003 Washington State has a Progressive Party again. In 2018 it endorsed one legislative and one congressional candidate (who, in a candidates' debate, called for "bold, progressive leadership" so many times that one of my students described it as a potential drinking game). There was a Progressive Party in the early twentieth century, and they contributed quite a bit to electoral reform and some level of regulation. However, as with most third parties, their good ideas were hijacked by the major parties. In the end some Progressives became Republicans and some became Democrats, adding their political DNA to the gene pool of both parties. The aforementioned Knute Hill, for example, was reelected to the legislature and then to Congress as a Democrat.

Although the new Progressives like to claim the mantle of the old Progressives, they're not quite the same. The old Progressives were not anti-business; they were against arrangements that limited competition. The new Progressives tend to sound anti-business, although surely they would deny that. Any close examination of what they say suggests that they are old-line liberals. Republicans in recent decades managed to make "liberal" sound like a dirty word, and so liberals appear to have adopted the Progressive label in an effort to rebrand themselves. Beyond them are the self-described "Democratic Socialists," a movement that seems to have grown out of Bernie Sanders's attempts at winning the Democrat nomination for president. Sanders was elected in Vermont as a real socialist; "democratic socialist" seems to be a cover for that, since a real socialist is unlikely to get elected president.

Other third parties crop up now and then in Washington State, including Socialists, the Socialist Workers, and various flavors of the American, Natural Law, and Constitutionalist Parties, who appear to hold an eclectic mix of beliefs about what the country ought to be. A recent version of the Constitution Party says that they believe government is doing too much and needs to get back to constitutional principles. One could argue that they have a very narrow interpretation of both the state and federal constitutions, and it's at least a debatable point. The party also is anti-choice, anti-gay marriage ("as divinely instituted"), and isolationist in terms of foreign policy. They also have an expansive view of property rights.[9]

On the other end of the political spectrum is the Green Party of Washington. "The Green Party is different because we are governed by our principles and values," unlike, oh, I don't know, every other party in the country. The party lists "10 key values": "Diversity, Gender Equity, Social Justice, Grassroots Democracy, Non-Violence, Ecological Wisdom, Decentralization, Community Economics, Personal & Global Responsibility, Future Focus." The Greens are understandably concerned about climate change and economic inequality, which are both serious issues.[10] Like the Constitution Party, there's some logic in some of the things they say; you have to decide whether this is a party that will both win elections and make things better.

For the most part, such parties tend to put up candidates for federal office, such as Congress and the presidency, without any success. Before the end of the Cold War there was always a communist candidate or two who generally didn't draw much attention or votes. For all these parties, their issues tend to be bigger, which doesn't necessarily lend itself to running for city council or even the state legislature. It was an occasional criticism of Socialist Seattle City Council member Kshama Sawant that she appeared to care more about geopolitics than she cared about the people in her district.

Perhaps the most interesting third party in state history was the OWL Party, which stood for "Out With Logic, On With Lunacy." Their motto: "We don't give a hoot." Jazz band leader Red Kelly, who ran a club called The Conservatory in Tumwater near the state capital, came up with this idea along with cronies late one night after perhaps too many drinks and not enough sleep. The Owls put up candidates for all statewide races, complete with voters' pamphlet statements. Their secretary of state candidate, "Fast" Lucie Griswold, was touted as a good choice because she knew shorthand and could take dictation. Fast Lucie got nearly 3 percent of the vote. The Owls got a lot of votes and so angered the major parties that state law was changed to make it harder for third parties to get on the ballot—either the filing fee of 1 percent of the expected salary for the office or signatures of registered voters equal to that number.

Still, people can often be heard to say that what we need is a third party, something other than Republicans and Democrats. Usually they don't understand that this basically won't happen under the electoral system that we currently employ. In 2017 former legislator and state Republican Party chair Chris Vance and former Democrat congressman Brian Baird launched the Washington Independents PAC, aimed at helping elect "centrist" candidates to state office. They endorsed three candidates in the 2018 election. All lost, two in the primary. One candidate, Dr. Ann Diamond, a physician in the Wenatchee area, actually survived the Twelfth District state house primary and got a respectable 44 percent of the vote in the general, losing to a first-time Republican candidate but doing better than most eastern Washington Democrats. But there are problems with running as an independent. First, you have no party organization to help with the election, although that's what Washington Independents was attempting to provide. Second, not having a party ID, particularly in a partisan race, robs voters of a key piece of information. What are they voting for? In an interview during the campaign, Dr. Diamond said she wanted to find out what people in the district wanted, and that's what she would try to achieve. With only one vote among ninety-eight and no party members, that would be a challenge for any legislator, especially a first-timer. But Dr. Diamond also said she was fiscally conservative but socially tolerant, and that she also hoped to lower health care costs.[11] Absent some widespread medical insurance plan, health care costs are not going to come down, and if you're truly fiscally conservative, then you're probably not going to want to raise revenue enough to pay for that. And that gets at the heart of what may have been part of the problem for Washington Independents and other "centrist" groups—this is basically warmed-over Republicanism without the social agenda. Washington Independents' statements tended to sound Republican from the start. This may be a good thing or not, but it's unlikely to win over a lot of voters, especially in western Washington, where some folks may see a more positive role for the state in addressing economic inequities. Like the liberals who claim to be Progressives, conservatives who claim to be centrists are usually not. More conservative voters, meanwhile, may feel like someone who identifies as a Republican is a safer choice.

American voters often express some desire for a centrist party, but this doesn't ever seem to happen, for a variety of reasons. First, although substantial numbers of voters across the country profess to be independents, they tend to vote Republican or Democrat.[12] Second, the presidential primary system and, to a lesser extent, state-level primaries tend to reward candidates at either end of the spectrum. As noted previously, the turnout is so low in primary elections that more radical candidates of both parties are rewarded by more radical voters because that's who shows up and votes. Third, centrist and moderate candidates are often just that—moderate. In trying to remain even-handed and fair, they sometimes fail to make a case why a moderate course of governing might be desirable.

If they survive the primaries, centrist candidates may have some success. In general elections the overall electorate swings back toward the center as voter turnout increases. So in recent Washington State congressional elections, "progressive" Democrats really didn't do all that well.[13] Some won, and some didn't.[14] Meanwhile, if as some are predicting, the Republican Party implodes in the wake of President Trump, a new party will arise, whatever it may be called. It will be pro-business and pro-free market, after a fashion, and there will be a struggle within it between doctrinaire social conservatives and slightly more pragmatic traditional conservatives. Unless those who are now advocating for a change in voting systems are ultimately successful, we will have a two-party system, whatever labels they end up wearing.

CHAPTER EIGHT

Interest Groups

THE POLITICS OF POWER

Interest groups are coalitions of individuals and organizations who unite in pursuit of policy goals. As noted previously, parties are a broad form of interest group, but there are key differences. Both interest groups and parties want policy outcomes, laws passed or rejected. But while parties seek to control policy by winning elections, interest groups just want policy, and they're less concerned whether that policy is enacted by Republicans or Democrats. Interest groups also provide evidence of pluralistic competition, in that groups may oppose each other over questions of policy. They also reflect how elites play such a large role in who gets what. Interest groups with money or significant economic impact tend to be elites, and hence can have a bigger impact on what happens in government and politics.

Interest groups are a ubiquitous and everlasting feature of American politics at all levels. Interest groups—special interest groups, often, if we don't agree with them—are formally organized collections of like-minded people who unite in pursuit of political and economic goals. Interest groups may include "organizational interests" (such as business groups and unions); "institutional interests" (large firms and various other government agencies); and membership groups (such as trade groups, senior citizens, and environmentalists).[1]

Interest groups help connect citizens to government. We are all part of interest groups, though oftentimes we may not realize it. As a professor, I certainly care about education funding, so I'm automatically a part of an interest group that might loosely be called "higher education." I don't belong to any organized interest group, but when I vote I'm going to think twice about somebody who says we should do away with public colleges—occasionally there's a candidate who says that. Students also care about education—what is tuition going to cost? Are all the classes you want available when you want them? Those are issues of funding. In high school, you probably cared about state testing—that's a matter of state policy. If you have a job, the issues surrounding your industry, such as work and safety rules, minimum wage levels, or who gets overtime and who doesn't—are all matters of public policy.

Pick a group of people—there's a group that represents it in politics. Businesses, unions, and consumers all are represented in some way. Usually groups are not trying to control everything that happens in government but rather get legislation pointed their way. Successful interest groups seek to influence policy to their advantage.

Interest groups try to affect policy in several ways. First is lobbying. Hired and volunteer lobbyists travel to state capitals and city halls to make their cases for their groups' positions. Large firms and organizations may employ full-time "in-house" lobbyists. Smaller groups may hire contract lobbyists when they need them. A contract lobbyist may represent several clients at once. Lobbyists can be lawyers, former legislators, other officials, or anyone with an interest and a knack for talking. They talk to elected officials and attempt to convince them that one policy is better than another. Successful lobbyists don't lie because if you get caught in a lie, doors close, and a lobbyist who can't get through the door is of no value. In fact, really good lobbyists tell elected officials both sides of a story so the official is ready for the questions that come when he or she votes one way or another. Lobbyists' chief job is to provide information that advances their clients' causes. In legislative government, information is power.

"A lot more knowledge is exchanged" through the efforts of lobbyists, one legislator said. "It's helpful to have them to talk to." That being said, not every lobbyist is to be trusted. "It takes time to tell which are the ones you can trust," the legislator said, "and which are the flim-flam artists." Still, she said, "They can be really helpful in getting stuff through," helping to convince other legislators that a bill is a good idea. Another legislator said it's important to listen to everybody, while remembering that every advocate is thinking about their clients' best interests first. "It's our job to weed through that and listen to a number of people and then come to a conclusion."

Interest groups also organize support for their positions, encouraging people to call and write legislators, to demonstrate, and to support the campaigns of like-minded legislators and other officials. As part of that, they may contribute money to party organizations and directly to candidates. They may also campaign on behalf of candidates and issues, directly and indirectly. Effective interest groups will also court the media, attempting to win favorable coverage for their positions. This sounds worse than it is, as most of that involves schmoozing reporters and editors and trying to ensure that a particular group's point of view gets covered. Media organizations generally have rules against accepting gifts from sources.

Part of this is getting out the vote. Interest groups reach out to their members, telling them who they should support and who they should oppose. Many interest groups offer "report cards" for elected officials, grading legislators based on how much their votes agreed with the positions of the interest group. They encourage members to vote and give money to campaigns and candidates. They often invite candidates for interviews or send them questionnaires and then endorse candidates as a sign to others that these candidates have made the grade.

Unlike parties, interest groups don't usually recruit and train candidates (although sometimes groups will try to find candidates to oppose someone who they really don't like). They make clear what flavors of candidates they will support. Interest group leaders will occasionally encourage someone to run who they believe will support the group's position.

Interest groups play a big role in Washington State, as they do in all politics. Hundreds of lobbyists work the halls of Olympia every session, from senior citizens to schoolteachers to dental hygienists to farmers. Agriculture, still one of the state's largest industries, is one of the state's more powerful lobbies. Any industry with that sort of economic footprint is going to be listened to by lawmakers. That's a lot of jobs and a lot of money at stake. Here again, this isn't necessarily evil. If you represent a district where a big chunk of your constituents work for business X, the fate of business X matters greatly to the people you represent. No eastern Washington legislator who wants to remain a legislator is going to consistently vote against farm interests. Second, while the farm lobby has paid lobbyists, they also send farmers in to testify in Olympia. And nobody really hates farmers (you don't hear many people say, "Those damn farmers, they're growing food again! I hate that!"). Farm laborers also have a lobbying presence. But they may not vote and may not be citizens. Also, they don't have as much money as the farmers. So the farm workers' lobby, while no less earnest, may not be as effective. Finally, while there are fewer rural and more urban legislators in the state, the rural legislators tend to be fairly well organized around farm issues, and the urban legislators tend to be largely unorganized. So the farmers tend to be more successful with their legislative agenda.

And yet agriculture, like any interest group, is not all powerful. "With the ongoing population shift from rural (agricultural) communities to suburbs and urban areas, fewer voters and fewer lawmakers understand or appreciate farm life or what it takes to feed a growing population," said one former farm lobbyist. "Consequently, urban lawmakers tend to favor environmental and labor groups to the detriment of farmers and ranchers. This can be seen on wage and hour issues where rigid work schedule requirements, minimum wages, and leave or health care benefit mandates don't align well with the realities of seasonal, weather-dependent labor needs, particularly where pay is based on production (piece rate, for instance). It is also evident on environmental matters—pesticide spraying or other agri-chemical applications, water rights and usage, land use, odors, dust, noise, and so on. Far too often, farm policy is being decided by those who may never have set foot on a farm, let alone raised any crops or livestock. As the number of farm-country legislators continues to decline, so too does power of the agricultural lobby."

Amid the current polarization of American politics in general, some legislators may not fully grasp rural issues.

"I think there's some difficulty in the city of Seattle legislators understanding that their way of life is not the same as ours," said State Sen. Curtis King (R-Yakima). "I probably saw more of that this last session [2019] than I've seen in the past. There was more anti-farmer talk this session than I've ever seen, which is too bad. Statements like 'Farmers don't pay taxes,' which was uttered on the Senate floor."

Even an important, longstanding lobby such as agriculture doesn't all hoe in the same direction. The Washington State Farm Bureau, perhaps the state's leading agricultural lobby, has forty-six thousand members, not all of whom are farmers. As with a lot of interest groups, people may join for reasons other than politics—insurance programs and member discounts, in the case of the farm bureau. That tends to undercut their political effectiveness because all the members may not be on the same page when it comes to politics and policy. In short, no interest group is a monolith.

But if you talk to enough interest groups, a common woe-is-me story starts to emerge: the other side has X, and we've only got Y. Apparently every interest group is at a disadvantage. But the real disadvantage may rest with citizens, who, despite the large number of interest groups, may not always be fully represented. As two scholars succinctly put it, "The major problem is they do not represent all segments of the population equally. Their bias is toward better-educated, higher income, white male segments of the population." The less well-educated, the poor, women, and people of color are either not represented or are represented by groups without the resources of the rich and the powerful.[2]

Boeing, unions of all sorts, businesses, trial lawyers, and the building industry also tend to be big players in Olympia. But it's not all about size and money. The petrochemical industry is well represented but not nearly as successful, despite the presence of several large oil refineries in the state. While the economic impact of an interest groups matters, that's not the only thing. Generally speaking, economic interests tend to be politically dominant to the extent that they are economically dominant. But that also depends on a number of other things—are they well regarded by the public? Do they have an effective lobbying effort? Do they pay well? Losing a Boeing facility would be a much bigger deal than losing a Wal-Mart because Boeing jobs tend to pay a lot better.

Environmental groups have long fared well in Washington politics, which is probably a combination of longstanding public regard for the environment, and the fact that a strong state economy generally means people are more willing to pay for a clean environment. Even though it can be argued that a clean environment tends to pay for itself, people don't always connect those dots. Washington Conservation Voters and its policy wing, the Washington Environmental Council, try to help voters make that connection.

"We're the state's political voice for the environment," said Nick Abraham, communications director for the conservation voters. "We work in elections across the state that we think are stronger on environmental issues. And we work to pass policy we think will benefit people's health and the environment." That involves a mix of lobbying, campaign contributions, and independent expenditures on campaigns and issues. Part of that is trying to "help people understand why these things are important—protecting Puget Sound, addressing climate change, and working on the millions of acres of forests across Washington," Abraham said. They're not always successful. While they didn't succeed in getting Initiative 1631 (which would have imposed a carbon emissions tax) passed in the 2018 election, they did help get a broad clean-energy bill passed in the 2019 legislative session. The initiative campaign played a role in that by bringing the issue to more people across the state.

"There were a lot of groups that had to wrestle and think about the issue," Abraham said. "That really elevated the discussion. It made it clear that if this doesn't get done, the legislature has to act." As the impacts of climate change become more obvious to more people, that makes their work a little clearer to voters, Abraham said.

"I think it does make the consequences more real for people and it does make the urgency more immediate," he said, pointing to such realities as changes in the weather, lower snowpack in the mountains, and more severe fire seasons. "But I also think that makes it harder from a physical standpoint. The less time we have, the quicker we have to transition to clean energy."

The group has also added a social justice component to its mission, he said. "The last five to seven years it's something we have been wrestling with and trying to address," Abraham said. "For a long time, the benefits of a healthy environment have not been distributed very evenly. People of color, poor people have been stuck with the most pollution. It's something that we wanted to make more explicit and have that be part of the lens we're viewing these issues with. We want to make sure there's a clean environment for everyone in Washington."

The more focused an interest group, the more successful it can be. For example, the Association of Washington Businesses represents seven thousand businesses in the state. It has paid lobbyists whose job it is to attempt to influence legislative outcomes to the advantage of its members. Their stated goal is achieving economic prosperity; their preferred path to that is lower taxes and less regulation. For example, they have opposed a capital gains tax. A capital gains tax is a tax on profit made from the sale of assets such as shares of stock. At present, most people in the United States would never pay this tax. But wealthy people might.

Sometimes they run up against opposition from a group such as the Washington State Labor Council. The labor council represents more than six hundred different unions in the state and pools their resources for political and economic action. They want higher wages for workers, driven in part by the ability to organize and bargain collectively with employers. They oppose the approach called "right-to-work," common in many states, in which even if the workers vote for a union, you don't have to belong. Whereas the liberal candidates that labor often supports generally favor government action to combat climate change, members of some unions may oppose such action because it could affect their jobs. Many groups have diverse memberships whose interests may not always coincide. In the end, a broad-based organization may keep quiet on issues about which its members disagree.

PEOPLE IN POLITICS: PATRICK CONNOR

Sometimes being small can be a little bit of an advantage.

Patrick Connor is the state director of the Washington chapter of the National Federation of Independent Businesses. Its seven thousand members are largely small, independently owned firms, averaging ten employees and $500,000 a year in sales. This fact tends to provide some clout with legislators.

"An advantage of representing small, independent firms is that everyone claims to support small business, especially when campaigning," Connor said. "As a result, our biennial voting record is important to most legislators, making our endorsements, as well as political contributions, desirable.

"And there is a certain amount of goodwill and desire to help 'small business' among lawmakers and, to some extent, regulators as well," he said. "Moreover, when we are able to connect lawmakers with small business owners from home, especially local small employers, those contacts tend to be more impactful than mass emails, postcards, or phone call campaigns.

It can make a tremendous difference when a legislator knows their local grocer, coffee shop owner, barber, accountant, shopkeeper, etc. is paying attention to how they vote—and will ask them to defend their position the next time they see them."

Connor got an early start in politics and stayed with it as a career. "A grade school teacher suggested I run for student council," he said. "I did, and won. That spurred an early interest in government and politics." Connor served on his local city council, as a congressional intern, and as an aide in the state legislature. "Most importantly, however, I spent several years working for my family's construction company," he said. "A much different perspective results from having actually prepared and paid local, state, and federal taxes; navigated agency rules and ensured compliance with overlapping (and sometimes inconsistent) local, state, and federal regulations; negotiated with suppliers, sub- and prime contractors, and labor unions; and managed cashflow and financing oneself rather than having little or no firsthand experience in business management.

"Far too often legislators and regulators simply do not understand what is involved in complying with the laws and rules they propose," Connor said. "My private-sector work experience allows me to be a better advocate for small business owners because I understand and can articulate the likely impact of policy proposals to legislators and regulators who may otherwise be unaware of the burden (or benefit) their proposals may cause."

As a lobbyist, he said, his job is to provide information. "Legislators simply can't be experts on every issue or bill that comes before them," Connor said. "Lobbyists play an important role in providing good information to help inform legislators' decision-making processes. A robust exchange of ideas, information, and experience should lead to better policy." And that means telling the whole story about a given issue. "Absolutely," Connor said. "It is my job to explain—and refute—the other side's arguments better than they can articulate their position themselves." Still, there are challenges to representing small business owners, he said. "Unlike unions, membership in NFIB is voluntary," Connor said. "We cannot deduct dues or political contributions from anyone's paycheck. Moreover, small business owners rarely have the luxury of closing up shop, or calling in replacement workers, to come to Olympia to testify or meet with policymakers. Consequently, we have a modest PAC and cannot regularly bus people in for mass demonstrations at the capital or neighborhood canvassing. This can make it challenging to get as much traction on our positions when opponents can generate hundreds of contacts on any given issue and can levy those forces along with tens of thousands of dollars to support or oppose candidates at election time."

Still, Connor and the federation persevere. "We hold an annual Small Business Day at the capitol that draws fifty or so small business owners, many of whom testify," he said. "Almost all of them also meet with their legislators while in town. In addition, we have members who come to Olympia during session to testify on priority bills affecting their operations, as well as members who serve year-round on various agency boards, committees, and work groups."

"NFIB is the nation's leading small business advocacy organization," he said. "It has lobbyists in Washington DC and all fifty state capitals. Our members are exclusively small, independent business owners. Each member has the opportunity to vote on our annual ballots about state and federal issues, which determine the position NFIB takes on those key issues. One member, one vote. Our state political endorsements are based on our biennial voting record; our position on key bills is communicated to legislators in advance of the vote, so they're all aware where NFIB stands on priority legislation."

More tightly focused groups can be more effective. Consider Boeing. Aside from its economic impact across the state, Boeing's public affairs effort has always been narrowly focused. While some observers have rather blithely asserted that Boeing watches everything that happens in the state legislature, the company mostly pays attention to things that will affect Boeing. They carefully reach out to legislators when necessary, explaining why they think a bill is good or bad. They make campaign contributions to Republicans and Democrats, showing no special favoritism, and haven't been known to target legislators who have been critical of the company—and some are.

Even then, with one of the best lobbing organizations in the state, Boeing doesn't always get its way. The Growth Management Act of 1990 required Washington cities to plan for growth; the result was that Boeing's plans to expand its plants in Renton and Everett pushed those cities to charge Boeing a lot of money (around $50 million between the two cities) to pay for the expected costs of growth—traffic, housing, school, and environmental impacts. The company wasn't happy, and a lot of arguing and posturing ensued, but in the end it was all worked out. Still, if Boeing was as all-powerful as it's often made out to be, the disagreement never would have happened in the first place.

The idea of trying to convince elected officials to do something for you may seem mildly heinous, but be real—this is what people do. This will never change. Anybody who tells you that we could have a system of government in which people aren't trying to get theirs is kidding themselves; that's not human nature. The results aren't always benign; business interests (or labor or environmental interests) could get legislation passed (or stopped) that would benefit them at the expense of others. But almost all legislation does this; very little is passed that is universally good for everybody. Furthermore, most of the ways in which you could curtail the power of interest groups would also curtail the political freedom we have worked so long and hard to create and preserve.

FOLLOW THE MONEY

As already noted, interest groups spend money on campaigns, either via contributions or independently on behalf of or against candidates. Most of the money interest groups give to candidates goes where we might expect it to go: to people who already agree with the group. "Most organizations that give you money know where you stand," said one legislator. The legislator reported receiving lots of questionnaires from interest groups, plus occasional telephone conversations and face-to-face interviews. "Most of the money comes from people who agree with you." Still, she said, "the government's not going to function if everybody's beholden to an outside interest." You've got to be able to take their money and still vote no.

We would be wrong to conclude that interest groups aren't powerful, or that some of them sometimes go too far in pursuing their own interests. They do. Do they have too much influence? Sometimes. It's a frequent feature of American political history to see interest groups exercising too much power at various points. Interest groups spent $1.1 million on the 2000 election in Washington State, mostly on independent political advertising. They spent $8 million in 2004; $5.8 million in 2006; $24 million in 2008; and $4.5 million in 2010. The average citizen doesn't have that kind of money or that kind of influence. For example, in 2007 opponents of Referendum 67, the Insurance Fair Conduct Act, spent $6.3 million. As this was a measure about the practices of the insurance industry, that money came from the industry, which doesn't want laws that limit how it does business. Consumer groups supported the measure. Despite the campaign against it, 56 percent of the state's voters approved. Meanwhile, expenditures on lobbying rose from $30 million in 2001 to $59.8 million in 2015. Spending by political action committees on campaigns rose from $10 million to $40 million over roughly the same time frame.[3] Costco wanted to get into the business of selling liquor, previously a state-run monopoly. They spent $20 million to get Initiative 1183 on the ballot in 2011, and now they're in the liquor business.

A lot of business-oriented money goes in the direction of Republican candidates and causes. Nonetheless, of the $105 million spent in the 2017–18 congressional election cycle, almost 69 percent of contributions went to Democrat candidates.

But groups are not all powerful all the time; as already noted, at the height of its power and influence in Washington State, Boeing, with a first-rate public affairs program, didn't win all of its battles with state and local government. When groups exercise too much power, citizens tend to respond accordingly and eventually reforms arise and circumstances change. Would you have guessed that railroads were the dominant political force for much of the second half of the nineteenth century? They were. They're certainly not now. One could argue that various interests are getting their way right now in Washington, but this too shall pass. If nothing else most interest groups that I've observed don't know when to say when, and eventually that will catch up with them.

SCORING GOALS

Interest groups tend to want a small set of things. Some interest groups coalesce around social issues. Anti-abortion groups are always very active; at the same time, pro-choice groups are arguing the other side of that case. Groups have pursued differing agendas relating to marijuana use, LGTBQIA rights, and gun control. Many groups have economic agendas, including businesses, labor, and consumers. For example, senior citizen groups have pushed for more options for people to fit dentures. They filed an initiative in 1982 to let people who make them also fit them for patients. More options tend to mean more competition and lower prices. Of course, dentists, who would stand to lose some business, opposed this measure. In the end the senior citizen lobby failed to gather enough signatures to get the measure on the ballot.

Similarly, dental hygienists pushed an initiative in 1997 to allow them to practice on their own, providing only services that they were qualified to provide and referring patients to dentists for anything beyond that. Dentists again opposed this measure, painting a picture of substandard dental care and public calamity. Even though the change in the law wouldn't have prevented anyone from sticking with their regular dentist, and despite the fact that not every hygienist was likely to want to go into business for themselves, the initiative failed.

This gets at the heart of why interest groups form and what they want. Licensing requirements for all sorts of trades and professions are a commonplace feature of contemporary life. They're a double-edged sword. On the one hand, licensing requirements demand a minimum level of competence and hence protect consumers. On the other hand, licensing requirements restrict the supply of a good or service, thereby ensuring higher prices. Both things are demonstrably true, and it's not immediately obvious if either option is better for consumers.

Consider the moving story of Uncle Mover. Uncle Mover, aka Mike the Mover, aka Michael Shanks, is a Washington resident who wanted to get into the moving business. But under Washington law, moving firms were regulated by the state. To legally get into the business, one had to apply to the regulatory agency, the state Utilities and Transportation Commission. Shanks applied, which produced a swift reaction from established and licensed moving firms: there were already too many movers; profits were thin; consumers could suffer at the hands of unscrupulous business people; the very fiber of the republic would unravel. The UTC turned Shanks down.

Shanks's response, in part, was to run for office (seventeen times at last count). He legally changed his name to Mike the Mover in part so he could get it on the ballot that way. At one point Mike had to flee the state because he had been operating an illegal moving business; later he got around this by having people make "donations" for his moving services. Eventually the state moved to deregulate the moving business, and Uncle

Mover continues hauling furniture in King and Snohomish Counties. His campaign hasn't brought him an elected office, but apparently it has brought him a lot of business.

Interest groups are an important and unavoidable part of politics at every level. The only country that doesn't really have interest groups is North Korea, which, by most accounts, is not a nice place to live. Everywhere else, groups of people compete to get what they want from government. That's all the more reason to pay attention to what's going on, especially in your city, county, and state.

PART III

State Government

OLYMPIA AND BEYOND

State government has multiple parts with which folks might be a little more familiar. The governor is the chief executive of state government. Like presidents, they get too much credit when things go right and too much blame when they don't. The legislature makes policy, and shares power with the governor. The court system completes the oft-cited checks and balances of the American system of government, compelling people—including those in government—to adhere to the law as written. But there is more to the top level of government than that. Stage agencies—the bureaucracy—have to put law and policy into practice. Like the rest of government, it struggles both to keep citizens happy while following the intent of the legislature while administering the law. Those things don't always coincide.

Much of what happens comes down to budgets, which are laws passed by the legislature detailing what the public's money will be spent on. Budgets are funded by taxes and revenue, again a matter of public policy as envisioned by the legislature but further constrained by the state of the overall economy.

In this section, we will explore how all of that fits together.

CHAPTER NINE

Where It Happens

THE LEGISLATURE

The Washington State legislature is the engine of government. It is the legislature that makes laws; checks the powers of the other two branches of government; and ultimately decides how the state will raise and spend money.

Legislatures are where policy is made. Legislatures make laws, levy taxes, spend money, and engage in oversight of other government agencies. Like the U.S. Congress, state legislatures are arenas for the articulation of conflict. This is where people can go to settle their differences with words and not weapons. That's gotten more difficult as compromise has become a dirty word in current politics, but many people are still trying.

Historically state legislatures were dominant in the post–Revolutionary War era, then were later dominated by governors and interests in the late nineteenth century. They were characterized by short sessions, high turnover, low staff support, and dominance by powerful interests. Legislatures became more sophisticated in the second half of the twentieth century. They got professional staff; they began to meet long enough to consider issues carefully; and they began to develop enough internal expertise to contend with governors and lobbyists. Naturally legislatures now are criticized (not by me) as being too professional. Professionalism sometimes means more challenges to legislative leadership from legislators bent on advancing their careers. But for the most part, professionalization has been a good thing. The addition of professional staff and resources gives the legislature a better chance of writing good law and of knowing when an interest group is pulling its collective leg. For example, Washington's legislature has created a fistful of special boards and panels to address ongoing issues and develop better information.

One thing to remember about government in the United States, including in Washington State, is that we live in a republic—not a democracy. Democracy means direct rule by the people. While Washington and other states have a bit of that in the form of initiatives and referenda, on the whole, we live in a republic. That means we elect people to make decisions our behalf. The people who make the biggest decisions serve in the state legislature.

The state is divided into forty-nine districts, with each district electing one senator and two representatives, who meet annually in Olympia to decide what is what. Don't confuse these with congressional districts, of which Washington has ten. Those folks are elected to the U.S. House of Representatives, and while they represent their districts and Washington State, they are not state officials. Neither are U.S. senators, of whom Washington has two, like every other state. Those twelve people serve in the U.S. Congress. Generally speaking, they have bigger cattle to corral than what happens here in the other Washington.

The state constitution says Washington must have between sixty-six and ninety-nine representatives in the house, with the state senate half that size. From 1933 until 1972 the state house had ninety-nine members, though no state senator was designated as a half. Representatives serve two-year terms, so every other year the entire house is up for election. Senators serve four-year terms, so roughly half the senate is up for grabs every two years.

State Sen. Hans Zeiger (R-Puyallup) previously served in the state house before getting elected to the senate. He said he noted "some cultural differences as well within the institution." "With the longer tenures in the senate, there's kind of a continuity, more of a sense of tradition and institutional continuity. The house is more concerned about their next election, which is intended."

Staggered terms provide a little more continuity, as the senate will see fewer new faces with each election. However, it is unlikely that all of the house would be new after any given election. The longer terms of the senate also tend to provide slightly more perspective on state issues. Many senate members will have served in the house before joining the senate, so new senators are likely to be more experienced when they take office.

Washington legislative districts are not subdivided. All three legislators, two representatives, and a state senator represent the entire district. By law (as a result of a pair of Supreme Court decisions, *Baker v. Carr* [1962] and *Reynolds v. Sims* [1964]), each district must be within 1 percent of population. If the districts had different populations, some voters would be advantaged, and some would be disadvantaged. In the case of *Baker v. Carr*, the state of Tennessee had not redrawn its own legislative districts since 1901. In the case of *Reynolds v. Sims*, the Alabama state senate featured two senators per county (and the counties had widely different populations). That tipped the balance of power toward rural districts.

Now every ten years following the U.S. Census, states redraw their legislative and congressional district boundaries to account for changes in population. The Washington State constitution has required this since its adoption in 1889, although it took until the 1970s for the legislature to finally adhere to this law. Legislators were unwilling to redraw legislative districts since doing so would probably cost some of them their seats.

In many states redistricting remains a partisan political exercise, as it was in Washington for much of its history. This is called gerrymandering, named after an early nineteenth-century Massachusetts governor, Elbridge Gerry, a signer of the Declaration of Independence. Overall, Gerry seems to have been a moderate and thoughtful politician, but this is what he's famous for. Gerry was governor during redistricting after the 1810 Census, and of course he wanted to help his own party. The state senate approved a redistricting plan that included a district that was long, narrow, and featured some twists and turns. As an artist was drawing a map of the district for the *Boston Gazette*, an editor remarked that it looked like a salamander. Someone else said, no, that's a gerrymander, and the name stuck.

Gerrymandering involves dividing up districts so that one party is limited to as few districts as possible while giving the other party majorities in as many districts as possible. At the congressional level, for example, that has led to Democrats regularly getting more overall votes for the U.S. House of Representatives but failing to gain majorities in the House because of gerrymandering. Washington suffered from this as well for many decades. By the 1930s voters were complaining that districts were badly apportioned, and by the 1950s, led by the League of Women Voters, people began to push for some kind of redistricting commission. A report by the league, for example, found that District Ten—Columbia, Garfield, and Asotin Counties—had just under 19,000 people in it. District Thirty-One in Seattle had more than 150,000.[1] The league even got a ballot measure, I-199, approved to reform the process, but the legislature quickly acted to gut it. A federal court ruled in 1957 that Washington's districts were discriminatory, although it took the legislature three years to address that.

The state house had ninety-nine members during this time until a U.S. District Court judge forced a redistricting plan on the state before the 1972 election, when the house was reduced to ninety-eight members—two per district. Following a rather messy partisan redistricting in 1980 (which was thrown out by the courts), the legislature proposed a bipartisan redistricting commission in 1982. The state's voters approved a constitutional amendment in 1983, making Washington the third state to adopt such a commission. It took up its job for the first time in 1991. The commission did away with the subdivision of Districts Nineteen and Thirty-Nine into A and B subdistricts for house seats, which critics had decried as unconstitutional.

The redistricting commission has five members: one appointed by each caucus of the state legislature: house and senate Democrats, house and senate Republicans, and a non-voting chair. This kind of design is aimed at forcing compromise and preventing gross partisan advantage. It's not perfect. Critics say it tends to protect incumbents, and districts, while equal in population, can still be a bit strained at times. And, as has happened on occasion, one strong personality on the redistricting commission can tip the scales in favor of one side or another. On the other hand, we don't see many gerrymanders crawling across the map anymore.

Even though the districts are within 1 percent of population, they're not all equal in terms of registered voters. For example, the Thirty-Sixth Legislative District, which includes the Ballard, Queen Anne, and Magnolia neighborhoods in Seattle, has 112,000 registered voters within its boundaries. Five other districts also have more than 100,000 registered voters. The Twenty-Ninth District, covering much of Tacoma, has just over 72,000 registered voters, with two others well under 80,000. The average is 90,000.

They're also widely different in geographic size so they can be equal in population. The Twelfth District in North Central Washington is 8,517 square miles. The Forty-Third District, in the middle of Seattle, is only 11.65 square miles. But each has a population of 137,250 people, give or take a few.

YOU'VE GOT A JOB TO DO

Once elected, legislators have a job to do. It has several parts. First, legislators make and revise laws. While governors can issue executive orders, the legislature can easily override those with a simple majority vote. Courts can invalidate laws, interpret them, and compel citizens and government to adhere to the laws as written. But the legislature can respond by changing the law, and it has a crucial role in amending the state constitution. At the end of the day it is the legislature that must decide what the laws of Washington will be.

They can't know everything, however, so successful legislators learn to develop areas of expertise and rely on the expertise of others to make decisions about subjects outside of their areas. "Members pick what work they can, but it's kind of like drinking from a firehose—the stuff keeps coming at you so fast," said one former legislator. Still, if you have an area of expertise, you can put it to good use. "The best thing is as a legislator you can ask rude questions, and then you can do something about it," said one legislative leader.

Second, the legislature is a check on the power of the other two branches of government. Governors can veto laws, but the legislature, with a two-thirds majority, can override the veto. In practical terms neither of these things happen very often. Smart legislative leaders—and smart governors—work together and try to figure out ahead of time what they both can live with. While you may hear inexperienced candidates saying they'll draw a line in the sand and dare the executive (the governor or the mayor) to step over it, that's not how most politics is done. Because this is an ongoing relationship, picking fights doesn't get much done and may make it harder to get support for something you really want. Meanwhile, if a law is invalidated by court decision, the legislature can simply rewrite the law.

And while courts can invalidate laws as unconstitutional, they can only do so if someone files suit. The state senate must confirm the governor's appointments, and once in a while they say no.

Third, legislators represent the interests of their constituents to the state. If your district is full of farms and orchards, you care about those issues because farmers and growers are your homefolks. If you represent the central Puget Sound region, you probably care a bit about traffic and transit. If your district is in the wooded parts of the state, you might care a little more about forestry and timber issues.

Part of this is providing assistance to individual constituents who may need help with specific issues with state government. This is something that good legislators learn to pay attention to. One legislator I once knew was approached in his district by a young man who had been injured in a logging accident and was getting some runaround from the state's workers' compensation program, which provides help to people who are injured on the job. The legislator, once a logger himself, simply responded, "You're lucky to be alive!" Not a very compassionate response, and that kind of thing gets around. The legislator lost his reelection campaign in the next election. And while that was not the only reason, it couldn't have helped.

Finally, and this is an area where the Washington legislature might fall a little short, is administrative oversight. An expected duty of legislatures everywhere is that, as the lawmaking body of government, they will communicate with the administrative arm of government to find out what's working and what isn't and try to ensure that legislative intent is being followed. Congressional committees, for example, conduct hearings for the purpose of communicating with federal agency officials to hear whether the laws as written are working as intended or if they need revision.

Washington's legislature, however, is a part-time citizen legislature. They meet every year, 105 days in budget-writing years and 60 days in the opposite years. They also meet occasionally throughout the year in what are called "committee weekends" (now reduced to a few days in November), when they take up issues but pass no bills. The logic behind a part-time, citizen legislature is that because they're not full-time elected officials, they will spend some time at home and not lose sight of their districts. It's a nice thought, but a bit of a challenge in practice. When the legislature's job was much smaller, because state government was much smaller, this probably worked okay. But since 1981, when the legislature began to meet annually instead of every other year, it has become increasingly difficult for just anybody to serve. While the standard schedule calls for the legislature to meet for two or three months, challenging economic times and government often divided between Republicans and Democrats means legislators can be in session for up to six months out of the year as they try to hammer out a state budget.

It's very difficult for small business owners to serve, because if you're in Olympia for up to half a year, who's minding the store? "My law practice kind of dwindled while I was in the Legislature," said one former legislator. "It had become a full-time job." That leaves state employees, employees of big companies (who can afford to have somebody gone for months at a time), and retired people. So rarely do we find farmers serving in Olympia—they're really busy with their jobs—and other business owners serve at their own risk. Consequently, Washington's citizen legislature may not be very reflective of the state's citizens, at least when it comes to occupations. Nor does it pay all that well. The annual salary is $48,731 a year, an amount set by a nonpartisan state salary commission. Plus they get $120 "per diem," or pay for expenses while the Legislature is in session. (The state is just big enough that most legislators must move to Olympia when the house and senate are open for business.) One legislator I knew supplemented his income by being a basketball referee.

If you work for a big company, that's all right, but it basically means sacrificing your career. "They were fine with you serving," one legislator said of his employer, a large Washington-based company. "And they never put any pressure on us to vote for the company. But you're giving up your career to do this. When your boss wants someone to head up a project, you're not there." Advancement then becomes very difficult.

State Rep. Tom Dent (R–Grant County) had to sell his business before he could afford to be a legislator. A competitor offered to buy out his crop-dusting firm. "I'm a political junkie," said Representative Dent, who was Grant County Republican Party chair before he ran for a Thirteenth District house seat in 2014. "I got interested in politics when I was ten. It was a lifetime passion, and finally the opportunity arose. Finally there came a time when things changed and I could run and serve." And so he felt compelled to serve in office. "I think that this country belongs to all of us, and I think we have an obligation to give back if we can," said Dent, who still maintains his ranch in Quincy, where he raises bison. ("They're easier than cattle," he said.)

PEOPLE IN POLITICS: KRISTINE REEVES

Kristine Reeves isn't getting rich being a legislator.

"I think often people assume that everyone there is paid a six-figure salary and that we have tons of staff to help us do our jobs," said State Rep. Reeves (D–Federal Way). "In reality I took a pay cut to become a part-time citizen legislator and really pay to do the job—whether in increased childcare costs or transportation costs not covered by the legislature. It is not the high-pay position people think it is.

"Therefore, I still have to work a full-time job to afford to serve in the legislature and I just don't think a lot of people know that or appreciate that about Washington's legislative structure," she said. "I only have one staff person to support the work and the ethics laws are very stringent (which is good) but makes it tough to do some things like use Facebook or Twitter as a legislator. We are in need of a modernization plan in the legislature."

Still, Reeves thought it was important to run. "I ran for state representative in 2016 because the biggest problem facing our state at the time was the full and fair funding of the K–12 system," she said. "It seemed like years were dragging on and folks in Olympia were not getting the solution to this massive problem nor its importance." Education had been Reeves's guardian angel in the past. "As the daughter of a single mother, who had grown up in and out of foster care for the first ten years of my life; as someone who was exposed to drug addiction, alcoholism, and domestic violence daily, I am sure my ACEs [adverse childhood experiences] scores were high, had I known what those were growing up," she said. "What I did know was that it was teachers who checked in on me, that it was my experience in Head Start that exposed me to early learning. My elementary teachers while I was in foster care that would expose me to food security and a sense of safety from an erratic parent. It was my high school English teacher, Mr. McCaffery, and my high school guidance counselor, who would expose me to hope—hope of college and hope from homelessness. So you see, I grew up believing that teachers were real-life superheroes, that they saved my life."

Reeves went on to get bachelor's and master's degrees from Washington State University and Gonzaga, respectively, and eventually became director of economic development for the military and defense sector for the state of Washington. She wanted the same kinds of chances for success for others. "And as a kid from a poor rural farming town, as a woman and person of color, I knew that access to a high-quality education would be the difference for kids like me and I wanted to ensure that all kids had access to that educational opportunity that would lead them to potential economic stability," Reeves said. "At the time, I had a two and a four year old. I wanted them to have a good school, of course, but it wasn't my kids I was most worried about as they lived in a stable two-parent home," she said. "It was those foster kids and homeless kids and kids of color who were farthest from opportunity that I was most worried didn't have a voice in Olympia fighting for them. So I ran."

Reeves was elected in 2016 and reelected in 2018. She became vice chair of both the House Consumer Protection & Business and the Commerce & Gaming Committees, and she served on the Housing, Community Development & Veterans Committee.

Despite having expertise in some of these issues, Reeves said the important thing is first to listen.

"I believe a good legislator is someone who can listen to those they represent, discern the real problem to be solved, and find the appropriate path to that solution," she said.

It's a difficult job.

"I have learned that this is the hardest job no one trains you for," Reeves said. "There is no degree you can obtain, no preparation you can do for the dehumanization an elected official title allows others to heap upon you, and nothing that is built into this system that supports the mental health and well-being of those we ask or those who seek this public service—particularly lacking for those for whom the system was not built—working moms, women or people of color.

"But in my second term, I can say without a doubt that it is the highest honor to serve my neighbors whether they agree with me or not," Reeves said. "The more you come to understand how the system truly works versus how it is supposed to work, the more effective you can become in fighting for the things your communities care most about and actually getting it done."

Whatever they do for a living, or what party they belong to, or what corner of the state they serve, it's important to remember that legislators are all just people. There are good ones and a few bad ones and a whole bunch in between. They're not on the take, or they'd probably dress better (and if you work in or around the legislature, you have to dress up). Some are nice people and some are not. One thing I learned from working there was that a bill is a good bill or a bad bill, regardless of the personality of the person who sponsored it. This was brought home to me in a conversation with an old school chum who was an attorney for a committee. A legislator we both knew came up. In my office, we couldn't stand the guy. He didn't know how to treat professional staff and he didn't treat us well. My friend, on the other hand, really liked him. "He pays attention; he reads his bills." In short, he was an ass, but he was a careful and effective legislator.

The recent make-up (2019–20) of the legislature mirrors the changes and divisions happening in the country at large. The House Democrat Caucus, for example, features twenty-nine women among its fifty-seven members, and eleven people of color. The House Republicans have ten women and one person of color out of forty-one people in the caucus. In the Senate twelve of twenty-seven Democrats are women, along with eight people of color. The Senate Democrat web page also features links to the Members of Color Caucus and the LGBTQ Caucus, which lists eight members from the House and Senate (all Democrats). Eight out of twenty Senate Republicans are women.

Does this diversity matter? People disagree on that. On the one hand, most of us hope to live in a world where we truly are judged on our merits, not how we look. On the other hand, throughout the history of our country, many groups have been excluded from full political participation. Women didn't get the right to vote in Washington until 1910. Nationally, Blacks didn't get the right to vote until 1870; Native Americans didn't get the right vote until 1924; and Chinese Americans in 1943. Having a more diverse legislature can serve to encourage more people to participate in voting and government, and thereby not neglect anyone's well-being.

"If you don't see someone in government who looks like you, then you need to be there," said one Black legislator.

Recent elections have begun to change that. "We have a much more diverse legislature, which brings a needed perspective," said another.

OVERSIGHT

Meanwhile, it's still a part-time legislature, even if for many legislators it ends up feeling like a full-time job. One thing that could suffer is administrative oversight, because the legislature and its committees just don't meet often enough to conduct oversight hearings. "After a couple of years, I got to know the names of a few agency heads," said one legislative committee chair. That's not exactly oversight.

The legislature's answer over the years has been to establish ongoing structures focused on oversight. In 1977 the legislature created LEAP, the Legislative Evaluation and Accountability Program. This bipartisan group has four senators, four representatives, and a staff of ten, and tries to be an "independent source of information and technology for developing budgets, communicating budget decisions, and tracking revenue, expenditure, and staffing activity. LEAP also provides consulting to legislative committees and staff and provides analysis and reporting on special issues at legislative request."[2] This gives the legislature more useful financial information when they're trying to build budgets.

The legislature's first attempt to get good information and to do some oversight came in 1951 with the establishment of what was then called the Legislative Budget Committee. In 1996 the legislature changed the panel's name to JLARC—the Joint Legislative Audit and Review Committee. Including both Republican and Democrat legislators and professional staff, JLARC "works to make state government operations more effective, efficient, and accountable."[3] The legislature as a whole, or the committee itself, may make audit assignments. The staff audits programs and makes recommendations for improvement. They also conduct "sunset reviews," which attempt to determine whether a program should be discontinued, continued as is, or modified. Meanwhile, the Joint Administrative Rules Review Committee (JARRC), established in 1982, reviews state agency rules to make sure they meet legislative intent. Finally, the Joint Transportation Committee, created in 2005, researches and reviews transportation issues and programs to try to provide policymakers at all levels with better information. The chairs of the House and Senate Transportation Committees are the co-chairs of the JTC.

Some of the oversight function occurs naturally, since a lot of legislation comes from the executive branch—all the state agencies who need the legislature to change laws and policy so agency officials can operate with an eye to the situation on the ground. As noted above the legislature also conducts what is sometimes known as a committee weekend, or committee days, currently between election day and Thanksgiving, when legislators return to Olympia for caucus meetings, committee work sessions, to hear from state agencies, and to review reports. They discuss new issues and get visits from lobbyists—generally speaking, preparation for the new session coming in January.

Some review function is built into new laws in the form of sunset clauses. After a specific number of years, any program undergoes a mandatory review by one of the legislature's research committees, which is then relayed to the relevant standing committee. "There are mechanisms for checking in," one veteran legislator said. Legislators also have the benefit of some full-time staff, the great majority of whom work for the institution and not for individual legislators. Legislative staff is under the direction of the Office of Program Research, a nonpartisan organization created in 1973 to provide legislators with year-round assistance.

When he first got to the capital, one legislator said his biggest surprise was "the incredible staff that was in Olympia," including the Office of Program Research (OPR) and the legislative assistants assigned to each member. He noted "how hard the staff works to support the members. They're such incredible people. Some of the brightest people in the world are there. They have the attitude that 'we'll get it done.'" If a bill needs revision, "They just fix it. They never complain. It just gets done."

INFORMATION IS POWER

It helps if the legislators understand what they're hearing, especially from lobbyists and agency officials. Experience and inexperience matter. It is naturally tempting to sing the praises of fresh voices and new ideas, and those voices and their ideas often do bring change over time. They might even be good ideas. But it takes experience at being a legislator to get anything done. First-time candidates, before they actually get elected, go down to serve and learn how it all works, can make claims that are ridiculous. This may lead voters to complain that they've been lied to, and that "politicians" break their promises with regularity.

If they serve long enough, legislators learn. State Rep. Tom Dent, a Republican from Grant County, had been involved in politics for a long time before joining the state house in 2014. "Having been the chairman of the [county] party for such a long time, I worked with all my legislators. Working in my industry organizations, I leaned toward the legislative liaison positions. I had a pretty good idea of what it was about. I knew a lot of legislators, I knew a lot of lobbyists," he said. And still, he found surprises. "It just comes together, and everybody works together to make it happen," Dent said. "That was a big surprise, how it all comes together."

Dent was pleased to find people he could work with. "I went over there with the idea of getting along with the other party, but I have to say I was surprised at how easy that was," he said. "Some of the people who helped me the most were from the other side, people who were way apart. There were some pleasant surprises that first year. . . . I think everybody is there for the right reasons. I may disagree with them, but we can work together." And that's one of the keys, legislators say. "In the legislature it's all about relationships. Politics is all about relationships," said Dent. "Relationships aren't friendships. They're so you can understand each other and work together." That being said, "One my best friends in the legislature is in the other party," he added.

Dent said a good legislator has to be honest with others about what you can support and what you can't. "I think it's important that you're who you are," he said. "I don't throw rocks at people, but by the same token I don't roll over. Don't blow smoke or BS people. Just tell them what you can and can't do." State Sen. Hans Zeiger (R-Puyallup) agreed. "When it comes to policy making, relationships are more important than policy," he said. "If you want policy you have to have good relationships."

"Relationships rule," said one former legislator. If you want to get something done, you have to build relationships with Republicans and Democrats alike.

The incoming Speaker of the House in 2020, State Rep. Laurie Jinkins (D-Tacoma), began her tenure by visiting every member of the house—

both Republicans and Democrats—in his or her district (which led to some long drives in eastern Washington). "She has a wickedly dry sense of humor, and that will carry her a long way," a colleague added.

Part of building relationships is about getting information. "Don't think you know everything—you don't," a former legislator said. Good legislators tend to recognize that they can't be experts on everything and to seek the advice of others who do know more.

"You have to find people you can trust, because you cannot know it all," said State Sen. Curtis King (R-Yakima). "You cannot be expert in every aspect of government, so you find those individuals on both sides of the aisle that you can go to ask questions and have discussions and know that the answers are [made] to the best of their ability and as truthful as they can be."

"It's about relationships and it's developing trust," King said. "In the committees you're on, you have to focus on those and try to get your beliefs across on what's going to move our state forward. But you don't do it in a confrontational manner. That to me is what makes the difference."

"Ninety percent of what we do is nonpartisan," one Republican legislator said.

"We try to find a path forward that benefits all of Washington," said another.

Legislators say that if you need somebody's vote, it's better just to be told no. "I'd rather have them tell me that," said Senator King. "When you're working on a bill and you need a vote, when I go to him and say, 'I really could use your vote,' and if he says, 'Let me look at it and I'll let you know,' I know that that 'no' is no. He just doesn't want to say no to your face." So then you know there's no point in pushing the issue with that legislator. "You treat people the way you want to be treated," King said. "You treat all people with respect, and it pays off." As many legislators have said, your opponent on one issue could be your ally on the next. Nobody is your enemy.

Many legislators do try to get their colleagues to understand the issues faced by their constituents. As a rancher and agricultural businessman, Representative Dent tries to help his urban counterparts understand the challenges faced by rural Washington residents. "When you come into an ag environment and rural way of life, it's different," he said. "Any legislator has to get out of his comfort zone and learn what other people experience." Consequently, Dent said he tries to "work with my colleagues from the city about what we do and why we do it." He has helped lead agricultural tours of eastern Washington. "We had four legislators from the urban side of the state, folks that didn't have a clue about this stuff but they're willing to come learn.... It's important that that you use your talents and your experiences."

One veteran legislator agreed. "You need to hone your interpersonal skills in order to get the job done," said State Sen. John McCoy (D-Tulalip). "It's all about relationships and how you interact with people." When he first arrived in the legislature, McCoy said, "I thought I was okay, but I recognized that I needed to get better."

LEARN TO COUNT

When you elect a state legislator, you're electing one voice among 147 people broken down in two chambers. Any number of the other 146 may have different ideas and priorities. People get elected to Olympia, saying, "I'm going to make this happen!" But nobody comes back from Olympia not having learned the first rule of politics: ya gotta have the votes.

The first lesson of politics is to count. If you have 50 percent plus one, you can pass a law. If you have 50 percent minus one, no how matter how astounding your idea, you have nothing. So all the grandstanding and indignant posturing of legislators (at any level) is meaningless if you don't have the votes. "It takes seventy-six votes to pass any bill [fifty-one in the house plus twenty-five in the senate] so it's very difficult to pass anything that's slightly controversial outside of the normal incremental paternalistic progress we usually see," said State Sen. Bob Hasegawa (D–Eleventh District). Part of this is by design. Legislative government is not designed for quick action. It is designed for patience and deliberation. It puts every proposed law—a bill—through a baptism by fire, and most of the bills get burned up. "It takes a long time to do things," said one former legislator.

PEOPLE IN POLITICS: CINDY RYU

After the mayor of her small town said he was tired of listening to constituents, Cindy Ryu decided she was tired of listening to the mayor. "I was living a normal, busy life of raising my family, working full time with my husband in a small insurance office, and attending and serving at our church several times a week," she said. "The city of Shoreline was in the process of redeveloping Aurora Avenue North, on which our commercial property is located. The city invited the public and property owners to attend various work sessions. I started making written and verbal comments, and after a while the mayor said he was tired of listening to the public—with which I took offense. I had become a U.S. citizen after living in other countries with military dictatorship and a sultanate, and I took representative democracy seriously."

She ended up running for city council. On her second try, she won, claiming the seat formerly held by the mayor. (Shoreline has a council manager form of government, meaning the mayor is chosen by the other council members and does not have executive authority in city government.) Her fellow council members chose her as the new mayor, making her the first female Korean American mayor in the country. Her time in city government was a bit rocky, with lawsuits over the city's handling of the Public Meetings Act and the Public Records Act. "I was even subpoenaed for my personal calendar dating back to three months before I was sworn in for the first time," Ryu said.

Ryu lost her bid for reelection but said her experience in city government has helped her as a state legislator. "I learned how and how not to approach my elected position," she said. "I was elected to the Association of Washington Cities Board twice, so that service helped me take broader views and understand other bigger and smaller cities' challenges."

Ryu was first elected a representative for the Thirty-Second District in 2010, where she has found her legislative career to be a better fit. "I enjoy the much broader policy issues at the state level, which I think comes through in my being a happy legislator and not a grumpy mayor," she said. "I appreciate having one dedicated legislative assistant in the legislature in addition to access to all other partisan and nonpartisan staffers, compared to no dedicated staff as mayor and very limited access to staff as a city councilmember."

But some of her approach to politics remains the same, Ryu said. "I ran on a platform of listening to everyone and considering constituents' opinions, so I continue to do that in my current position," she said. "My experience as an insurance agent for twenty-four years is very helpful in constituent relations. I struggled much more with local issues of land use and local taxes than I do with the broader issues at the state level. Also, I am not personally attacked at the state level as I was at the local level, including at my children's schools. Local politics is not for the faint of heart."

Working with ninety-seven other representatives is a little different than working with six other council members, she said. "At the state level, and specifically in the ninety-eight-member house, I learned to appreciate the citizen legislators who bring various life experiences, personalities, and views, as well as how each of us behave uniquely, even in how we 'wear' our elected positions," Ryu said.

In the 2019 session she worked on a number of bills relating to mobile home parks, including several that got rolled into SB 5183, providing more assistance for mobile home owners who have to move because the park they are renting in is closing. "Even though there were increased fees and taxes, many Republican members voted for it," she said. Even in a time of sharp political divisions, Ryu said it is possible to work with people from the other party. "The divisions do show up," she said, "especially when the camera is turned on." But, she added, "I am able to work with my Republican counterparts, especially when we focus on the policy and the people. I also co-led the weekly Tuesday morning fellowship and the annual Governor's Prayer Breakfast the past three years, so my engagement with certain members has an added layer and understanding, even though we might be polar opposites on voting records. On certain issues, such as facial recognition usage, I've been able to partner up with the most conservative members—each of us arriving at similar positions for polar opposite reasons—what I call the horse-shoe effect," Ryu said.

"As a former member and chair of the Color Caucus, current chair of a committee, and sitting on the Executive Board of the House Campaign Committee for Democrats, I am sensitive to how certain members may need to have at least one bill pass or predict how their floor speeches will go. So I've worked closely with my ranking member (the top Republican in her committee, Community Development & Veterans) to at times negotiate how we hear or pass certain bills in committee or even on the floor."

Like any field, experience helps legislators get better at their jobs, Ryu said. "What the public may not realize is that because we don't have term limits, many of us stay long enough to learn about other members' way of doing things and their viewpoints—critical especially for the opposite chamber (the state senate) which has to consider our bills," she said. "We also develop certain reputations and specialties, so that while all of us vote on all policies, we may rely on certain members' opinions on issues we are not as conversant in." The legislature is ultimately about information, she said, and ordinary citizens have a role to play in that.

"The house, with ninety-eight members, is a very interesting organization in which to serve," Ryu said. "I love the information and knowledge that is shared among ourselves, from the constituents in hearings and in individual or group visits, as well as the deep bench of dedicated partisan and nonpartisan state staff members. I describe it as being in grad school every day.

"The majority party caucus briefings and discussions are truly interesting and democracy in action with a whole bunch of other dynamics," Ryu said. "So I've counseled constituents that it may take just one legislator to move or kill a bill, and many times citing one constituent's experience or example can make that difference. So they must tell their own stories to specific legislators."

MAKING LAW

As noted earlier, legislatures write laws. It's their single biggest job. Anyone can introduce a bill; all you need is a legislator to sponsor it. Thousands of bills get introduced every year. Most of them don't become law. That's a good thing because they're not all great ideas. In even-numbered years (the 60-day session) over the last twenty-five years, an average of 1,463 bills were introduced. Some handful of those are "title-only" bills, blank bills put in the hopper before the deadline, ready to be used if legislators should need to rewrite an important budget or revenue bill in a hurry. Such bills will say nothing more than "a bill relating to the state budget." Of all the bills introduced, an average of 312 become law. In odd-numbered years (the 105-day session), the average number of bills introduced goes up to 2,430, with an average of 460 becoming law. Ideas for bills come from all over: citizens, lobbyists and the interest groups they represent, legislators themselves, and lots from the executive branch, the governor, and the many state agencies.

Bills also get cosponsors, other legislators who sign on to show their support for the bill. Being a cosponsor doesn't require anything more than a signature, but sometimes cosponsors are very important. Let's say you have a bill, a good bill, and it's not a partisan issue. But you're a member of the minority caucus (the caucus with fewer votes). The majority doesn't want the minority to look too good, so it's harder to get a bill through when the committee chair is not from your party.

A resourceful legislator finds a friendly member of the other party, and gets her or him to be the prime sponsor. You sign on as a cosponsor, and you'll probably end up doing most of the leg work to get it passed, but if you want the bill, that's what you may have to do. Legislatures tend to feature two kinds of people: show horses and workhorses. Workhorses get things done. Show horses sponsor "hero bills," legislation that has no chance of passing but looks good to the folks back home.

If you're serious, get your bill in early. Bills can be pre-filed a month before the start of session. Session starts on the second Monday in January and runs for 105 days (odd-numbered years) or 60 days (even-numbered years). The longer session is when the budget gets written, so that puts even more pressure on the legislature to get things done. It's a tight schedule, featuring a series of cut-off deadlines when your bill has to have cleared committee, house of origin, and then the opposite house. Bill filing is only the first of many deadlines your bill faces.

Every bill faces a series of readings, a formality that lends a little elegance to the process and also speaks with some irony to the number of bills that legislators don't actually manage to read. The first reading is a bill's introduction. In the house, for example, the Speaker or his or her designate stands at the podium while the clerk reads the title of the bill. The Speaker says, "The clerk will read the bill," and the clerk literally starts reading the bill out loud. The Speaker then rapidly interrupts: "The clerk will read the last line," which he or she does. The bill is then assigned to a committee.

Your bill's fate in committee is never certain. It may get a hearing; it may not. In years when the legislature prefers subcommittees, it may be assigned to a subcommittee, in which it may get a hearing. Or not. Does the subcommittee chair want to take up this bill? Is this a bill the majority caucus is interested in? All of this matters because there's a deadline for your bill to be voted out of committee.

Most of the work is done in committees. Within committees the legislature used to have more subcommittees but has largely done away with them in recent years. Legislators decided that subcommittees were an unnecessary step since committees could do pretty much the same thing and move bills on to the next step. In short legislative sessions that can be very important. "The subcommittee process created more hearings, more work for members and staff, more hearing room conflicts, for too little gain," said one former high-level staffer. "The full committee still had to meet and act on the recommendation."

Committees are where the real work on legislation is done. Bills can be introduced into either the house or the senate, and from there are assigned to committees by subject. A bill altering laws relating to colleges might go to the house's or the senate's Higher Education Committee. The bill may get a hearing; it may get amended or rewritten. If the committee votes to move the bill on, it will go to the Rules Committee. More on that in a moment.

Hearings are held on some but not all bills. People come to testify before the committee—citizens, lobbyists, legislative sponsors, other government officials. Anyone can testify; just show up on time, sign in, and you get three minutes to have your say on the bill. It's actually a remarkably open and accessible system. In committee your bill can (and often will) get rewritten. What was originally House Bill (HB) 1123 turns into Substitute House Bill (SHB) 1123. This can happen twice, turning your bill into Second Substitute House Bill (SSHB) 1123. It's a rare thing for a legislator to get a perfect bill, one that is not amended in any way and is voted into law.

If it's time for a vote, the committee may go into executive session. In the legislature that simply means the committee is done taking testimony. Committee members can still talk about the bill, but the time for public comment is over. But your bill won't come to a vote unless it has the votes to pass. This is because of McCrone's Rule, named for Donald McCrone, the University of Washington professor who first suggested it: nothing comes to a vote that hasn't already been decided. If your bill comes up for a vote and fails, it's dead. Why bother? Better to wait until you have the votes. If your bill survives the committee vote, and it has a budget or revenue impact, it will have to go through one of the fiscal committees. Here again, it might never get a hearing or a vote, and it dies.

COMMITTEES

The house of representatives has twenty committees. The number and the names of the committees can and do change as new groups of legislators decide to rearrange the furniture. The names tend to reflect the flavor of the month when it comes to policy priorities. Every member serves on multiple committees, two to four depending on the member's other obligations. The Speaker of the House, for example, serves only on the Rules Committee. There are policy committees that consider changes to existing laws, and fiscal committees that deal with taxes and spending. Recent house committees include:

Appropriations. This is the main budget-writing committee. It has thirty-nine members, Republicans and Democrats from around the state. It also has seventeen staff members. The majority party chooses the committee chair and vice chair. Any bill with a fiscal impact—increasing spending—must go through a budget committee. Most go through Appropriations, but some will go through either the Capital Budget Committee or the Transportation Committee, which deal with separate budgets. Why are so many people on this committee (thirty-nine out of ninety-eight house members)? This is either a plum assignment or a lot of work, depending on your point of view. Appropriations holds the state's checkbook in its collective hands, and this committee has a lot of power. The state budget must go through this committee, as well as its counterpart in the senate, in order to become law.

Capital Budget Committee. This committee deals with capital projects. Capital projects are land, building, and equipment you expect to last longer than five years. School buildings and other public facilities fall under this budget. This includes new buildings and repair of old ones, as well as money given to local governments for infrastructure work. This committee also deals with debt. Capital projects typically involve hiring private contractors who have to pay for materials and pay their workers up front. As a consequence, the state borrows money through the sale of bonds, using the proceeds to pay for the projects and using state tax revenues to pay off the bonds.

Civil Rights & Judiciary. This deals with the state court system—basically anything that could end up in court—as well as human rights and other legal issues. As we saw in chapter 1, a bill dealing with the rules for mobile home parks ended up here first.

College & Workforce Development. What used to be called the Higher Education Committee probably got this name thanks to pressure to ensure that state colleges are turning out people qualified for jobs. It regulates all higher education in the state, including licensing of private colleges and schools.

Commerce & Gaming. This sort of falls under the category of things that have to be regulated, therefore we need a committee. This committee's assignment includes alcohol, tobacco, and cannabis, as well as legal gambling, including agreements with Native American tribes.

Consumer Protection & Business. This committee has been known by various names over the years, once carrying the label FIRE—Finance, Insurance, and Real Estate. Now it oversees regulation of businesses and professions, licensing, consumer protection, and sometimes still sets things on fire.

Education. This is the committee that oversees the state's K–12 education system.

Environment & Energy. The environment committee got energy added to its portfolio after people began to figure out that this climate change thing is for real. It covers a host of environmental concerns, including the above-mentioned Growth Management Act, as well as issues surrounding renewable energy resources.

Finance. If you have a budget, you have to have a way to pay for it, and the Finance Committee deals with revenue. We'll talk more about this later when we talk about the state budget.

Health Care & Wellness. Here again, even though health care is supposed to lead to and preserve wellness, somebody thought this should be added to the sign out front. This committee oversees the licensing of health-care practitioners, the regulation of pharmacies and drugs, as well as state health-care programs, and accessibility and affordability.

Housing, Community Development & Veterans. Another catch-all committee. The committee "considers a broad array of issues relating to housing, including accessibility and affordability, homelessness, state assistance to low-income housing, housing authorities and the Housing Finance Commission. The committee also considers issues relating to community development, community investment programs, underrepresented communities, veterans and military affairs, parks and recreation, and emergency management preparedness and response."[4] That would definitely qualify as a broad array.

Human Services & Early Learning. Another "broad array" committee (it says just that on its webpage), it covers a host of topics relating to children and family services, including welfare, juvenile justice, and childcare.

Innovation, Technology & Economic Development. Another trendy title. Once upon a time economic development was covered by the Commerce Committee, but that was before the internet became a thing. So now the committee covers not only trade and tourism but also digital communications and, they hope, emerging technologies.

Labor & Workplace Standards. This committee "considers issues relating to industrial insurance, unemployment compensation, collective bargaining, family leave, safety and health standards, occupational health, and employment standards such as wage laws and employment discrimination. The committee also considers issues relating to the building and construction trades."[5] Not necessarily a broad array because these things are all related.

Local Government. Although federalism describes the relationship between states and the national government, local governments are not a part of the federalist equation. So the state has a lot to say about what cities and other local governments can and can't do and it starts in this committee.

Public Safety. This committee oversees law enforcement (which happens largely at the local level), as well as crime prevention and sentencing.

Rural Development, Agriculture & Natural Resources. As wide-ranging and diverse as Washington's economy is, this committee has to cover a lot of ground—both literally and figuratively. The committee deals with issues relating to rural development, as well as "issues relating to agricultural production, marketing, and sales; food policy; animal and plant disease control; fisheries and wildlife; forest practices and forest fire protection; water; and mining. The committee also considers the management of certain state-owned lands."[6]

State Government & Tribal Relations. Like Sesame Street, two of these things don't have to be together, but they're not entirely unrelated. So the committee considers state agency rulemaking and performance audits, as well as elections and campaign finance, plus relations with the state's twenty-nine Native American tribes, which, as we'll see, are states within the state.

Transportation. This committee oversees the transportation budget, including both spending plans and revenue, as well as transport regulations and the Washington State Patrol.

Rules. Really important and less known outside of the legislature itself. The Rules Committee is the traffic cop of legislation. Your bill might get through committee, but it doesn't go to the floor unless it gets through Rules. The house version has twenty-five members. They tend to be the heavy hitters among the legislators, and the Speaker of the House, the highest-ranking official in the chamber and the head of the majority caucus, is the chair. Recent Rules Committee procedures specify that any member can "pull two bills," which means they go to the house or senate floor for action. But as one observer noted, "The Speaker gets his bills."

"You have to make a deal with somebody unless you're on the committee" to get your bill out of Rules and to the floor, one legislator said. "It's considered bad form to pull your own bill. We try to make gentlemen's agreements" to move bills on to floor debate. As the session winds down, non-controversial bills can get moved to the consent calendar (and hence to the floor), and majority leadership may also pull bills to get them to the floor without requiring a full committee meeting.

The senate, with only forty-nine members instead of ninety-eight, has fewer committees (fifteen versus twenty in the house) and fewer people on them. Most senators serve on at least three committees. The names of the committees are also sometimes slightly different. The Appropriations Committee in the senate is called Ways & Means, an old-school term for budget committees, and it handles revenue as well as spending. Also in the senate, early learning moves to Early Learning and K–12 Education, while Labor and Commerce covers parts of the portfolios of its house counterparts in one committee. As in the house, the budget-writing Ways & Means Committee has the biggest membership with twenty-seven senators, more than half of everybody there, plus twenty staff members. The

Senate Ways & Means Committee also oversees the capital budget, which gets its own committee in the house.

By 2022 the legislature had shuffled the deck yet again. Among other changes, Housing was moved to its own committee, and the rest of it became Innovation, Community & Economic Development & Veterans. Because, you know, innovation!

Every committee has staff assigned to it, lawyers, analysts, researchers, all of whose job is to help legislators make better laws and put their agendas into practice. The staff is nonpartisan, so they're able to work with both Republicans and Democrats (and they really do). The senate also has a Rules Committee, which performs the same gatekeeping function as does the house version. It has seventeen members, again featuring the major players on the legislative stage, with one difference. The presiding officer is the lieutenant governor, whose one actual job is to be presiding officer of the senate. And like every other member of the Senate Rules Committee, he or she can also pull two bills to send to the floor.

What should be clear from all this discussion of committees is that the legislature can organize its own affairs. It determines what legislation will be considered, where it will go, and what the rules are for it to become law. All the committees and their processes mean that, in a broad sense, legislative government is more about stopping new laws than it is about passing them.

THE READING RAILROAD

Remember our first reading, when your shiny new bill was introduced and assigned to committee? Let's say through your careful efforts and the brilliance of your idea, your bill survived the carnival of committees and ended up in the Rules Committee, where it gets pulled and sent to the floor of the house. If the bill is uncontroversial and nearly certain to pass, it may go on the suspension calendar (as in suspension of the rules) in the house or the consent calendar in the senate. In either event that sort of bill is advanced to third reading for final passage. Otherwise, if your bill gets pulled, it's on to the second reading.

The house and senate chambers are large auditoriums with enough seating for all the members. There are offices and hallways out in the wings, and galleries up above where people can watch. The only meetings that happen in private are caucus meetings, and those rooms are in the wings of the chambers as well. Pages—high school students from around the state—scurry on and off the floor, relaying messages to legislators, who may be at their desks or may be in the wings. Not just anybody can go on the floor when the house or senate is in session. On rare occasions, the Speaker (or the president of the senate) may say, "Call of the house," which means every member must come to the floor and the doors are locked. When this happens it means there's a tough vote coming, and the majority caucus leadership has to put pressure on enough people to go along with the vote. (On one such call in the early 1980s, we were there all night. It was a very difficult budget year, and they needed all the votes they could get. The bill still failed.)

A position called "the whip," elected along with the rest of the caucus leadership, is supposed to count the votes. "Sometimes we put a bill on the calendar and then pull it because we don't have the votes," said one legislator. Each caucus also elects a floor leader, who manages the bill's life on the floor of the house or senate. "The floor leader decides in the end if it's go/no go," the legislator said.

In second reading the bill is reintroduced. The sponsor is recognized by the Speaker or president of the senate, rises, and talks briefly about her or his bill. And then come the amendments. They are briefly described by the clerk, and the sponsor of the amendment is recognized and rises to address the group. Not all amendments are created equal. Sometimes amendments are offered by the minority party that will gut the bill, contradicting its original purpose. Sometimes amendments are offered just to gum up the bill so much that nobody will vote for it. Amendments like this will provoke a response from the majority floor leader, who will be recognized and then rise and say why legislators should vote against this amendment. Sometimes amendments from the other party really are intended to make the bill better, and the amendment sponsor will indicate this by saying, "I intend this as a friendly amendment."

Unfriendly amendments can have a big impact on what gets passed. "If you have three to four hours of debate, you're killing a lot of bills" that you can't then get to, one legislative veteran said. "Sometimes you have to say to the minority, 'What will it take for you to pull your amendments?'" The usual answer is to get one of the other side's pet bills through so you can get back to work. Horse trading is often how politics is done. This isn't necessarily a bad thing because it means everybody gets something.

The amendments will be voted on, one after the other, until they've run out or the Speaker cuts off debate. If the bill hasn't been too badly trashed and they have the votes, the bill will be advanced to third reading. Third reading is the final vote. As with executive session in committee, there can still be debate, but the vote is now up or down; no more amendments will be considered. Any bill is less likely to come to the floor at all if the majority doesn't feel it has the votes to pass the measure. This is McCrone's Rule: nothing comes to a vote that hasn't already been decided. But sometimes there is a trial run, just to see who's playing along. One member of the majority caucus will vote no. As the votes are tallied—electronically in the house, by voice vote in the senate—when it appears that the measure has failed, the designated "no" voter will rise and be recognized. That member will say that having voted with the majority (no), she or he asks that the bill be removed for consideration for reintroduction at a later date. So the bill gets pulled back from the precipice, and the majority caucus leadership knows who they need to lean on.

The House has a large electronic readerboard with every member's name on it, with a light that shows green for a yes vote and red for a no vote. (The senate still conducts votes by voice vote and roll call.) An old tradition is that when a new legislator is about to get his or her first bill passed, everyone in the chamber votes no, showing a reader board with one green light and ninety-seven red ones. The Speaker leaves the voting open long enough for everyone to have a chuckle and change their vote.

So your bill has passed the house! It's a great moment; you've done something positive for the people of the state of Washington. And now you get to start all over, because it's going to go through all the same procedures in the senate. Careful representatives find a friendly senator and get them to introduce a companion measure, the same bill but starting its life in the senate (and vice versa). If your bill stalls in the house, perhaps you switch your attention to the senate version and see if you can get that rolling. Either way, your bill is going to have to pass the house and the senate—in no particular order—in exactly the same version. If that happens, it's sent to the governor for their signature. The governor can veto all or part of the bill (a line-item veto). Vetoes are not all that common. If the governor vetoes a lot of things coming from the legislature, they are less likely to get cooperation on things that they want. Moreover, effective legislative leadership will work with the governor ahead of time and find out what the governor can live with. They don't regularly send bills to the governor that they expect to get vetoed. You hear that kind of talk on the campaign trail, particularly from rookie candidates, vowing to draw a line in the sand and force the governor (or the county executive or the mayor) to see things the right way. But you don't see it in practice. In politics, compromise is not a dirty word. It's how things get done.

We've talked about all the opportunities a bill has to die, but in some ways a bill is never really dead. Sometimes a bill passes one house but not the other, in which case it may be kept on life support, resurrected next session, and taken up again. Even if your bill never makes it out of committee, it can still rise from the grave—as an amendment to a bill that's still alive. As the bill cut-offs arrive, legislators begin to scramble to find a live bill to which they can attach their own as an amendment. This is trickier than it may sound because the Washington legislature is constitutionally bound by a germaneness rule—an amendment must relate to the subject of the original bill. So you can't tack an amendment relating to school funding to a bill dealing with health care. Still, sometimes there's a bill so broad that it invites amendments, which can end up being known as a "Christmas tree bill," because everybody's hanging an ornament on it.

In an odd-numbered year, if your bill passed the house but didn't make it through the senate by the end of session, it is returned to the house for reconsideration in the following year's short session. The same is true for a bill that passes the senate but dies in the house. It then goes back to the senate, a process called carryover. In the short session the bill could be advanced to third reading and sent straight back to the senate (or the house), or it could be sent back to committee and the process starts all over again. At the end of the two-year cycle, however, if a bill has not been passed by the legislature and signed by the governor, it's dead. You will have to reintroduce it in the next odd-year session.

Passing a bill can take a while. State Rep. Tina Orwall (D–Des Moines) needed three tries to get a bill through improving the rights of adoptees. "Bills can get stuck in all kinds of places," said Orwall, herself an adoptee.

One year it passed 98–0 in the house but couldn't get a hearing in the senate. Still, she persevered, and in the end her bill passed.

Sometimes the house and senate versions of a bill are slightly different. Each side will ask the other to recede from or concur with the amendments enacted by the other side. If that fails, they call a conference committee, which includes Republicans and Democrats from all four caucuses. Their job is to hammer out a compromise. They issue a report on the bill, and the house and senate must both vote to approve the report, which in effect says they're now both approving the same version of the bill. And then it's off to the governor. The governor can veto all or part of it or sign it into law. If the governor vetoes the bill, the house and senate can override the veto by a two-thirds vote.

The house and senate chambers are located on opposite sides of the capitol dome. Their main entrances are on either side of the chambers, but in the middle in the back of the auditoriums are pairs of large brass doors. When the legislature is finally set to adjourn, the doors are opened, and across the floors and the dome, the Speaker of the House and the president of the senate can see each other. They pronounce the session ended, "Sine die" (with no scheduled resumption), and bring down their gavels at the same time. Honestly, it's kind of cool.

The governor can call the legislature into special session for up to thirty days at a time. This can happen if there's some kind of emergency. The legislature can also call itself into session with a two-thirds vote of both chambers. It most often happens if the legislature has finished its regular session and hasn't passed a budget. That might happen when state tax revenues are down, typically as a result of a recession.

This can be very frustrating to watch. Republicans took control of the house and senate in the 1980 elections, and for a while things went smoothly. But then the bottom dropped out of the economy, and the sales tax had been removed from food and medicine so that the revenue stream was more susceptible to reductions in consumer spending. The legislature had to go back into session twice to address revenue shortfalls, and ultimately the Republican majority temporarily put the sales tax back on food. They got hammered in the 1982 elections, but majority Democrats didn't have an easier time of it, as the economy hadn't really recovered by the time they went back into session in 1983. But having learned from the

Republican experience, they stayed in session (the regular session plus two special sessions) for 136 days. The joke making the halls among staff that year was, "What's the difference between the legislature and a Boy Scout troop? A Boy Scout troop has adult leadership."

Sometimes the legislature, called repeatedly into special session, stays in Olympia and keeps plugging away. Other times most legislators are sent home while leadership of the four caucuses attempts to forge a compromise. The longest the legislature has been in session was probably 2017, when it met for 193 days—the regular 105-day session plus three 30-day special sessions. The legislature was under a court order to comply with the McCleary decision and amply fund K–12 education. Democrats, who had a majority in the house, and Republicans, who had a majority in the senate, had a very difficult time agreeing on how to do that. That meant the budget wasn't actually passed until after the June 30 end of the fiscal year, which had never happened in Washington before. Nonetheless, it's still important to remember that most legislators believe they're doing the right thing, as easy as it might be to disagree about what is best.

State Sen. Hans Zeiger (R-Puyallup), said you have three things to think about when you vote: "Your district, your conscience, and your party. Most issues are not conscience issues." So, he said, you apply "your best judgment given limited information at the time. There are times when you have to vote for your district and go against your party."

Another Republican, State Sen. Curtis King of Yakima, agreed. "Most of us can work well together, most of us try to look at both sides of an issue and try to make the best decisions we can for our constituencies and for our state," he said. "At times I've taken votes that are best for the state but not necessarily the best for my district."

As one veteran legislator put it, "We're all just folk trying to do the best we can, but with different life experiences informing our decisions."

"This job is what you make of it," said another. "If you want nightmares, you can generate all that kind of stuff. But if you want to have a good flow and want to do good work, you can make that happen."

CHAPTER TEN

The Gang of Nine

THE EXECUTIVE BRANCH

The executive branch is all the people in charge of running government on a day-to-day basis, including the people who work for them. The executives oversee and manage all the state employees who put the legislature's work into action. Washington has nine statewide elected executives, all elected to four-year terms in presidential election years (yet another reason why we have some of the longest ballots on earth). Thirty-six states elect governors in off-year elections, opposite the presidential cycle.

Governors are the chief executives of states. Their roles are not completely unlike those of presidents, though the specific tasks and powers of governors vary from state to state. Governors have term limits in some states but not others (Washington has no term limits). It's a job that pays, on average, a little over $147,000 a year (as low as $70,000 and no higher than $225,000) yet is required to manage multi-billion-dollar budgets and large payrolls (average fifty-five thousand people), while engaging in salesmanship, politicking, ribbon cutting, and general running around and being chief symbol and cheerleader for the state. Take a vacation at your own risk, and no pay raises should be expected. A CEO of an organization that large in the private sector would get millions of dollars a year in salary for giving up a normal life but governors are stuck with it. Yet people run for governor regularly all over the country; in my experience half of Washington's state legislators, at any given time, think they should be governor (and most of them shouldn't). Like all political jobs, it retains an appeal for people who want to do politics.

The governor's current salary is just north of $187,000 a year, plus they get to live in the governor's mansion on the Capitol campus, which makes for a very short commute. The governor's office has an $18 million annual budget, including a $4 million strategic reserve account. (In terms of the $99 billion state budget, this isn't much.) The governor's budget covers the operating costs of his office and the mansion, plus the Women's Commission, an oversight board, and three ombudsmen's offices.

Washington's governor has a number of duties as specified by the state constitution: The governor can require written reports from other state officials and "shall see that the laws are faithfully executed." Some governors appoint numerous other statewide positions; some, like Washington's, appoint relatively few. Washington's governor can appoint people to fill vacant offices, including judges and Washington's members of Congress. Appointees to elective office must run for the unexpired portion of that term at the next available election. Washington governors tend to appoint more than a few judges. Judges may retire midterm, allowing a like-minded governor to put someone in office in line with the governor's political philosophy. Overall, in a four-year term, the governor will appoint more than 1,600 positions, including management-level state jobs as well as filling court vacancies. Every time the legislature creates a new board or commission the governor will have to fill it. She or he must provide information to the legislature every session as to the "state of affairs" of the state and what might be done about it. This has become known as "the state of the state" speech, and the governor generally gives it in person. She or he can call the legislature into special session, generally for thirty days at a time. In difficult budget years, that happens quite a bit. He or she is commander in chief of "the state militia," according to the state constitution. Realistically governors can call out the National Guard in case of emergency but can't really be said to command them. The president remains the commander in chief of the armed forces, of which the National Guard is a part.

PEOPLE IN POLITICS: JAY INSLEE

Like a lot of people in government, Jay Inslee's career started when he saw a problem and tried to fix it. "I got involved by helping to pass a school bond measure to build a new high school in Selah, Washington, and when the legislature cut the funding formula so we couldn't build the school, I ran for the legislature to fix the problem," he said.

Inslee was a high school basketball star who later went to law school. He ended up working for a firm in Selah, in Yakima County, and in 1985 worked on the school bond campaign. He was first elected to the state house in 1988, serving two terms before getting elected to Congress from the Fourth District in 1992. He lost his seat in the Republican wave of 1994, taking a job with the federal government afterward.

That moved him back to Seattle, where he ran for governor in 1996, losing in the primary, and then for Congress from the First District in 1998. He won that race, getting reelected five more times. In 2012 he ran for governor and won, winning reelection in 2016 and 2020. In 2019 he launched a campaign for president, promising to address climate change but dropped out after not making any headway in the polls.

Inslee said being governor of Washington has some peculiarities, in particular sharing power with eight other statewide elected officials. "Having multiple statewide offices often provides challenges citizens don't see," he said. "Sometimes a citizen will ask me to fix a problem and it turns out there's another elected official who has as much or more control over that issue, so I have to try to explain that."

Having served in both Washingtons, the governor said the states are playing a very important role in current U.S. politics. "Right now, the balance of power is in the states rather than the federal government because it's only in our state that we're making progress," he said. Inslee pointed to a number of policy innovations in Washington State. "First public option [for health insurance], first long-term care plan, 100 percent clean energy, gender pay equity, net neutrality—we've demonstrated that power through the actions in the state," he said. "Between the legislature and the executive, I think our system is pretty balanced, and we're lucky to have it."

But, he said, you don't have to occupy the state's highest elected office to have an impact on government in our state. "What people should know about government is that you can make a difference," he said. "Anybody can make a difference in a whole variety of ways by becoming involved, starting with voting."

Washington governors have the power to pardon convicted criminals and also to forgive fines and forfeitures. The governor has a limited ability to issue executive orders, directing state agencies to make policy changes, which are in force until the legislature or the next governor says otherwise. She or he can veto bills passed by the legislature. Washington's governor, like all but seven in the United States, has line-item veto, by which the governor doesn't have to veto the whole bill. But the governor can only veto an entire section; he or she can't veto a word and change the meaning of the bill. Washington governors can veto a single budget item from a bill. They cannot, however, simply reduce the amount of spending authorized in a bill; it's all or nothing. Nor does the governor have a pocket veto, by which she or he simply ignores a bill without signing it after the end of the session. If the governor doesn't sign the bill, it still becomes law.

The legislature can override a veto by a two-thirds vote of both chambers. As noted previously, this doesn't happen all that often. Governors have to be careful with vetoes because if you start vetoing anything with a bill number on it the legislature probably won't give you the things you do want. Between 1983 and 2018 Washington governors partially vetoed an average of 7.5 percent of the bills that passed and applied full vetoes to only 1.3 percent of bills. (Contrast that with former New Mexico governor Gary Johnson, an eventual Libertarian candidate for president who vetoed hundreds of bills a year in a somewhat quixotic quest to shrink state government. You might think that's a good idea, and you might think that's not really governance.) If the governor vetoes a bill, in current circumstances you'd be hard pressed to get a two-thirds vote to agree that Olympia is the state capital. If things are working as they're supposed to, the governor and legislative leaders communicate ahead of time to see what everybody can live with. A successful governor learns how to work with legislators to get what he or she wants. They're expected to be "legislator-in-chief," setting a policy agenda for the state.

The governor also presents the legislature with a budget. All state agencies funnel their budget requests to the governor's office by September where it will get hammered into something like the governor's priorities. Catty legislators will sometimes declare the governor's budget "dead on arrival," but in reality, the broad outlines of the budget don't change that much. Whether the governor gets what he or she wants in that budget will depend in part on how the governor engages with the legislature. Does he or she get in there and get involved, working with legislators to fashion a budget that reflects priorities and provides some benefit to the people of the state? Or does the governor stand back and let things happen?

We've had both kinds of governors. Before Inslee, Dan Evans (1964–76) was the only consecutive three-term governor in the state's history (Arthur Langlie served 1940–44 and 1948–56). Evans had served in the legislature so he knew how the game was played and how to play it. Evans got a lot done. Christine Gregoire (2004–12) also got points for being involved and helping the process along. Current governor Jay Inslee (2012–present) is sometimes criticized for not being more engaged, but he earned compliments for taking charge amid the COVID-19 pandemic in 2020. Booth Gardner (1984–92) was very popular when first elected and by many accounts was a good guy, but by the end some of his most ardent partisans had concluded he wasn't actually that good at the job. "He didn't care to get his hands dirty," one legislator confided at the time.

And this gets at the heart of what makes a good governor, what the elder George Bush once derisively referred to as "that vision thing." Does the governor have a vision for what the state could be, and can she or he make that happen? Governors can issue executive orders, but real policy change involves convincing a majority of the legislature to say yes, both to policy direction and the money to pay for it.

While governor, Evans got the legislature to create the Department of Ecology, the first such agency in the country and a model for the Environmental Protection Agency. He oversaw the founding of the state's community college system. Legislators recalled that Evans, an engineer, when confronted with claims presented by legislators, would simply whip out a slide rule (an early calculating tool), do the math, and tell them where they'd gone wrong. He had a gift for getting things done, but it shouldn't be overlooked that he served five terms in the state house before becoming governor. He knew the players, and he knew where the bodies were buried.

Jay Inslee began his third term facing the COVID-19 pandemic, a struggling state economy, and various uncertainties left over from the Trump years. With Democrat majorities in the house and senate in 2019–20, he was able to push quite a bit of his legislative agenda, despite spending a fair amount of time running for president. Like every elected state official, his name on the official webpage is prominently displayed.

Inslee succeeded Christine Gregoire, who served for two terms. She previously served as attorney general and emerged as the Democratic frontrunner in the 2004 campaign. In the 2004 election, she narrowly defeated Republican Dino Rossi. The Rossi campaign alleged vote fraud, but by the model for counting votes that the Republicans proposed in court, Rossi still lost. She beat Rossi by a larger margin in 2008. Gregoire had the misfortune of being governor during the Great Recession, which meant that state tax revenues were down. She weathered the storm in pretty fair shape.

Gregoire succeeded Gary Locke. He previously served as a state legislator and King County executive before being elected governor in 1996 and reelected in 2000. Locke was a liberal Democrat who reinvented himself as a pro-business centrist. On the whole he had a successful two terms as governor, mightily frustrating Republicans by carefully managing state finances (they have a harder time running against somebody who's doing a reasonably good job at that).

Locke replaced Mike Lowry (1993–97), a former congressman, state senator, and King County councilman. Lowry's term was tarnished by accusations of sexual harassment by a former aide; he did not seek reelection. He succeeded Booth Gardner (1985–93), a decent man who was not, by some accounts, very good at politics. Gardner defeated Washington's last Republican governor, John Spellman (1981–85). Spellman, a former King County executive, was an able politician, an environmentalist, a former labor lawyer, a civil rights advocate, and he helped clean up King County and get it on a firm financial footing. But as one Democrat legislator later put it, "He was governor at the worst possible time." Spellman served during the recession of the early 1980s, the steepest downturn between the Great Depression and the Great Recession. During those years neither Republican nor Democrat majorities in the legislature looked very good in trying to sort out the state's sorry finances, and Spellman became one of many fall guys.

Spellman replaced Dixie Lee Ray (1977–81), Washington's first woman governor. Ray was elected in 1976, a year in which, following Watergate, voters began their curious obsession with outsiders. Ray had been director of the Pacific Science Center and chair of the federal Atomic Energy Commission, but she had no real political experience. As the Democrat nominee she defeated Spellman in the general election, and things went downhill from there. She couldn't get along with the legislature, even when her party had majorities in the house and senate. She had no understanding and no feel for politics, and by the time the 1980 primary came around, the rallying cry for many voters was ABD—Anyone But Dixie.

Ray replaced the retired Dan Evans, giving Washington the opposite side of the coin when it comes to governors. Evans, as noted, understood politics, knew how the system worked, and had a clear vision for the state.

Outsiders, particularly populists—who claim to represent the common people as opposed to the rich and powerful—don't have a great track record as government executives. Jesse "the Body" Ventura had a steep learning curve in his one term as Minnesota governor. He got some things done but might have done more had he learned to work with legislators.[1] Arnold Schwarzenegger had a very rocky start to his career as governor of California, but he eventually learned that he had to work with the California legislature to get anything accomplished. Meanwhile, consider the argument that you should "vote for me; I'm an outsider." Is there any other job where lack of experience is considered a plus? I can't think of one, but in politics at present, some candidates rely on a pitch that amounts to converting "I have no experience at any of this whatsoever" into a selling point. Dino Rossi ran for governor on this platform in 2004 and again in 2008. He claimed to be an Olympia outsider while taking credit for writing the 2004 state budget while serving as a state senator. How can both of those things be true at the same time?

Governors also have several informal duties. Governors are the leading pitchmen for their states. They lead trade missions; they push their states' prospects in regional and national arenas; they are looked at to take charge of efforts to revitalize sagging economies and manage booming ones. Witness Governor Locke's efforts to land Boeing's 787 production for Washington State, which kept jobs and taxes in the state in the 1990s. In recent years Washington governors regularly lead trade missions to Asia, pushing Washington products to new markets. And they're the de facto leader of their political party.[2]

If something happened to the governor, she or he would be succeeded by the lieutenant governor. This is the single strangest office in the state. The lieutenant governor is the president of the state senate and hence presides over meetings of the senate as a whole, as well as being chair of the Rules Committee. In that capacity the lieutenant governor can pull two bills for floor action like everybody else. But this is where it gets odd: the lieutenant governor can vote to break a tie in the senate. The senate has forty-nine members. It is very unlikely that there will be a tie vote in that chamber (and in the past, senators have been dragged in from their sickbeds to make sure that doesn't happen).

Other than that the lieutenant governor has no duties (except "as proscribed by law").[3] Consequently, the lieutenant governor also sits on the State Finance Committee, State Capitol Committee, the Washington Health Care Facilities Authority, the Washington Higher Education Facilities Authority, and the State Medal of Merit Committee.

Early in the twentieth century, two lieutenant governors stepped up upon the death of the sitting governor, but other than that the office has been of little significance. Consequently, the position doesn't attract a lot of attention, nor is it an office often desired by candidates with higher ambitions. But it has been held by some interesting characters. Jazz bandleader Vic Meyers held the post for twenty years, 1933–53 (followed by eight years as secretary of state). Known as "the clown prince of politics" for some of his antics, he apparently learned the job and took it seriously. In 1956 the voters chose ex-Husky football coach John Cherberg, who served until he retired in 1988. Cherberg also sold ads for KIRO TV on the side, as the salary for lieutenant governor wasn't much.

Cherberg was succeeded by Joel Pritchard, a state senator and U.S. congressman who pushed a referendum to legalize abortion in Washington State and, with some friends, invented the game of pickleball. Pritchard, a relative short-timer, only served two terms as lieutenant governor. His successor, Brad Owen, was elected four times beginning in 1996. Owen, a conservative, anti-choice Democrat, was criticized for all kinds of things, including not working very hard, but he never attracted a serious opponent. In 2015, however, as presiding officer of the state senate, he disallowed a rule passed by senate Republicans that required a two-thirds vote to advance a revenue (tax) bill. Owen ruled it out of order, as the constitution specifies that bills only have to pass the legislature by a simple majority. (A separate state supreme court case reached the same conclusion about a Tim Eyman–sponsored initiative that would have done the same thing.)

Owen was succeeded by Cyrus Habib, elected in 2016. Legally blind and highly educated (an Oxford master's degree plus Yale Law School), Habib is a former legislator; with Jay Inslee away running for president, he was apparently quite busy filling in for the governor in 2019. After Habib declined to seek another term, he was replaced in the 2020 election by Denny Heck, former legislator, chief clerk of the house, and former congressman. Maybe he thought this would look good on his resume.

The secretary of state, unlike her federal counterpart, is not the state's chief of diplomacy and foreign affairs. Washington's secretary of state, like most of those around the country, is the state's chief elections officer. The constitution says the secretary of state is the official record keeper of the legislative and executive branches. Maintaining the state archives remains one of the duties of the office.

But since 1889 a lot has been added to the office's menu: chief elections officer; registering charities, domestic partnerships, in-state business trademarks, and corporations; managing the state library; and being the general keeper and disseminator of state arcana large and small. Need an apostille—an authentication for documents to be used in countries that subscribe to the rules of The Hague Convention of 1961? They can get that for you too.

The current secretary of state is Steve Hobbs, a former state legislator who was appointed to the job when his predecessor, Kim Wyman, took a job with the Biden administration. Wyman, like her predecessor, Sam Reed, previously served as Thurston County auditor (county auditors also run elections). Wyman, a Republican, worked hard to increase voter turnout and was generally supportive of measures to make it easier to register and vote. On the other hand, like a lot of people on this list, she seemed to be engaged in a permanent reelection campaign, as her signature was effectively a part of the logo at the top of every page on the office's website. Hobbs has a picture on the office's front page but his name is relatively small. Hobbs was elected in his own right in the 2022 election.

The state treasurer is the state's chief financial officer and essentially the state's banker and investment manager. Money comes to the treasurer's office through taxes, fees, and fines, and goes out to state agencies to be put to work. Combining the management of state finances in one office saves money. But not all of the more than $300 million that rolls in on an average day has to go out to be spent, so part of the treasurer's job is to invest the extra funds short-term, so as to increase the amount of money the state has available. The office manages all the state's retirement and insurance funds, which means investing them to maximize returns before the money has to be paid out as pensions and claims. It is also the treasurer who issues bonds that are used to pay for capital projects and issues warrants so that the state's bills can be paid.

The most recent state treasurer is Mike Pellicciotti, a former state legislator who was elected in 2020. He defeated Duane A. Davidson, besides Secretary of State Wyman, the only other Republican recently in statewide office. In 2016 Davidson, then the Benton County treasurer, got a plurality in a five-way primary and faced another Republican in the general election after the three Democrats split the majority of the vote. It's worth noting that Davidson was endorsed by nearly every other county treasurer, not all of whom are Republicans.

The office managed $246 billion in transfers, deposits, and withdrawals in 2017, 95 percent of it electronically. It managed surplus funds for all levels of government, earning interest on money that somebody doesn't need right away. Davidson was out front on cannabis banking reform, calling it a safety issue. Many commercial banks won't take money from marijuana stores as long as the evil weed remains a controlled substance under federal law. That means they do business almost exclusively in cash, which is both challenging and makes them a target for criminals. Davidson, along with other state treasurers, lobbied for a change in U.S. law.

On behalf of the state and many local governments, the treasurer's office has an average of $6 billion invested every day, pooled from five hundred separate accounts managed by the treasurer. The treasurer is bound by state law and by accepted accounting principles, so you don't find the state's portfolio holding junk bonds and placing risky bets on the market. The money goes into U.S. Treasury securities and similar investments, chosen so as to maximize return and minimize risk. In 2018 the treasurer invested $33.3 billion in state funds and $531 billion in local government funds, earning a 1.43 percent yield. That's not a great return, but it's a good return considering both current rates and the constraints placed on state investments.

The treasurer's office also manages Washington's debt. The debt comes from the sale of bonds to finance construction projects such as roads and schools. People who do the work expect to get paid up front, so bonds allow governments to raise capital in a hurry, then pay them off over time. Bonds are sold on the open market, meaning anyone can buy one. Bonds are basically a form of loan by which the investor gives the borrower money in exchange for regular interest payments and eventual return of the initial investment. Bonds are affected by inflation. If inflation is high, bonds must pay a higher rate of interest to attract investors. If it's lower, the interest rate falls. The treasurer's office will refinance when interest rates fall, once again saving taxpayers money. States (and other borrowers) get bond ratings from rating firms such as Moody's and Standard & Poor's. These attempt to judge a state's ability to support its debt. Washington's ratings are generally excellent, meaning the state has to pay less interest on its bonds because they are a less risky investment. Once again, this saves taxpayers money.

Washington has around $21 billion in bond debt; servicing the debt consumes 5.8 percent of the general fund budget. If you just look at total state and local debt, Washington ranks somewhere around ninth among U.S. states (and it's a little hard to tell just what numbers the rankings are using, as everybody seems to be measuring debt differently).[4] But if you take debt as a percentage of a state's economy as measured by GDP, Washington falls to thirtieth.[5] And doing Ryan one better, Davidson's name on the webpage was actually bigger than the line that said "Washington State Treasurer." Ditto for Pellicciotti, and his picture is the biggest thing you see on the page.

PEOPLE IN POLITICS: MIKE PELLICCIOTTI

Mike Pellicciotti wants to help children who haven't been born yet—or even conceived. Pellicciotti, elected state treasurer in 2020, spent a chunk of 2022 traveling the state to push a program for "baby bonds," an investment aimed at addressing the wealth gap in Washington State. Upon his election, Pellicciotti said the first order of business was to shore up the state's finances. "In my first year and a half in office, our office has refinanced existing debt so that $385 million goes to the people of Washington instead of Wall Street profits," he said. "We have successfully privately financed other budget obligations to navigate a budget shortfall and avoid a $300 million government bailout after the COVID economic recession.

"We have convinced the legislature to follow our responsible budgeting recommendations that ensure Washington has the third-best-funded pension in the country because $800 million went to pension needs instead of corporate tax cuts," Pellicciotti added. "Washington has a low debt-service ratio on our capital budget, and Washington has returned our budget reserves to pre-pandemic reserve levels so that we can better weather future economic downturns and not increase tax burdens on working families if that happens. We have budget surpluses now after having a several billion-dollar budget hole when I first came into office."

That, he said, has allowed his office to focus on longer-term concerns. And that led to baby bonds, an idea developed by New School (New York) economist Dr. Darrick Hamilton. The basic premise is that government would create small trust funds for every child below a certain poverty threshold, so that when they came of age they would have resources more like those available to children of wealthier families. For example, the average white family has eight times more wealth than the typical Black family in the United States.[6]

In Pellicciotti's version, any child born under Apple Health—the state's low-income Medicaid insurance program—would qualify. To qualify for Apple Health, a family of four would have to earn less than $36,000 a year or a little over $17 an hour. About two million state residents and about forty thousand newborns qualify.

A Washington Future Fund recipient would be able to access their trust fund between the ages of eighteen and thirty-one for education, buying a first home, or starting a business. Pellicciotti has suggested fund sizes of $10,000 to $25,000. The state would have to invest $125 million in the program to start, with unclaimed funds reinvested into the program.

"Nearly half of newborns are born into low-income households in Washington," Pellicciotti said. "These numbers are closer to two-thirds or three-quarters in rural Washington and communities of color.

"The Washington Future Fund would reserve surplus money now, allow for its investment in the economy for two decades, and then provide sufficient funds to provide each of these newborns $10,000 to $15,000 or perhaps up to $25,000 when they become adults, in a way that lightens future Treasury budget obligations and also interrupts the wealth gap, while injecting capital into rural Washington in a way that can support a purpose-driven life for many."

Pellicciotti started his career with the state attorney general's office, working on economic fraud and corporate financial crime cases. He has both a law degree and an MBA. He later served two terms in the state house before deciding to run for treasurer in 2020. "It became clear to me that my background and interest in government, finance, economic development, and the law were well-matched for my vision of the office," he said of the treasurer's job. "I thought and continue to believe it is one of the most important positions in Washington State government and believe there are few opportunities to be more impactful in achieving good government aims, greater public confidence in government, the creation of laws that serve the financial interests of working families and retirees instead of corporate interests, and ways to protect the long-term policy interests of the people of Washington." And so he's pushing baby bonds, which have been adopted in Connecticut and Washington DC. "If the legislature funds our Washington Future Fund, after twenty consecutive years of funding, as many as a million low-income children will have their lives transformed," Pellicciotti said. "It is the initiative that has the potential to help the most amount of Washingtonians—and ultimately better secure greater stability in government, society, and our state treasury during the twenty-first century."

The state auditor makes sure the money goes where we think it's going. State agencies must file regular reports with the auditor's office, carefully documenting that all the money is accounted for in state expenditures. Every state agency and all 2,400 local governments get audited, filing financial reports annually and getting a full audit every three years. The auditor's office also runs the Employee Disclosure program (whistleblowers) and investigates when citizens report shady government dealings. If government is as corrupt as many people claim, everyone in the auditor's office is a liar. This seems unlikely.

One of the jobs of the auditor's office is performance audits, required by the citizens via the passage of Initiative 900 in 2005. "Performance audits evaluate the efficiency and effectiveness of government programs with the goal of making them work better," according to the agency's website.[7] They do this by comparing what the agency is supposed to be doing with what it's actually doing, but they also look for solutions if there are areas for improvement. They have added cybersecurity performance audits to their portfolio.

The current auditor is Pat McCarthy, a Democrat, whose name on the webpage is about the same size as the one that says "Auditor." McCarthy is a former Pierce County auditor and was elected to the state job in 2016 and reelected in 2020. McCarthy succeeded Troy Kelley, a former Democratic legislator who held the job for one term before he was convicted of possession of stolen property, making false declarations in a court proceeding, and tax fraud.[8] He did not seek reelection.

Although the auditor's office is supposed to audit every government in the state, some of them have been declared "unauditable." As of 2019 some forty local governments had not complied with state reporting requirements, relatively small entities such as diking and drainage districts. Moreover, they don't have to hold elections if no one files for office.[9] One such district in Enumclaw hadn't had an election since 1988 or been audited since 1986.[10] Media reports and public outcry led to a former commissioner being arrested for mail fraud in 2019, with the county council appointing new commissioners soon after. Part of the challenge has been that the auditor's office lacks enforcement power; all they could do was ask the state attorney general to dissolve the district, "the death penalty or nothing," as one official put it.[11] Legislators were able to push through a new law in 2020 that allows counties to withhold funds from districts that are not filing financial reports. Some districts are so small that they lack the expertise to properly file the forms. But by 2020 the number of unaudited districts had fallen to fifteen.[12]

The office of attorney general has been described as head of "the largest law firm in the state of Washington."[13] It has twenty-eight divisions, ranging from Agriculture and Health to Washington State University. It has 600 attorneys, 650 staff, and thirteen offices around the state. The attorney general and her or his designates represent the state in court, defending state agencies and, in recent years, challenging actions by the U.S. president in court. They are the legal representation for two hundred state agencies, boards, and commissions, including public colleges. The attorney general enforces the state Consumer Protection Act, advises other officials of government on legal matters, enforces laws on anti-competitive business practices, and can investigate and prosecute persons accused of criminal activity if asked by the governor or by a county prosecutor.

The current attorney general is Bob Ferguson (name slightly smaller than "Attorney General" on the webpage), a Democrat most noted for taking on the Trump administration on a host of issues and usually winning. He is frequently rumored as a future candidate for governor, a career path that worked for Christine Gregoire (attorney general, 1998–2005; governor, 2005–13). That didn't work as well for her successor, Rob McKenna (attorney general, 2005–13). Whereas Attorney General Gregoire led a lawsuit that got $206 billion settlement from Big Tobacco (turns out they had long known that cigarette smoking kills people), McKenna was most notable for joining the suit by some states against the Affordable Care Act. In this suit Republicans tried to overturn the health care plan they themselves once proposed. McKenna lost the governor's race to Jay Inslee in 2012. Fellow Republican Slade Gorton, however, parlayed his time in the AG's office (1969–81) into a couple of terms in the U.S. Senate.

The superintendent of public instruction oversees the state's K–12 education system. The office oversees around 45 percent of the state general fund budget, which goes to 296 school districts and around one million public school students. More than seven hundred thousand private school students also are under OSPI jurisdiction, although the state does not fund those schools. This includes certification for teachers, administrators, and other school employees; developing curriculum guidelines; administering school accreditation (which means your school meets certain standards); and setting regulations for everything from programs for the disabled to food service. However, like some other state agencies, the office lacks much enforcement authority when it comes to schools.

The top issue for K–12 education is always funding, especially given the constitutional imperative to amply fund the common schools. A number of other issues also show up on the K–12 blackboard as well, however. For decades, some people have campaigned for a voucher system, all in the name of "school choice." This would allow people to take their tax dollars and apply it to whatever school they wanted, either the local public school or a private school. This often runs into the U.S. Constitution's separation of church and state, since some private schools, many of which are academically very good, are affiliated with churches. Going back to the 1990s, people campaigned for charter schools—privately run schools paid for with public money. Again, the stated logic for charter schools was that parents could choose and schools would improve because they would be forced to compete for students.

It should be no surprise that most of the people pushing for charter schools are Republicans because charter schools tend to be non-union and teachers unions generally support Democrats for office. Washington State voters approved charter schools via initiative in 2012. Meanwhile, studies have shown that charter schools don't perform better than public schools, and if you standardize for family income levels, they perform worse. They also serve lower percentages of lower income and special needs students than do nearby public schools.[14]

Which leads to another issue for schools in general, which is standardized testing. Historically, American students have never done well at standardized tests, which had more to do with how we do education compared to other parts of the world. But when policymakers woke up to this fact, something had to be done. This brought us the No Child Left Behind Act of 2001, a congressional requirement that local school districts had to show improvement in standardized test scores or risk losing their federal funding. (Which is only about 7 percent of a typical school district's budget.) It should have been called No Rich White Child Left Behind, because if you account for family income levels, or the percentage of homes in a district where English is not the first language spoken, you account for most of the variation in test scores. By 2015 Congress had largely dispensed with the act, but Washington and other states persist in applying standardized tests to K-12 students. (The state has only recently broadened the ways in which schools can show that their students are succeeding.) This compels teachers to teach their students how to pass this test, which is also true for students taking Advanced Placement and International Baccalaureate exams. I've never met a student who said they thought the tests were useful or worthwhile. But teaching is one of those rare professions where the people who do it are presumed to have no special knowledge of the field. Then again, those who can, teach, and those who can't make education policy.

The current superintendent is Chris Reykdal, a former legislator from the Olympia area. He was first elected in 2016 and reelected in 2020. He was once a public school teacher and also served as a school board member. Having an actual teacher in charge of the schools simply cannot be explained.

The commissioner of public lands oversees the state's Department of Natural Resources, which has 1,500 employees and a $2 billion budget. Among other things, that means management of about 5.6 million acres of state land. It's a tricky task. On the one hand, people want to see some of the state's natural beauty preserved; on the other hand, economic use of those lands generates revenues that support school construction and funds for other state and local agencies. Consequently, commissioners are regularly criticized for either allowing too much logging and development or not enough.

The department is supposed to regulate logging practices, including reforestation. It has the state's largest fire department, crucial in a time of increasing forest fires, and oversees a network of Natural Area Preserves and Natural Resource Conservation Areas. It oversees 2.6 million acres of aquatic lands; state recreational areas; and the Washington Geologic Survey, which keeps an eye out for earthquakes, volcanic eruptions, and landslides.

The current commissioner is Hilary Franz, a Democrat who was first elected in 2016 and reelected in 2020 (since we're keeping score, small name, picture on the first webpage; like Attorney General Ferguson, a presumed future candidate for governor). She has said it's her goal to help Washington's public lands survive climate change, which is a worthy objective. Climate change has meant drier winters, which increases the risk of forest fires, producing hazy summers from all the smoke. She has also spearheaded the Rural Communities Partnership Initiative, which aims to boost economic development in the state's rural areas. Historically, the economies of those areas have been driven by resource extraction (such as logging and mining), and unlike central Puget Sound, they've been hurting for a long time.

The insurance commissioner was first created to register insurance companies that wanted to do business in the state. This job originally went to the secretary of state. The legislature created a separate, statewide post in 1907. Now it regulates anybody who sells insurance here, including "testing, licensing and oversight."[15] The office's Consumer Protection Division gets two hundred thousand complaints a year.

The agency's stated mission is consumer protection, and anyone in Washington can file a complaint with the office. The commissioner and company investigate unpaid claims, insurance fraud (by both people and companies), and tests and licenses thirty-six thousand insurance representatives and firms each year. They help senior citizens learn about health insurance, and they also collect $100 million a year in insurance taxes, which goes into the general fund.

The current commissioner is Mike Kreidler, an eye doctor, former state legislator, and U.S. congressman who has become something of a bulldog in regulating the industry. Reading in between the lines on his 2016 opponent's campaign statements, the industry probably thinks he's doing too much. This isn't necessarily a bad thing. He didn't have an opponent in 2020.

"Number one by far is to be a consumer advocate," said Kreidler, Washington's insurance commissioner since 2000. "You're there to be sure that for the consumer, insurance is available and affordable. And that those insurance products are delivering on the promises made."

The commissioner said people often lose sight of the fact that his office regulates all kinds of insurance. "I think there's a perception here, at least in some circles, that I am the health insurance commissioner in the state of Washington," he said, and he's even been introduced as such. Nonetheless, health insurance is a major part of what they do. "The number one driver for my interest in this office when I ran for it in 2000 was the focus on what we could do with health insurance coverage and how we could make it available for more people," he said. Now he finds himself in the position of trying to defend the Affordable Care Act, the Obama-era prescription for broader health-care coverage for all Americans.

That includes concerns from prominent Democrats who want to completely change health care insurance in the country. "My frustration now, even among the Democrats, you have no idea how difficult it is to eke out a major reform," Kreidler said. "The idea that you could come back and totally revamp the system in a new fashion without having huge resistance—you're just not being realistic." He said it's much more politically possible to continue to try to improve the ACA. "We're much more likely to say we don't like the ACA but we can work with it," he said. "I think in many ways you can get to the same kind of principles [such as universal coverage] without making people unduly nervous about so much change.

"We have an opportunity to do that now," Kreidler added. "The Trump administration was unable to destroy the ACA. Now what can we do to make it better? What discourages me the most is that you're going to make the good the enemy of the perfect," he said. "In 2021 we're going to have a window of opportunity. We should not just fritter it away. We've got to focus on what we can achieve and what will be sustainable. I love being in the center of that storm."

Kreidler got credit for taking on the insurance industry, such as forcing them to cover contraceptive care, but then took some heat when insurance companies raised rates in 2017 and 2018. He was also criticized for not doing more to help boost coverage for the mentally ill. Finally, in 2022 he came under fire for using racist language and frequently mistreating staff (confirmed by a former staffer I know). Governor Inslee and state Republican and Democrat leaders called on Kreidler to resign. The commissioner apologized for his language but said he would not resign. He said he would hire a consultant to investigate workplace conditions in his office.

CHAPTER ELEVEN

All Rise

THE COURTS ARE IN SESSION

The courts are the third branch of government at both the state and national levels. Courts resolve disputes and decide matters of law, but only if someone files suit. Courts at all levels in the United States cannot take action on their own; they can only decide on that which is brought before them. But in those decisions, they can force governments and citizens to adhere to the laws as written. They are a check on the power of the other two branches of government. Washington's court system has generally fulfilled that role, although judges have often complained that the legislature is a bit stingy when it comes to funding.

With all the pieces in place, the checks and balances are easy to follow. The legislature makes laws, and dissatisfied citizens can ask the courts to overturn such laws as unconstitutional. The governor must sign bills for them to become laws, or can veto them, and the legislature can vote to override the veto. And if the courts invalidate a law, the legislature can write a new one. What they can't do, however, is ask for a court opinion ahead of time. So while Washington courts have the power of judicial review—the ability to overturn acts of government as unconstitutional—that only happens if someone files suit. The courts cannot issue advisory opinions or take on a law all on their own.

State courts handle most criminal trials, and more trials than federal courts in general. Criminal defendants have the right to trial by jury, although jury sizes vary from state to state (anywhere from six to twelve). Criminal trials must be decided on the evidence as presented. Civil cases—

disputes between two or more people—can go to judges or juries depending on the state.

State courts are roughly organized in the same way: a high court (usually called the supreme court), appeals courts, trial courts of general jurisdiction, and trial courts of limited jurisdiction (such as traffic courts). State supreme court decisions are usually final. The U.S. Supreme Court, if asked, could review a state supreme court decision, but rarely does.

Judges are chosen in several different ways, again varying from state to state. Some twenty-one states elect judges, including Washington. Another twenty-four use a merit plan in which an expert panel reviews possible judges and forwards a list to the governor whenever there's a vacancy. The governor can choose from that list. In four states judges are appointed by the governor, and in Virginia, they're chosen by the legislature.

Judicial elections are somewhat problematic. Citizens obviously exercise more control in electing judges, but if they don't know who they're voting for, it's hard to say what value that control is. (Of course, appointing judges doesn't guarantee that the process will be any less political.) In judicial elections, voters may lack good information about judicial candidates. Judges in Washington and many other states are chosen in nonpartisan elections. Originally elected by party, Washington citizens changed that via constitutional amendment in 1912. Parties nonetheless routinely endorse and support judicial candidates.[1] Meanwhile, races may or may not be contested, so that little is written about them. Judicial candidates are not supposed to campaign on their positions on issues, since that would indicate they might decide a case based on their ideology rather than on the facts presented in trial.

That doesn't stop some from doing so, however. Former Washington Supreme Court justice Richard Sanders was a self-professed property rights advocate, which is to say that he didn't believe government can limit what people do with their land. Something of a Libertarian, he was nonetheless anti-choice when it came to abortion. After being elected in 1995 Justice Sanders spoke at a March for Life rally, after which complaints were filed and he faced a disciplinary hearing for failing to display the required impartiality. The state judicial conduct commission said, "In this case, the Washington Commission on Judicial Conduct determined that Justice Richard B. Sanders did not exercise sufficient restraint." But, they added, his actions did not require sanction, noting that "judges do not forfeit the right to freedom of speech when they assume office."[2] On another occasion Sanders was reprimanded for visiting prisoners at McNeill Island State Penitentiary, unknowingly meeting with some inmates who had cases coming up before the court. Nonetheless, Sanders was reelected in 1998 and 2004, in part because of a quirk in Washington election law. In judicial races, if one candidate gets more than 50 percent of the vote in the primary, they are declared the winner and do not have to stand in the general election. Sanders had only one opponent in the 1998 election. He was reelected handily in 2004, but lost in 2010 and again in 2012. In the 2010 election he blamed the *Seattle Times* for reporting that he had said there are more Blacks in prison because they commit more crimes. (As in much of the rest of the country, the number of Blacks in prison is wildly out of proportion to their actual percentage of the population.) Sanders said the article misrepresented what he said, and to his credit he has argued against three-strikes-and-you're-out laws.[3] Sanders also supports judicial elections.[4]

The only people who might really know whether someone would make a good judge—other attorneys—typically say little about judicial candidates for fear of later running into them in court as judges. Lawyers typically want someone who is fair and impartial and pays attention, not someone who shows up on St. Patrick's Day in a green robe and cancels everything early (this happened to a friend of mine). One local judge got unelected after she insisted that women attorneys had to wear dresses when they came before her. That didn't go over so well.

Bar association ratings are of some help, but on the whole many voters are probably guessing when it comes to choosing judges. In one Washington State election, the sitting state supreme court chief justice was defeated by a little-known lawyer from Tacoma. There was very little campaigning by either man; voters apparently liked Charles Johnson's name better than they liked Keith Callow's. Justice Johnson remains on the court.

On the other hand, sometimes the voters are paying attention. In the 2018 election incumbent supreme court justice Steven Gonzalez was challenged by attorney Nathan Choi. In his first election in 2012, Gonzalez had been narrowly elected, defeating a candidate who did not actively campaign but who had an Anglo surname (Danielson). Gonzalez actually lost in twenty-nine counties but carried Puget Sound. In 2018 Choi's voters' pamphlet statement painted him as a seasoned attorney with experience in business and real estate, with a law degree and an MBA, plus the usual pabulum about being fair and honest and working for you and not for special interests. Gonzalez cited his experience as a judge, attorney, and prosecutor, and had a somewhat Democrat-leaning list of endorsements. Choi, however, often campaigned as "Judge Nathan Choi"—he'd never been a judge—and his license to practice law had been suspended in his home state of Hawaii. Meanwhile, in one court session, he said that he didn't understand Washington law and mostly worked on immigration cases. His website highlighted a number of off-the-wall conspiracy theories. Early on in the campaign it looked like Choi was outpolling Gonzalez. But come election day, Gonzalez got 67 percent of the vote, winning in every county in the state.

And yet two-thirds of judges in this state are appointed, as judges tend to retire midterm, allowing the governor to appoint someone who then must stand for election for the unexpired portion of the term they are filling. Most of those who are appointed subsequently are elected.

Washington's court system has a four-level structure. At the top of the heap is a nine-member state supreme court, which meets in Olympia. It hears direct appeals when actions of state officers are involved; constitutional questions; or issues of broad public interest. It also administers and makes procedural rules for the state court system; lower court rules must not contradict what the high court has decreed in terms of operating process. It also oversees disciplinary activity of the state bar association. It generally meets in the Temple of Justice on the state capitol grounds but has conducted hearings at various locations around the state. Justices are elected to staggered six-year terms, so a third of the court is up for election every two years. As with other staggered elections, this provides some continuity for the institution. The justices themselves elect one of their members as chief justice, and that person serves a four-year term, attempting to lead the court through its responsibilities. Washington is the first state in the country to have a majority of women sitting on the high court. It also ranks dead last in court funding, which has led judges throughout the system to criticize the legislature for its lack of financial support.

The state supreme court has discretionary jurisdiction, meaning they can decide whether to take a case on appeal. A five-member panel of the justices must agree unanimously to hear an appeal. They get about one hundred cases a year. Cases are decided based on what's already happened in the lower courts, along with written and oral arguments. They don't call witnesses and new evidence is generally not introduced. For most cases, they are the last word. "The supreme court isn't always right, but they're final," said one lower court judge.

The court can have major impacts on state policy. For example, eighteen state high courts have invalidated school-funding plans as unconstitutional (including Washington in 1978 and 2007). State courts have played a big role in this policy area, forcing states to revamp programs to provide more equal funding for all school districts. It's important to remember, however, that in every one of these instances, someone in that state filed suit, challenging the government's policies. The courts acted only to decide those suits. While this judicial power forces governments to obey their own laws, it also sometimes puts judges in a position to make policy on subjects about which they may know little.

Courts are sometimes criticized as being "activist," inventing law rather than applying it. This seems to have everything to do with how the critic feels about the decision. Property rights advocates and anti-tax conservatives have supported candidates who promise to do something about those issues, with limited success. Whatever you feel about their decisions, courts do make law, and this is nothing new. When the state supreme court decides a case, at least one of the justices in the majority writes a decision. This is published and then may be referred to by judges in other state courts. This is known as case law, and it's as old as our legal system.

The court of appeals has seventeen judges in three divisions, Seattle, Tacoma, and Spokane, and only hears appeals from lower courts. The need for an intermediary court between the supreme court and the superior courts was proposed as early as 1929, but it took until voters approved a constitutional amendment in 1968 and legislative enabling action in 1969 to create the court.

If you are dissatisfied with a lower court decision, you can appeal, but the court of appeals only hears cases with a value of more than $300. So it's less likely that you get to appeal a traffic ticket all the way to the top.

An appeal basically argues that the trial judge has made a mistake. You can't introduce new evidence. The court of appeals, however, must consider all qualifying appeals. "The court of appeals has authority to reverse (overrule), remand (send back to the lower court), modify, or affirm the decision of the lower court."[5]

"It is the only appeal as a matter of right," said appeals court judge Marlin Appelwick. Nonetheless, 95 percent of cases are not appealed. The appeals court also does not hear tax cases, death penalty cases, or constitutional challenges. They still get four thousand cases a year. "If a case is filed with us, it will get to us within a year," the judge said. The whole appeal could take two years if the case is heard. The judges hear cases in three-judge panels. "A decision of any three judges is a decision of the whole court," Judge Appelwick said. On the court, judges read legal briefs on the case, hear oral arguments from attorneys, and then the panel meets in conference. A judge is randomly assigned to write the opinion of the court. "In a sense, I'm correcting papers," the judge said. "The trial judge—did you get it right? Is it a serious enough mistake that we need a do-over?" That produces a lot of concentrated work, he said. "There's only twenty-two of us, so we weed out a lot," Appelwick said. "I have to have a written opinion out every three days. We pedal pretty fast. We have to pay attention and we have to stay on task."

For all its important work, the appeals court is under the radar for many people. "The focus is on the supreme court," Judge Appelwick said. "We don't mind that a bit."

The twenty-two judges are elected to staggered, six-year terms, so that the court never faces 100 percent turnover in any election. Incumbent judges frequently face no opposition as despite the court's importance, it is often overlooked. The three divisions of the court are Seattle (Division I, ten judges), Tacoma (Division II, seven judges), and Spokane (Division III, five judges). Division I covers Seattle and northwest Washington. Seven judges must be elected from King County, two from Snohomish, and one from Island/San Juan/Skagit/Whatcom. Division II covers southwest Washington and the Olympic Peninsula with similar election requirements such as three judges from Pierce County. Division III covers everything east of the Cascades, with a geographic distribution of judges among the counties.

The state superior court features 147 judges in thirty districts. Superior court judges are elected to four-year terms; if you live in one of the larger counties, you'll see a lot of them on the ballot nearly every year. Large counties have their own superior court districts and every county has a courthouse. A handful of small counties have been joined in multi-county districts. These courts hear cases involving felonies, civil actions over $100,000, juvenile matters, domestic violence and harassment orders, appeals from lower courts, and property, tax, probate and domestic cases. Only 16 percent of cases filed in superior court involve criminal charges; the rest are civil cases, covering everything from adoptions to probate.[6]

Among the courts of limited jurisdiction are 60 district courts and 134 municipal courts, which hear misdemeanors, domestic violence protection orders, traffic and parking cases, civil actions under $100,000, small claims up to $5,000, and preliminary felony hearings. Municipal judges can be elected or appointed, depending on local laws. District court judges are elected to four-year terms. Each county has at least one district court, and many cities have their own municipal courts. District courts cover parts of counties while municipal courts cover cities and generally deal with municipal law.

The lower courts—superior, district, and municipal—are trial courts, the places where lawsuits begin their lives. Court sessions are generally open to the public, though they can be closed for protection purposes (generally only in adoption cases). Civil cases involve disagreements between private citizens, businesses, and governments, including divorce, landlord-tenant disputes, personal injury, business disputes, and professional liability. Decisions are based on the weight of the evidence—whose case is more convincing? Criminal cases, on the other hand, involve violations of the law and are brought by local prosecuting attorneys. Such crimes are generally divided into felonies such as arson, assault, burglary, murder, and rape, and misdemeanors, which can include disorderly conduct, prostitution, and thefts worth less than $250. Defendants can opt to stand trial before a judge or a jury. In either case the prosecution must prove beyond a reasonable doubt that the defendant committed the crime. But most cases don't go to trial—only 2 percent in superior court and 0.25 percent in municipal court. They are largely settled by negotiation outside of court.[7]

PEOPLE IN POLITICS: VERONICA ALICEA-GALVAN

When she was young, people judged Veronica Alicea-Galvan. They did not support her career and educational goals and did not encourage her. Today she judges the actions of others from a seat on the bench of the King County Superior Court. Galvan was born in Bremerton and grew up in Yakima, where her father picked fruit for a living. "I was the first [of her family] to graduate from college," she said. "I knew that a formal education was necessary if I wanted to have greater opportunities for success. I had great mentors and individuals, particularly teachers, who encouraged me constantly. I was very fortunate. I also tuned out a lot of the negative expectations individuals had of me."

She earned a bachelor's degree in sociology with an emphasis in criminology from Western Washington University, then earned her law degree from the University of Washington Law School. "I am—and have always been—an avid reader and naturally curious," Judge Galvan said. "I love to learn and am lucky that it came easily to me. I have always been a planner and think of my time in terms of five- and ten-year goals. This helps me pave the way to gain the necessary education and experience to succeed in accomplishing those goals."

After law school Galvan worked as an assistant city attorney in Seattle, and then an administrative law judge for five years before being appointed to Des Moines Municipal Court, where she created the only Spanish-language traffic court in the state. "The thing about the law is, not only does it have to be fair, it has to appear fair," she said. "Perception is very important."

In 2014 Galvan was appointed to fill a vacancy on the King County Superior Court, getting elected in her own right in 2015 (the remainder of the term) and reelected in 2016 and 2020. The job of a superior court judge is "to decide legal matters, to interpret the law, to apply constitutional principles, and to effectuate justice," she said. "These duties cannot be abrogated to popular sentiment, political pressure, or personal desires." Having been a municipal court judge was good training for her current job, the judge said.

"Contrary to some peoples' perceptions, constitutional principles apply to cases in municipal courts as well as superior courts," Galvan said. "Furthermore, the calendars in municipal courts are often much larger, requiring a judge to develop skills in quickly analyzing, deciding, multitasking, and time management. Indeed, there are certain calendars here in superior court where those skills come in particularly handy, such as my current assignment as assistant chief criminal judge, presiding."

But as with any job, it's a learning process, she said. "Judges do not know every area of the law," Galvan said. "While I understood this in theory, I understand even more in practice as a superior court judicial officer. Civil law in particular is very nuanced and contextualized, and while legal issues may be similar on their face, the facts and context of a particular case may lead to what may seem to be different results. Because of the breadth of issues I am addressing in superior court, I am in constant learning mode, making this work very intellectually stimulating as well as challenging."

She is not opposed to seeking higher office in the court system, she said. "The more I engage in this work, and in particular with the nature of some of the cases I have been assigned, I find myself interested more and more in the 'weeds' of the law," the judge said. "I liken our trial courts to emergency rooms, where we make quick decisions, triage cases, and move them on, while appellate work is more like a specialty where you are allowed to really ruminate about the issues before you."

What happens in court is only part of what really goes in the system, however, Galvan said. "The bench is not where most of our work is concentrated," she said. "Frankly, before we make decisions there is a lot of reading and preparation that is undertaken. I often take work home, and even while on vacation find myself reading pleadings on the plane." Judge Galvan said no one should look at her career and say, "I can't do that." "You can," she said. "You have to commit yourself to that path, it takes dedication and hard work, and for some it may take more time than others. As a law student I had outside pressures that inhibited my ability to truly engage and appreciate my time in law school. I did fine, but I know I was doing what was necessary to get out and begin practicing. Your grades are not correlated to your ability to succeed. No judge or jury will ever ask to see your transcript. You must however have an excellent work ethic to succeed in practice."

The jury system is a longstanding feature of law in the western world. In Washington people are called to jury duty based on Washington driver's license lists. Courts in Washington used to select juries from lists of registered voters which discouraged some people from registering to vote. Lawyers, however, say that using the driver's license rolls brings in more jurors who may not understand the law. The prosecution and the defense interview prospective jurors, a process called voir dire, with an eye to weeding out potential jurors who may be less than impartial. Each side gets three objections, though the presiding judge must decide if the objections are valid. Juries have twelve members in superior court and six in municipal and district courts. Trials have a common pattern: Attorneys make statements, evidence is presented, witnesses are interviewed under oath. After closing arguments, the judge instructs the jury on how the law applies in the case. Jurors retire to a private room and thereupon decide the outcome of the case.

In criminal trials, if the verdict is guilty, the judge sentences the defendant using a determinate sentencing system. This puts boundaries on the judge's discretion but doesn't erase it. The goal is that people who commit similar crimes in similar circumstances receive similar sentences. Factors include the seriousness of the crime and the defendant's criminal history, if any. The judge can deviate from the standards under special circumstances, though such sentences can be appealed. The judge also can order restitution. Washington law generally seeks to protect witnesses and victims, both from threats of violence as well as employment impacts of a trial.

Washington law also provides for alternative dispute resolution which doesn't involve a trial. This can include mediation (a neutral third party tries to help the two sides work out a solution) and arbitration (the third party weighs the competing claims and makes a decision). Both parties must agree to submit to either of these alternatives. Arbitration can be either binding or non-binding by prior agreement.

PEOPLE IN POLITICS: THE NOT-SO-GOOD, THE BAD, AND THE UGLY

While Washington politics overall has been pretty clean for decades, there were darker periods in the past. Scandals great and small pop up across the state's history. Some seem nearly comic in history's rear-view mirror; others should make you growl and grit your teeth while several are just tragic. For example, real estate developer Corliss P. Stone was elected mayor of Seattle in 1872. That only lasted a year. In 1873 he absconded to San Francisco with $15,000 of his business partner's money and somebody else's wife. He was replaced as mayor that year, but still has three streets named after him in one of the neighborhoods he helped create—Stone Way North, Stone Avenue North, and Corliss Avenue North, all in Wallingford.

Some scandals damaged multiple people's lives. Albert Canwell, sometime photographer, aspiring writer, and long-time hunter of communists, managed to get elected to the state house of representatives for one term, 1946–48. With the Cold War heating up, Canwell managed to convene the Legislative Joint Fact-Finding Committee on Un-American Activities in Washington State, often called the Canwell Committee. Canwell's panel hauled in busloads of suspected communists, particularly targeting labor unions and the University of Washington. The committee ignored actual evidence and sometimes prevented people from speaking in their own defense. Three UW professors were fired. Canwell was easily defeated in the next election but continued his professional red-baiting for most of the rest of his long life. He targeted an eastern Washington attorney, John Goldmark, who successfully sued Canwell for libel in 1963. Sadly, a deranged ultra-conservative read about Goldmark from Canwell's perspective and ended up killing Goldmark's son Charles and his family in 1985.

Some people can't resist the lure of money. Troy Kelley was elected to the state's most important watchdog post, state auditor. There was just one problem: he'd been robbing his clients for years—as much as $3 million. A three-term legislator, an attorney, and a lieutenant colonel in the Army National Guard, Kelley appeared to have all the right stuff when he won election as auditor in 2012. However, in 2015 U.S. attorneys indicted him on multiple counts of possession of stolen property, making false declarations in a court proceeding, and tax fraud. He was sentenced to a year in jail and restitution.

Charles O. "Chuck" Carroll was, for a time, "the most powerful man in Seattle and King County."[8] He had a say—and a hand—in a lot of what went on in the 1950s and 1960s and some of what went on was outside of the law. An all-American football player at the University of Washington, Carroll served as King County prosecutor for twenty-four years. Under Carroll gambling and prostitution were tolerated under the excuse that doing so was keeping bigger, badder organized crime at bay. That led to police payoffs and an uneven application of the law. It's worth noting that one of the scandals involved pinball, on which people used to gamble, and which was long regarded as a thoroughfare to moral decay for America's youth. Carroll wasn't a pinball wizard, but he was apparently on pretty good terms with the guy who was—at least until Ben Cichy drowned near his home on Lake Washington. Meanwhile, the prosecutor had so much dirt on everybody that at the height of his power, he could veto any political appointment, including to the courts. By the late 1960s this house of cards and pinball began to tilt as media investigations mounted and federal prosecutors began to get involved. Carroll was never formally charged with anything, but he lost his last bid for reelection in the 1972 Republican primary.

Not to be left out, Pierce County saw fourteen people convicted of racketeering-related crimes in 1978, including the county sheriff, for assisting in a protection racket that saw payoffs made and businesses firebombed.

Washington legislators have had their troubles too. State Sen. August Mardesich, a Snohomish County Democrat, was acquitted by a federal jury on charges that he had extorted $10,000 from a couple of garbage haulers, on the very day the state senate passed bills the firms wanted. Mardesich, the senate majority leader, admitted to taking the money but said it wasn't related to the legislation. Voters didn't believe him, and he lost his next election.

The paths of two rising stars in the Democratic Party were derailed in 1980, when they got caught up in a federal sting operation that became known as GamScam. State Rep. John Bagnariol (D-Renton), Speaker of the House, was considered a front-runner for governor, while State Sen. Gordon Walgren (D-Kitsap) was expected to be the next attorney general. But when FBI agents posing as representatives of the gambling industry alleged that the pair asked for bribes in return for pro-gambling legislation, their careers took a detour. The pair and a lobbyist eventually all served two years in prison.

Sometimes it's sex that does an official in. Brock Adams was a pillar of Washington politics for much of the second half of the twentieth century. He served as a member of the U.S. House of Representatives, the U.S. Senate, and transportation secretary in the Carter administration. But beginning in 1987, allegations began to surface that Adams was given to drugging and assaulting women. Although he denied the allegations, he withdrew from his 1992 reelection campaign and largely retired from political life. He died of Parkinson's complications in 2004.

Some things once regarded as scandals now are kind of sad. For so much of our history, different sexual orientations were not widely accepted and in many instances were effectively criminalized. In the early 1980s, a state legislator, a local businessman, and a lobbyist were sharing an intimate moment in a men's room in Olympia. One of the trio propositioned the next man who came in who happened to be an undercover police officer. Unfortunately, when gay people couldn't be out, that kind of thing happened. The legislator resigned soon after.

Another somewhat sad case involved former Spokane mayor Jim West. West was an ex-cop who became a state legislator; he was one of the people who I worked for. One day West came into our office; greetings were exchanged in the normal way. And then, out of the blue, Representative West announced, "I'm not gay. A lot of people think I'm gay, but I'm not." We nodded and said nothing until after he left, at which point we looked at each other and jointly concluded, "He's gay." Not that we much cared.

West, a Republican, was elected to the house twice, then elected to the state senate in 1986 where he eventually became majority leader. He was noted for sponsoring anti-gay legislation. In 2003 he became Spokane's mayor. A newspaper investigation turned up allegations of misusing his office. These were not proven and no charges were filed. In 2005 West was outed, and 65 percent of Spokane voters voted to recall him. His apparent hypocrisy was probably more concerning to voters than the fact that he was gay; he was a fairly effective mayor. Some said he had used the mayor's office to find partners, although the FBI later concluded no wrongdoing had been done. He died of cancer a year later. It's hard not to imagine that in a more open and forgiving society, Jim West just would have been gay and everything might have turned out differently.

On the other hand, former legislator and Seattle mayor Ed Murray was openly gay, and nobody seemed to care much about that. But in 2017, amid his term as mayor of the state's largest city, allegations of improper sexual activity began to surface. Murray denied them all but resigned as mayor in September 2017. King County judge Gary Little hanged himself in his office in 1988 after he was accused of abusing juvenile offenders for two decades. This led to amending the state constitution to unveil the judicial discipline process to the public. Little had been admonished for his behavior some years before.

One of the greatest scandals in Washington political history was the internment of fourteen thousand Japanese Americans during World War II. Although this was a federal policy, this wasn't a time when the state tried to stand up to the federal government. As in our time, racism reared its ugly head; near the end of the war, one Kent man posted a sign in his business window declaring: "We don't want no Japs back here, ever." The internment tore the heart out of communities up and down the coast; Japanese Americans were generally forced to sell their homes and businesses at fire-sale prices. It took until 1988 for the U.S. government to formally apologize for this terrible act. When I was growing up, a Japanese American friend of mine said that her father, a decorated veteran of World War II, had told her, "Never trust a white guy." As I learned about what happened, I can't say that I blamed him.

So Washington's political history isn't spotless, and some of the low points are pretty low. While acknowledging the bad things that have happened, we might first vow to prevent their reoccurrence and secondly remember that there are high points too.

Another key piece of the legal system, particularly with regard to criminal law, are the prosecuting attorneys, elected officials in all thirty-nine counties. Prosecutors must be attorneys. County prosecutors are the state's advocate in all prosecutions occurring within that county, which may include child support cases. They represent the county in civil cases, as well as providing legal advice to county officials. They may also administer various funds, including victim compensation funds.

King County prosecutor Dan Satterberg was among a group of county prosecutors who are trying to keep more people out of jail. "Mass incarceration and racial disproportionality are undeniable mathematical facts," Satterberg said. "They undermine the credibility of the legal system and threaten the legitimacy of our authority in the communities most impacted by crime. These are my motivations to reform all aspects of the criminal justice system to make it smaller and more fair."

King County Superior Court judge Veronica Alicea-Galvan agreed. "You can't throw people away, and our justice system is starting to recognize that," she said.

Although Washington ranks forty-second in incarcerations, the prisons are still over capacity, "with no plans to build new ones," Satterberg said. "The best strategy to avoid that would be to build a comprehensive reentry support system to improve the chances of people who come out of prison. Today, one in three who are released will be back in prison in just three years, half by five years out."

Satterberg said one of the key elements is drug policy. "Creating a sensible policy toward drug addiction is my key area of focus and has been for the past ten years," he said. "I am on the boards of several national organizations that bring together progressive prosecutors to explore new alternatives to the courtroom and the prison cell. There are some newly elected prosecutors in Washington, especially on the I-5 corridor, who are interested in replicating our LEAD [Law Enforcement Assisted Diversion] program and in pursuing various reforms. I am the seasoned veteran of this group, but not the only or last one to work toward reform."

The practice of law is regulated at the state level; here that's done by the Washington State Bar Association. It's an "integrated" bar, which means the association licenses attorneys and you have to be a member to practice law (hence the phrase "admitted to the bar," not quite the same as being let into a tavern; if you want to practice law in another state, you have to pass the bar exam there). The profession basically regulates itself but must answer to the state supreme court. The bar association administers the bar exam, adopts and enforces rules of conduct, investigates complaints, and levies penalties for violations. Attorneys can be disbarred but can appeal. In recent times, the bar association's board of directors has been embroiled in controversy, with allegations of sexual harassment and a hostile work environment.[9] Sounds like they're going to need a lawyer.

CHAPTER TWELVE

Turning Policy into Practice

STATE AGENCIES AND WHAT THEY DO

Washington State employs about 65,000 people, excluding higher education, which adds more than 50,000 to the total. Around 63,000 people work for the executive branch; fewer than 1,000 work for the legislature and fewer than 500 for the court system. The executive branch includes 193 different state agencies, from the State Board of Accountancy to the Washington Wine Commission, and from the 2 people who work for the State Commission on Asian Pacific American Affairs to the 16,870 who work for the Department of Social and Health Services. The University of Washington alone employs 25,000 people, and the Community and Technical College system employs another 15,000.

Many of these agencies are small and narrowly focused. There are eight boards aimed at establishing licensing requirements, from accountants and architects to pharmacists and psychologists. Four are focused on issues involving race and ethnic groups within the state, while fourteen are aimed at helping key agricultural sectors within the state. For example, the aforementioned Wine Commission represents the more than one thousand wineries (and 350 grape growers) in the state. Self-funded but established by the legislature in 1987, its goal is to help all those folks sell more wine, particularly out of state.

Government agencies operate in a form of organization known as bureaucracy, yet another term that has unfortunately taken on the feel and taste of a dirty word. In fact it's the way most things are organized in the postmodern world, done so for some good reasons. Bureaucracy involves a defined chain of command, organized in a hierarchy of control, with specified tasks and roles for employees and adherence to established rules. This was done because giving people in large organizations leeway to decide how to respond to a given situation can result in uneven results, and at worst, favoritism. As always, there are trade-offs. Ideally we'd probably like to see people in government exercise reasonable judgment in dealing with any situation. On the other hand, we probably don't want to see them helping some folks while playing hardball with others. In a perfect world bureaucracy makes things predictable and treats everyone the same. That doesn't mean state agency workers can't apply judgment, but it does provide them with guidelines and boundaries. As with anything, if you want something from somebody in government, treat them nicely. That usually helps a lot.

Some people have argued that privatizing state agencies (turning their duties over to a privately owned, for-profit business) would make them more efficient. Others argue that it tends to mean less service and more poorly paid public officials, which tends to invite graft and corruption. Government doesn't work as well in places where public officials are poorly paid. In any event, research shows that privatizing government functions does not in fact save money.[1]

The largest agencies include the Washington State Department of Social and Health Services, or DSHS, as it's usually known, along with the Department of Corrections; the Department of Transportation; Labor & Industries; Children, Youth & Families; and the State Patrol. The agencies overlap a little bit—health care can fall under DSHS, the Department of Health, and the insurance commissioner's office. Support for children can come under DSHS and Children, Youth & Families. And both Transportation and the State Patrol have a role to play in highway safety.

DSHS is the biggest state agency (after the University of Washington), with more than sixteen thousand employees working with one of the biggest slices of the state budget. The agency oversees food, cash and medical assistance; housing assistance; child support; youth services; adult care; mental health and addiction services; and support for the disabled. Put another way, DSHS works on aging and long-term support; behavioral health; aid to children; developmental disabilities; economic assistance;

and rehabilitation. Its secretary is appointed by the governor, subject to confirmation by the state senate. Its budget for 2019–21 was $13.8 billion.

The fact that so many Washington residents qualify for public assistance tends to provoke a couple of reactions. Conservatives tend to ask why people don't get jobs and argue that giving people assistance discourages them from working. And there's some truth to that. But it's also true that the great majority of people getting public assistance would have a hard time getting work—the old, the ill, the disabled, and children. The other question we might ask is what kind of economy Washington has if that many people are that poor—once upon a time that wasn't true. Some 13.5 percent of Americans—forty-three million people—live in poverty. The United States ranks seventeenth out of the world's nineteen biggest economies for poverty. With 11 percent of our citizens living in poverty, Washington ranks thirty-seventh among U.S. states. The federal poverty level is $25,750 for a family of four, so we're not talking about very much money. In the Seattle area it would be difficult for one person to live on that, let alone a family.

Meanwhile, the myth of the welfare mama is largely not true. This myth painted a picture of a woman who kept producing babies so as to get more public assistance. This has probably happened somewhere. The only longitudinal studies done of welfare recipients—following people over many years to see how they behaved—found that almost nobody got on welfare and stayed there for life. If people got work, they got off welfare. If they lost their jobs, they got back on.

Nonetheless, in 1996 Congress and President Bill Clinton agreed on the Welfare Reform Act, which put limits on how long someone can receive welfare. Aid to Families with Dependent Children (AFDC) was replaced with Temporary Assistance for Needy Families (TANF). TANF requires recipients to get training and look for work. Unlike AFDC, however, recipients can't just enroll in college and find a direction; they are required to enroll in a short-term training program that ends in a job. Any job. No matter what it pays. Be that as it may, the Brookings Institution reported in 2006 that caseloads were the lowest since 1969.[2] Of course, this was just before the Great Recession, which took a hammer to the economy for several years.

But the declining number of caseloads may simply mean that fewer people are seeking assistance, not that it's putting people back to work. Just because they're not receiving welfare doesn't mean they're working. Many families in some parts of the country report incomes of $2 per person per day, affecting three million children. Apparently, in the age of TANF, many people simply go without cash for months at a time.[3]

Washington has less poverty than other parts of the country, but even in the booming Seattle-Bellevue-Tacoma area, it's 9.6 percent. Historically, that's not very good, and is probably a contributing factor to the estimated 12,500 homeless in King County. Despite an often-booming economy, average wages haven't changed much in forty years in the United States, leaving most working people actually poorer than they (or their ancestors) were in the 1970s.[4] The numbers are bigger, but if you factor in inflation, purchasing power has not changed.

Despite the relatively high level of poverty, only 0.8 percent of Washington residents get TANF, an average of 57,432 per month in 2018, including 15,374 adults and 42,058 children. Around 16 percent get food assistance from SNAP (Supplemental Nutrition Assistance Program), the program once known as food stamps. Recipients tends to be clustered around the state's most populous areas—central Puget Sound, Spokane, and Vancouver. The ABD program—aged, blind, and disabled—helps about 24,000 people a month.

The Department of Corrections employs 8,500 people. With a $1 billion budget, it operates the state's prisons and supervises parolees. Washington has twelve state prisons, including two for women, housing around 19,000 inmates and 20,000 people under "active community supervision" by the department.

Prisons exist to improve public safety by getting offenders off the street. U.S. prisons have also generally aimed to rehabilitate offenders with mixed results. Washington's department has done a number of things to address this, as numerous studies have shown that people are less likely to reoffend if they learn how to make a living doing something other than crime.

"The Department of Corrections has, in recent years, invested heavily in work that will yield beneficial results for those who are reentering our communities," said Jeremy Barclay, engagement and outreach director for the department.

"There has been a focus on providing increased academic and vocational education opportunities, and more employment training and skills leading up to release," including job training and mock interviews. The department also works with the state departments of Veterans Affairs, Social and Health Services, and Employment Security and the State Board of Community and Technical Colleges "to create more interagency processes and tangible results."

One ongoing impact on the state prison system has been the three-strikes-and-you're-out-law, passed by initiative in 1993. Three-strikes laws basically say that if you commit three felonies, you will go to prison for life. As noted previously, this measure and others like it were pushed across the country by the private prison industry. In many states the influx of prisoners after the adoption of three-strikes laws pushed them to contract with private prison firms to develop new facilities. Washington did not go that direction, but it has caused 288 more people to become lifers in Washington's system (40 percent of them Black versus 4 percent of the state's population).

Three-strikes laws have a number of strikes against them: they're not a deterrent to crime; they can send someone to jail for life who has turned their life around and makes one bad mistake; and they're expensive.[5] Crime rates, for example, were already falling well before three-strikes laws took effect. New York did not adopt the three-strikes law, and its crime rate fell more than California's, which did adopt.[6]

In 2019 the Washington legislature altered the state's law, removing second-degree burglary from the list of offenses that reach the three-strikes threshold. Second-degree burglary does not involve weapons, assault, or robbing a financial institution such as a bank. The legislature also overwhelmingly passed a bill that makes it easier for ex-convicts to regain their civil rights, such as voting, and expands the list of crimes that can be vacated from one's record. The intent was to make it easier for someone who's done their time to rejoin society in a productive way.

The Washington State Department of Transportation (WSDOT) covers a lot of ground, from managing 18,600 lane-miles of roads and 3,300 bridges and other structures, to managing the state ferry system and those handy WSDOT online cameras that tell you how the freeways and mountain passes are doing. It has 6,700 employees and a $9 billion budget. The department also assists thirty-one public transportation systems in the state, which account for 220 million passenger trips a year. It owns three trains that operate in the Amtrak Cascades fleet and manages the Palouse River and Coulee City Rail system, which carries freight in five eastern Washington counties.

The Aviation Division runs sixteen state airports. Most of these are in out-of-the-way locations, from Copalis Beach on the Olympic Peninsula (don't land on the light-colored sand) to Sullivan Lake in the far northeast corner of the state. Most are better described as runways than as airports, and the runways themselves are likely to be either turf or gravel. The Woodland State Airport, however, has grown into a community airport, with a paved, two-thousand-foot lighted runway and amenities within walking distance. Then again, landing is not advised when the level of the nearby Lewis River is higher than the runway.

The department also runs Travel Washington, which has resurrected several intercity bus lines around the state. Greyhound used to run buses all over, but in 2004 they opted to cut back to their most profitable routes. The state interceded in 2007 and was able to leverage money from Greyhound and the Federal Transit Administration to eventually create four new lines: the Apple Line, which runs from Ellensburg to Omak with several stops along the way; the Dungeness Line, from Port Angeles to Sea-Tac Airport; the Gold Line, from Spokane International Airport to Kettle Falls; and the Grape Line, from Tri-Cities Airport to the Walla Walla Airport. All the lines connect with other modes of transportation, including Greyhound—hence their incentive to put up some funds. The bus lines are operated by private firms and contracts are awarded based on competitive bids.

"The Travel Washington ICB Program began as Greyhound pulled out of rural routes nationwide, leaving many rural communities without service," said Greg Wright, community liaison for the program. "And as states are required to spend 15 percent of their 5311 funding [a federal program that supports rural transportation options] on intercity bus services, it made sense to look at picking up these abandoned routes in an effort to meet the transportation needs of individuals needing to get to more urbanized areas for services and connecting with the national intercity bus network." The lines collectively carry thirty-one thousand passengers a year, including sixteen thousand on the Dungeness Line. Travel Washington conducted a study and had a series of hearings in 2018, with a goal of changing the service as seems warranted in the future.

WSDOT is governed by the secretary of transportation, who is appointed by the governor, subject to senate confirmation. That doesn't always happen. In 2016 majority senate Republicans rejected the confirmation of Lynn Peterson, who had been interim secretary for three years. She appeared to be a scapegoat for all that's wrong with Washington traffic, as I-405 tolls slowed down some traffic and Peterson wasn't anti-transit enough for some. Some Republicans who earlier praised her voted to oust her. She was replaced by the deputy secretary, Roger Millar. The other piece of transportation governance is the Transportation Commission, a seven-member board appointed to six-year terms by the governor. They establish toll rates on bridges and highways; produce a long-range transportation plan; and "provide an open public forum for transportation policy development."[7]

The Department of Transportation also runs the largest ferry system in the country, which moves 24.2 million passengers and 10 million vehicles a year. It has twenty terminals and ten routes, linking Pierce, King, Snohomish, Kitsap, Skagit, Island, San Juan, and Jefferson Counties, and reaching from Tacoma to Vancouver Island in British Columbia. Like everything involving transportation, the Washington State Ferries are not without controversy: people who use them, rely on them but don't like to wait in lines; people who don't use them claim the system costs too much money. But with Puget Sound to cross and multiple islands to be reached, it's probably necessary.

Ferries and boat transportation were essential in the early development of western Washington, including the Mosquito fleet—dozens of privately owned ships that carried freight and folks around Puget Sound. The beautifully restored *Virginia V*, anchored at the Museum of History and Industry on Lake Union in Seattle, is the last of the fleet still afloat. The fleet reached its peak of activity between World War I and World War II. After the war more people began to drive; bridges were being built; and the call was for ferries. But the last two Puget Sound ferry firms went out of business in the early 1950s, in part because of labor troubles, and the state bought the assets of the last one, the Black Ball line, in 1951 for $5 million. (Black Ball still runs a ferry service from Port Angeles to

Victoria, British Columbia.) From there the system grew; ferry employees became state employees in 1957; and the state steadily added boats and routes. Plans for bridges across Puget Sound sank as engineers figured out it couldn't be done.

The ferry system's operating budget is around $220 million a year, which covers 1,800 employees and the operation of twenty-two ferries. It was twenty-three until the legislature didn't provide funding for a second relief vessel (necessary because despite the department's best efforts, ferries do break down). Add to this the capital budget, which varies greatly depending on whether they're buying new boats or overhauling old ones. Recent capital budgets have reached $210 million, as the system needed to rebuild the Colman Dock in Seattle (some of the pilings have been in the water since the 1930s, and they don't last forever) and replace the 1950s-era Mukilteo terminal.

The ferry system tries to get sixty years of service from a boat. Given the ups and downs of state finances, the system can go a while before the legislature floats enough money to buy a new boat. Between 2000 and 2010 no new boats were built; since 2010, seven have been added and placed in service, with one more on the way. A new ferry can cost $160 million. The average age of the fleet is thirty years, from the sixty-year-old *Tillicum* to the one-year-old *Suquamish*.

The system doesn't quite pay for itself, but it does cover 75 percent of its costs from ferry fares. Adjusted for inflation, fares are about the same as they were in 1951.[8] Washington State Ferries have adopted a reservation system, which has done a lot to cut back on the endless lines at several ferry terminals. Reservations were first added to the Port Townsend–Coupeville (Whidbey Island) run in 2012 and expanded to Anacortes–San Juan Islands in 2015. "We consider the reservation system a success, with record numbers of people using it year after year," said system spokesman Ian Sterling.

The Washington State Patrol has 2,300 employees, including about 1,100 commissioned officers. In 2016 they took nearly six hundred thousand 911 calls, receiving more than three thousand contacts a day. They do a lot more than write tickets on the freeway, however.

The state patrol includes the State Fire Marshal's Office, which provides training, certification, licensing, and inspection services across the state.

This includes training for various levels of firefighter certification, such as dealing with hazardous materials, and creating standardized educational materials for training. Overall, the State Fire Marshal and Fire Protection Bureau try to ensure that fire safety is more than a slogan, via development of fire codes, emergency mobilization, and regional fire protection services. The Fire Training Academy, near North Bend, provides firefighters with live fire-training opportunities. The Prevention Division inspects licensed care facilities, reviews school plans, and certifies fire sprinkler systems around the state. It also regulates the fireworks industry.

The patrol inspects commercial vehicles and school buses for safety. A school bus that's been in a collision can't go back into service until it's been cleared by the patrol's inspectors. Enforcing size, weight, and load regulations helps protect the state's roads and bridges (heavy trucks take a heavy toll on state highways), done through regular audits and inspections.

The state patrol is in charge of keeping the governor and her or his family safe wherever they are (home, business, and travel), as well as the lieutenant governor if he or she is filling in. They also patrol the Capitol Campus in Olympia. Various state patrol crime labs assist law enforcement agencies with forensic investigations, including the Toxicology Lab, called upon when alcohol or drugs may be involved in a fatality. The Criminal Investigations service collects records, such as criminal histories; does background checks; investigates auto thefts; and maintains a fingerprint database. The Homeland Security Division works on counterterrorism, crime prevention, and emergency management. The patrol provides security to the state ferry system and has the largest K-9 team in the state. Other divisions offer technical services to other law enforcement agencies; maintain 911 services; initiate emergency services when and where they're required; and maintain statewide communications networks. And they look for missing persons and try to get them home.

In 1911 Washington became one of the first states to enact an industrial insurance program. More than a century later the 2,800 employees of the Department of Labor & Industries are "dedicated to the safety, health and security of Washington's 2.5 million workers."[9] As of 2018 that number had risen to 3 million workers, plus 179,000 employers. L&I's programs include maintaining health and safety standards, including workplace inspections. They administer the state's workers' compensation program, which assists people who are injured on the job with medical insurance and limited wage-replacement. They attempt to ensure that workers get paid what they've earned (wage- and tip-theft by employers is an endemic problem in several fields). L&I officials collected $5.5 million in unpaid wages in 2018. They enforce child labor and building safety standards. That year they also inspected 251,000 electrical wiring jobs, nearly 19,000 boilers and pressure vessels, 8,700 elevators and escalators, and registered 5,500 new apprentices statewide.

The Department of Ecology is assigned to preserve the state's environment, which makes it a paragon to some folks and a pariah to others. Its mission and vision statements sum up the perceived dichotomy in its role. On the one hand, the department says of its vision: "Our innovative partnerships sustain healthy land, air, and water in harmony with a strong economy." On the other hand, its mission is: "Protect, preserve, and enhance the environment for current and future generations."[10] Some folks argue that preserving the long-term viability of the environment is in fact good economics; others see the short-term costs of complying with regulations.

The department's portfolio includes air and water quality; shorelines; and waste, toxics, and spills. The agency says 66 percent of its budget is "pass-through," money that goes to local governments to pay for local environmental projects such as water pollution control; hazardous waste cleanup; stormwater treatment; watershed health; and managing solid waste and recycling. Its work includes assessment, monitoring, research, and when needed, getting their hands dirty cleaning things up.

For example, Puget Sound has five major oil refineries, and a serious oil spill could cost the state $10 billion and 165,000 jobs.[11] Testing shows that oil spilled in Puget Sound would pretty much just stay there, damaging the local ecosystem for a long time to come. Consequently the department spends much of its effort on preventing spills and maintains twenty-four-hour response teams in six locations around the state.

The state's Department of Agriculture aims to support Washington's $11 billion agricultural sector. It does this by conducting quality inspections, testing and produce grading; providing workshops and technical assistance for regulatory compliance; and trying to "raise the profile" of Washington's more than three hundred different agricultural commodities. Its $151 million annual budget includes around 750 employees.

In case you're wondering, apples are the state's top crop at $2.4 billion, followed by $1.2 billion worth of milk and dairy products. Washington ranks first in the country for production of apples, hops, spearmint oil, pea seed, concord grapes, sweet cherries, pears, raspberries, blueberries, and aquaculture, and it's second or third in the country in an additional twelve commodities, from asparagus to potatoes. Washington is the second leading wine producing state in the country after California. Fish and seafood top the state's agricultural exports at $1.2 billion, followed by $756 million worth of frozen french fries. Washington has almost thirty-six thousand farms, 95 percent of which are family owned. There are at least one hundred farms in every county in the state.

By way of marketing, the legislature and the department have established twenty-one different commodity commissions, covering everything from alfalfa seed to wine. Thirteen were established by the department director under authority from the legislature, and she or he sits on the boards of all of them. They are all funded by the industries themselves, and chiefly engage in product marketing and research. Agriculture department officials, meanwhile, attempt to link up Washington farmers with international buyers through a variety of programs.

The Department of Fish and Wildlife has one of those curious jobs: keeping more animals alive so that people can kill more of them. Of course that's an oversimplification, and not everyone who values fish and wildlife necessarily wants to harvest them. As the department puts it on its webpage, they are "dedicated to preserving, protecting, and perpetuating the state's fish, wildlife, and ecosystems while providing sustainable fish and wildlife recreational and commercial opportunities."[12] The department tries to protect wildlife habitats and preserve endangered species; enforces fishing and shellfish regulations, including comanaging fish stocks along with tribal nations; regulates hunting and educates hunters; and issues licenses and permits. The agency is governed by a nine-member commission appointed by the governor. They set policy for the department and also hire and fire the agency's director, who is in charge of the day-to-day operations of the department. Its $437 million budget includes around 1,500 employees.

The department tracks hunting numbers and wildlife populations, with an eye to striking a balance between killing too many creatures and letting a population get out of hand. Absent predators to keep their numbers in check, creatures such as deer can go from pretty to pestilent. Fish and Wildlife also keeps track of and attempts to save endangered species, from the American white pelican to the Yuma skipper, a small orange moth found in the western United States. They've had some success. Fishers, a member of the weasel family, have been successfully reintroduced after having been trapped out by 1900. Sea otters were also successfully reintroduced in 1969–70, with positive impacts on the marine environment. Otters keep anemones in check, which means they don't overgraze the kelp beds, a good thing for everything else in the sea.

Another relatively small but important agency is Washington State Parks. It is governed by a seven-member commission, appointed by the governor to staggered terms. They hire an agency director, who oversees the day-to-day operation of the system. Washington has 124 state parks ranging from the twelve thousand acres of Mt. Spokane State Park to less than one acre for the Ranald MacDonald's Grave State Park Heritage Site, which is near Curlew State Park in far northeastern Washington, near the town of Republic. In case you're wondering, this is not the grave of the red-haired burger king but the final resting place of a pioneer in the opening of relations between Washington State and Japan.

Parks have both economic and environmental benefits. A 2015 study done for the commission showed that state parks generated $64 million in tax revenues for the state (all the things that people bought because they were going to a state park). That also included $1.5 billion in consumer spending and fourteen thousand jobs.[13] It's especially important to rural communities, because that's so often where the parks are.[14] The parks draw thirty-eight million people per year.

The parks' budget was one of the big losers during the Great Recession, when the legislature had to cut billions in spending. Its budget in 2017–19 was only $166 million, nearly 70 percent of which came from user fees, including $13 million in donations from people renewing their driver's licenses. Out of a state budget of nearly $100 billion, we spend next to nothing on state parks. You could close every park in the state and the budget wouldn't notice. But people would. The park system did a little better for 2019–21, with a budget of $181 million, including more money for equipment, resource protection, orca recovery, and other ongoing costs. They also got $104 million for capital expenses, including two new state parks, trail work, and fish barrier removal. The department has 600 year-round employees and another 300 to 350 in the summer.

Parks became a thing when people began to notice that open space was vanishing. Yellowstone was the first national park set-aside in 1872. Mt. Rainier became the fourth national park in 1899. The legislature created the first parks board in 1913 but provided no funding or directions as to what it was supposed to do. Two properties were donated in 1915, including what is now Larrabee State Park in Whatcom County. The legislature finally got around to providing some authorization and guidance in 1921, and soon the park system was on its way. Except for the tenure of Republican governor Roland Hartley (1925–33), who vetoed every parks bill that came his way. Hartley battled against "waste and extravagance," which in his mind covered a lot of ground. The parks were all closed and fell into disrepair. His successor, Clarence Martin, got the parks reopened when he took office.

The first donation to the park system was the John R. Jackson House. This was the homestead of Mr. Jackson near Chehalis. He was one of the first Euro-Americans to settle north of the Columbia River and later served as sheriff, assessor, tax collector, territorial representative, and justice of the peace. Residents gathered at Jackson's house in 1852 to call for a new territory separate from Oregon. Jackson's home remains a state park, and the house was restored by the department in 2017.

The Department of Children, Youth & Families was created by the legislature in 2017, and although its services are not new, it is the newest state agency. It was created following a report from a special commission created to find a more effective way to provide services to children. And anytime you split something off into its own agency, you're saying "this is a priority," in this case "the well-being of children. Our vision is to ensure that Washington State's children and youth grow up safe and healthy—thriving physically, emotionally, and academically, nurtured by family and community."[15] The department's portfolio includes child care, early learning, foster care and adoption, child welfare and support, juvenile services, and support for various service providers.

PEOPLE IN POLITICS: ROSS HUNTER

Like a number of people, Ross Hunter quickly ran out of things to do once he retired. "After I had retired from Microsoft, it was pretty clear to me that I needed something to do," he said. "After about six weeks, my wife said, 'You can be retired but you can't be in the house during lunch time.'"

Hunter began doing volunteer work and ended up working on a school levy campaign. That led him to conclude that the school funding system, which relied heavily on local property tax levies, "was insane. In addition to being inadequate, it was poorly designed." That led him to run for the legislature, whereupon he became the first Democrat elected from the Forty-Eighth District. "I spent most of my time in the legislature trying to make the funding system work better," he said. He rose to become chair of the House Appropriations Committee but stepped aside in 2015 to take over the state Department of Early Learning.

What Hunter learned there was that problems of at-risk youth were not being addressed in a comprehensive way, which eventually led to a seat on a special panel ("blue ribbon," in the language of government) assigned to make improvements. The end result was the Department of Children, Youth & Families, combining the Department of Early Learning and pieces of the Department of Social and Health Services.

"I shared the broad interests of that commission," Hunter said. "I had a couple of core beliefs. One was that DSHS was too big to manage effectively." DSHS's size made it hard to both plan and manage at the same time. The goal became "getting something that it's small enough that you can manage but big enough that you can bring interests into one place."

Hunter said this was important because the myriad programs aimed at troubled youth were not seeing the whole picture. "Eighty percent of the kids have a CPS finding [Child Protective Services, meaning a child who has been in a dangerous situation at home]," he said. "Seventy percent have been in foster care. When you look at the Venn diagram of the population, they are the same children. We have to get ahead of this. We can't have forty different systems serving these kids."

Hunter said his previous work helped prepare him to be secretary of a cabinet-level state agency. "There's different things you bring from those experiences," he said. Working at Microsoft, Hunter said, gave him "the perspective that you can change the world." But it also made him realistic.

"When you look at a particular action, you ask, 'Is that going to move the needle? Is that going to work? My time at Microsoft gave me the insistence that we actually plan our activities to achieve our goals." Microsoft gave him that confidence, he said.

"The legislature taught me the value of building coalitions," Hunter said, "about making sure that you are not just paying lip service to bringing people along, but that you really listen to constituencies, understanding what they need, making sure that it [a policy] is going to last."

Being in charge of the newest state agency puts him in a position of helping to drive "policy for at-risk children in the state, which I'm excited to do. My interest is in pursuing outcomes for children." And they've had some early successes. "My early realization was that we have too many kids in foster care," Hunter said, so from 2018 to 2019 foster care was reduced by 7.5 percent. They have reduced the number of children placed out of state by more than 60 percent. "We can run a good system, but don't serve more kids than you need to serve," Hunter said. "You can make the system work better."

One agency is assigned to keep all of this functioning, the Department of Enterprise Services. Welded together by the legislature in 2011, the department combines the functions of a number of existing programs, all aimed at making state and local government work a little bit better. For example, the agency's 1,100 employees and $185 million budget help provide printing, fleet services, facilities and leasing, accounting and human resources, risk management, contracting, and managing the Capitol campus in Olympia. "We bring together the policy, planning and oversight of such services and are constantly working to improve their value and effectiveness and reduce the overall cost of government operations," according to the department's webpage. "Services provided by Enterprise Services allow state agencies and municipal governments to focus on their core missions."[16] By putting all these services in one basket, the agency tries to realize economies of scale to save the state and its taxpayers some money. Economies of scale are long run decreases in the cost of production brought about by gains from specialization, automation, and leverage. So, for example, one state agency in charge of buying or leasing vehicles will buy or lease a lot more at once, allowing the agency to bargain for a better price. By charging various agencies in government for its services, the department is essentially self-funded, which encourages more efficiency on both sides of the equation. The department will be as efficient as possible while its client governments and agencies won't buy more service than they need.

CHAPTER THIRTEEN

Where It Comes from and Where It Goes

THE BUDGET AND TAXES

Whatever they do, governments can't just decide to spend money. Spending money and raising the taxes to pay for it requires approval of legislatures—Congress at the federal level and state legislatures at the state level. The same is true for cities and counties via councils or commissions. At the state level the money to pay for all the things that state agencies do cannot be spent without authorization from the state legislature. This takes the form of the budget, a series of bills passed by the legislature that allow state agencies to expend funds. The budget is hammered out by legislators and signed by the governor. It authorizes the spending of state money on everything from promoting Washington's agricultural produce to funding for the Workforce Training and Education Coordinating Board (whose title more or less describes what they do).

Washington uses a biennial budget, meaning a two-year spending plan that is enacted in odd-numbered years. This now includes a plan for years three and four (the next biennium). In even-numbered years the legislature passes a supplemental budget, a much smaller plan to alter the existing budget based on changing circumstances. In good years this may mean money is added to one account or another; in bad economic years it could mean reductions to what's already been approved. An odd-numbered year may also see a supplemental budget, making adjustments to spending at the tail end of the last biennium but passed at the start of the new legislative session.

There are three state budgets: the operating or general fund budget; the capital budget; and the transportation budget. The general fund budget pays for most of what state government does, including schools, social services, higher education, and prisons. The capital budget pays for land, buildings (including repairs), and equipment expected to be in use for more than five years. The transportation budget pays for roads, bridges, and traffic safety improvements. Each budget is separately funded, so it's not easy to short one budget so you can build up another.

The budget process begins with state agencies forwarding their requests to the governor's office. Agencies look at what they spent last time around; what needs more; what new programs they want to pursue. The governor's office then takes all of this and puts together a budget proposal, which is sent to the legislature at the beginning of each session. Although legislators will make adjustments, the broad outlines of the budget generally don't change that much. Most of what's in the budget is dedicated, meaning that for one reason or another, it's difficult to change. For example, the constitutional mandate to fund the public schools means that it's hard to make substantial cuts there. Many social service programs rely on federal matching funds; cutting part of a program can threaten all of its federal funding.

At the legislature, budget bills go to the budget committees, most recently called the House Appropriations Committee and the Senate Ways & Means Committee. There are separate house committees for the transportation and capital budgets. The Senate Ways & Means Committee also handles the capital budget, although there is a separate chair for the capital budget among the committee leadership. The house and senate alternate on who starts the budget process. Budget committees will conduct hearings, taking public testimony from citizens, lobbyists, and agency representatives who will tell legislators why their program should be funded (and not cut). This can take several hours. A house Appropriations Committee budget hearing in 2019 went on for six hours; as a staffer, I once sat through a budget hearing that went on overnight.

PEOPLE IN POLITICS: CHRISTINE ROLFES

Regardless of what you do with the state budget, you're never going to please anyone, says one budget committee chair. "Following each of the two budgets that we've passed, I've spent months listening to people tell me that people are dying because of decisions that I made, which is a somewhat unpleasant part of not being able to fund everything that people want, even the stuff that is very important," said State Sen. Christine Rolfes (D–Bainbridge Island). "Also, advocates will say, 'Thanks for the funding, but . . .' Because no matter what item is being supported, it is NEVER ENOUGH."

Rolfes chairs the Senate Ways & Means Committee, one of two major budget-writing committees in the legislature. The budget begins with forecasts—how much money is expected to come in and how much will need to be spent. "Both the revenue and the caseloads are predicted by independent councils—the Economic and Revenue Forecast Council and the Caseload Forecast Council, which are staffed by professional economists," Senator Rolfes said. "The ERFC estimates what the revenues coming into the state will be over the next four years based on existing taxes and economic projections, and the caseload forecast council predicts what the maintenance level for state services will be if no policy changes happen (how many children will enter kindergarten, how many people will need Medicaid services, etc.).

"The legislature doesn't just pick numbers out of a hat," she said. The next step is the governor's budget. "The budget chairs in both houses introduce the governor's budget as a bill and traditionally hold hearings on the bills during the first week of session," said Rolfes, who started her political career as a Bainbridge City Council member. "Then we rewrite it. It's a good starting point for discussion."

Putting a budget together means talking to a lot of people and figuring out what everybody wants. "As chair, I work with my caucus to determine our top priorities for funding and meet regularly with the house and the governor's office to determine their top priorities," she said. "After outlining a framework, I work with senators from across the aisle to determine their priorities, as well as their priorities for their districts, and make sure that the budget that leaves the senate reflects statewide priorities and values.

"Last year [2019], for example, we needed to finish McCleary funding obligations (public schools) which took up a lot of the resources," Rolfes said. "There was a bipartisan consensus on priorities related to mental health funding and wildfire suppression and prevention."

Even on the budget, there are some issues that Republicans and Democrats can work on together. "I understand that Republicans will never (rarely) help with increasing the revenue needed to fund their priorities, and rarely have ideas to cut spending to the extent that might be needed to fund their priorities," Rolfes said. "So, I take it as a given that they will not vote for an operating budget that directly includes increased taxes if they know the Democrats will do their dirty work for them.

"Having said that, having different perspectives on how to tackle challenging problems is helpful to laying out strategies—like how to improve the mental health system, for example," she said. "One technique is to create a bipartisan team and say something like, 'You have $80 million to fight crime, what are your priorities?' So, I try to get many different perspectives when designing the spending plan."

Rolfes was first elected to the state house in 2006 before being appointed to the senate in 2011 and winning the election there in 2012. She took on one of the biggest jobs in the legislature in 2018. But being committee chair doesn't give her total control over anything. "The power that a committee chair has is limited—at least in my caucus," she said. "The chairmanship of the Ways & Means Committee is granted based on trust, and I wouldn't want to breach that trust by overstepping my authority. Ultimately, the responsibility to craft a budget that can get at least twenty-five votes is up to me, and I make sure that I have lots of check-backs with my caucus on that. It's less about power and more about responsibility."

When a budget committee has approved a plan, the bill moves to the Rules Committee, and from there to the house or senate floor. Each side will offer amendments to the budgets. As with any bill, amendments are sometimes intended to improve the bill. At other times amendments may be designed to make it so unwieldy that no one will vote for it. After second reading and all the amendments have been dispensed with, the budget may be advanced to third reading and final passage. As always, you only bring the bill to a vote if 1) you know you have the votes or 2) you want to see who will vote for it just to be sure.

If it passes, the budget bill then moves to the opposite chamber, and the process is repeated. Eventually the house and senate will have to agree on exactly the same budget bill, down to the penny, before it can be sent to the governor. That can involve a bit of arm-twisting and horse trading, and a skillful governor can try to work with the two sides to iron out a compromise. The governor can veto items within the budget but can't alter the spending totals except by vetoing whole programs. Good legislative leadership will have already consulted the governor to try to avoid this. If the governor and the legislature are picking fights over the budget, something has gone wrong.

Cooperation doesn't always happen, however. At the end of a long, contentious session in 2017, in which Republicans and Democrats alike struggled to come to grips with the McCleary decision—the state supreme court's order to boost spending on K–12 education—majority senate Republicans held the capital budget hostage until the legislature also resolved the Hirst decision. That ruling affected the water rights of many rural residents, many of whom are constituents of Republican legislators. Both the Hirst decision and the lack of a capital budget held up public construction projects all over the state. The issues were not resolved until the legislature went back into session the following January, allowing the water and the money to both start flowing again.

THE BUDGET

The general fund budget was $89 billion for 2017–19 and $99 billion for 2019–21. That includes about $30 billion from the federal government, most of which is dedicated to specific programs. Washington ranks nineteenth in the country for per capita state spending.[1]

For the 2017 budget, if we include federal funds, $40 billion (44 percent) went to human services. This includes health care, welfare, long-term care, and prisons. Much of the federal money is matching funds, which compels states to match the federal money or lose all of the funding. This makes these programs, such as SNAP (formerly known as food stamps) and Medicaid, very difficult to cut unless you want to throw the young, the poor, and the disabled out on the street. One out of every three residents of Washington gets something from one of these programs, including one million children. It's worth noting that overall, 57 percent of the human services budget goes directly to assistance, and 23 percent goes to salaries and benefits.

K–12 education is 28 percent of the budget at $25 billion. If we take out the federal funds, this makes up about half of all state expenditures. Given that the state constitution makes education "the paramount duty" of the state, this is also very difficult to reduce, and the McCleary decision compelled the legislature to increase funding.

Higher education, $15 billion (16 percent), comes in next. Part of the cost of a college education is paid by state funds and part by tuition and fees. Students' share of the cost of their education has risen sharply in recent years. As one public college president said, "We're no longer a state-funded college. We're a state-supported college." During leaner budget times following the Great Recession, tuition rates went up nearly four times the rate of inflation as higher ed became the ATM of state budgeting. Tuition at community and technical colleges, for example, was about $100 a quarter in the mid-1970s. If you factored in inflation, the comparable figure for now would be about $550. Instead, it's about $1,250, and even more than that at four-year and graduate schools. As the economy and state finances improved, the legislature reduced tuition a little. In the same budget they also cut funding for the State Need Grant Program, which helps the poorest of the poor and always runs out of money before all the eligible people are helped. In essence they cut tuition for people who could afford it while reducing help for people who couldn't. The legislature in 2019 replaced the State Need Grant with a more generous program aimed at ensuring that all lower income students will be able to afford college. However, the recent flood of calls for free college largely ignore the fact that tuition only pays for part of a college education, and every state, including Washington, would have to come up with the money to pay for the rest of the cost.

Government operations came in next at $4 billion (5 percent). This includes everything not in the first three categories, from the Department of Commerce to the Department of Revenue. Another $2 billion (2 percent) goes for natural resources, which includes environmental protection, land management, and recreation. Another $4 billion (5 percent) for the ever-present Other, which in this case includes the legislature and the court system. The legislature's budget, for the record, is tiny, about $220 million for 2019. While $220 million is a lot of money, it's still only 0.2 percent of the whole budget.

Washington does not have a balanced budget requirement other than a law passed by the legislature in 2012. And yet the budget always ends up balanced; so far, legislators from all sides have agreed that the state should not engage in large-scale borrowing like the federal government. They have played tricks to get the budget balanced. Back in the 1970s and 1980s when times were tighter, public employee pensions were underfunded. Since then, guaranteed-benefit pensions have been largely replaced by guaranteed contribution retirement plans, with the state matching employee contributions up to a certain level. Advocates of old-style pensions don't like this, but financially it's a more sustainable model. In the early 1980s, amid the previous great recession, the legislature even counted the first month's revenue of the next biennium, "the twenty-fifth month," but as the economy improved later in the decade, the legislature was able to pay off that marker.

Could state government be more efficient? Probably. But probably not enough to greatly reduce spending. Regular calls for eliminating "waste and corruption" are fairly ludicrous. If nothing else that suggests that everybody in the state auditor's office is a crook, which seems unlikely. State agencies get audited every year, and they must be able to account for every dime of public money they put to use. Every so often someone advocates for "zero-based budgeting," which suggests that every budget be built from scratch. The idea here is that by starting from zero, this will eliminate some of the organizational inertia that is presumed to keep programs going long after their pull date. This was tried in the 1970s and found to be impractical. Government budgets are generally big enough that starting over from scratch wouldn't leave enough time to actually run the government. Like a lot of states, Washington also has a "sunset law," by which all agencies are periodically reviewed to see if they're still needed. But because somebody benefits from every agency, it's difficult to demonstrate that something isn't needed anymore. In the early 1980s, for example, legislators debated whether the state still needed an Asian American Affairs Commission. Its budget was tiny. People campaigned to keep it, and it stayed. In light of the great influx of immigrants that followed, and the return of public racism, that turned out to be a good choice.

The second budget is the capital budget: this pays for land, buildings, and some long-term equipment. It was about $4 billion for 2017–19, $5 billion for 2019–21. The kinds of projects it pays for include state buildings, college and university facilities, prisons, parks, K–12 schools, affordable housing, water quality and supply, and flood control.

About 31 percent of the budget is paid for from a variety of sources, including fees and taxes such as public timber sale fees, which are dedicated to capital projects, plus federal funds, and even a little slice of college tuition that is dedicated to college capital projects. The rest comes from general obligation bonds. The state sells bonds—$2.9 billion for 2017–19—to get funds up front for capital projects. These projects generally involve private contractors, chosen through competitive bidding, who expect to get paid up front, or at least by the time the project is finished. By selling bonds the state borrows money in the financial markets to meet these immediate expenses, using tax revenues to pay off the bonds over time, plus interest. Investors find government bonds a safe place to park their money while earning a little interest. The interest rate is set in advance, so the market value of the bonds can vary depending on inflation and the state's bond rating. Investors often buy and sell bonds in anticipation of what inflation will do, so there's a big aftermarket for these kinds of securities.

This isn't a bad sort of debt for the state to have. Public facilities, such as new schools or other government buildings, matter. It's more like borrowing to buy a house than running up your credit card to buy a lot of new clothes. A recent candidate for state treasurer criticized the state for having a high level of bond debt (he was apparently adding together state and local bonded debt), but the states with low levels of bond debt tend to be the states with low quality-of-life scores—more poverty, lower levels of education, more teen pregnancy, and lower incomes. Those states are not investing in themselves.

The third budget is the transportation budget, about $9 billion 2017–19, almost $10 billion for 2019–21. As you might imagine, it pays for roads, bridges, traffic safety features, and transit. Funding for the transportation budget comes from the gas tax, 45 percent; licenses, permits, and fees, 23 percent; tolls, 6.4 percent; ferry fares, 6.3 percent; and the remainder comes from other fees and sources. Just under 9 percent comes from the sale of construction bonds for capital expenditures. Federal funding makes up about 16 percent of the budget, with local government funds coming in at less than 2 percent. A little over half the budget, 52 percent, goes for capital costs (building things), while the rest goes for operating expenditures (keeping things working).

One challenge faced in transportation funding is that as people drive higher mileage vehicles, especially electric vehicles, they're buying less gasoline. That has led to the start of calls for a different financing model since it's expected that everyone who drives on public roads will contribute something to their upkeep. That could include mileage charges, but nothing is imminent in Washington. It's being proposed and tested in other states, so don't be surprised to see this coming down the highway, along with the usual arguments about how this is a violation of all that is good and decent in America.

REVENUE

Americans have never liked paying taxes. Some conservative economics texts even go so far as to count corporate tax burdens as "deadweight loss," as though the money spent is simply burned in some great bonfire. But the money goes somewhere for something somebody wanted, even though we might disagree about the value of that something. People who don't have to drive as much tend to say transportation improvements are a waste of money; some people who don't have children in school can't understand why they should pay taxes for education. But in the end, it all matters.

"Taxes are what we pay for a civilized society," in the words of the U.S. Supreme Court justice Oliver Wendell Holmes Jr.[2] Or, as one Washington legislator put it, "Taxes are great. Taxes make sure that lights on intersections work, that potholes get filled." Without them government cannot provide the services and things people say they want. And yet, like many Americans, Washington citizens seem to want a small, inexpensive government that somehow provides a high level of service.[3]

Writing in 1973, scholar Mary W. Avery described a situation no different from today: "It has been pointed out that, as government services have increased, local and state taxes have mounted to the point where legislators are urged by many groups to curb public expenditures. Yet, when they attempt to reduce spending by abolishing government services, they discover that it is extremely difficult to find an agency sufficiently unpopular that people are willing to give it up."[4]

As much as people like to complain about taxes, our state's tax burden is fairly middle of the road. According to the Tax Foundation, 9.3 percent of personal income in Washington goes to state and local taxes, ranking us twenty-eighth in the country.[5]

Washington is one of only three states without an income tax, as voters have consistently turned down proposals for anything like that. State income tax would be deductible from your federal income tax, but sales tax wasn't until recently, a tax break that may yet go away. Moreover, you only get a deduction if you happen to buy something big in any given tax year.

Since 1921 eight citizen commissions have studied the tax system; every one said Washington's system is unfair since it taxes the poor more than the rich; and seven out of eight recommended some kind of income tax. The legislature first passed an income tax in 1931, but it was vetoed by Gov. Roland Hartley, the same guy who tried to close all the state parks. It's often reported that the income tax has been ruled unconstitutional in Washington State, which is not correct. What the state supreme court said, way back in 1933, was that a graduated income tax was unconstitutional, following overwhelming citizen approval of personal and corporate income taxes via initiative in 1932. The court said that income is property, and property in Washington must be taxed at a uniform rate. Treating income as property was and is a legal interpretation nearly exclusive to Washington, even at the time.[6]

Washington started out with nothing but the property tax. High property tax rates helped produce the tax system operating now. By 1932 the effective property tax rate was 3 percent, which would be roughly triple what property taxes are today. When they approved the income tax, voters also approved big reductions in the property tax. The property tax measure was not invalidated by the courts, so it stayed on the books. This left state government desperately short of revenue in the middle of the Great Depression. It also undercut support for the income tax, as property tax relief was the main driver of tax reform sentiment.[7] Washington residents have been saying no to an income tax ever since. Between 1929 and 1982 the legislature passed fourteen different income tax bills, all but one of which (1932) were rejected by the voters.[8]

Now we have more than sixty different taxes.[9] In terms of the general fund budget, about half the money—$45 billion—comes from state taxes; $30 billion (34 percent) from the federal government; $11 billion (12 percent) from state college tuition and fees; and around $4 billion (4 percent) from the ubiquitous Other. Washington's current biggest source of revenue is the sales tax. The basic state rate is 6.5 percent; counties and cities add their own little slices so that the effective rate is higher but varies by locality. The average sales tax rate in the state is 9.18 percent, fourth highest in the country. Oregon has no sales tax, which affects retailers along the border. So while the total tax rate in the city of Seattle is 10.10 percent, it's 8.4 percent in Vancouver, Washington. Border towns generally get a little tax rate break so that everyone doesn't drive over the state line to shop.

The sales tax comprises 45–49 percent of state general fund income. If you count federal dollars, in 2016, it provided 37 percent of overall state money, or more than $22 billion. The forecast was for $21 billion in 2017–19; state revenue forecasters have learned to be cautious in their estimates. That would be about 46 percent of state general fund revenues; it ended up being 49.5 percent as the state's economy improved and people spent more money.

As always, there are trade-offs here. Sales tax is regarded as a regressive tax because it impacts low-income people more than high-income folks. The sales tax is only charged if you buy something, which some folks see as a virtue; on the other hand, a 9 percent sales tax is a much bigger deal to someone making $50,000 a year than it is to someone making $100,000. Voters removed the sales tax on food and medicine for just that reason in 1977, but it made the tax a much less stable source of revenue. (People still buy food in a recession, but they stop buying other things.) Many services do not have to collect sales tax but may pay a higher B&O tax (see below). The sensitivity of the tax system to economic fluctuations is plain to see. In 2014, adjusted for inflation, state tax collections were still lower than they were in 2007, just before the Great Recession.[10] The economic downturn wrought by the COVID-19 pandemic in 2020 punched another multi-billion-dollar hole in the state budget, which went away as the economy recovered.

Sales tax receipts are particularly susceptible to recessions, defined as at least six months of economic contraction. In a recession some people lose their jobs and other people worry about it. As a result, most people cut back on spending, particularly on items such as cars, appliances, and clothing, all of which are subject to sales tax. State and local governments collect less money just when they face higher demands for government services.

Overall, Washington State has one of the most regressive tax systems in the country. The lowest 20 percent of family incomes in Washington—those making less than $24,000 a year—pay 17.8 percent of their income in state and local taxes. At the other end, the top 1 percent, those making more than $545,000 a year, pay 3 percent of their income in state and local taxes.[11]

Washington economist Dick Conway has gone so far as to say Washington has the worst tax system in the country. Conway looked at five criteria: fairness, adequacy, stability, transparency, and economic vitality. Fairness covers the aforementioned regressivity of the state's tax system: the poor pay more. In terms of adequacy, it doesn't keep pace with economic growth, making it more difficult to pay for things people generally say they want. By Conway's measure, Washington's average state and local tax burden, 9.4 percent of income, is a full point lower than the national average of 10.6. Washington had the forty-seventh most stable tax system in the country from 1995 to 2011 because of the volatility of the sales tax in the face of changing economic conditions. The lack of an income tax and reliance on the sales tax also gives Washington the second least transparent tax system in the United States. Unless you keep track of everything you buy, how much sales tax are you paying? As for economic vitality, despite occasional high rankings for a good business climate, Conway concluded that there's no correlation between the so-called business climate and job growth. For example, Oregon has an income tax and no sales tax, and yet the two states' economies have grown at the same pace. Conway's answer is a flat-rate income tax of 10.6 percent, which would redistribute the tax burden toward the wealthier people in the state. This might be a good idea, but no one fights harder against taxes than the rich.[12] (And the rich tend to have political power because of their wealth.) The usual conservative argument against an income tax is that it may start out as a small tax on upper-income earners, but it will inevitably expand to the point where the state will perform a total cashectomy on each and every person in the state. You will probably someday get the chance to decide whether that's true.

One commonly proposed alternative to an income tax is a capital gains tax. Capital gains taxes are levied on income derived from the sale of assets, in particular shares of stock. Governor Inslee proposed such a tax for the 2019 budget; as you might imagine, the idea is more popular with Democrats than with Republicans. The governor's plan would have levied a 9 percent tax on proceeds from capital gains, exempting houses, farms, and forestry. The tax was expected to raise just under a $1 billion in its first year, and affect about forty-two thousand taxpayers, or about 1.5 percent of households in the state.[13] The tax was not adopted. At a policy conference before the 2020 session, a liberal policy analyst said that a capital gains tax would begin to address the regressive nature of the state's tax system, while making that system more stable. Forty-one states already have capital gains taxes. A representative from a conservative think tank said that they had researched a capital gains tax, and their "number one finding" was that "a capital gains tax is an income tax," the evilness of this truth apparently being self-evident. His other complaints included that it will be unstable; that the legislature won't manage it properly; and that the threshold for paying the tax will eventually fall. Both of these viewpoints have some truth to them; you will have to decide who is most right. As one legislator at the conference pointed out, simply adopting Idaho's tax system—which includes a capital gains tax—would bring about $10 billion more per biennium. Idaho, it should be noted, is one of the more conservative states in the country. Meanwhile, in the 2019 session, the legislature set a four-year tax study in motion, with the goal of a new state code to be proposed by 2024.

"We built this tax code over the last one hundred years," one legislator said. "It makes sense that we should need four years to fix it."

Majority Democrats in the 2019 legislature trotted out a couple of versions of a capital gains tax, with the idea of using the modest amount of money raised ($49 million—less than the state lottery) to provide some tax relief for low-income families and small businesses. The tax bills went nowhere, but the legislature did pass some tax increases on some of the largest firms in the state with the least political clout—large banks, oil companies, and tobacco producers. These measures were supported by Democrats but opposed by Republicans.[14] And as usual, money was allocated for another study.

Then, in April 2021, the legislature enacted a capital gains tax on gains above $250,000 a year, which means most people will never pay anything. The 7 percent tax is expected to raise $550 million a year. The tax was levied on capital gains of more than $250,000 a year, not including real estate, retirement accounts, small businesses, or cattle and timber. Opponents challenged the tax in court, but the state supreme court upheld the tax as constitutional in March 2023.

Another major source of state revenue is the property tax, which is a tax assessed on the value of land, buildings, and taxable personal property. According to one study, including local governments, Washington gets 28 percent of its revenue from property tax.[15] In another way of looking at it, Washington collects $1,436 per capita in property tax, ranking twenty-fourth in the country.[16] From 2017 to 2019 the tax was expected to bring in $5 billion, or 11 percent of general fund revenues; it came in at 13.7 percent.

Everybody pays the property tax. You pay it whether you're an owner or a renter. If you think your landlord is eating the cost of the tax and not passing it on to you, you're dreaming. Like nearly every state in the country, Washington has a cap on the growth rate of property taxes. Washington's limit is 1 percent per year, which is generally less than either inflation or the growth rate in population. This tends to limit money available for local services, shifting the tax burden to sales tax and fees, which disproportionately impacts low-income taxpayers. The impact is particularly hard on smaller counties in the state, which may have less recourse to alternative tax sources.

The business and occupations tax, or B&O, is one of the strangest taxes in the state, if not the country. It's a tax on gross receipts—in other words, you pay the tax whether your firm makes a profit or not. The rate ranges from .015 percent for services to .0484 percent for manufacturing and wholesaling. Thirty-nine cities also levy a B&O. In 2011 Washington got $3 billion from the tax, which in terms of the budget is real money. From 2017 to 2019 that was $9 billion, 19 percent of general fund revenues, so you can see how much difference a strong economy makes to state tax revenues.

It's harder on small business, though if your firm grosses less than $50,000, you are exempt from the tax. But it's supposed to be better for large firms (think Boeing), who might pay more if it were a tax on corporate profits. Although many people agree this is not a great tax, the number of exemptions built into it make it more difficult to change or repeal and replace, because every firm or industry that benefits from the hundreds of exemptions fears that they would pay more under a new tax.

Other major tax sources include real estate taxes, $2 billion (5 percent); state insurance premiums, $1 billion (3 percent); utility taxes (everything from cell phones to electric bills), $1 billion (2 percent); tobacco taxes, $1 billion (2 percent); and the ever-popular Other, $5 billion (12 percent).

Washington has the eighth highest cigarette taxes in the country at $3.025 per pack. It's not difficult to get cigarette taxes pushed through; without any tobacco farmers, the only organized opposition tends to come from the owners of convenience stores. It's very difficult to argue that we should support a product that kills people. Research shows that every time the price of cigarettes goes up, people quit.[17] That tends to produce societal savings in health care costs and gains in productivity (no more smoke breaks), but it does mean that tax revenues will fall. Meanwhile, high cigarette prices tend to tempt people into smuggling untaxed cigarettes into the market, which further decreases revenue.[18]

Washington adopted a lottery in a somewhat desperate attempt to balance the books amid the early 1980s recession. It gave some folks the impression that this would solve all our tax woes. The lottery was launched amid much fanfare in 1982, but despite some clever advertising campaigns, it has never generated that much money. In 2017, based on $736.7 million in ticket sales, the lottery paid out $457.9 million in winnings. It turned over $134.2 million to education programs in the state (the gift of a 2000 voter-approved initiative). That's about 0.3 percent of the state budget. No one who had to write a budget would want to give away $134 million, but in terms of overall state spending the lottery is peanuts. And maybe just the shells. Another $12.6 million went to help pay for Century Link/Lumen Field, $31.2 million to the general fund, $4.6 million to an economic development account, and $400,000 to the Problem Gambling Account.

Amid all the struggles of the early 1980s recession, the legislature created the Economic and Revenue Forecast Council to try to get a handle on how much money was coming in before they tried to write a budget. The council has three members appointed by the governor and four appointed by the legislature, with the chair coming from the legislative appointees. The council includes the state treasurer, the director of the Department of Revenue, and the director of the Office of Financial Management. The heavy lifting is done by the executive director, the state's chief economist, who also hires a staff. They make quarterly revenue forecasts. In tough years the legislature has held off on the budget until March or even June in hopes that the forecast will get a little better. The forecast includes pessimistic and optimistic outlooks for the state's economy. Its first chief economist was Dr. Chang-Mook Sohn, who pioneered some computerized modeling programs for estimating the impact of various economic possibilities. Because Dr. Sohn started his career during hard times he was often referred to as "Dr. Doom," but overall his work and the council's has provided policymakers with a better view of how much money is available every year.

TAXES AND THE BUDGET

The state budget rarely shrinks. The state keeps growing, bringing more demands for government services. Inflation, even when it is relatively low, means that over time everything gets a little more expensive. The legislature, for better or for worse, finds new ways to spend money. And as noted before, everything in the budget is something somebody wanted. In crafting a budget, the governor and the legislature must consider what people want.

Sometimes, however, the budget must be cut. This happened with the 2009–11 budget, coming on the heels of the Great Recession. State tax collections fell by 8–12 percent (as usual, the numbers reported vary), and overall spending fell by $10 billion. That meant people losing assistance, such as drug subsidies for low-income seniors and basic health care coverage for low-income families, childcare assistance, and income support for people too disabled to work; college tuition hikes and less financial aid; and fewer K–12 teachers and more crowded classrooms.[19]

Spending goes up more when Democrats control the legislature; it doesn't go up as much when Republicans are in charge. Democrats are more likely to raise taxes; Republicans would rather do anything but.

When they're in the minority, Republicans often criticize Democrats for budgeting at "unsustainable levels," and this is one of their more apt if somewhat shortsighted critiques—as we've noted before, states that don't spend are not investing, and their citizens tend to suffer. The problem all Washington legislators face is that when things are good—when the economy is strong and people are spending money—state revenues are also strong. Inevitably, however, we get a recession, tax revenues tumble and the legislature finds itself scrambling to keep the budget ship afloat. The legislature has on occasion built a "rainy day fund," salting away a few billion in case of a downturn. Here again there is disagreement. The Republican perspective often appears to be that it will take biblical plagues and Armageddon before the fund can be tapped; Democrats are a little more ready to put it to work. On the whole it's probably a good thing that the two sides don't have consensus on this: it keeps them from using it too freely but not from never using it. As of 2019 the legislature succeeded in rebuilding the rainy day fund to a record $3 billion. But even that is only a small slice of the roughly $50 billion annual budget.

Clearly the state's tax system isn't the best thing about Washington State government. Although many people on both sides would agree that it could be made better, this speaks to the difficulty of getting something done. Many things about Washington's tax system benefit some people, like the sales tax exemption on aircraft sales. As long as Boeing is building planes in Washington State, that exemption will remain. Too many good jobs are at stake. The folks who benefit from our tax system will work to avoid changes that impact them. Changing the mix of taxes will also mean that some folks will pay more, and they'll be against those revisions as well. The one change that could (and should) happen is a sales tax exemption for feminine hygiene products since those purchases aren't optional. Tax reform will come up again in your lifetime. It will be up to you to decide if any changes should be made.

PART IV

In Your Neighborhood

LOCAL GOVERNMENTS

Local governments are the governments closest to you. There are more than 90,000 in the United States, and Washington State has its share: 39 counties, 281 cities and towns, plus 1,511 special purpose districts and 29 federally recognized Native American tribes, each with their own governments. "I see local government as the 'people's business,'" said one county official. "Not only in the aspect as it's their business to know what is going on because we are a public entity, but also in the sense that they are shareholders in the business of their local government."

Local governments play an important role in the wider picture of government. They deliver services; they deal with everyday issues such as police and fire protection; they are the level of government you turn to when you want a traffic light and a crosswalk at a busy intersection. Citizens have a role to play in those decisions.

"People can have more influence on local government than they realize," said one former city official. "Someone once said 90 percent of life is just showing up, and much of local government is designed to be accessible and engaging. I understand people have busy lives.

"What I worry about is cynicism and disengagement because people think they aren't welcome or aren't informed enough or that it won't matter if they participate," the official added. "And especially I worry that people get convinced that public policy decisions are all about the winners and losers and the battle, rather than the tough task to allocate precious resources, make fair decisions and think long-term. Government can and does work, especially at the local level, and people participating can and do make it even better."

"Most of these local elections have more direct effect on your life every day," said another state official. And you can be there when it happens. Washington State law features the Open Public Meetings Act, which requires that all governments in the state conduct their meetings in public, with formal announcements of where and when ahead of time. The only two exceptions are for personnel matters—so a city council, for example, can chew on the city manager without publicly embarrassing her or him—and real estate transactions. That was written into the law for school districts. If a school board had to discuss a potential piece of property for a new school in an open meeting, a real estate speculator could swoop in, buy the property, and jack up the price. Otherwise meetings must be open.

For the most part, local governments borrow power from states, aside from the handful of cities and counties with home rule charters, which in effect gives those entities constitutional status and an ability to order their own affairs without direct state permission. Six counties in Washington State have home rule charter; a dozen others have tried but were turned down by voters. Even under home rule charter, local laws must comply with state laws, and the state sets boundaries on what local governments can and cannot do. They can even make them disappear.

Like Lester. Lester, on Stampede Pass, south of Snoqualmie Pass, started as a logging camp and then a way station for the Northern Pacific Railroad. At its peak in the 1920s, it had a thousand residents. Over the years this dwindled. Scott Paper closed its logging camp there in 1978, and the Burlington Northern mothballed its Stampede Pass rail line in 1984. The population fell to twenty-two, and all that was left was the school district. Virtually everybody who lived there worked for the school district, which was largely state funded. With only a handful of students, on a per pupil basis it was the most expensive school district in the entire state (by a factor of four). Finally, in 1985, the legislature passed a law disbanding school districts with fewer than five students and Lester was no more (students were sent to a nearby district).

Today, Lester is one of the state's only ghost towns. Most local governments are in better shape than Lester, and they still provide an array of services to Washington residents. The governments include counties, cities, special purpose districts, and tribal governments.

CHAPTER FOURTEEN

County Government

REGIONS WITHIN THE STATE

Washington has thirty-nine counties, ranging from two thousand people in Garfield County to two million in King County, and from the 175 square miles of San Juan County to the 5,268 square miles of Okanogan County. Clark County, established in 1845, is the oldest in the state, and Pend Oreille County is the newest, established in 1911. Two counties, Ferguson and Quillehuyte, were created in the 1860s, then merged back into Walla Walla, and Clallam and Jefferson Counties, respectively.

Article XI, section 1 of the state constitution recognizes counties as "legal subdivisions of the state," which means they have no power of their own. That's not precisely true given that a county can adopt home rule charter and alter its precise form of government. Counties also must provide roads, a county courthouse, and sewage and water treatment. The state constitution also specifies that a new county must have at least two thousand people. From time to time people in eastern King County have made noises about breaking away, usually over disagreements on land use. Oftentimes, urban people tend to want to see some wilderness preserved, while rural landowners would like to make some money off their land. Once again we have a trade-off and logical arguments can be made on either side. In the 1990s citizens floated proposals for Liberty County in eastern Pierce County, Freedom in northern Snohomish, Pioneer in eastern Whatcom, and Skykomish in southeastern Snohomish and northeastern King Counties. "Although proponents of the different new counties had varying motivations, all expressed frustration that laws governing rural areas, especially land use regulations and restrictions, were passed by governing bodies dominated by politicians from urban areas, leaving rural residents feeling unrepresented."[1] But in 1998 the state supreme court ruled that only the legislature has the power to create new counties, and a six-year battle to carve "Cedar County" out of eastern King County was brought to an end.

In some senses, counties must put state policies to work. "Counties are creatures of states and state law has counties here do land use planning, public safety, courts, some records, elections, and taxes (assessment and collection)," said Whatcom County councilman Todd Donovan. "Land-use planning, land-use regulations, and implementing the state GMA [Growth Management Act] are the most contentious issues, given conflicts between development interests and environmental concerns."

Counties in Washington State have eclipsed an intermediate form of government between counties and cities: townships. Townships are more common back east. They are generally bigger than a city and smaller than a county. In Washington they provided services such as roads, animal shelters, cemeteries, and business licenses. Over time, cities and counties took over these functions. Spokane and Whatcom Counties were the last to include townships, which were all gone by 1969.[2] The state constitution originally specified that a commission form of government was to be used in all counties. Sometimes this is called the "plural executive" form of government because the elected commissioners have both executive and legislative powers. If the county's population goes over three hundred thousand people, the commission may be expanded from three to five members. Thirty-two of Washington's counties employ this form of government. The other seven counties—King, Pierce, Snohomish, Clallam, San Juan, Whatcom, and Clark—have home rule charters, a possibility created by the legislature in 1948 but not adopted until King County voters said yes in 1969. Clark was the most recent to adopt this in 2015; voters in another dozen counties have just said no. You'll notice that most of the home rule charter counties are larger in population. In King County a three-member commission seemed inadequate to managing a jurisdiction with a million people in it. Home rule charter allows county government to change its form by adopting a constitution (a home rule charter) within the boundaries set by state law. King County couldn't, for example, decide that what they really need is a king.

Counties play a bigger role in the western United States than they do back east, providing services and serving as regional governments in larger metropolitan areas. King County, for example, provides wastewater treatment and transit services through King County Metro. The Municipality of Metropolitan Seattle, more commonly known as Metro, was created by voters in 1958 to provide sewage treatment. In 1972 voters authorized Metro to create a countywide transit system. Metro's governing council eventually had forty-two members, representing county government and cities large and small. A 1989 court case in New York made clear, however, that such an arrangement violated the one-person, one-vote rule, since every Metro councilmember had one vote but each one represented a constituency that might be large or small. Voters approved a merger in 1992, and Metro was merged into King County.

With more than 2.2 million people, King County is the thirteenth largest county in the United States. Counties do things that don't make sense for cities to do on their own, as one county official said. King County's other services include police; regional planning; running local elections; maintaining county parks; providing some public health services; handling licenses, permits, and records; and maintaining county roads. The county effectively is the local government for unincorporated areas of the county—areas that are not part of any city. Beginning in the 1990s county leaders began to push for more incorporations and annexations by existing cities, so as to get out of the business of local government as much as possible and to focus more on regional issues.

Though not as large, other counties provide similar services to their residents. Cowlitz County, in southwest Washington, has around 110,000 people. Its list of services is roughly the same as that of King County. Asotin County, in southeast Washington, has around 21,000 people and lists a very similar set of services on its government webpage. So while often overlooked and misunderstood, county governments in Washington State provide an array of things people tend to say they want.

County governments are increasingly hamstrung by the 1 percent property tax lid, diverting money from other programs to maintain law enforcement. Even there, many counties have had to make staffing cuts.[3] The recently elected sheriff of one southeast Washington county said his biggest problem was lack of staffing. One of his answers was to call for volunteers.[4] Counties are particularly hit hard by the property tax cap because most rely on property tax and sales tax for revenue, in some cases making up two-thirds of a county's budget. Moreover, the 1 percent cap rarely tracks either increases in expenses, inflation, or the growth of population. Counties also complain that the state is saddling them with more requirements but not providing the money to pay for them, with some county officials threatening to sue the state over "unfunded mandates."[5] Counties can ask voters to approve a levy lid lift, which can be a challenge at a time when people are often opposed to all taxes.

Nonetheless, citizens may have unrealistic expectations about government finances. "There is a public perception that all levels of government are able to do whatever is desired, and funding is never an issue, because it's 'government money,' which we all know is unlimited," said one county commissioner. "Or just go out and 'get a grant,' because they grow on trees as well.

"I actually have had people ask what we do with all that money we collect in taxes," the commissioner added. "One has to bite one's tongue to keep from saying, 'Well, we spend it all every year.' I am frequently told we should hire more deputies for the sheriff's office to cut down on crime. I try to explain that a deputy costs about $150,000 per year in salary, benefits, training, car, uniforms, and so forth. The sheriff already spends 40 percent of our budget, and if we add in the prosecutor's office, the judges, and the rest of what would be termed 'law enforcement' it comes to about 67 percent of the budget. Trying to find money to mow the lawns in our parks, let alone fix up the buildings and make improvements, is a real challenge."

COUNTY OFFICES

Counties may separately elect a sheriff, clerk, treasurer, assessor, coroner, and auditor, once again demonstrating the state founders' inclination to break up power in government whenever possible. In some instances it's also questionable why some of these seats should be up for election. Jobs such as coroner are positions that ostensibly require some technical knowledge and to some extent so do the other positions. This should raise the question of why hiring for a job that is essentially apolitical should be reduced to a political decision. On the other hand, keeping these elected offices insulates them from pressure from other parts of government, allowing them to be more focused on the needs of the people.

Tiny (but important—they grow a lot of wheat) Garfield County elects three county commissioners, plus a prosecuting attorney and coroner, auditor, clerk, treasurer, sheriff, and county assessor. Assessor is another technical job—figuring out how much property is worth for tax purposes. But across the state, every four years voters in every county elect an assessor. All but four counties elect a county clerk; only King County doesn't elect an auditor. Only six counties don't elect a coroner or medical examiner; only King County doesn't elect a treasurer. King County voters decided to make sheriff an elective office in 1996, a measure pushed by local Republicans as it got harder to elect any Republicans in the county. In 2020 voters made it an appointed position once again. All counties elect a prosecuting attorney, and that status cannot be changed even if the county has adopted a home-rule charter. Charter counties may decide to have partisan or nonpartisan elections; noncharter or "general law" counties generally have partisan elections. King County voters opted to make all county offices nonpartisan in 2008, again pushed by Republicans who were on the verge of not being able to elect anyone to the county council. All these offices are elected to four-year terms. In some counties these elections take place in odd-numbered years. In many smaller counties, county elections coincide with off-year federal elections (the year when the presidency is not on the ballot).

Among the offices, only four Washington counties have an elected county executive: King, Pierce, Snohomish, and Whatcom. As noted previously, voters in several counties have turned back efforts to adopt home-rule charters. The county executive is the top official of county government and is technically in charge of overseeing the day-to-day operations in government. Given the number of elected positions in county government, like the governor, there's a good chunk of county government that the executive does not control. And also like the governor, the county executive is expected to lead, to be a policy entrepreneur, and to have a vision for what the county could be. Like governors, they propose budgets and they (and their staff) oversee the regular operations of some portions of county government.

PEOPLE IN POLITICS: JACK LOUWS

In some ways, Jack Louws was born to politics. His father also served as executive of Whatcom County. "Dad served on the Lynden City Council when I was young," Louws said. "I remember traveling with him on Saturday mornings to the hardware store, which was owned by the mayor. They talked city business; roads, water, sewer, problems concerning citizen complaints, etc. As with most kids, I probably intuitively picked up hints of a skillset that I have used throughout my adult life."

After serving a term as a Lynden city councilman, and two terms as mayor, Louws decided to run for executive in 2012. "I felt that I could be of service to Whatcom County citizens," he said. Having experience eased his transition to become the county's fourth executive. "My four years as councilman was a great lead-in to be mayor of a small community. Being mayor gave me a very good understanding of municipal finance, a great introduction in union negations, and a strong realization that you need to rely on professional staff to get the work done," Louws said. "Couple that with my business background [he ran a family manufacturing business for eighteen years], and I'm hopeful that I've made a positive impact in my years as an elected official.

"Being exec is a full-time job that requires more time than I'd like analyzing the political aspects of decisions, but my past experiences have given me good insight into the ramifications of decisions and how to hopefully be a good boss."

As a charter county, Whatcom has a county council, which has legislative power and hence controls the budget. "I've learned that as much as I might wish to move some initiatives forward, that I can only provide as much information as I can and hope for a positive outcome," Louws said. "Often other branches of government have ultimate control over decisions." The executive oversees the "efficient and economical" operation of county government. That includes appointing people to boards and commissions; enforcing state and county laws; estimating quarterly revenues, proposing a budget to the county council and making sure that the budget isn't out of whack once it's enacted; representing the county to the rest of the state and the country; hearing people's requests and complaints; and administering the county economic development program.

All of these might explain why he didn't seek a third term. "I feel that it is time to retire, travel, and enjoy being a grandfather, father, and husband," Louws said. He had a little bit of advice for whoever succeeds him. "Listen twice, then act decisively," Louws said. "Clear direction is imperative for staff to be effective. Always share the 'we' in the successes, and only say 'I' in the failures."

"He is a very good boss," said one of his aides. "We'll be hard pressed to replace the wealth of experience and savvy."

In a government with a county executive, the county council is the legislative branch. They will have final say on budget and policy and will need to work with the executive to craft spending plans and program directions. Like the legislature, the council has the ability to make law. The King County Council has nine members, elected by district on a nonpartisan basis. The council once had thirteen members after the merger with Metro and before voters agreed to shrink it. Councils in Pierce and Whatcom have seven members, and Snohomish has five.

County councils, like city councils but unlike the legislature, meet year-round. A year-round session means lawmaking takes more time, said one county council member. The smaller number of people creates a different working dynamic as well. "Personality matters much more than at the state level," said the councilmember. "If they're [another member] a difficult personality, it doesn't matter. You gotta deal with it." On the other hand, the council member said, "Even though the scope of our work is smaller [than the legislature's], our ability to influence is greater."

In Whatcom County, where the executive is full-time and the county council isn't, the balance of power tips toward the executive a little bit. "The executive directs most departments (those not separately elected), and has control over several hundred staff," said Whatcom County councilman Todd Donovan. "The council is part-time, has no policy staff, and is mostly unable to affect budgets and contracts apart from when adopted every two years. We give direction, pass ordinances, resolutions, place things in budgets, but largely depend on the executive to make it go—not easy if it's not his priority."

Most counties in the state are governed by county commissions, in which legislative and executive authority is combined in an elected body of three or more people. In fact, aside from Clark and Spokane Counties, which have five-member commissions, every other county government features a three-member commission. San Juan County has a three-member council. If a county's population rises above three hundred thousand, the county can choose to increase the commission to five. While a three-member commission may be a little more focused and certainly less expensive, it poses a challenge in that no two commissioners can meet outside of official business. Two out of three makes a quorum, and Washington's open public meeting laws make it clear government bodies can't meet without saying where and when they'll meet and inviting everybody in.

Commissioners in some noncharter counties appoint a chief administrator. Like a county executive, an administrator oversees the day-to-day operations of county government. Unlike a county executive, the administrator, while able to recommend things to the county commission, does not play a direct role in setting policy for the county government other than through recommendations to the commission.

PEOPLE IN POLITICS: FRANK WOLFE

Frank Wolfe retired from the U.S. Merchant Marine but sailed into a new career in politics in Pacific County. "I ran in the 2012 election cycle and decided to run about eighteen months earlier. I was retired at the time," he said. "My motivation for running was a longtime friend was finishing up a twelve-year run and was planning on not running again. I didn't see any viable candidates looking at the position and thought it was something I could do for the community to give back."

Despite no prior political experience, Wolfe said his work in the Merchant Marine was good training. "It takes a lifetime of interaction with people to manage the job I presently hold," he said. "Many folks are angry or feel victimized. They can be belligerent. I can say, dealing with twenty-two other folks trapped on a ship for months at a time can be said to have prepared me for this."

One of the challenges Pacific County faces is the 1 percent lid on property taxes. "Property tax is the single largest and only predictable revenue source for the county," Wolfe said. "Having it pegged at 1 percent (plus new construction—about 0.2–0.3 percent for Pacific County) is disastrous for us. With a CPI [consumer price index, a measure of inflation] in the range of 3.2–3.4 percent, our main revenue source is worth about 2 percent less each year. Our workforce is unionized and deserves (and expects) a raise of at least the CPI each year. That works out to deciding what services we can cut each year to be able to make ends meet.

"If the legislature would at least adjust this to the CPI, at least we would have a less catastrophic outlook. Meanwhile, the state adds more and more mandates with no (or inadequate) funding. Example: Indigent defense costs the county about $340,000 per year for which we are reimbursed about $30,000. Yes, those figures are correct. So the legislature is the key to fixing this."

Although in theory the commissioners have both executive and legislative authority, Wolfe said the county commission's job is to set policy for county government. "In Pacific County much of the executive authority is administered by specialists. They follow the ordinances the commissioners pass, and hammering out any conflicts or problems that show up is a collaborative activity," he said. "Essentially, the legislative part is setting policy, and the various departments then carry it out. The commission has a role then in ironing out any inconsistencies that arise."

Although he ran as a Democrat, Wolfe said party politics is somewhat less important at this level. "While the partisan label has a role in the election dynamic, in a small county (twenty-one thousand citizens and fourteen thousand voters) each candidate is looked at individually," he said. "We have a number of independent candidates in our races."

Wolfe said the best part of being a commissioner is simply helping others. "I enjoy being able to really help people," he said. "Making things work out for others is very satisfying. It really does seem that in a small-town environment, one individual can make a real difference.

"The most challenging part of my job is dealing with people who have unreasonably high expectations. I had a fellow the other day call me on the phone demanding to know how I was going to stop his neighbor from opening a vacation rental in the house next door. He phrased it as though it was my fault that the neighbor could even do this. I let him vent, then explained the process his neighbor would follow to get a permit for this activity. The permit would have to be renewed each year," Wolfe said. "I was able to turn him around to submitting a letter to the hearings examiner detailing his specific objections (not just a blanket 'not in my back yard' statement). I spent almost an hour on the phone (my home phone) with him, getting him turned around to having specific conditions that could be incorporated into the permit that would be issued for the rental. He finally grasped the two facts that 1) his neighbor had a right to open the rental if he chose to and 2) if the rental tenants were to violate any of the conditions that would give him and the county leverage later to shift the problem onto the neighbor. He took my suggestions, preparing a letter and also attending the hearing with a few of his other neighbors," Wolfe said.

"He later called me back and was very positive and thankful. Apparently the hearing had gone very well from his perspective, and he now felt his voice had been heard, and he had some assurance that the rental would be compatible with the neighborhood. This turned a possible bad situation into one that should turn out better. Educating the public is an important part of the job. It also makes me feel like I've made a positive difference."

PEOPLE IN POLITICS: MARY KUNEY

Mary Kuney thinks a three-member commission is better than a five-member commission, especially when there's no executive involved. "I think as a commission of three people I think we can" provide a vision for the county, said Kuney, a Spokane County commissioner and Republican. "From what I've seen so far, I think we can. You're still there for the greater good of the entire county. If you add five and you don't have that [an executive], you lack that vision."

The commission has a hired chief executive to oversee daily operations of county government. The full-time commission, meanwhile, sets policy and approves budgets. "The city of Spokane has districts, but one council member is elected at large and so is the mayor. Unless you have that countywide elected, I think you lose that ability to be as visionary as you can be. . . . Trying to herd five cats would be a little harder."

The issue was on the table because a pair of Spokane County legislators, a Republican and a Democrat, in 2018 managed to push through a bill that changed the form of county government from a three-person to a five-person commission. Spokane County's population is now 514,000 people, making it the largest county in the state to still be governed by a three-member commission.

"The system worked decades ago but doesn't work for the current situation, and I think that's why you saw such a bipartisan push to get this out of the legislature," said State Rep. Marcus Riccelli (D-Spokane). "I think that our democracy should be about getting representation closer to the people. . . . Our county has outgrown the current form of government."[6]

Nonetheless county voters said no to a five-member commission in 2015. That has led the Washington Association of Counties as well as two of the three current commissioners to file suit to overturn the law. They argue such a change has to come via a vote of the people, not by an act of the Legislature. Kuney noted that under the new system, which took effect in 2022, the five commissioners would be elected by district. As it is now, commission candidates run by district in the primary, but at-large in the general election. "I would only be representing 20 percent of the people," she said. "You're going to have people who are there to do the right thing. But you're going to have people there who are there because it's their job, and if it's your job, you're going to be thinking about where things go" to benefit your district and not necessarily to benefit the whole county.

The other problem is the added expense of two more commissioners, Kuney said. The county budget is already tight. "It's just more money," she said. "Knowing what I know sitting here, where do we put them? We're already strapped financially, we have to find more money, and where do we take it from?"

Kuney knows something about finance, having worked many years as an auditor, first for the state, and then for Spokane County. "I got to know the county from a different perspective," she said. After a failed run for county treasurer, she was appointed to fill a commission vacancy by Gov. Jay Inslee, and then was elected in her own right in 2018.

As for many counties in the state, tax revenues are an increasingly difficult issue. Like most other counties, Spokane is partially dependent on property tax, increases in which are limited to 1 percent a year. "For us, that's about $500,000," Kuney said. "For that you can't cover cost of living increases. There's got to be something to help us. One of our other big expenses is our criminal justice system, and that's all on the county. There's not revenue generation that you can get from that. It's one of those hard things, as expenses keep going up there's no way for us to keep up. I don't want to put a lot of taxes on our citizens, but it's a delicate balance."

Spokane County's growth has meant and will mean more incorporations and annexations, Kuney said. "You get more developments in the outlying areas, the roads are getting stressed," she said. "As people go to the city, that revenue goes to the cities. Those things make it harder on the county because there's still so many services that we provide no matter what."

Still, she likes her job. "It is really fun," Kuney said. "You really go from one topic to another to another that has nothing to do with each other. Truly, the local elected officials have more influence on your everyday life than national or statewide officials do," she said. "The elected officials in county government actually have more effect on your daily life than I think most people understand—roads, land use, parks, people things really want to have."

And Kuney likes being able to make a difference. "I'm happy to be here," she said. "I'm blessed that I don't have to be here, so I truly look at it as community service."

The county clerk is easy to overlook but is actually very important. "The position of County Clerk is best characterized as the administrative and financial officer of the Superior Court."[7] The office oversees the local courts' records, managing the jury system and notifying jurors, and files cases in superior court. The clerk supervises the court reporters who transcribe court hearings.

Independent of the courts and separately elected, the clerk is in a position to protect all sides of "the judiciary from the appearance of impropriety or unfairness in the settling of cases, implementation of orders, or investment of funds." The office ensures that people have access to the courts' opinions and rulings.[8] In issuing writs and subpoenas, the clerk acts in a quasi-judicial manner. The clerk also holds bonds for public officials and maintains records for some special purpose districts. Clerk is an elected office in all counties except King, Pierce, Whatcom, and Clallam, all of which are charter counties.

PEOPLE IN POLITICS: KYM FOSTER

Kym Foster went into a local government office for some help. When she didn't get any, she decided that the office needed some assistance. "I came into the office in February of 2015 looking at how to file for a divorce. I was treated less-than," Foster said. "They were rude. There was no eye contact or smile. When I asked questions, before I could get the question out of my mouth, the clerk cut me off and said she wasn't a lawyer and couldn't help me. I was humiliated and embarrassed."

Three years later, the incumbent Grays Harbor county clerk decided not to seek reelection. Foster, a part-time legal assistant and schoolteacher, saw an opportunity. "While in the office on Friday, May 18, my lawyer was talking about the current clerk and how horrible if the person who was running unopposed were to win," Foster said. "The clerk's office was terrible. I remembered how they made me feel."

Still, running for the office was a big step. "I had zero experience," she said. "The person running had been in the office for twenty-eight years." The incumbent clerk had been caught up in a scandal in which she appeared to tip off a suspect, someone she knew, before the county sheriff was able to take them in. The FBI investigated, but no charges were ever filed.

Foster had no experience running for office, but she had the support of friends and family, and her boss, who was also the mayor of the town of Montesano. She won election in November 2018 with a little over 51 percent of the vote. "It was tough while on the campaign. I tend to not use my filter. I don't like to BS or take the long route while dealing with issues," she said. "People now know me as the person who will get stuff done. I like that and hope I can keep the momentum."

In her first five months on the job, she said it's been a learning experience. "This position is a lot more than I knew coming in," Foster said. "I am not surprised, per se, just didn't know the extent. I know the voters wanted change. I was not the only one who had the encounter that I experienced.

"Once it got out that I was running I had tons of support from voters I had no tie to," Foster said. "They didn't know me, they knew the office and wanted change. I am very active in my community with my kids, working at the school, the Elma Chamber of Commerce. I am very outgoing and friendly. It wasn't difficult to go to all the events and campaign and talk."

Foster ran as a Democrat, while her opponent, nominally also a Democrat, specified no party preference. But, she said, party doesn't enter into it when you're serving the public. "When you come into my office seeking help, it does not matter your political affiliation," she said. "We help all with the same respect and dignity everyone deserves.

"That is a tough pill to swallow for some," Foster added. "I attended a Republican county meeting and gave my speech at the same time as my opponent. I had devout Republicans who said they love me, love who I am, but would not vote for me because I am a Democrat. I was asked several times why I filed as a Democrat and not NP or Independent. I didn't want to start my career with a lie. I am a Democrat that carries a gun and prays on occasion. I wasn't going to change to win an election. I knew once I got out there and chatted and got to know the voters and who I was, I would get the votes needed. I did have many Rs who took my sign and said it was the only Democrat sign they would ever own. That was a plus."

Assessors are in charge of valuing real and taxable personal property for tax purposes. Real property includes land, improvements, buildings, and some equipment attached to buildings. Taxable personal property can be things used in the conduct of business, such as furniture and equipment. Residential personal property is generally excluded from that calculation. Assessors have to keep records of property values. They also administer exemptions such as those offered to low-income senior citizens.

By law, property in any county must be reassessed every year, and someone from the office has to physically see the property at least every six years. Assessments are generally based on what's there—how big is your lot, your house, and its location—and what's happening with property values in your neighborhood. If houses in your neighborhood start commanding higher prices, chances are the assessed value of your home will go up as well. Counties generally have an appeals process if you think the assessor has gone too far.

By law, county assessors must appraise all property at its "true and fair market value . . . according to the highest and best use of the property."[9] "Highest and best use" means that even if a piece of land is vacant, it could be taxed at a higher rate if it was, for example, a piece of prime commercial property. This put pressure on suburban farmland going back to the 1960s and 1970s; in 1979 King County voters authorized county government to buy up the development rights of existing farmland so as to preserve it. In the 1980s they acquired development rights to 12,600 acres of farmland in south and east King County. Nonetheless, the Green

River Valley, once one of the most fertile places in the country, is now one of the biggest concentrations of warehouse and industrial space in the country. It generates more money than did the farmland, but it's not as pretty. As always, there are trade-offs.

The property tax rate is determined in part by the value of the tax levy. The assessor looks at the size of the levy—the total amount to be collected from taxpayers—be it for a school district, a fire district, or county government. "The county assessor then calculates the levy rate necessary to raise that amount of revenue by dividing the total levy amount by the assessed value of taxable property in the district."[10] The basic formula is to divide the levy by the assessed value of the taxing district, producing a rate per $1,000 of assessed value. So a $10 million school levy in a district with $100 million worth of taxable property would produce a levy rate of 10 cents per $1,000 of assessed value. So on a $100,000 home, it would cost $10,000 a year in property taxes.

PEOPLE IN POLITICS: PETER J. MCENDERFER

Peter J. McEnderfer started out building houses. Now what he says about home values is the law. McEnderfer was elected Franklin County assessor in 2018, after working in the assessor's office for more than fifteen years. He earned bachelor's degrees from Washington State University and worked as a certified residential appraiser before joining the assessor's office in 1999. "I enjoy the appraisal profession and community service," he said. "The position of Franklin County assessor is an opportunity to fulfill that desire." The assessor's job is determining what things are worth for tax purposes, and then levying taxes fairly for everyone. "It can be challenging to not be influenced by factors that might cause the assessor to do otherwise," McEnderfer said. "However, the oath taken by the elected official requires the duties be performed in compliance with the laws and rules of the state of Washington, in my case the equitable distribution of the property tax burden.

"As a separate and independent elected official, the assessor is empowered to fulfill the obligations of the office without the influence of other entities in the county," he said. "As assessors, we strive to perform the functions of this office in a professional manner and benefits all of the constituents in all counties."

An assessor must have knowledge of appraisal, real estate transactions, land use, the parcel layer, mapping, segregations and combinations, current use, personal property, senior exemptions, the Board of Equalization, Board of Tax Appeals, and the levy process, McEnderfer said. And that's not always easy. "Everyone hates taxes, and Washington State has a complex property tax system," he said. "One of the main tasks of the assessor's office is to educate and clearly communicate the process to the public."

McEnderfer said he and his predecessor, who first hired him, have tried to make information available to the public via the county website. "With the growth of Franklin County and real estate market fluctuations it was necessary to transition from cyclical revaluation (four years or one-quarter of the county every year) to annual revaluation (inspect one-sixth of the county every year and statistically update the entire county annually)," he said, which is now the law statewide.

The assessor doesn't determine tax rates. Other governments, such as the state, counties and school districts, set the rates. Based on those rates, McEnderfer's office "must determine the assessed values for the properties in each district. Next the taxing districts provide the assessor with 'budget resolutions' which the assessor must review to determine the amount that can be collected (subject to limitations). Then the assessor calculates the levy rate, when applied to the assessed value of the district, to collect the district's revenue. Then individual district levy rates are combined, and the combined levy rate is applied to the assessed value properties in that taxing district (tax code area). Lastly, the assessor 'rolls' to the county treasurer and tax statements are created."

McEnderfer, who ran as a Republican, said that assessor being a partisan office doesn't change anything. "Regardless of my party affiliation, my obligation is to serve all of the constituents of Franklin County (regardless of their political, social, or religious ideals)," he said. "My goal is to equitably distribute the property taxes in the most efficient manner possible. Through innovation, technology, and education, the assessor's office can continue to provide professional valuation and taxation to the citizens of Franklin County."

Auditors cover a lot of ground. They oversee elections in all counties, but they also may be responsible for overseeing county finances; recording documents such as marriage licenses; handling auto and boat licensing; and handling public records requests. In many noncharter counties, the auditor runs the accounting system for county government. They may issue licenses, from adult entertainment to pets. An auditor may in fact audit county expenditures on a regular basis. Whatever needs to be done in county government but doesn't have a home may end up on the desk of the auditor.

"The stewardship of a county auditor in Washington State is important to society," said longtime Douglas County auditor Thad Duvall. Duvall's position includes responsibility for elections, vehicle and vessel licensing, recording documents, accounts payable, budgeting, and payroll. Each of those items is important to how things work in the county, he said. "Elections provide the very basis for grass roots democracy," Duvall said. "We would not have our current form of government without elected officials. Recording provides the basis for private property ownership in a free society and also issues and records marriage licenses. Vehicle and vessel licensing facilitates the ability to track ownership and allows our customers to drive legally with current license tabs. For most people the purchase of a home or a vehicle are the two largest investments made in a lifetime. The accounting department tracks spending of public dollars and produces the warrants (checks). Accounting makes sure that all expenditures have appropriate documentation, are approved and within budget and facilitates the budgeting process for the whole county.

"This is indeed a full plate. Each separate function is governed by a different set of Washington State laws (RCWs [the Revised Codes of Washington]), has totally different software, and provides a unique set of challenges," he said. That means an auditor will have to rely on professional staff for much of the work. "Most county auditors in Washington State initially have some technical knowledge in one or more areas covered by the duties of the office," Duvall said. "Over time each auditor will typically gain a working knowledge of each area. However, it is more important to hire good staff who become experts in their job and provide good knowledgeable customer service. The county auditor is primarily an administrator charged with making sure that county auditor staff have the training, equipment, and working environment necessary to provide excellent customer service to all."

Duvall said he relies on his own staff to keep things working. "Even though the job is very challenging, it is manageable because I am blessed with good staff who take their job seriously, strive to be experts, and give good customer service," he said. "While training staff, I like to emphasize the importance of our jobs to the county and all its citizens."

PEOPLE IN POLITICS: SANDY JAMISON

Sandy Jamison thought her decades of private sector experience could make a difference for the people of Whitman County. And when the job of county auditor came up for election, she gave it a try. "I am a CPA with an MBA and have over thirty years of accounting and management experience," Jamison said. "I have also been on many community-related committees, boards etc. and have seen where I felt that improvements in the county government level could be made."

After her predecessor decided not to seek another term, others approached Jamison about entering the race. "They felt (and I agreed) that my accounting and management experience would greatly benefit the county through my election to this office," Jamison said.

Jamison was elected for the first time in 2018 and took office in January 2019. She said she learned a lot in her first several months on the job. "Many things," she said. "Trying to utilize efficient time management; juggling twelve staff who do a variety of unique tasks and have their own opinions; utilizing the media to my advantage and trying to anticipate what its needs are before anything 'monumental or negative' comes out; trying to meet the needs of fifteen small towns within our county—whether it be helping folks file for a public office, guiding them through an election cycle, or walking the special taxing districts through our county's accounts payable process."

It's government, so there's politics involved, Jamison said. "I'm also learning courthouse politics—how to not only get along, but to work toward the common goal of making this county better, with all of the other county elected officials. Overall, though, we have very little drama here—I hate drama. Our electeds are good folks," she said.

The auditor's office covers a lot of territory, Jamison said. "There isn't an easy way to characterize the job description of county auditor," she said. "Counties differ, to some degree, as to what the duties of an auditor are, but most are pretty similar. This position, in Whitman County, is responsible for the oversight of all of the elections, vehicle and vessel licensing, recording, and accounting functions. This includes payroll, accounts payable, and year-end financial statement preparation.

"Our department is also the hub for any state audits that occur—counties are audited on several fronts, and it is the county auditor's office that is the liaison for all of them," Jamison said. "As you can see—these duties are quite varied, and the umbrella over them is quite large. It may seem daunting, but I really like it. No two days are the same, and when I come into my office each morning, I hit the day with a 'what new item will I deal with today?' I find that the day goes by really quickly, and it usually ends on a positive 'checked that off my list' feeling as I head home."

Jamison credits her staff for keeping all this working consistently. "I realized early on that I am blessed with a knowledgeable and dependable staff," she said. "They know what they are doing and feel comfortable rolling forward with their assigned tasks each day. I have two supervisors that work under me, so they handle some of the employee management items, but I am quite involved with the administration of policy, personnel, and media tasks. I think I am very organized and prioritize which items I will take on myself and which ones I assign to my staff. I don't expect them to work any harder than I do, but I do expect them to work as hard as I do. Mutual respect goes a long way, and it has proven to be quite effective in our office."

The position is elected on a partisan basis, but it's not really a partisan job, Jamison said. "While this office is a partisan office per the ballot, I believe that the duties performed by the auditor are truly nonpartisan in nature," she said. "In our county, the reality is that in order to get elected the person filing for the election needs to declare a party. That is just our county history. I could have filed Independent but I may not have won, and my general political leaning is toward the Republican side so I went ahead and filed as an 'R.' But this position could be handled just as well by a Democrat, and I work with many Democrats on a daily basis.

"Since I've been in office, I cannot think of one time where the partisan line has even come into play—neither in discussion nor action," Jamison said. "This is truly an administrative position that needs organization and common sense—which folks on both sides of the line have."

Jamison said she thinks her office is making improvements. "I have instigated several changes since I became the auditor—mostly procedural within the department and in-house with the other electeds," she said. "They have been met with positive reviews—I'm excited to continue to move forward."

Coroners—sometimes called medical examiners—are assigned to determine the "cause and manner of death" for anyone who dies within that county. The coroner investigates any death that is "unattended"—someone who dies not under a doctor's care. Accidents, suspicious deaths, and crimes leading to death also get the coroner's attention. Most counties elect a coroner; fourteen combine the office of prosecuting attorney and coroner, "a practice that has drawn scrutiny in numerous studies and is rejected in national standards."[11] As you might suspect, the training required for the two positions does not overlap. If the county population surpasses forty thousand people, the coroner must be elected.

Nick Henderson became the first elected coroner of Kittitas County in 2018. The job of a coroner is to figure how someone died. "It may sound corny, but as coroners we speak for the dead and are their voice," he said. Cause and manner of death could affect insurance claims or criminal charges. Henderson was elected as a Republican, but he said that isn't important. "You are never conservatively dead or liberally dead," he said.

"My job and the others in the field are to determine cause of death and manner of death," he said. "The other day we had a case that looked like a suicide but after the autopsy it is looking like a drug overdose. We are waiting for toxicology tests to come back. In that case it would change the manner of death from suicide to accident."

The largest counties in the state—King, Pierce, Snohomish, Pierce, Spokane, and Clark—have medical examiners, who are forensic pathologists or medical doctors who are qualified to perform autopsies. Elected coroners in medium-size counties may or may not be qualified to do autopsies, in which case they bring in someone who is.

PEOPLE IN POLITICS: HAYLEY THOMPSON

From the time she was a child, Hayley Thompson had a fascination with human anatomy—and with mysteries. "I grew up watching shows like

Unsolved Mysteries, Rescue 911, and operating shows on TLC. I loved to read books by R. L. Stein and Nancy Drew," she said. "As I grew older I started to read Patricia Cornwell books and learned more about forensic pathology and death investigation.

"For my high school job shadow requirement, I visited the Washoe County (Nevada) Medical Examiner's Office and met with the medical examiner about her position and the role of her office. I was intrigued and felt that this would be something I would be happy doing as a career."

Thompson studied forensic anthropology at the University of Wyoming with a minor in criminal justice. Eventually she earned a master's degree in anthropology as well. Following internships and jobs as a deputy coroner and death investigator, she eventually ended up working at the Snohomish County Medical Examiner's Office. As she lived in nearby Skagit County, in 2016 the county commission appointed her coroner, and she kept the job via election that fall. She was reelected to a full four-year term in 2018. "I enjoy what I do every day that I come to the office," Thompson said. "The position is challenging with regards to the administrative work involved, but overall I have been able to build this office up in a way that we are respected by other agencies and the community."

Like many coroners around the state, Thompson has turned her attention to preventing deaths as well as investigating them. She did this by changing the way the office worked and by building partnerships with other organizations. "Prior to my appointment as coroner, my predecessors were not as involved or as knowledgeable about death investigation. There was no comprehensive death investigation and no teamwork with our partnering agencies," she said. "When I came into office in mid-2016, I erased the platform that this office had been running on and started things over. I immediately went around to the various agencies in the county and tried to involve myself in every group that I could.

"In July 2016 I was asked to join a group of professionals in the county to begin examining and discussing the opioid problem in our county. Today, our group has grown to almost forty members and the information that our office has been able to provide on the deaths that have resulted from opioids has been an essential key into understanding the problem," she said. "I know that I will always have a job, as death is part of life. However, many of these deaths brought to our attention are deaths that could have been prevented in some way," Thompson said. "I think that it is important for offices like mine to get involved with the community and share information that will help in the prevention of these tragic deaths."

She said she doesn't let the fact that it is a partisan, elected office get in the way of the job. "The political nature of this position has always been something I do not understand," Thompson said. "There is nothing about my job that requires politics. However, the law has never been changed and therefore, the position remains an elected position."

She's also trying to change the public perspective on her office's work. "Over the last three years I have attended various meetings to educate our community on what the coroner's office is and how important our role is when it comes to a death," Thompson said. "I was amazed at how many people in this community did not know what the coroner is and what we do. I feel that the community is now more informed of our importance and how we can be of help in providing useful information. I plan to continue to be involved and help bring answers to the families and the communities."

Prosecuting attorneys, as noted previously, must be elected in every county. They represent county government (and school districts) in civil and criminal litigation and may offer legal advice to officials from other parts of county government, including law enforcement. They prosecute on behalf of the county and the state in criminal trials, and they represent the county if it is being sued in a civil trial. The state legislature has limited the ability of county governments to seek outside legal advice from anyone but the prosecuting attorney. All of the prosecutor's duties are laid out by state law and can't be altered, even in charter counties.

In most counties, it's still a partisan office, although that has changed in King County. "The prosecuting attorney is a minister of justice and thus the last elected office that should be influenced by partisan politics," said King County prosecutor Dan Satterberg.

Satterberg was appointed chief of staff to then–King County prosecutor Norm Maleng in 1990. He was appointed prosecutor when Maleng died in 2007, then was elected in 2007, 2010, 2014, and 2018.

Charter counties have the option to make the office nonpartisan. "I led that effort two years ago," Satterberg said of the change in King County.

"Then, last year when I ran in the first nonpartisan race, I was repeatedly asked what party I belonged to. My opponent claimed that he was the only D in the race. My personal belief system and values have always aligned much more closely with the Democratic Party, which is especially true now in 2019. I announced that I was a D, which surprised few people who knew me. I recognize the irony that in making the office nonpartisan that I created the need to declare a partisan affiliation. That is more about the times we live in and the place I represent."

The bigger the county, the bigger the office and the more administrative work a prosecutor must take care of. Satterberg said he hasn't tried a case since 1990. "The reason I have not tried a case since 1990 is that the job of administration of a five-hundred-employee public law office leave little time for the immersion of trial work," he said. "I am involved in individual case decisions on most homicides and other high-profile cases, and policy, training, legislative, intra and inter-governmental relations, and building better community relations."

PEOPLE IN POLITICS: JAMES KENNEDY

James Kennedy got out of the military amid bad economic times and wasn't sure what came next. "I left the army in 2009 not knowing exactly what I wanted to do, but because the economy was in a recession I thought it best to go to graduate school to ride out the bad economy," he said. "After toying with various ideas I decided to attend law school," Kennedy said, which eventually led to an internship at the King County Prosecutor's Office, "which ended up being the only office to offer me an internship. As it turned out though I really enjoyed being a prosecutor, and this is what I have done since 2012." He was elected Jefferson County prosecutor in 2018.

Kennedy's job is half administration and half litigation and case management. He hopes to reorganize some things so that he can spend a little more time on administrative chores. Because Jefferson is not a large county (around thirty thousand people), he does double duty as prosecutor and coroner. "For my office, the deputy prosecutors are all also deputized as deputy coroners," Kennedy said. "I have also deputized the sheriff's deputies as deputy coroners. We work closely with our local funeral home for retrieval and transport of bodies. We make the call when to autopsy an individual, but the autopsies themselves are performed by contract forensic pathologists at the funeral home. We rotate throughout the year when we are the on-call coroner."

Kennedy said that electing a prosecutor serves to remind the person in that job of why they're there. "There are both virtues and challenges with this being an elected position," he said. "The challenge is when you have to take the morally right but politically unpopular position. The virtue is that we work for the people and if none of us were elected, we would probably forget that. Having at least one person who is directly answerable to the public is a helpful reminder to the rest the office of where our values should be."

Kennedy said he doesn't see the position as a terribly partisan one, even though it's a partisan office in Jefferson County. "I don't think that prosecution should be partisan, but these days everything is," he said. "But having participated in the political process I appreciate how, in concept, political parties serve to screen qualified candidates and put their seal of approval on people to keep some patently unqualified individuals from getting too far in the process. Of course, any casual observer would note that this doesn't appear to be functioning too well anymore, at least not on the national scale. Competing philosophies on the criminal justice system have strong correlations with certain political parties. Whether we like that or not, it is a fact. And by declaring for one party or the other it can save the candidate from having to explain where they are on every position, but that also cuts both ways."

Sheriffs are the head of law enforcement in every county, and nearly every county elects one, and mostly on a partisan basis. Sheriff's departments provide law enforcement services in unincorporated areas. In some counties they also may provide police services in cities within those counties on a contract basis. Burien, Covington, and SeaTac all contract with the King County sheriff to provide dedicated police service within their borders.

Most of the sheriffs in the state are Republicans, and Republicans typically cast themselves as the party of law and order. But that may depend on what law and whose order. For example, in 2018 voters approved Initiative 1639, which raised the minimum age for gun ownership to twenty-one, imposed tougher background checks, and instituted safe storage requirements. The measure passed overwhelmingly in larger, western, and more urban counties; it failed in the rural areas of the state. Sheriffs, suddenly saddled with part of the responsibility of enforcing the law, often reacted negatively. Some said they wouldn't enforce it because it is unconstitutional (sheriff, of course, being one short step from constitutional scholar); others pointed out that the issue will likely be decided in the courts, and counseled caution on everyone's part. The official statement from the state county sheriff's association said, in part, "In recognition of this separation of powers we encourage all residents of our state to join us in balancing our opinions and beliefs on this issue with our commitment to our Oath of Office and to the Rule of Law, and ask that you work alongside us to resolve our differences within the framework of the Constitution."[12]

Police at all levels have a difficult job, given that society's problems are often allowed to roll downhill to the cops, exacerbated by throwing more people into prison and underfunding mental health care since at least the 1980s. Also in 2018 voters approved Initiative 940, which changed the standards for the use of deadly force and also required police to receive training in de-escalation and mental health. These things might prove to be beneficial to police officers, but then again, they must be funded to work.

PEOPLE IN POLITICS: JOHN AND ROBERT SNAZA

If you're running from Sheriff Snaza in Thurston County, don't head south to Lewis County. You might run into Sheriff Snaza. John Snaza is the elected sheriff of Thurston County, and his twin brother, Robert Snaza, is the elected sheriff of Lewis County. John Snaza initially followed his brother into law enforcement, then got elected county sheriff in 2010. Robert Snaza was first elected sheriff in 2015. "He's really the one who got me into law enforcement," John Snaza said. "I got recalled to active duty [to the navy]" after working as a longshoreman in Tacoma. After serving in Germany, he returned to Puget Sound. "I came back and followed him right into law enforcement and got hooked."

Robert Snaza said it was a career he had long wanted. "I have always wanted to be in law enforcement since I was a young kid," he said. "I can't tell you why, it was just something I wanted to do. I knew my skills were not in the field of carpentry or mechanics. I can barely pound a nail right or change the oil in a car. I know my limitations."

Robert Snaza served in the cities of Shelton and Napavine before joining the Lewis County Sheriff's Department in 1995. Although the sheriff's offices in each county covers a lot of ground, both Snazas say the key is being out in the community. "The job of sheriff varies, depending on what kind of sheriff you want to be," said Robert Snaza. "When I became sheriff, I wanted to make a change, become more involved in our community, working together to solve the problems we all face, whether it is opioid abuse, mental health, or homelessness. As an active sheriff, I am involved in many community events, parades, sitting on various boards, or just being out there. I believe a sheriff needs to be truly involved in their community."

John Snaza tells much the same story. "The first thing is that you want to make sure that you stand up for the men and women of your agency, and make sure that they're being taken care of, and making sure that they're taking care of the citizens of our community," he said.

Consequently, John Snaza also serves on the boards of several community organizations, participating in fundraisers and community events, all the while overseeing the patrol officers, the county corrections facility, and the civil administration of the department. "It is a lot but it's one of those things where you hope that people know that we really do care about the community that we live in and work in," he said. "It's getting out there and letting people know that we live, work, and play in this community and want everybody to be safe."

Drug addiction is a problem even in a largely rural county such as Lewis, Robert Snaza said. They're trying to tackle it directly by getting people the help they need. "I am very proud of our corrections side," he said. "We have twenty-four-hour medical, addressing mental health and drug addiction head on with a staff of mental health professionals. Our goal is to get those who want off of drugs, get them the meds they need and the resources that allow them success when they leave our facility."

Both sheriffs say they try to spend regular hours with their officers, learning about what they're seeing in their daily rounds. "I try every day at least to get out two to three hours a day to be with our folks," Robert Snaza said. "Leadership is huge and as you know it's important to lead from the front."

John Snaza also spends time with his deputies and the folks working in corrections. He also meets with other government officials across Thurston

County. "Every year I go to the city and meet with the mayor and with the city manager," he said, and has breakfast with local city police chiefs. "I really like to hear from the city managers and the mayor about how Thurston County is working with your city—the good, the bad, and the ugly. Am I really hearing what's going out there on the road?"

John Snaza said there's a balancing act in representing the administrative side of things in contract negotiations while still trying to take care of his employees in terms of pay and working conditions. "It's kind of a double-edged sword," he said. "It makes it kind of difficult at times, making sure the men and women are paid fairly. That can make things a little tense."

Robert Snaza agreed. "The challenging part in my agency is I know everyone, which can be good or bad," he said. "I feel I haven't changed who I am, just a new position, but with that it's challenging when dealing with leadership and how I would like to see the agency going. Visualize a big wheel going in one direction at a fast rate, then getting on top of the wheel and try to get it going in the other direction—that's how it feels at times, but I will say it's been great."

John Snaza said it's also challenging to keep the community linked in with what the department is doing. "After 9/11 we could do no wrong, but over time we became a bunch of thugs," he said. Consequently, his department has no designated public information officer, using a variety of officers to perform that function.

"A hard part about law enforcement is being out there and making yourself known to the younger generation for recruiting," he said.

John Snaza is also the president of the Washington Association of Sheriffs and Police Chiefs and the Washington State Sheriffs Association, via which he spends some time lobbying the legislature over laws that impact law enforcement.

"I don't know if I'm putting out more fires or starting them," he said. And the time that takes also is a balancing act because minutes spent on lobbying are minutes not spent on something else. "That's one way of getting unelected, if you're not there and visible in the community."

Although Robert Snaza was elected as a Republican, both Snazas agree that sheriff should be a nonpartisan office. "I do believe at some point being sheriff should be nonpartisan," Robert Snaza said. "A sheriff represents everyone in the county, no matter what your political status is.

"With that being said, I am a conservative sheriff with conservative values," he added. "However, I would also consider myself progressive in the way we help our community with the many issues we face. I ran as a Republican partially because it is a Republican county and my values align with the Republican Party."

John Snaza decided to run as an independent. That didn't impress a few folks, he said. "When I first started running I was told it was the stupidest thing I could have ever done," he said. "But I don't think that the office of sheriff should be partisan. I don't get to pick who I serve and protect."

Naturally, people do ask: Who's the better sheriff? "We're always competing," John Snaza said. "It wouldn't be fair to say. I have more dents and scrapes than he does. As a first-year sheriff when he first got elected he had a lot of questions, so it's cool to see him come into his own."

"I am glad to have my brother as sheriff," Robert Snaza said. "He has been a great resource when I encounter challenges and have questions."

Robert Snaza said it's clear who's the better sheriff, however. "I think we are both great sheriffs who truly love our communities and the people we work for," he said. "Thurston County is totally different than Lewis, population wise, more diverse groups, and the list goes on. For the size, John does a great job, a lot more administrative work. With that being said I will concede that he is the better sheriff, he is in his third term and ran unopposed. But most important, he is fourteen minutes older than me."

And they like what they do. "I never looked back and have had a great career," Robert Snaza said. "I am truly blessed."

"It's the best job I ever had," John Snaza said.

County treasurers are the bankers for county and local government. All thirty-nine counties have one; only King County's is not elected. Treasurers manage accounts for funds for all kinds of local governments, including school districts and other special purpose districts. Treasurers also collect taxes (again, they don't set the tax rates), disburse funds, and manage investments. They "redeem warrants," which are orders to pay whomever the government owes money to.

As far as investments, governments at all levels collect a lot of money, not all of which goes out the door as it comes in. These temporarily surplus funds get invested, with the earnings going to defray the cost of operating whichever governments the funds belong to. Treasurers help local governments manage their debt by facilitating and keeping record of bonds issued by local governments, such as school districts, which are used to pay for construction projects. Treasurers also administer the disposal of surplus county equipment at auction. This system saves local governments money, if only because, unlike a commercial bank, county treasurers aren't in business to make a profit for shareholders.

"The simplest way I can describe the treasurer's office is that we are the bank for the county," said Kayla Meise, Adams County treasurer and its financial manager.

Meise said there are advantages to this being an elected office, despite the technical skills required. Meise had a solid career in banking before she took a job in the treasurer's office and then ran for the job when it came open. "With the treasurer being an elected position there is a lot of accountability involved," she said. "If it was not an elected position then the treasurer would only have the Board of County Commissioners to answer to. With it being an elected position, you have the public as a whole to answer to. I think it is good for this to be an elected position because the public elects a treasurer that is going to safeguard their public funds."

But it does take some skill to do the job, she added. "This position does require a lot of technical knowledge," Meise said. "I do not think the voters understand the importance of the technical knowledge we need. Our software system, for example, is something that we have to be very knowledgeable of. Not just on what information to input in a certain box, but how the behaviors of our software are set up so that we can ensure our accuracy. We also have to know how to perform different calculations with a calculator so that we can set up formulas in spreadsheets. The public may think that we just plug numbers into a computer and that's how our accounting is done. That is incorrect. Because we are managing public funds, everything has to be checked, verified, and balanced by our staff every day."

PEOPLE IN POLITICS: STACIE PRADA

Hard times forced Stacie Prada to think outside of the box. "I hadn't intended to pursue this career," said Prada, the Jefferson County treasurer since 2014. "Rather my career path was one of taking the best possible option at each opportunity.

"My education was in business with a major in marketing. I also studied heavily in the journalism school, intending to go into advertising," Prada said. "I graduated in 1991 at the tail end of a recession and had difficulty getting interviews. After working in the service industry, I became self-employed for a few years, took jobs in retail and real estate, and eventually secured an entry-level position in a county community development department. There I moved up through the department to eventually become the second in command for the department and even filling in as the director when vacant.

"It was at that point that the existing county treasurer observed my ability to present complicated statistics and analysis to frustrated citizens and satisfy their concerns," Prada said. "Upon her retirement, she reached out to me to ask me to run for office."

People must have approved because Prada ran unopposed for treasurer in 2014 and 2018. "I credit others for seeing potential in me along the way and pushing me to pursue positions I hadn't considered. My current position is a job that is perfectly suited for me that I enjoy," she said. "I've realized over the years that it is important to me to serve my community and give back in my life, and being a public servant accomplishes that daily. I will add that in high school, I distinctly remember thinking that I didn't know what I wanted to do for a career, but I knew I didn't want to be involved in politics. As an adult, I grew to know politics affects every aspect of our lives and there are roles at every level that can suit a person's interests and personality."

Prada's role is to lead the office that serves as the financial manager for the governments of Jefferson County. "The county treasurer serves as the bank for county government entities," she said. "In addition to the county departments and offices, this includes schools, hospitals, fire districts, ports, libraries, and parks among others. All revenue must be deposited to the county treasurer, where funds are held and invested on behalf of those entities. Debt is managed on behalf of those entities as well. Most citizens are familiar with the collection aspect of the county treasurer. We bill and collect property taxes owed and ensure that funds are distributed to each entity. Along with that role, the treasurer's office processes and collects excise tax for real estate transactions."

Every county treasurer's office is different, but it helps to understand finance and accounting, she said. "The day-to-day tasks and specific technical skills required to be a county treasurer vary given the size of each county, but knowledge of finance, accounting, and government operations is imperative," Prada said. "Public presentations, meeting regarding legislation, and working on spreadsheets at my desk are frequent tasks. Management skills regarding personnel, budgeting, and office operations must be sharpened continually. All of this comes into play once a person successfully campaigns and is elected. Interpersonal skills go a long way to facilitating all aspects of a career path to the position and getting reelected."

People's appreciation for her work makes the job even more rewarding, she said. "In conversations with voters, I've found many aren't confident in their ability to analyze and be responsible for finances," Prada said. "They want someone who they trust. I encounter gratitude from many people frequently that I serve in this position for our county."

Prada said she thinks it's good to have separate elected offices at the county level. "I think a crucial benefit to this being an elected position is that there is independence and autonomy for fulfilling the duties of the office," she said. "When a position is appointed, it is likely appointed by a person holding an elected position," which puts a layer between the citizens and the office.

"Department directors appointed by county commissioners serve at the will of the commissioners," Prada added. "As an independently elected official, I serve the residents of my county directly. It is my integrity and interpretation of laws that direct my actions, not desires of other officials who may have different priorities or preferences. I believe the separation of duties for safekeeping of funds (treasurer), budgeting and spending of those funds (commissioners), and auditing of financial activity (auditor) is well managed with independently elected officials."

Prada suffers from multiple sclerosis (MS), a disease of the central nervous system that disrupts the flow of information between the brain and the body. She has been upfront about her condition since she first ran for office. "I have been open with my MS diagnosis from the beginning," Prada said. "Shortly preceding diagnosis, I spent three days in the emergency room at Harborview Medical Center, and my coworkers were part of my support network in knowing something was wrong. Upon diagnosis weeks later, I briefly considered whether to disclose my condition. For some it can sabotage their standing and opportunities at work. I considered my position as a manager in a county department to be one where accommodations I may need would be offered and employment regulations would be followed, so I didn't feel nervous that I would be fired. I've also believed for a long time that I wouldn't want to keep working somewhere where I wasn't wanted. As such, I was open with my boss, my coworkers, and the county commissioners that I had MS in 2008."

Confronting it directly helps, she said. "I know for sure that disclosing my condition helps me do better," she said. "I'm not hiding or making excuses for needing to manage my health and energy exertion. Doing that would be an added level of stress that would drain me. I feel that sharing my experience offers an opportunity to see an example of vulnerability and strength coexisting, it can demystify a very scary condition, and it can provide a resource for others in their own individual journeys. I do feel that I set an example for self-care and prioritizing health over work. That said, there are times I push too hard and need to follow my own advice."

Prada said she does try to be an example for others who may face similar challenges. "I believe the best thing I can offer and receive is a kinship with others for each of our conditions, struggles, and accomplishments," she said. "My hope is that others who receive an MS diagnosis or know someone who does will be able to see that MS is serious and changes everything, but it can also drive a person to lead to a really great life."

Prada has made helping others a part of her life. "Most people are surprised to learn I have MS, and it usually increases their respect for me," she said. "Often, people learning I lead the local MS self-help group believe that I'm being selfless in serving. It sometimes takes a couple corrections to let them know that I'm a member with MS and not just a volunteer.

"Many assume I have a mild version because I look like I'm doing well. I've even had people say they forget I have MS because they don't see it," Prada said. "Therein lies the basis for me being so open. It's a constant factor in all I do because I'm affected daily with physical challenges that are invisible. My success at living well with it makes it easy for people to assume that it's easy for me. It's been difficult, and I have designed my life to accommodate my health as best I can. I believe I'm doing as well as I am precisely because I have adapted to my limitations and accommodate my MS fatigue with daily midday rest. I'm fortunate that these changes have improved my health and allowed me to remain very active. It seems to be working for now, and I anticipate constant adaptation in coming years to maintain my health and career."

As you can see, county government does a lot of things for a lot of people, even though for most of us it may not be obvious. As we shall see, local governments inside counties are governments that we do see, even though we may not recognize what they're doing.

CHAPTER FIFTEEN

Cities

POLICE, PLANNING, PARKS, AND POTHOLES

A city must have at least 1,500 people to incorporate, but there are lots of existing cities that are smaller than that (they formed before the law changed in 1994). The largest is Seattle with more than 700,000 people. The smallest is the town of Krupp, more commonly known as Marlin, which has around 50 people. Vancouver is the oldest Euro-American settlement in the state, but Steilacoom in Pierce County is the oldest city, having incorporated in 1854. Spokane Valley (2003) is the newest. Some 65 percent of Washington residents live in the state's 281 cities, so they matter to a lot of people.

Cities are general purpose governments. They provide a variety of services and have the ability to choose what services they will supply. Generally speaking cities are 4P: parks, planning, police, and potholes. Cities typically run local parks. They also issue building permits and decide what can be built where. "Planning is what makes a city feel like a place," said one Washington mayor. "It's control over what things look like." Cities also provide police protection inside city boundaries. And they take care of local roads.

In Washington State, cities do not run schools. Schools are run by school districts, which are separate local governments with their own elected boards. (This has to be stressed because the number of people who think otherwise is fairly astounding.) Each city has its own mix of services so that no two are exactly alike. But the 4P rule is a reliable starting point.

"The city is where the rubber meets the road," said one former mayor. "You see the services the city provides."

"We provide about 90 percent of the services people care about," said another former mayor.

Some cities have airports; some have their own water or sewer utilities. Seattle and Tacoma provide electric power. Many cities have their own fire departments. Some newer cities in King County, such as Burien and SeaTac, contract with the King County Sheriff's Department to provide police services.

City governments also come in a variety of formats. Cities can have separately elected mayors and councils, such as Seattle (a strong mayor form of government, because the mayor has executive power), or a weak mayor form, in which the mayor is ceremonial and is elected by his or her fellow council members, plus a hired city manager. In Washington, 227 cities have a mayor council form of government; 54 have the council manager or weak mayor form of government. (My friends who are or have been weak mayors don't really like that term.)

In a strong mayor form of government, the mayor is elected by the people and is the chief executive of city government. They are expected to manage the day-to-day operations of the city, including hiring and firing department heads. They can propose legislation to the city council, but the council has the final say on budgets and ordinances. The city council is the legislative arm of city government. The mayor can veto acts of the council, but the council can vote to override.

In the weak mayor or council manager form of government, the council has both legislative and executive power. They hire (and fire) a city manager, who oversees the day-to-day operations of the city. The council sets policy and approves budgets and ordinances (city laws). They typically choose one among their number to serve as mayor, often for a two-year term. The mayor chairs the council meetings and represents the city in ceremonial and regional affairs. But the mayor has no more power than any other member of the city council—hence the term weak mayor.

In this form of government, it's the city manager who makes sure it all works. "City managers are responsible for all city policy and operations, so a lot of 'managing down,'" said Kamuron Gurol, former city manager of Burien. "But they report to a council and it can take a lot of time and adaptive leadership skills to 'manage up' successfully."

Either way, city managers serve at the pleasure of the city council, which isn't necessarily job security. "There are a number of local examples of city managers that retire after a long stint at one city, but it is also common to work for several agencies across a thirty-year career," Gurol said. "I was attracted to the job because of the opportunity to make a real difference for a community that deserves great public services, and to take responsibility to do so." And for a while, he and the council were on the same page. "I left because a majority of the council decided to make a change," Gurol said. "My opinion is that the council I worked for struggled to find consensus on just about every front, and giving me clear direction was not really possible. Others might have a different opinion. The saying in the industry is that you have to 'count to four everyday' [the majority on a seven-member council], and one day I couldn't do that."

There are distinct trade-offs in having a council manager or a strong mayor form of government. Having an elected chief executive gives the voters some additional say, although given the appallingly low turnout for city elections they don't seem to be taking advantage of that. An elected mayor also is in a better place to have a vision for the city and to drive policy in a way that could make the city work better. City administrators recommend but don't make policy, and if the executive is seven different people (the city council), that vision may be harder to realize.

On the other hand, does your city possess someone with the talent and skill to be mayor? Or, as one opponent of a recent effort to adopt a strong mayor form of government put it, "How do you go from running a small print shop to managing hundreds of employees and a multi-million-dollar budget overnight?" It's a fair question.

In 2013 citizens of Pacific, a city of 6,900 that straddles King and Pierce Counties, voted overwhelmingly to recall Mayor Cy Sun. Recall means citizens vote to remove someone from office. First elected as a write-in in 2011, Sun had fired or chased off most of the city department heads; ordered police to conduct a private, out-of-state investigation related to Sun's business; called people in one meeting "savages"; and pretty much drove the city to the edge of bankruptcy and dissolution. So the notion that all these relatively small cities have the native talent to find someone who not only can but wants to be mayor is at least debatable. (It might also be fair to ask this about certain large cities as well.) Meanwhile, many of these cities still have to hire a city administrator to help with the actual work, which makes this form of government potentially more expensive. And yet the great majority of Washington cities have the strong mayor form of government.

Tacoma (209,000) is the largest city in the state with a council manager government. Meanwhile, tiny Krupp and its 50 people have a mayor and a five-member council, which means that 10 percent of the entire city is involved in city government. Starbuck (Columbia County, population 130) and Hatton (Adams County, population 110) are listed as having council mayor governments, but a little digging reveals otherwise. As it turns out, Hatton doesn't have a strong mayor. It has a five-member council; one member of the council is the mayor. It takes three votes to get anything passed. Starbuck lists five council members and a city clerk, but no mayor. And no Starbucks.

Many of these cities were incorporated before city managers became a career choice. Newer cities tend to have the council manager form of government. Staunton, Virginia, may have been the first city to employ a manager in 1908. Dayton, Ohio, hired a professional manager in 1914. Damaged by a flood, the city commission decided they needed a good manager to help sort things out. It was also a choice because it took administration out of the hands of party bosses, meaning that there was a better chance that city government would work the same for all the citizens.

Outside of big cities like Seattle, most city council positions are part-time. They may get a few hundred dollars stipend a meeting, but it doesn't add up to enough to live on. "The council doesn't make a lot of money," said one city council member. "But my colleagues and I don't do it for the money."

Washington law also allows for government by city commission, in which three commissioners are elected to fill specific roles—public safety, finance and accounting, and public works. Shelton was the last Washington city to use this system, switching to a council manager government in 2017. Like counties, cities can adopt charters that allow them to alter the form of government.

Washington has different classifications of cities: first class (6 cities total), second (5), town (68), code (147), and unclassified (1)—Waitsburg of Walla

Walla County, population 1,230, founded in 1865, which still operates under its territorial charter, passed by the territorial legislature in 1886. In a way that's kind of cool. First-class cities have a population over 10,000 when organized or reorganized. A second-class city has 1,500 or more people and isn't a charter or code city, meaning they can't greatly alter the form of city government. A town has less than 1,500 people. Since forming a city now takes at least 1,500 people, you can no longer form a town. Code cities operate under the state's Optional Municipal Code, which specifies a population of at least 1,500 people. The code aims to offer broad statutory authority to allow cities to do what they see fit.

First-class cities include Seattle, Tacoma, Everett, Spokane, Yakima, Vancouver, Aberdeen, and Bellingham. Second-class cities include Davenport and Wapato. Code cities are the majority of the cities in the state, including relatively large cities that started small, such as Bellevue and Kent, and areas that incorporated late, such as Federal Way. Towns tend to be very small, such as wealthy east–of–Lake Washington enclaves such as Yarrow Point, Hunts Point, and Beaux Arts Village. Founded as an art colony, Beaux Arts Village has three hundred residents and at 0.1 square miles is the tiniest town in the state. Unlike other mayors, town mayors don't have veto power over city council decisions. In recent years more than a dozen second-class cities and towns have changed to code cities, presumably giving those local governments more flexibility.

Incorporating a new city requires a few steps. First you must have 1,500 people within your proposed boundaries, 3,000 if you're within five miles as the eagle flies of a city of 15,000 or more. You're going to need signatures of registered voters representing 10 percent of the new city's population, and the Boundary Review Board or the county government must examine and approve the proposed borders. Then the majority of the citizens have to vote yes. A new city council must be elected, and the city must incorporate within 360 days of the incorporation election.

PEOPLE IN POLITICS: FRANK KUNTZ

Frank Kuntz likes helping others. As mayor of Wenatchee, he's found a way to do that. Kuntz ran for mayor at a time when the city was struggling a bit. "I ran for mayor as our public facility district and the city were defaulting on bonds issued to build a sports arena," Kuntz said. "The city was preparing for bankruptcy, and I thought we should find a different path, so as a CPA and former council member and someone who loved the city, I felt it an obligation to run and try to help." His favorite part of the job is "Helping people. Solving problems. Trying to make your community better. I just want to leave the city of Wenatchee better than I found it," he said.

Wenatchee has a mayor council form of government. The seven-member council has five district-based seats and two at-large, and it has legislative authority. The mayor is the chief executive of city government. "I would say being the mayor of Wenatchee is a lot like being the CEO of a company: 165 full-time employees running a $100 million budget," Kuntz said. "We do water, sewer, garbage, stormwater. Police, building, planning, environmental. We fix roads, plow snow, maintain parks, program parks. We do a lot." That being said, there are challenges. "Not having enough resources to do everything that you think needs to get done," Kuntz said. "That will always be an issue. And secondly, I would say trying to make sure that we keep our homeless population in check."

Meanwhile, the city only recently adopted district-based elections, so that hasn't all shaken out yet, Kuntz said. "I do like the fact that if citizens have issues, they can contact the councilmember from their district." He said that people should know that city government is doing its best. "I would say that generally speaking the mayors, councils, and department heads really care about your city and want to make it better," Kuntz said. "And they do listen to their constituents."

As a part-time mayor, Kuntz maintains his practice as a CPA, which he said is not a bad background for his city job. "I think owning a business and having accounting and budget experience was very helpful," he said. "Also, and equally as important, was I was a city council person for four years before I became mayor, so I already understood the city budget and departments. I would also add that I think maintaining your current job while still being mayor is important," Kuntz said. "I think our founding fathers thought we should be able to keep our regular jobs while being in government. It allows you to make decisions that are in the best interest of the city and not necessarily in the best interest of getting reelected." It's "challenging to do both but still possible," Kuntz said. "Tax season is the hardest time. But the rest of the time it's very manageable."

Kuntz said he's in the place where he wants to be. "The best job in government is a strong mayor in the strong mayor form of government when the council and the mayor agree. You can accomplish a ton," Kuntz said. "I look at all of the local elected government jobs—county commissioner, state legislator, etc. I would not trade my job for any of those. It really is the best job in government."

Most cities in the west elect city councils on an at-large basis, a legacy of the Progressive movement of the early twentieth century. At-large elections mean the entire city votes for each member of the city council. In a district- or ward-based election, citizens vote for someone to represent their district. Such a city may have six districts, plus one at-large seat voted on by the entire city. The Progressives battled with urban political machines backed by large immigrant populations in many U.S. cities. By making city elections nonpartisan and ending district-based elections, they were able to reduce the machines' power. In large cities this can be a concern, as in citywide elections minority groups can be excluded as a result. At one point in the 1990s eight out of nine Seattle City Council members lived in the same upscale neighborhood, but voters repeatedly turned down efforts to create ward-based elections until they finally said yes in 2013. Seattle now has seven district-based seats and two at-large seats.

Federal courts forced Yakima to adopt district-based elections because although half the city was Latinx, with at-large elections they had never elected a Latinx council member. The city spent $3 million of taxpayer money fighting this in court and lost every step of the way. The very first district-based elections elevated two Latinx citizens to the council, and the sky hasn't fallen. Meanwhile, this kind of thing matters. First, in most situations people naturally look for other people who are like themselves in some way. We all do that the first time we walk into a room. So if we want people to participate in and support local government, they have to feel like they can belong. We can all dream of a day when what you look like won't matter, but we're not there yet. So electoral systems that exclude different ethnic groups don't tend to make government run better. Wenatchee and Pasco have each adopted district-based elections on their own.

Unlike other parts of government, we do occasionally get new cities. Fifteen cities have incorporated in Washington since 1990, driven by growing suburban populations and a strong economy in Spokane and the Puget Sound region. Incorporations in Washington State have come in three waves: a bunch in the decades after statehood; a bunch more in the baby boom years after World War II; and the most recent wave in the 1990s. As previously noted, the King County Council began to push for more incorporation into cities in unincorporated but heavily populated suburbs. Eventually voters agreed to create cities in places such as Federal Way and SeaTac (1990), Burien and Woodinville (1993), Newcastle (1994), Covington and Maple Valley (1997), Kenmore (1998), and Sammamish (1999). Pierce County added University Place (1995) and Edgewood and Lakewood (1996), while Spokane County welcomed Liberty Lake (2001) and Spokane Valley (2003).

These incorporations represent classic trade-offs in government. On the one hand, inside a city citizens have more control over the places where they live—zoning, parks, how much police protection they are willing to pay for. And that's the trade-off: residents of cities typically pay higher taxes in order to get more government services. Voters have a hard time making those choices; Federal Way voters turned down cityhood five times before finally saying yes in 1990. Federal Way's first incorporation try was 1972. The yes campaign, as always, stressed the higher level of services and control over zoning that cityhood would bring. But "no" voters simply didn't want to see higher taxes. By the time voters said yes, Federal Way had somewhat missed the opportunity to create an attractive, functional downtown against which city government has struggled ever since. The key may have been finally excluding the Redondo neighborhood, which eventually became part of nearby Des Moines. The move toward creating more cities also led to bigger cities; Kent, Des Moines, and Tukwila all began significant annexations in the 1980s and 1990s, adding to both their tax bases and obligations. In urban and suburban areas, however, one can still find little chunks of unincorporated land, unwanted because cities think the taxes from those parcels will not pay for the services that will have to be provided.

Don't get too excited over those annexations: they require petitions from a majority of landowners within a target area just to get started. Annexations are not unlike the incorporations that start new cities. At some point a majority of the affected people have to say yes to the idea of joining a nearby city, beginning with some formal indication, such as a petition, that the people who live in the annexation area want to join the city. A petition, in whatever form, has strict legal requirements, and gets examined by the county prosecutor, the affected city council, and the Boundary Review Board.

Several different methods may be used to confirm an annexation proposal. Property owners representing 60 percent of the assessed value of the annexation area may approve the annexation. Alternatively, property owners representing a majority of the land and the residents of the annexation area can approve the annexation. Or you can have an election, and a simple majority must vote yes. In counties under the jurisdiction of the state Growth Management Act, areas may be annexed only from a city's designated growth area. Cities generally weigh the costs and benefits of annexation—will the new area generate enough tax revenue that the city will be able to afford to provide it services? If the answer is no, city government may not be interested.

PEOPLE IN POLITICS: LUISA BANGS

Luisa Bangs thought the community where she lived needed help. She decided to run for city council. "I decided to get involved in my local city government because I wanted to be part of the solution to the issues we had, versus part of the problem," she said. And Des Moines had problems. Years of questionable policy by the city government had brought the town of thirty thousand to the edge of bankruptcy. A largely new city council, including Bangs, rolled up its sleeves and started to find solutions.

"We accomplished a sustainable and solvent budget for the long term with healthy contingencies," she said. "We secured financing with new bonds for our marina bulkhead replacement in our state Legislature in the amount of $2 million. The total to replace the bulkhead will be closer to $12 million, but this is a start.

"Our police department is now fully staffed and is implementing successful, innovative programs and strategies to assure safety in our city. We have paved our first road in over ten years, and we will continue as our capital projects are completed. The Des Moines Business Park is 100 percent occupied and bringing in long-needed revenues that will be ongoing."

Bangs previously was a senior manager for the Port of Seattle, which she said was not bad training for a job in city government. "That management experience was a great help in my time on council," she said. "I managed over one hundred people, and I managed a budget of $15 million primarily made up of salaries and operational issues. I understand capital budgets and how to work various teams to prioritize the expenditures. Very challenging at times. These responsibilities did steel me for work on council."

Despite that experience, Bangs said she found there was plenty to learn. "The intricacies surrounding the roles and responsibilities of council members versus city staff is eye-opening," she said. "The city manager's role is to run the daily operations of the city. Council members are responsible for council meetings and agendas, administrative duties, also assuring municipal codes are updated, staffing council committees (Environment, Municipal Facilities, Public Safety & Emergency Management, Transportation, and Economic Development), and enacting ordinances, resolutions, and motions."

Despite the council's progress, there are still issues to address in Des Moines. "I believe we still need to work on noise and environmental mitigation from the airplanes that fly over our city, of which we are disproportionately impacted by," Bangs said. "We also need to revive our downtown district, working with property owners to see a 'vision' that will bring people here as a destination city rather than a 'drive-through' city. The Des Moines Theatre is progressing and will be operational in 2020, if not sooner. We are looking at plans and ideas for the Marina and Beach Park that will also provide a draw to our Marina District. These are exciting times and I look forward to being a continued part of moving our city forward."

CITY BUDGETS

City budgets reveal quite a lot about what cities actually do. Generally speaking, the larger the city, the more revenue, and the more programs they will be able to engage in. And it's never enough, at any level. "It's a constant struggle for cities and counties to get the revenue to provide the services," said one former mayor. "In every city there are a lot of competing commitments," said one city council member. "Where those show up is in the budget. Some people say we need more police. Some people say what are the causes? People really do care and that's why they get upset."

Spokane is in many ways a typical big city. It was incorporated in 1881, meaning the city was there to provide services for a long time. Older cities tend to provide more services. It has almost 230,000 people and covers 69.5 square miles, so it has a larger tax base than many smaller cities but also greater demands for services. Spokane's city budget for 2018 was $975 million. Every city budget is a little bit different, and city budgets tend to be quite a bit different from state budgets. Out of Spokane's budget, $189.3 million was the general fund budget covering the police department and criminal justice, fire and emergency services, streets, parks, libraries, planning, community, and economic development, among other things. As a point of comparison, note that Spokane spends about 29 percent of its operating budget on police. In smaller cities police tend to take a much higher percentage of the budget (not because they need more police, but because their budgets are so much smaller).

Spokane's budget also includes $370 million for "enterprise funds," which are funds that pay for themselves through the sale of services. In Spokane's case this includes water, sewer, garbage pickup, and a golf course. Not every city has a golf course. Another $310 million goes to "special dedicated funds," which includes streets, public works, debt service, pensions, and a lot of miscellaneous things that need to be done. Finally, $104 million goes to "internal services funds," by which city departments charge other city departments for services such as vehicle fleets, information technology, and accounting. This is much like the state's Department of Enterprise Services. By bundling these things together the city will save money because it gains leverage with outside suppliers.

To pay for this the city takes in $152 million in taxes. That includes $43 million (29 percent) from sales tax; $42 million (28 percent) in property tax; $38 million (25 percent) in public utility tax; and $26 million (17 percent) from a B&O (business and occupations) tax on private utilities. Many smaller taxes, fees, and other funds make up the rest. It doesn't all go in one large pot; the budget breaks down where every dollar comes from and where it will go. For example, arterial work is funded in part by $7 million in federal grants and $9 million in state grants. The bulk of the water department budget comes from $40 million in water sales and fees.

The sewer department takes in $56 million. The city solid waste utility takes in $47 million to pick up the garbage and $19 million to get rid of it.

Smaller cities tend to do similar things but on a smaller scale. Longview, in Cowlitz County, has about thirty-eight thousand people and covers a little over fifteen square miles. It became a city in 1924. Its budget includes $39 million in the general fund, of which $13 million (33 percent) goes for police and $9 million (23 percent) goes for the fire department. Special revenue funds take another $11 million, which includes street work at $5.2 million and the transportation benefit district at $2.9 million. That district was created to ensure funding for maintenance of city streets not covered by the arterial fund. Longview's enterprise fund reaches $57 million, with about half, $29 million, taken up by sewer and water service. Longview has a municipal golf course, but it also contributes more than $11 million to RiverCities Transit, the Cowlitz County bus system that the city first took over in 1975.

To pay for this the city expects to collect $29 million in taxes, including sales, property, utility, and B&O taxes. Another $1 million comes from licenses and permits; $2.5 million from intergovernmental funds such as state and federal grants; and $3.4 million from charges for services. That can include fire service fees for fire coverage outside of city limits, for example.

Now consider a much newer city, Covington, twenty thousand people tucked into six square miles in southeast King County. It incorporated in 1997. Newer cities typically incorporated long after special purpose districts had been created to provide services such as fire, sewer, and water to the areas that are now part of the city. Like several other cities, Covington contracts with the King County Sheriff's Department for police services. It also contracts with the Puget Sound Regional Fire Authority for fire protection.

Covington's budget includes $21 million in its general fund, plus $1.5 million for its street fund, and $10.5 million for surface water management. This is perhaps a bigger issue on the west side of the state where surface water runoff can be a problem and a major source of pollution for lakes, rivers, and the ocean. All those little drips of gas, oil, and whatnot from people's cars and homes add up; cities now try to take care of this by managing surface water runoff so as to minimize the impact. The biggest fund is $31 million for the Capital Investment Program Fund. At first glance one might be tempted to ask, "What are they building?" but this just shows how different cities slice the pie a little differently. The fund pays for improvements to bridges, streets, public buildings, water and sewer systems, and heavy equipment. Spokane and Longview, by contrast, folded some of this into their enterprise fund budgets.

In line with other small cities, Covington spends more of its budget on police—35 percent—than do larger cities. That number would probably be even higher if it did not contract for police service with King County. Covington also speaks to the advantages of living in a city instead of in an unincorporated area. In seventeen years the city has gone from zero parks to five and made numerous road improvements that might not otherwise have happened. The city also provides arts and cultural programming and operates and maintains the Covington Aquatic Center.

Covington's chief sources of revenue include sales tax, $4.5 million; property tax, $2.7 million; and utility tax, $2.3 million. Other, which includes real estate excise tax (a kind of sales tax), licenses and permits, and shared funds from the state, comes in at $3.1 million.

Overall, cities provide a basic set of services, with variations from place to place. Their sources of tax revenue are remarkably similar, with the B&O generally the one tax a city may choose not to have.

CHAPTER SIXTEEN

Special Purpose Districts

SERVICES WHERE YOU LIVE

Special purpose districts exist to provide one or more services such as water, sewer service, and education. They have elected boards of commissioners or directors, and they hire full-time managers to oversee the day-to-day operations. Sewer and water districts are funded from sales of their services; other districts may be funded by local property taxes and money from the state.

Such districts provide "localized services where they're needed, with a specialized focus," as one utility district official put it. They are usually formed by petition or resolution of county government, typically with a vote by the affected residents to approve the formation.

Common kinds of special purpose districts include school districts; port districts; utility districts, including water, sewer, and electricity; fire districts; transportation districts; public hospital districts; park districts; cemetery districts; and agriculture and environmental districts, such as irrigation districts and mosquito control districts, respectively. One could argue that we probably have too many of these governments. King County commissioner Ed Munro, way back in 1965, pointed out the inefficiency of having more than two hundred taxing districts in King County.[1]

Constitutional scholar and UW professor Hugh Spitzer agrees. "With local government, one of the problems is it is much too easy to create too many different kinds of local government," he said. "We have per capita in terms of the number of local governments, we are either number one or number two [behind Illinois]. It makes it easier to tax and it makes it easier to borrow. So we create a whole lot of entities, and the problem with that is it confuses voters. They have no idea where to go."

But while there has been some consolidation among local governments, don't expect them to go away. Organizations tend to find a reason to exist long past their pull date, and people do often value local control. Back in the 1980s, a failing water district in King County refused to join a larger, better funded water district next door until it literally ran out of water.

School districts run local schools. K–12 school districts in Washington employ around 118,000 people, including 64,000 teachers, educating more than 1 million students a year in 294 school districts across the state, from Aberdeen to Zillah. Seattle is by far the largest district, with more than 50,000 students. The Stehekin District in Chelan County has 4 students.

Schools in Washington are funded 68 percent by the state and 22 percent from local taxes. Another 7.8 percent comes from the federal government, with the rest from Other, including self-raised student body funds. Local taxes come from levies and bonds, approved (or rejected) by voters at the polls. Levies are supposed to be for special programs, but realistically school districts often have to use them in order to provide all the programs people say they want. Bonds are used for financing construction projects. The bonds are sold to investors, giving the district cash up front to buy land and pay contractors. The investors get interest payments over the life of the bond (typically twenty years) and get their initial investment back at the end. Both levies and bond issues add a little bit of tax to the property tax, a few cents per $1,000 of assessed value.

For most of the state's history, school levies had a turnout requirement, meaning that even if the levy passed, it would fail if enough people didn't vote. That led to plaintive campaigns by levy supporters to encourage people just to show up and vote, even if they voted no, so as to meet the turnout requirement. But if you opposed the levy, your best strategy was not to vote. This was fundamentally undemocratic, as not voting shouldn't be rewarded. Meanwhile, some school districts were failing levies despite getting 70 percent approval. The legislature finally did away with the turnout requirement in 2007.

Bonds, however, still have a validation requirement, plus they a need a supermajority to pass. A bond election means the yes vote has to equal 60 percent plus one, with 40 percent of the turnout of the last general election.

The logic of all these hurdles for school funding was that it would "force" the school districts to justify their expenditures to the voters. What in fact happened was that communities with aging populations tended to take the "I don't have any kids in school" view of bonds and levies and just say no. The other problem with levies is that they are based on the property values in the district. So a small, rural district, or a district that is largely residential—without a lot of valuable property like a Boeing plant—can't raise as much money as a district with large and valuable properties inside its borders. Legislative efforts to reduce the turnout requirement for bonds so far have failed.

School district governments are somewhat like council manager governments at the city level. Voters choose a board of directors, often in district-based elections. The four-year terms are staggered, with elections in odd-numbered years. School board members may get a small stipend for meetings, which might take place two to four times a month. Most are citizens with day jobs who think they can make a difference for their local schools. As with any kind of office, once in a while somebody gets elected who, for example, thinks public schools are a bad idea, but most seem to have their heads and their hearts in the right places. The board sets policy and approves budgets and hires and fires the superintendent. That's it. The superintendent oversees the day-to-day operations of the district; the board doesn't fire teachers or discipline the custodian. If the board doesn't like what the superintendent is doing, they can fire her or him.

PEOPLE IN POLITICS: CHERYL REID-SIMONS

Cheryl Reid-Simons thought the school district where her two sons were being educated could do better. So she ran for school board. "I saw the way the previous board operated and while it was not bad, it wasn't proactive either," she said. "They were somewhat removed from the community and were rarely at school events. I thought as someone who was involved in the schools, I could bring a fresh perspective and also be a good representative to the public."

In 2017 she was elected to the Fife School District Board of Directors. Reid-Simons stresses that schools really matter. "Public schools are the heart of any community, but especially a small one like Fife-Milton-Edgewood," she said. "Over the years I've seen boards in other districts taken over by ideologues who are interested solely in promoting a particular agenda, regardless of whether it was backed by educational research. I have also seen that as local newspapers die, there is precious little oversight of things like school boards and city councils in small towns and cities," Reid-Simons said. "So we desperately need to make sure they are filled with people with integrity. If not me, then who? I don't mean that to be self-serving. There are plenty of good, bright citizens of integrity. It's just that too few of them actually run."

Reid-Simons had earlier run for city council in a campaign she described as "half-assed." But she learned from the experience, first that "you can't fake enthusiasm," and second that she knew and cared a lot more about schools than she did about city government.

The school board, like the city council in a council manager form of government, hires and fires the superintendent, who manages the daily operation of the district. "It [the board] sets policy for the district and sometimes acts as a quasi-judicial body for appeals of various sorts. But let's be honest. Most policy—like 99 percent—is boilerplate drafted by WSSDA (Washington State School Directors Association). And if you're hiring and firing superintendents very often, you're doing something wrong," she said. "We are, for the most part, not professional educators," Reid-Simon added. "We don't and shouldn't try to make decisions about how professional educators do their jobs."

Being a Fife school director is strictly volunteer. But they have an important job, nonetheless. "I think one of the biggest roles is just to be the eyes and ears of the community. To be a liaison between members of the community and the schools. We don't get into personnel disputes, despite the calls I get when parents are mad at coaches, teachers, or principals."

Reid-Simon said the board has pushed for some changes, however. "For example, last year we decided that just saying that standardized test scores aren't a good metric of success wasn't good enough. You can't just say test scores don't paint the full picture—show us (and the community) what does," she said. "So we told the superintendent that he had to work with his building leaders and come up with other ways to measure success (or failure). He was a little taken back by that, but over the course of the year it's proven to be really valuable as we take a hard look at how we know we aren't failing kids," Reid-Simons said. "I think those sorts of exercises that essentially come from 'outsiders' help the professional educators step back and see things differently."

The board also pushed through a bond measure with the voters to help replace and renovate some aging school buildings. "We also have an increasingly diverse student population," she said. "That's not a bad thing—it's a good thing. But the challenge is in recruiting teachers of color so that those kids see themselves reflected."

People should remember that there's a process in whatever happens in the school district. "When things seem completely insane, there's almost always a reason," she said. "That reason usually has a law degree. It's not always a reason we can talk about because of privacy laws, but there's a reason. . . . People don't seem to understand that school employees have a right to due process. And sometimes that takes a while. And sometimes things are not what you've heard through the grapevine."

Lurking in the shadows of the state's educational system are nine educational service districts created by the legislature in the 1970s. Each district encompasses many local school districts. They replaced county-level intermediate school districts and now allow individual school districts to purchase goods and services collectively, saving them all money, as well as assisting districts with everything from curriculum development to implementing new state programs.

Public utility districts (PUDs) supply services to the majority of Washington counties, including electricity, water, sewer, and telecommunications. There are twenty-eight PUDs in the state, plus more than 170 water and sewer districts. They are typically run by elected boards of commissioners who hire and fire a general manager (and sometimes a general counsel) to oversee the day-to-day operations of the district.

Public utility districts are generally self-supporting—they charge people for the water, electricity, and telecom service they use, and they generally charge a flat fee for an ongoing sewer connection. The districts have a limited ability to levy taxes when they start up, but they basically thrive or dive on sales of whatever services the district provides.

Sewage treatment is one of the great marvels of modern life, as much as we may not like to think about it. Before sewage treatment, waste was pumped into rivers, lakes, and shorelines, with the theory that nature would take care of it. As populations grew, nature's answer wasn't always a happy one. For example, in the 1950s, cities around Lake Washington were pumping their sewage into the lake. This was fouling the lake, killing fish, making it unsafe to swim in, and slowly turning it into a swamp. Civic leaders began to campaign for a solution, and in 1958 voters created Metro, which stopped the dumping into the lake and also treated sewage flowing into Puget Sound. Sewage treatment is pretty simple: You pump the effluent into a large vat, where an impeller stirs it, and let bacteria do their thing. Doing that once is called primary treatment; pumping it into a second vat is secondary treatment. The water isn't drinkable, but it's much less nasty than when it started the process. That's the required standard in most of the country. Third-stage, or tertiary treatment, could render the water usable by people, but it's not in widespread use so far.

In other parts of the country, water and electric service may be sold by private businesses, usually operating as regulated monopolies. That's because utilities such as water, sewer, and electricity are regarded as natural monopolies—the market is effectively better served by one firm. This isn't hard to grasp: it wouldn't make economic sense for competing water companies to build separate lines to their customers' homes. If a private firm provides the service, they're usually regulated at the state level and must apply to change their electric or water rates. In Washington that is handled by the Utilities and Transportation Commission when a firm such as PSE or Avista, which sell electricity in King County and the Spokane area, want to raise or even lower their rates. But if the water or electricity is provided by a special purpose district, the elected commissioners ultimately decide the rates and the voters can throw them out if they don't agree. Rates are nearly always lower under public power and water—public utility districts don't have to satisfy shareholders or help the CEO make his bonus. Several states have attempted to deregulate their electric markets with promises of cheaper prices for consumers. The promises have been universally unfulfilled, and electric rates are higher in unregulated states for all but the biggest customers.

Nonetheless, public utility districts have to operate in the black—they have to show a profit. The profit is what pays for the upkeep of and improvements to their systems. They're not non-profit; they're not-for-profit—

they're not just in business to make money. In effect, their shareholders are the people who live in the district.

Public utility districts got their start because it wasn't economical for private firms to serve rural areas. Selling electricity in cities was easy—lots of customers, all nearby. Private firms were generally only interested in bringing electricity to the hinterlands if government was willing to pay them to do it.

In 1929 the Washington State Grange—the people who brought us the blanket primary and, much later, the top-two primary—sent an initiative to the legislature to allow communities to form their own public utilities. The legislature did nothing (the private power industry spent half of the twentieth century trying to convince people that public power was the first step on the road to socialism, communism, and Godless humanism, all the while illegally charging their customers for the cost of those campaigns). The initiative then went to the ballot, and voters approved the measure in 1930, and the law went into effect in 1931. RCW (Revised Code of Washington) 54 authorizes utility districts to "conserve the water and power resources of the state of Washington for the benefit of the people thereof, and to supply public utility service, including water and electricity for all uses." The law was amended in 2009 to allow utility districts to provide wholesale broadband telecom service.[2]

The first PUDs in the state were Mason County No. 1 and Mason County No. 3, approved by voters in 1934. (There was a brief campaign for Mason No. 2, but those folks eventually decided to join the campaign for No. 3.) Others followed throughout the 1930s, as voters opted to supply their own power. The PUDs generally bought the assets of whatever private power company was already there. They also got a boost by the federal Bonneville Power Act of 1937, which gave them preferred access to cheap hydropower from the Columbia River dams.

One of the challenges faced by all electric utilities, public and private, was rising postwar demand for power. With so many more people having access to and using electricity, demand soared after World War II and on into the 1960s. Power planners became concerned and created what amounted to straight-line projections for future demand. In 1953 the legislature authorized joint operating associations, and seventeen PUD and electric utilities, including Seattle City Light, joined to create the Washington Public Power Supply System, better known as WPPSS (eventually to be pronounced WHOOPS). It became one of the grand debacles in state history. The agency built a dam at Packwood near White Pass in 1964, during which there were hints that perhaps this new agency wasn't very good at project management. Then, with the specter of blackouts haunting their mutual vision, the agency decided to try to build five nuclear power plants at once.

After the war, the promise of nuclear power seemed nearly limitless. Experts predicted that power would be so cheap we'd be able to heat highways to prevent black ice. The possibilities looked endless. And it was clean! No smoke, no fish-killing dams, no muss, no fuss. And then when people began to build plants, all of the complications became apparent. To this day nuclear power is actually one of the safest options—if you could figure out what to do with the waste (spent nuclear fuel)—but also one of the most expensive. WPPSS's lack of construction management skills, constant rebuilding as safety standards changed, and simple economics eventually doomed much of the project. As electricity prices rose, consumers started finding ways to use less electricity. Public and private utilities eventually realized that it was literally cheaper to pay people to use less electricity (like financial support for insulation and retrofitting) than it was to produce new generating capacity.

WPPSS, since renamed Energy Northwest, eventually stopped construction on all but one of the five plants and defaulted on $2.25 billion in construction bonds. At the time it was the largest municipal bond default in the history of the country, and it led to a flurry of predictions that Washington was headed for a depression because no one would ever lend the state money again. This doesn't seem to have happened. Meanwhile, lawsuits were filed and settlements reached, and bond investors got somewhere between 10 and 40 cents on the dollar.

The state's newest PUD was formed in Asotin County in 1984. For much of its history, the county got its water from a private firm, Washington Water Power (since renamed Avista, because, you know, that's so much more descriptive of what they do). But in 1993 Avista sold the system to General Waterworks Corporation, a privately held firm. Usually when this happens the buyer has borrowed money to make the acquisition, and they have to pay back the loans. Even if the acquisition is self-financed, they expect to make a profit. Designating the subsidiary as the Clarkston General Water Supply Company, they started raising rates. Soon after, their customers started raising hell. Voters thought the local firm was charging too much for water. They approved the PUD in 1984 and it acquired the assets of the system. After a couple of years of lawsuits, it started service in 1987. It has since added electricity and sewer service to its portfolio.

PEOPLE IN POLITICS: RON NOWICKI

When Ron Nowicki retired, he needed something to do. Having worked in the power business, becoming a utility district commissioner seemed like an easy step. "I like to tell people that my wife put my name in for the open commissioner position because she didn't want me at home after I retired," he said. "While that is true, I was involved with the district for several years prior to my retirement on a citizen's advisory board and part of my consulting business was tangential to the district as I worked with Tacoma Utilities in both power and water."

Nowicki has been one of five commissioners with the Lakehaven Water and Sewer District since 2006. The district covers the city of Federal Way and small parts of surrounding communities. Lakehaven got its start as a sewer district in 1956, merging with a contiguous water district in 1987. The district covers 35 square miles and serves 112,000 people, with 400 miles of water line and 350 miles of sewer line, 22 wells, and storage for 31 million gallons of water. It pumps more than 10 million gallons of water a day, and its two sewage plants can treat an average of 14 million gallons per day.

Nowicki's engineering background has been very helpful in being a commissioner. "Most people do not realize the technical nature of the water and/or wastewater industry," he said. "But in my case I have a wider background. I spent a number of years in the electric utility industry so long-term planning and rates and finance are in the background. Also I have an MBA in finance and accounting and ran my own business for over twenty years so there is a business background. We need people with a wide background experience as Lakehaven is actually a midsized business."

Still, it's sometimes a challenge to get the district's residents—the people who effectively own the district—to understand how it all works. "The biggest challenge is having the general population understand the complexity and necessary function of water and wastewater service," he said. "The people in our service area own the district and that it is a very valuable asset."

To that end, the commission is "working on developing a major capital improvement program for the next ten to fifteen years, which should go on longer," Nowicki said. "This plan must also include personnel, financing, and operational options. Also I have been working for at least six years to get [the nearby] Highline Water District to buy water from us to save their ratepayers significant money."

Fire districts provide fire protection service to areas that are not or previously were not incorporated into cities. While many cities have their own fire departments, areas outside of cities need fire service of their own. And although some areas where fire districts were created later became cities, there's little sense in a city reinventing the fire truck wheel.

Washington has 344 fire districts and 12 regional fire authorities. Fire districts are organized like other special purpose districts: a board of three to five fire commissioners, usually elected to six-year terms, set policy and budgets and hire and fire a fire chief. The largest district in the state is Central Pierce Fire & Rescue, created from the merger of three different districts in 1996. It has 212,000 residents in eighty-four square miles, including the cities of Puyallup, Parkland, and Spanaway. For both financial and service reasons, fire districts have been consolidating in recent years, leading to fewer, larger departments.

That has led to the creation of regional fire authorities, which were first authorized by the state in 2004. They are created by a vote of citizens within the area of the proposed authority and may combine fire service for cities, traditional fire districts, port districts, and tribal nations—really, any entity that wants fire service. The fire authority's board must consist of elected officials, either elected by the citizens of the authority or by its constituent entities.

This can take some different shapes. Puget Sound Regional Fire Authority got its start as the Kent Regional Fire Authority in 2010, when citizens voted to combine the fire departments of Fire District 37 and the city of Kent. Kent's mayor at the time later said they just got tired of having the firefighters be the last employees to settle their contracts. Fire District 37 already provided fire service to people living in the city of Covington, and then the city of SeaTac decided in 2013 that it would be cheaper to contract with the fire authority than to run its own department. Finally, Fire District 43 from the Maple Valley area signed an interlocal agreement with the fire authority in 2018. The authority covers 108 square miles and provides service to 226,000 people, covered by sixteen fire stations.

This amalgam has resulted in a nine-member board—three voting members from the Kent City Council; three voting members from the Fire District 37 board of commissioners; and nonvoting members from the SeaTac and Covington City Councils and the Fire District 43 Board of Commissioners. Having an even-number of voting commissioners is uncommon, but in creating the fire authority, its founding members didn't want either the city of Kent or Fire District 37 to dominate the arrangement.

"Since the city of Covington had annexed into Fire District 37 when they incorporated in 1997, they had no direct voice on the District 37 Board of Commissioners," said Larry Rabel, division chief for assessment and planning for the fire authority. "During the discussions that created the Regional Fire Authority Plan to be submitted to voters, it was decided that the board should have a representative from Covington and the solution was to have a nonvoting member. While the Covington board member has not had a direct vote on the RFA's board, they have been a very important voice in many discussions and debates of the governance board. They are afforded all of the rights to speak and debate just as any other board member. This has allowed the direct interests of the city of Covington to be heard and considered at each vote. The city of SeaTac also has a non-voting member on the board as has King County Fire District 43 (Maple Valley Fire and Life Safety) as contract agencies."

Having an even number of voting members hasn't been a problem, Rabel said. "In fact, we feel that the even number of votes has been a strength of the RFA. This format seems to have brought both sides together. To date we have never been at an impasse and all of our major decisions have been 6–0 votes," he said.

Annexation to the fire authority would have required a public vote in SeaTac or District 43, whereas contracting with the authority could be accomplished by the city council or board of commissioners. In the case of SeaTac, contracting with the fire authority meant a higher level of service. A bigger fire department can add services more efficiently than a smaller department can. It will enjoy economies of scale since it will have less overhead and enjoy some leverage with suppliers as it will order more equipment and supplies at once.

The fire authority also has a slightly different funding model compared to traditional fire districts. While it gets part of its budget from the usual property tax levy, a big chunk of its financing comes from a fire benefit charge. This mechanism assigns a fee based on the property being covered, almost like an insurance policy. So a structure that houses a lot of flammable materials will be charged more than an empty concrete building.

All fire agencies and the people they serve benefit from the 911 system. Washington was an early adopter of the 911 emergency call system, augmented by the creation of Medic One in Seattle in 1970. At the time, King County had no paramedics, and ambulances still tended to be glorified station wagons that didn't provide much room to work on a patient. That changed when two physicians and the Seattle fire chief got together to create Medic One. With the cooperation of citizens, the system developed in a way that greatly reduced the number of deaths from cardiac arrest, as well as other serious injuries. It now covers the entire county via six different departments, supported by local taxes, and features fifty paramedics trained by experts such as physicians from Harborview Medical Center, one of the world's leading trauma centers. That also led to widespread training in CPR and broader general knowledge of lifesaving techniques among ordinary citizens. The end result is that while the national survival rate from cardiac arrest is 5 percent, in King County it's 60 percent.

Meanwhile, firefighters no longer fight as many fires as they once did. The raging infernos of Hollywood fare are increasingly rare. Sprinkler systems and other safety advancements mean that most fires are small and easier to contain. The big blazes you sometimes see on the news are relatively uncommon. Fire departments are increasingly adding social service officers to their menu since so many calls they get are from people who just need help.

"Eighty percent of our work is helping when you're sick or injured," said Capt. Jeff Bellinghausen of South King Fire and Rescue, which covers Federal Way and Des Moines. "We have people who call us a lot, sixty to ninety times a year," he said, people who are just having trouble with life. "We have a team of firefighters and social workers who respond to those folks." By narrowing this list down to the neediest people—thirty-eight individuals—and connecting them with social services, they "greatly reduced calls to the fire department," he said. The program may expand to all of King County in the future.

Like other special purpose districts, public hospital districts are created by local communities, in this case to provide health care services. The legislature approved creation of such districts in 1945; now there are fifty-eight in Washington State. Nearly half of all hospitals in the state are run by public districts. Forty-four districts feature full-on hospitals; others have created health clinics, ambulance services, urgent care clinics, and nursing homes to serve local residents. Many, though not all, are located in rural areas that might not otherwise have health-care options, and thirty-one are designated "critical access hospitals," specifying that they are crucial for rural health care needs.

Like other special purpose districts, they are governed by elected boards of commissioners, who hire and fire an executive to oversee the day-to-day operations of their facilities. They are largely funded by patient and insurance payments. Although they have taxing ability, usually only 2–3 percent of a district's budget comes from property tax.

PEOPLE IN POLITICS: MALL BOYD

Mall Boyd had the right experience and, as a recent retiree, had some time on her hands. "I retired as director of marketing at Wenatchee Valley Medical Center (now Confluence Health) in 2011 and in 2014 saw an article in the local Leavenworth weekly newspaper asking for interested parties to apply to fill a vacant seat on the hospital board," she said. "I applied and was selected and since then have been elected to my current term. It has been a good fit. A small critical-access hospital is very different from a large physician-owned multi-specialty clinic or hospital, but many of the issues facing health care are similar."

The five-member board for Chelan County Public Hospital District No. 1 provides strategic planning, quality control, and financial oversight. Its facility, the Cascade Medical Center, provides family practice and emergency care services. The center, on the edge of downtown Leavenworth, serves 1,200 square miles in North Central Washington, including the towns of Plain, Peshastin, and Dryden.

There are trade-offs to having an elected board overseeing the hospital, Boyd said. "It may be more challenging to create a board with a good balance of strengths or skills," she said. "For example, if the board is lacking expertise in a specific area such as in finance, they can't recruit a member with those skills unless someone resigns and there is an opportunity to make an appointment. An advantage is that a person with interest in the hospital, whose interest and expertise might not be known to the board, can be elected. Likewise, a board member that is elected is more readily accountable to the community."

As for all governments, finances remain a challenge, Boyd said. "Payer mix, health-care reimbursement, constantly changing payment models—one size doesn't fit all hospitals," she said. "And staffing—finding enough nurses, a problem nearly everywhere. We rely too much on agency nursing as we can't fill our open positions. Housing in Leavenworth is limited and expensive and Confluence Health's starting salaries are impossible for us to match and they are thirty minutes down the road," Boyd said. They also must often rely on part-time physicians to cover their emergency room. Nonetheless, Boyd said they are able to provide quality care. "We have excellent providers who provide high-quality care," she said. "There's usually not much of a wait in the emergency department.

"One doesn't need to see a specialist for everything," Boyd said. "Family physicians provide a broad range of services." Boyd said they do a lot of outreach to stay connected to the community, including a citizens advisory council, "generating ideas and providing feedback on what we're doing." The community in turn passed the latest emergency medical services levy, and the medical center has added a behavioral health practitioner and a chief clinical officer. The community seems happy with what they're doing, Boyd said. "Our patients usually give us rave reviews."

Washington has thirty-one irrigation districts, all in eastern Washington (there's one affiliate member of the Washington State Water Resources Association, located in Sequim). They have elected boards of commissioners, and members jointly fund development and operation of irrigation, mostly for agricultural purposes. Irrigation is a problem going back to the 1800s when Euro-Americans first started trying to farm in eastern Washington. A series of extraordinarily wet years in the late 1800s convinced farmers they could make a go of it. When the normal dry weather returned, it got a lot tougher. That led to the push for the Columbia River dams, among other projects, and citizens voted to create irrigation districts to pump water from the ground and the rivers.

It wasn't always an overnight success. The Greater Wenatchee Irrigation District was formed in 1922 but didn't start delivering water until the 1960s. It took a lot of work and a fair amount of federal help via Washington members of Congress before the project became a reality. Today it supplies water to 9,700 acres of agricultural land in the "apple capital of the world," as Wenatchee likes to be known.

Water issues are becoming one of the driving problems in the state. Water is needed for farming, for residents, for electric power, and for salmon. As the state's population grows, this gets trickier, especially as the forces of climate change keep shrinking the winter snowpack in the Cascades, which is crucial to water users in much of the state. Even on the rainy Olympic Peninsula water is becoming an issue. In 2013 the State Department of Ecology issued the "Dungeness water rule," which basically acknowledged that something had to happen to ensure enough water for both people and fish in the Sequim Valley. The Dungeness River is home to four species of protected fish, while Sequim's popularity as a retirement destination (it's actually quite dry there in the rain shadow of the Olympic Mountains) meant more residences and fewer farms. It's not an unsolvable problem, but it does require action. The Dungeness River Agricultural Water Users Association has been replacing irrigation ditches with underground pipes as farmers take up more efficient irrigation systems. Then again, less leakage from the ditches lowered the water table, meaning some well-water users had to drill deeper to keep their wells from running dry.[3]

Water districts in eastern Washington are facing similar issues. "We face many challenges within our district because of the different types of customers that we serve," said Shelbea Voelker, public relations coordinator for the Kennewick Irrigation District. "Many agricultural lands are becoming residential. With that, many new residential customers do not understand where KID's water comes from, our water rights, the amount of acres we serve, and our aging infrastructure that breaks and needs repairs as time progresses."

The president of the district's board of commissioners, Dean Dennis, first got involved "because he was a home owners association president (HOA) and felt there was no residential or urban representation on the board of directors at KID and wanted to know how KID operated and where the water was coming from," Voelker said.

The headwaters of the irrigation district reach back to the late 1800s, but the district got its formal start in 1917, created to help farmers water their land. The canals used today to draw water from the Yakima River were built with help from the U.S. Bureau of Reclamation in the 1950s. But now most ratepayers (what public enterprises often call their customers, since their customers also own the enterprise) live in residential areas, "and the change from farmland to urbanization is expected to continue into the foreseeable future," according to the district's website.[4] Farmers now have to order their water days in advance, while residential customers expect what we've all become used to—as much water as you want whenever you want it.

As Kennewick and the whole Tri-Cities area has grown, pressure on water resources has grown along with it. The first thing you find on the district's webpage is advice on how to conserve water. "Whenever a new customer comes into the district, customer service sends a welcome packet with information to help educate customers about the district," said Voelker, whose job was created specifically to connect with district residents about what's happening with their water and why. "To keep customers up to date on the status of their water, the GIS [geographic information system] analyst has developed our water status map that customers can access at any time to see if they are experiencing an outage and why," she added.

Getting people to conserve water is a major emphasis of the district. "We try to remind customers all throughout the water season to use water wisely and retrain their lawn to need less water, so their lawn can survive in times of drought," Voelker said. "We have created Retrain Your Lawn brochures, hold community events, post on our website and online, and run commercials on local TV stations to educate customers on this topic. Our land and water resources manager also tracks our water supply and presents the status of our water at every board meeting. We think it works to put the message out to our customer base. Some follow what we say and others continue to water whenever they would like to, but we do feel it's important to consistently remind customers."

Water supply will continue to be one of the major issues of our time. For example, water issues came to a head in 2016 with the state supreme court's ruling in *Whatcom County v. Hirst*, often known as "the Hirst decision," in which the court ruled that counties couldn't issue building permits if there wasn't enough water. To be precise, the court said building permits could not be issued unless counties demonstrated that new wells won't hurt stream flows or infringe on existing water rights. In some counties, such as San Juan—parts of which are very dry—this has long been true. If you can't demonstrate that you have sufficient water flow from a well on your property, you can't get a building permit. Supporters of the Hirst decision said it would preserve water for farmers, tribes, and fish, while opponents saw it as yet another blow to rural communities (and the building industry). In 2017 legislative Republicans blocked the capital budget at the end of session, holding it hostage to a resolution of the Hirst case. That finally happened in 2018, giving counties something of a workaround, but the underlying issue—not enough water—isn't going away.

Port districts grew out of Progressive efforts to reclaim waterfronts from private interests. Private firms developed the waterfront haphazardly, substituting short-term gain for long-term prosperity. For example, James J. Hill, developer of the Great Northern Railway, got covenants placed on Seattle waterfront land, which dictated that anyone who owned the land could only ship via the Great Northern. Waterfront cities on Puget Sound and the coast felt like they were being held back because of the unorganized and restrictive nature of private waterfront development. After several tries, the legislature authorized the creation of public port districts in 1911, and local voters made the Port of Seattle the country's first public port district later that year. The Port of Grays Harbor was created soon after, and other communities followed suit over the next decade. The ports quickly annoyed their private competitors by offering cheaper rates for moorage and cold storage. But legislative efforts to eviscerate the ports' newfound clout were overturned via referendum in 1916.

Washington now has seventy-five port districts, twice as many as any other state. Some port districts cover an entire county; others are much smaller. Grant County has seven different port districts within its borders and Kitsap has eleven. Naturally, many ports are on the water, but not all. Nearly all have industrial property available. Many have airports. Ports in eastern Washington may have rail lines and grain silos. Several operate hotels and restaurants.

When a shortage of railcars for grain cropped up in eastern Washington in the 1990s, the Port of Walla Walla bought eighteen grain cars and rented them to local farmers. After a railroad company abandoned the line in 1979, voters in Pend Oreille County voted to create a port district just to save a railroad. The Port of Pend Oreille exists solely to operate the Pend Oreille Valley Railroad, which serves firms in northeast Washington by shipping their goods to Newport, Idaho, where the cars are transferred to Burlington Northern Santa Fe. They have since added locomotive repair and painting facilities, which they do on a contract basis. It's one of the only port districts in the state that doesn't collect any property tax, subsisting on its freight and repair business.

Port districts around the state step in to make things work when others have given up. The Port of Coupeville on Whidbey Island stepped in to take over nearby Greenbank Farm when Chateau Ste. Michelle pulled out in the mid-1990s. The winery sold its Whidbey's Port from the site, along with other products, but didn't make enough money to satisfy its corporate parent. "The port purchased the property in 1997 and made the last payment in December of 2017," said port executive director Chris Michalopoulos. "The port is fully managing the property with its own staff and volunteers from the community. We have brought farming back with the Boots to Roots Veteran Farming Programming, Salty Acres Farms, Community Pea Patch, Greenbank Garden Club, and a bean producer, Lesedi Farms. We hold events in the historic barn and have one of the busiest event schedules in decades. The farm is doing well and progressing in many areas, though our need for maintenance is a constant." In short, they try to create and help enterprises that bring jobs and dollars to their communities.

"The role of a more typical WPPA [Washington Public Ports Association] port is to provide the infrastructure needed in a community that enables economic development while being respectful of the environment and the cultural character of the community," said John Mishasek, president of the

Coupeville Port Commission. "Our port is located in a national historic reserve with defined cultural guidelines plus many challenges that do not exist for other ports not based on an island, that is, inexpensive land for industrial park development."

Coupeville, with around two thousand people, was incorporated in 1910. With its 1905 wharf slowly falling apart, voters created the Port of Coupeville in 1966 to address that problem and others. In 1978 Congress created the Ebey's Landing National Historical Reserve, which includes all of the town and more than twenty square miles of surrounding land. Tourism is a major industry in the community, and the historic wharf is a big draw. It was repaired in 1986 and 1996, but the port is facing another renovation.

"The primary role of our port of improving the economic health of our community has been hampered by high maintenance costs of its assets and limited revenues from its assets," said Mishasek, who brought long business experience in the health care industry to the port commission when he was first elected in 2016. "Only after a change in 2015 to have direct management by the port of one of its properties has the port been able to create a positive financial cash balance. Prior to that change the port was barely hanging on and failing to do proper maintenance of its assets.

"With direct management of its Greenbank Farm property, the port has been able to clean up the facility, do proper maintenance of the farm's infrastructure, and provide the tenants with a better location for their businesses," he said. "Now the wharf is targeted for its delayed maintenance issues to be addressed."

Mishasek credited an interim executive director, Jan-Marc Jouas, for helping stabilize the port's finances and also with helping to recruit Michalopoulos, "who has helped the port to create positive relationships in the community, heal wounds from the nonprofit time period, and put solid business practices in place for our port to move forward in a professional manner. Cash reserves now exist for emergencies and for matching funds for grants."

The port gets about $400,000 from its property tax and another $230,000 in revenues from its properties, including nearly $40,000 in rent from the wharf. But it also gets Rural County Economic Development Fund grants, a nine-tenths of a cent rebate from state sales taxes collected in Island County, which can be used to help keep jobs or create new ones. That's good because it's going to take some cash to fix the wharf again.

"The wharf renovation will be costly, and significant funds, millions of dollars, need to be secured to accomplish this critical task. Our executive director has funding of the wharf renovation as his top priority as he continues to manage the day-in, day-out operations and staff," Mishasek said. "However, this special funding is supposed to sunset in 2035. While this sounds like a long time off, one needs to remember that repair and renovation at the wharf is a forever project, not a once every fifty to one hundred years," he added. "It is wood sitting over the water. The wharf is battered by winter storms and wind waves. A repair done today may need redoing in a year or two or three. Or less. Something at the port is always breaking or failing or leaking or blowing away in the wind or getting stolen or being damaged by vandals. That's the reality of having any real property, much less historic property that is over one hundred years old."

The wharf will have to be rebuilt, including replacing the old pilings, at an estimated cost of $1.2 million. Port officials may seek a higher property tax levy from voters, as well as the rural development grants. The port also is looking at developing fiber-optic capability on the island.

"The state legislature gave Washington ports the legislative authority in July 2018 to build dark fiber-optic wholesale infrastructure to be leased to ISPs [internet service providers]," Mishasek said. "By partnering with the city of Oak Harbor, the town of Coupeville, Whidbey Telecom, and Island County to have a CERB-funded [Community Economic Revitalization Board, a program run by the Washington Department of Commerce] planning study done, the port can investigate the reality of this type of infrastructure project.... The port could explore how it could be a partner in a public-private partnership for improving internet connectivity and over time have a new source of funds that pay for wharf repairs. Maybe," Mishasek said. But, he said, it will be worth it. "The historic wharf is an economic engine for the community as one of the most highly visited attractions in the area."

The port districts range from the tiny to the giant. The Port of Tracyton, established in 1929, lists its assets as "temporary restroom facilities, viewing bench, kayak rack, garbage receptacle, local area directory, breathtaking view." Tracyton is an unincorporated community near Bremerton. Like other ports in Washington, it is governed by an elected board of three commissioners.

The port once had a dock—the original reason for creating the district was to acquire the pier, which had been abandoned by two sawmills—but it's now gone, not having been maintained after a bridge was built nearby and the Mosquito fleet flew away. The port attempted to repair the dock in the 1950s, but nothing came of it. The port commission didn't actually meet from 1965 to 1993. In the late 1980s state officials recommended that the port be dissolved. One commissioner argued for dissolution of the port in the early 2000s, complaining that they were collecting taxes but not doing anything with the money. Ultimately officials farther up the food chain concluded that only the port could dissolve itself, and the commission majority did not favor that action. Citizens urged the port to continue. In 2011 the port attempted to annex some nearby land, but the voters there said no thank you. In 2014 they added the bench. More recently, port commissioners are planning to repair the kayak rack, which was damaged; to erect a shelter near the boat launch; and to shore up the bulkhead near the same.

On the other end of the spectrum is the Northwest Seaport Alliance, a cooperative agreement between the ports of Seattle and Tacoma. After years of poaching each other's shipping business, they finally buried the boathook and agreed that it made more sense to cooperate (which would mean no pressure to undercut each other's rates). "For almost one hundred years, we competed with the Port of Tacoma," said Eric Schinfeld, senior government relations manager for the Port of Seattle. "All we were doing was negotiating against our own region."

Together these ports are the third largest containerized shipping facility on the West Coast (behind Long Beach, California, and Vancouver, British Columbia) and the sixth largest in the country. Puget Sound is fortuitously well-located for access to Asia from the west and to the rest of the Americas in the east. Easy rail connections make it relatively simple to move shipping containers (those boxcar-like structures you see stacked up all over the Seattle and Tacoma waterfronts) from ships to trains and vice versa. State and local agencies in the 1990s put their heads and wallets together to create a "fast-freight corridor," so that trains leaving the ports don't have to stop for automobile traffic. Time, as they say, is money.

Between them, the two ports account for more than $12 billion in economic activity, supporting fifty-four thousand jobs and $4 billion in personal income. The twenty thousand direct jobs average $95,000 a year, meaning these are the coveted "family-wage" jobs. Top imports include machinery (including automobiles), furniture, plastics and rubber, and metals. Top exports include oil seeds (such as canola and mustard), prepared food, and wood. At one point Washington's second leading export after aircraft was hay (and it still ranks highly). Somebody figured out that you could fill otherwise empty shipping containers with hay pretty cheaply, sending it to cattle operations in Asia, where land is more precious and hay not as economical to grow.

The Port of Seattle's portfolio includes more than just containerized shipping at four deepwater marine terminals (which allow larger ships to dock). It also operates Seattle-Tacoma International Airport; three marinas; Fisherman's Terminal in Ballard, home of the Alaska fishing fleet; two cruise ship terminals in Seattle; the Bell Harbor convention space; and a foreign trade zone designation, which simplifies the import and export of goods. At more than four thousand acres, it is the second largest landowner in King County. It has its own police and fire departments. The airport alone generates more than one hundred thousand jobs, $7 billion in income, $22 billion in business activity, and $425 million in state taxes. The port says its mission "is to create good jobs here and across the state by advancing trade and commerce, promoting manufacturing and maritime growth, and stimulating economic development." All told, the port and its economic activities generate more than two hundred thousand jobs in King County. "We're a gateway for people and things to get in and out of Washington State," said Eric Schinfeld. "It's a billion-dollar business run by a government."

The port has five elected commissioners. They hire and fire an executive director, the person who is in charge of the overall operation of the district. The commissioners set policy and approve budgets.

For all its positive economic impact, the Port of Seattle is frequently cast as an evil empire in some circles. Local officials can be heard to say that the port is difficult to deal with and untrustworthy. Some voters have been frustrated when "reform" candidates get elected to the five-member Port Commission but think differently when they learn what the port actually does. Other critics ask why the port still collects a local property tax when other West Coast ports do not. Port officials reply that the port leverages property tax proceeds into activities that generate more jobs and income. One former local mayor opined that the port would generate more wealth by developing a waterfront more like San Francisco's, with housing and tourism as focal points. (Not necessarily the best idea: a working port isn't as pretty, but it generates many more good jobs.)

Perhaps the biggest source of flak for the port is one of its main operations, Seattle-Tacoma International Airport. Although the Port of Tacoma was an early contributor to the startup of Sea-Tac, it is run by the Port of Seattle. It is the thirtieth busiest airport in the world and eighth in the country. No airport with similar passenger numbers is as small as Sea-Tac's 3.9 square miles. It is served by more than thirty passenger airlines and a dozen cargo lines. It served nearly fifty million passengers in 2018 and moved more than four hundred thousand metric tons of cargo.

Seattle's first real airport was King County International Airport, better known as Boeing Field. The Port of Seattle built Sea-Tac in a then-less-populated area in 1944 after the military had taken over Boeing Field for the war effort. Commercial service commenced in 1947, and by 1971 scheduled commercial service had ended at Boeing Field. As the region grew, Sea-Tac got busier. It became clear by the 1980s that Sea-Tac was outgrowing its space, and then the skies got very cloudy.

Following lawsuits from impacted neighbors, by the mid-1970s the port had begun retrofitting homes and schools to decrease noise impacts and buying up properties that were too close to the airport to be effectively insulated. But that took time and still the noise bothered a number of the airport's neighbors. Once again we find a trade-off—the port's statutory mission to spur economic development versus homeowners' understandable longing for a little peace and quiet. (Before the port started insulating buildings at Highline College, where I teach, you could be on the ground floor of a two-story building, and if a jet were to fly over, all conversation would have to stop. You could not hear yourself, let alone anyone else.)

Port of Seattle officials proposed a third runway, which put local citizens and nearby governments in a tizzy, upset as they already were with the noise from jets taking off and landing. Coalitions were formed; lawsuits were filed. The fact that no airport expansion had ever been stopped anywhere in the United States did not discourage airport opponents from keeping up the fight. In the early 1990s a study group was formed to explore alternatives. The Flight Plan group, which included representatives from the four-county region, local governments, business, and environmental and labor groups, looked at alternatives for two years.

In the end alternatives were hard to find. Even without commercial service, Boeing Field is one of the busiest airports in the country. Commercial service could have been added to Paine Field in Everett, but all the Flight Plan representatives connected to Snohomish County were opposed to that. Service could have been added to McChord Air Force base in Pierce County, as there are lots of dual-use airports in the world, but Pierce representatives were opposed to that. The commission looked at alternative locations such as the Enumclaw plateau in southwest King County, but research revealed that the area is frequently subject to wind shear—unpredictable and forceful downward bursts of air that make flying a very risky proposition. People suggested moving cargo flights to Moses Lake, which has a large, less-used airport, but more than half of all air cargo moves in the bellies of passenger jets. Someone even proposed building a high-speed rail line from Moses Lake to Puget Sound. But the cost, aside from the relative inconvenience of a long train ride after a long flight, was $10 billion (about $17 billion in 2019), or more than building a new airport. In the end the commission concluded that the third runway was the least bad option. The Port of Seattle, which has no authority outside of King County, decided to go ahead and build a new runway.

In other parts of the country where there may be lots of available flat land, local governments have built new airports. But the Puget Sound region is land-constrained—the Cascades to the east and Puget Sound to the west. A Des Moines city manager once said to me, "They're land-banking in Toledo," as though that were a realistic option. Toledo, Washington, population eight hundred, is 106 miles and a two-hour drive from Seattle. That's the difference between people doing business in your town or not. Toledo is actually closer to Portland, Oregon, than it is to Seattle. There were certainly moments when one might have been tempted to ask, "If you're bothered by airport noise, why did you move near an airport?" But that usually doesn't go over so well. Then again, this happens as rural areas become more residential: people move near farms for a little rural splendor, then complain that the farms are noisy and smell bad.

The third runway opened in 2008. Port officials had promised that it would only be used during inclement weather, which quickly proved not to be true. Port officials claimed they never made that promise, but I was at meetings where they did. "Yes, somebody did say that," a port representative later admitted when I asked. Since then the airport has only gotten busier, and residents' complaints have resumed. Some say the port should change flight patterns to and from the airport, but while directives on landing and take-off heights could limit noise in some neighborhoods, the direction flights take is certain to impact somebody if not somebody else. In 2018, commercial service came to Paine Field in Everett, which is much more convenient for anyone living north of Seattle. In 2019 the legislature passed a bill calling for a fifteen-member commission to "review options and make decisions on potential sites for future aviation facilities."[5] The commission was to have eighteen months to identify two potential sites for new airports. In the land of process, that's as good as it gets.

SUPER-REGIONAL GOVERNMENTS

Rising population in the central Puget Sound area has produced its share of challenges and rewards. Growth is always a double-edged blade. On the one hand, a growing population tends to mean more jobs, more opportunities, and civic and cultural amenities. But it also means more traffic, more pollution, and higher housing prices. That has spurred the creation of a series of super-regional governments, which cross county borders to try to find regional solutions to problems that also cross county boundaries.

The Puget Sound Regional Council was started in 1956, with a few name changes along the way. It tries to plan for growth management, transportation, and economic development. Its latest plan is Vision 2040, which presumes that the region (King, Pierce, Snohomish, and Kitsap Counties) will have a population of five million people by then. This is not beyond the realm of possibility; four million people live there now.

The council includes eighty entities among its members, representatives of whom compose the general assembly. Member entities include the counties, cities within them, along with port districts, tribal governments, transit agencies, and other institutions and interest groups. The assembly meets annually to elect leaders and set a budget. It has a number of policy boards and committees, covering everything from freight mobility to special needs transportation issues. The council's $26 million budget is funded by a mix of federal, state, and local funds.

The council helps its members do a lot of planning, which keeps them in compliance with state and federal laws and also helps them get state and federal funding. Vision 2040, for example, suggests channeling all the expected growth into urban centers scattered across the region, some of which is already happening. "Centers, with a compact, walkable urban pattern tend to support more vibrant communities and better connections to transportation options," said Paul Inghram, growth management director for the council. "Since the 1990s there have been lots of successes around the region, like growth in downtown Seattle and Bellevue, downtown Bothell, and recent development in downtown Lynnwood."

Regardless of what you think of this, it's probably inevitable. As land becomes less available and more expensive, the only way to grow is up. Meanwhile, the council tries to help secure federal transportation funding and engages in long-term transportation planning for the region. It has also created an economic development plan intended to "sustain job growth and global competitiveness."[6] The council is already at work on the next plan, Vision 2050.

SOUND TRANSIT

Sound Transit (ST) is the regional transit agency for King, Pierce, and Snohomish Counties. It manages the ST bus system, Link Light Rail, and Sounder Commuter Rail, serving 40 percent of the state's population. Link Light Rail runs twenty hours a day, with an average of seventy-seven thousand daily boardings. The ST Express bus system covers twenty-eight regional routes, with bus rapid transit on the way. It will run from Burien through Bellevue up the eastside to Lynnwood. Sounder trains run on Burlington Northern Santa Fe tracks from Lakewood to Seattle and from Seattle to Everett. The system expected to carry more than fifty-two million passengers in 2019, up from forty-nine million in 2018.

Sound Transit is governed by an eighteen-member board of directors, drawn from elected officials in the three-county region, roughly proportional to their populations, plus the state secretary of transportation. Like other local government boards, it sets policy, engages in oversight of the system's operation, and approves budgets. Its $96 billion budget is funded by fares, property tax, sales tax, car tab fees, and a tax on car rentals. Overall, 66 percent comes from taxes; 14 percent from the sale of construction bonds; nearly 12 percent from federal grants and loans; 7 percent from fares; and 1 percent from interest earnings. Some 52 percent of that goes to ST's construction projects; 25 percent operations and maintenance; 16 percent to debt service (paying the interest on those constructions bonds); 6 percent to "state of good repair" (replacing equipment); and 1 percent in reserve. The agency has 3,800 employees.

Transit has an uneven history in the Puget Sound region. Voters have said no to transit multiple times, and some interests in the community are against anything but more roads. Voters said no to a widespread transit system in 1969. It would have cost $1.15 billion, or $8.2 billion in today's dollars. (Sound Transit's most recent expansion plan will cost $53.8 billion, so this would have been a relative bargain.) Perhaps even more galling is that by saying no, voters left another $730 million in federal funding on the table, meaning that in essence Atlanta got King County's transit system. Despite that, voters said no again in 1970.

People say they don't like transit because it is publicly subsidized, but realistically there is no transportation system on earth that isn't. Even automobiles are heavily subsidized, from the oil depletion allowance tax credit that keeps gasoline cheap in the United States to public construction and maintenance of roads and bridges and traffic systems.

And then there is the ever-present local inertia. In the early 1990s, Burlington Northern, owners of a rail line that runs from Tacoma to the Port of Seattle, said they could accommodate commuter trains without compromising their freight business. A week-long test run in the mid-1990s was packed every day, while studies continued. And continued. And were done again. As one local mayor put it, "For the price of these studies, we could have had this line up and running." Then again, as a Bellevue official said at one meeting, "Why would we want light rail to South King County? Nobody lives there." This was quite a surprise to those of us who did.

Voters in King, Pierce, and Snohomish Counties finally said yes to transit in 1996, and ST began operating buses and trains in 1999. The agency was in danger of derailing for several years: new taxes are never popular, federal funding was at times uncertain, and overlaying a transit system on top of a fully developed urban area turns out to be really expensive. Management was uneven, and a lot had to be corrected. Throughout its history, residents in areas that Sound Transit's light rail system hasn't yet reached have complained that they're paying taxes and still don't have service. (Remember, this is 'Murica. We want it all, we want it now, and we want it for free.)

Eventually, voters said no, yes, and yes to two more ST expansion plans, which will eventually connect much of the three-county area via light rail, buses, and the Sounder commuter line from Everett to Tacoma.

Now Sound Transit says its trains are on time 90 percent of the time, and the money is all accounted for. "ST is one of the most audited public agencies in the state," said Chelsea Levy, director of government relations for the agency. They have the best credit rating of any transit agency in the country, meaning they will pay less to borrow money to fund construction projects. Most recently, the system has suffered from a shortage of fare funds, as it's pretty easy to get on the train without a ticket, and fare enforcement is spotty at best.

The Puget Sound Clean Air Agency was created by state law in 1967. It covers King, Pierce, Snohomish, and Kitsap Counties, home to 4.1 million people. Their job is to monitor air quality; educate folks about clean-air choices (and help them make changes); and follow and enforce clean air regulations. It has about a $12 million budget, coming from federal, state, and local funds, plus some fees. The agency's board includes county executives and other government officials, along with ordinary citizens; an advisory council that includes representatives from business, education, tribal nations, ports, and environmental groups, plus a professional staff of seventy-five to do the work. A lot of their work is trying to get people to change their behavior—fewer backyard bonfires, idling their cars less, even fueling up at night since cooler temperatures mean releasing less ozone-depleting gases into the atmosphere. One of the challenges presented by climate change is that a big contributor is non–point source pollution—it's no one thing that's at fault. A polluting factory is easy to fix; millions of automobiles, each one adding a bit to air pollution, is a more difficult problem to address. Whatever you think of climate change (and you should think about it a lot, as anybody who's not effectively on the payroll of the traditional energy industry understands that it's real and largely manmade), air pollution is bad for the environment, including people's health.

CHAPTER SEVENTEEN

Tribal Governments

NATIONS WITHIN THE NATION

As noted earlier, Washington State has twenty-nine federally recognized tribes. They are effectively states within the state and nations within the nation. Enrolled tribal members have dual citizenship. Native Americans pay federal income taxes, as they are citizens like anybody else. In states with income taxes, tribal members don't have to pay taxes on income earned on the reservation but do for income earned off it. The tribes themselves generally don't pay taxes on tribal incomes and, in most states, don't pay sales tax on items sold on the reservation.

Native Americans were here long before Euro-Americans showed up. Although the traditional grade-school version of history is that North and South America were sparsely populated when Europeans arrived, more recent scholarship indicates that there were in fact substantial states across the two continents before disease decimated their populations.[1] In the Northwest, the economy east and west of the Cascades was built on salmon, of which there were a lot, and which Native people were very good at catching and preserving, supporting a high population density before diseases introduced by Euro-Americans took their toll.[2]

Nonetheless, Native Americans helped keep the first Euro-American settlers alive. In return settlers often treated Natives with "contempt and hostility."[3] As with the rest of the country, as the Euro-Americans arrived they banished the tribes to reservations, which were not the best land available. They were promised, via treaty, the right to their usual catch of salmon, and to fish, hunt, and gather in their usual places. The treaties were rapidly and increasingly ignored, and even more land was taken than had been first agreed upon. Some tribes fought wars to try to preserve their claims to the land, but they were outmanned and outgunned.

Today the tribes range from the seventy people who live on the Shoalwater Reservation on Willapa Bay to the more than ten thousand on the Yakama Reservation, and from the 12 acres of the Jamestown S'Klallam on the Olympic Peninsula to 1.4 million acres of the Confederated Tribes of the Colville Reservation (which comprises much of Okanogan and Ferry Counties). Today's tribal nations were somewhat forcibly amalgamated from hundreds of existing tribes and languages. For example, the Muckleshoots came from the Duwamish and the Upper Puyallup people, "Muckleshoot" having been their name for the prairie where the reservation is now centered.

In 1854 and 1855 territorial governor Isaac Stevens negotiated treaties with two groups of Puget Sound-area tribes (the Medicine Creek and Point Elliott treaties), with the tribes giving up land in exchange for reservations and traditional harvesting rights in the area. He then crossed the mountains and negotiated with two groups of Columbia and Snake River Basin tribes. More land was promised to the tribes than was ever delivered, and the tribes were left with very little.

The story only gets worse. Beginning in 1860 on the Yakama Reservation, the federal government established the first Indian school, by which generations of young Native Americans were to be taken from their families and sent to boarding schools in order to "civilize" and assimilate them. Students were barred from speaking Native languages and were sometimes beaten if they did.[4] Assimilation wasn't really aimed at making Native Americans part of the fabric of the country, however; it was pursued with an eye to reducing Natives' desire for land, leaving more for Euro-Americans.[5] Of course, even for those students who tried to make it work, they were generally not accepted into white society, on top of the disruption and destruction this visited upon Native American families and culture. (If you're tempted to think this is just a historical artifact, this continued into the 1970s. A few such schools apparently still operate.)

In the 1880s the government began a program of allotment, in which tribal members were given parcels of land and other reservation lands were sold off, all in an effort to take more land from the tribes. The allotments were typically too small for someone to make a living on. Some reservations were completely allotted. Many tribes eventually fought the uphill battle of buying back their land.

Native Americans, the people who were here first, didn't even become U.S. citizens until 1924, when Congress passed the Indian Citizenship Act. Nonetheless, the Washington State constitution barred Native Americans who didn't pay taxes—basically those living on reservations—from voting. It took until 1935 for the state attorney general to note that everybody pays some kind of tax and hence everybody should get to vote.[6]

For many years government didn't ever seem to feel it had done enough to hurt Native Americans. At various times, traditional ceremonies were banned; plans were launched to take reservations away from tribes; and frequently the federal Bureau of Indian Affairs tried to dictate how Native Americans would live. Ostensibly, the Indian Reorganization Act of 1934 was intended to end assimilation as a policy and to serve as a sort of New Deal for the tribes. The law was supposed to let Native people manage their land and mineral assets, as well as restore self-government to the tribal nations. It was a start, but it didn't work quite as planned. Economic opportunities for tribal people were still limited. Among other things, the act said that tribal government must follow a prescribed federal model. In 1953 Congress adopted a "termination policy" that sought to end all reservations and tribal governments. This was finally reversed in 1970, and in 1975 Congress passed the Indian Self-Determination Act, which "gave tribes more power to govern themselves."[7]

The tribes finally caught a break in 1974. Those old treaties from the 1850s included the right to fish in their "usual and accustomed places." This lasted into the 1880s; for the first few decades, Native Americans did most of the fishing because they were so much better at it. But eventually Euro-Americans took over that industry too, leaving many tribal members without a way to make a living.

Following protests in the 1960s, including fish-ins that led to arrests, a U.S. attorney sued the state of Washington for failing to follow the treaties. Federal judge George Boldt ruled that the treaties meant the tribes had a right to 50 percent of the catch, a decision upheld by the U.S. Court of Appeals and the U.S. Supreme Court. Although the issue continued to be litigated and argued about, in the end Native Americans got to catch more fish.

The second big change also came in the 1970s when the U.S. Supreme Court unanimously ruled that states could neither tax nor regulate activities on reservations. That opened the door to Native American gaming operations, beginning with bingo halls and eventually leading to casinos. Despite frequent state actions to shut down these gaming operations, subsequent court decisions established Native American sovereignty relative to the states, leaving only the federal government to regulate their activity. In 1988 Congress adopted the Indian Gaming Regulatory Act, which further defined tribal sovereignty but also compelled state-tribal compacts, in effect forcing the two sides to talk about what could be permitted. In some states, state governments have confiscated gaming revenues. Fortunately, this didn't happen in Washington. Native American and federal conceptions of sovereignty still differ however. Sovereignty means that a government has the right to rule and is the supreme authority within its borders. While Native tribes regard themselves as sovereign, both by treaty and by having been here first, the federal conception seems to imply that they're sovereign to the extent that Congress says they're sovereign.

Gaming at last gave many tribes a chance at economic opportunity. Across the country 283 tribes are running 460 gaming operations, generating $32 billion in revenue in 2017. The influx of cash has been a great benefit to many tribes who have been able to leverage that money into jobs and opportunities for tribal members. The success of individual gaming operations varies by location. A 2015 study found that 6 percent of Native casinos brought in more than $250 million each, whereas 20 percent made less than $3 million.[8] Washington's tribes operate thirty-five casinos in the state, although not every tribe has a casino.

Native Americans have the misfortune of being the poorest minority group in the country.[9] A 2022 report found that Washington tribal members made less than half the income of other state residents; were three times as likely to be unemployed; and were four times less likely to have finished college.[10] It's not hard to see why. The historical reduction of tribes to reservation status effectively limited what tribal members could do for a living. It was as though an outside force had come into the country and told Euro-American farmers they could no longer farm their land. And by the way, we don't want you around much anyway. Given that set of circumstances—loss of land, loss of traditional occupations, and general exclusion—economic opportunity appears to have been one of the great challenges of Native people, a fact reflected by the number of tribal governments that are now called business councils.

For many tribes the gaming industry has provided some initial leverage by which tribal nations can provide employment opportunities for tribal members, plus develop other industries to offer opportunities for tribal citizens. The impact in Washington State has been substantial. A 2012 study found that tribal economic activity had contributed $3.5 billion to the state's economy, including $2.4 billion in goods and services purchased; $1.3 billion in wages and benefits; $259 million in capital spending; and $267 million in state and local taxes paid. Of the more than twenty-seven thousand tribal employees, eighteen thousand were not tribal members, and several tribes are the largest employers in their counties. Tribes can point to millions in contributions to charities and to support various state and local projects, including $6.5 million in community contributions and $7.8 million in charitable contributions. The tribes also have put a lot of effort and money into fish hatcheries and restoring fish habitat.[11] The Kalispel Tribe, for example, working with the state's Department of Fish and Wildlife, has spent more than a decade working to eradicate the northern pike, an introduced species that threatens salmon in the Columbia River system.[12]

As the economy recovered from the Great Recession, the tribes' enterprises prospered as well. A 2017 study found that the tribes employed more than thirty thousand people in Washington, making them collectively the eighth largest employer in the state and paying more than $1.5 billion in total compensation. Seventy percent of those workers were not tribal members, and yet incomes for tribal members living on reservations rose by 30 percent from 1990 to 2017. Tribes invested more than $374 million in enterprises, facilities, and other infrastructure. Together, they purchased $2.8 billion in goods and services, nearly all off-reservation. Tribal activity generated more than fifty-five thousand jobs, producing $6.6 billion in economic activity in the state and $1.2 billion in state and local taxes.[13]

For example, the Makah Tribe created the Neah Bay Chamber of Commerce, representing local tribal and nontribal businesses, and paved the four-mile-long road out to Cape Flattery, the northwestern most point of the continental United States.[14] This may seem like a small thing, but making that road easier to drive encourages tourists who want to say they've been there. Tourists tend to stop and spend money, which tends to be good for the economy.

PEOPLE IN POLITICS: CECILE HANSEN

Cecile Hansen has spent most of her life trying to get the federal government to acknowledge the sovereignty of the Duwamish Tribe. The Duwamish—"the people of the inside," a reference to their location inside Elliott Bay—were the among the first people of Seattle; Chief Sealth, for whom the city is named, was a Duwamish, and Hansen is descended from him.

Now there are around seven hundred enrolled tribal members, up from five hundred in 2004. "They must be having babies," Hansen said.

Hansen has been tribal chairwoman since 1975, making her perhaps the longest-serving public official in the state. Like many officials, she didn't set out to be a leader. She grew up in Burien in a working-class family, got married, and had a family of her own. "I was minding my own business," Hansen said. "I loved taking care of my family, and my husband said I didn't have to work.

"My brother was fishing on the Duwamish with a bunch of Indian guys [an action that could land one in court, if not jail]," she said. "One day he was irritated and he was mad. He said, 'You know what? You've got to get involved.'" Hansen started attending meetings of the tribal council, working with then-chairman Willard Bill, and going to meetings with the Department of Fisheries with her brother. "He was fighting for fishing rights," Hansen said. "And the following year they had a meeting and they elected me chair."

Since then Hansen has helped lead the fight to get federal recognition for the tribe. The Duwamish were one of the original treaty tribes. They were promised a reservation in what is now West Seattle, but then they were told they had to relocate across Puget Sound to the Suquamish Reservation. Some went; others said no, as the Suquamish hadn't always been their friends. "It wasn't big enough and there wasn't enough food," Hansen said.

Some Duwamish joined the Muckleshoots, others the Tulalips. Many stayed in Seattle, hanging on how and where they could, several times coming frustratingly close to getting their own reservation. They drafted a constitution, still in effect, and created their first tribal council in 1925. With Hansen as chairwoman, they collected evidence to prove that they were a distinct nation and worthy of recognition, then petitioned the government once again for treaty status. The Bureau of Indian Affairs said no again in 1996, before the Clinton administration finally said yes on its last day, January 19, 2001. Two days later the Bush administration rescinded the recognition.[15] A total of four Washington tribes had their petitions denied during the Bush years.

In the Point Elliott Treaty of 1855, the tribe gave up fifty-four thousand acres, land that became the city of Seattle. In 1971 the federal government gave one thousand tribal members $64 each for the land. Hansen said that's not enough. "You give up fifty-four thousand acres and we're treated like foreigners," she said. Meanwhile, the Seattle School Board decided in 2019 to not include the idea of Duwamish sovereignty in its state-mandated Native American school curriculum.

Nonetheless, the tribe has not stood still. They established a social service agency to help tribal members and they have worked with other groups to restore the Duwamish River, heavily polluted from industrial use. In 2009 they opened a longhouse near the river, the first traditional longhouse built in Seattle in more than one hundred years.

Hansen also spent fourteen years as chair of the Small Tribes of Western Washington, a group that provides services and support to several tribes west of the Cascades. Recently her granddaughter joined the group's board. "I was delighted that she wanted to learn something," Hansen said. "I hope that she will hang in there for a while."

And the tribe keeps up the fight for recognition, in Congress and in the courts. Recognition would mean federal assistance for tribal members and the chance of reservation land, a key to preserving the tribe's culture, identity, and fishing rights. Recognition is not just about the economic opportunity it could offer, Hansen said; it's also about being acknowledged as a separate nation worthy of formal status. "Every Indian tribe, when signing a treaty with feds, should be rightfully acknowledged and recognized by signing off a treaty," she said. "But the BIA and government were 100 percent phony and played that card. They did not honor their part by taking our land, some fifty-four thousand acres. We have been treated awful bad."

And yet, they persist. "We are still here," Hansen said. "I told them [the tribal council] many years ago, if they give us recognition, I'm going to call them all together and tell them they need to elect a chair—to deal with the federal government."

STATES WITHIN THE STATE

Every reservation overlaps other governments, both counties and cities. This produces an environment where it could be fair to ask, "Who's in charge?" It appears from the outside that both tribal governments and local governments often make an effort to find common ground. "Our local tribal governments work with us on some issues and less so on others," said Whatcom County executive Jack Louws, whose county includes both the Lummi and the Nooksack nations. "As sovereign governments they have their own goals and objectives and those at times don't align with the county's. We strive to have good relationships even when we disagree and usually find a way to come to terms on issues."

Whatcom County councilman Todd Donovan said relations between the county and the tribes are "vastly improved . . . in the past decade vs. say the 1990s but could be better. A member of the Nooksack Tribe was elected and served in the early 2000s (he quit to become Nooksack chair), and a former chair of the Lummi Nation business council served on the [county] council last year.

"Water and access to tribal lands for our ferry and other facilities are challenging issues," Donovan said. "I think the tribes may see higher levels of government and courts as being an alternative to the county on advancing their interests with water. We try to invite them to have representatives on lots of advisory committees (probably not enough); sometimes they participate. They seek government-to-government relations, not just advisory roles, which I appreciate."

The state has taken some steps to acknowledge both the tribes' sovereignty as well as their importance in the overall picture of government in the state. As the state's centennial neared in 1989, a group of tribal leaders and officials from the Washington governor's office began to meet. With input from people all over the state, they forged what became known as the Centennial Accord, which acknowledged that the state would respect the sovereignty of tribal nations. Sovereign states are the ultimate authorities within their own borders, and their neighbors respect those borders. The accord put tribal nations on a stronger footing since their relations with the state were now government to government. The agreement was reaffirmed and expanded in 1999, with another state-tribal summit planned for 2019.

Since 1969 the state has had some version of the Governor's Office of Indian Affairs, which serves as a liaison between state government and the tribes. It also works to educate state officials about tribal nations and their people. The current director, Craig A. Bill, has been in that position since 2005 and is a former director of intergovernmental affairs for the Lummi Nation in Bellingham. He is an enrolled member of the Swinomish Tribe in Skagit County. In addition, nearly sixty other state employees, covering more than three dozen different state agencies, are designated as tribal liaisons.

It's still not a perfect arrangement. While tribes have civil jurisdiction over members and nonmembers alike on reservation lands, tribal criminal authority doesn't often extend to nontribal members, even when they're on tribal land. Tribal police forces can now be certified just as nontribal officers are, and there is some cross-deputization between county sheriffs and tribal police. But if a nontribal member commits a crime on tribal land, they still end up in the nontribal legal system.

The two sides—state government and the tribes—have continued to try to develop their relationship. In 1999 tribal leaders and state officials formalized the Millennium Accord, which called for further cooperation and consultation on issues of mutual concern while maintaining recognition of the tribes' sovereign status. This was to include education of young people on the history, role, and importance of Washington's tribes.

In 2004 the accord was expanded to address relations with non-Washington tribes that have treaty rights within Washington. In May 2019 state attorney general Bob Ferguson said that his office would henceforth obtain "free, prior, and informed consent" before doing anything that directly affects tribes and their lands, rights and sacred sites. He also promised to engage in "meaningful consultation" to resolve disputes between the state and tribes. Ferguson said he would seek legislation in the 2020 legislative session to formalize the policy.

A number of tribal officials welcomed the announcement. "Today is a day to celebrate," said Frances Charles, Lower Elwha Klallam chair, on the day of the announcement. "Attorney General Ferguson made a meaningful and historic step towards recognizing and honoring the full sovereignty of Washington's Tribes."[16]

"Through his actions today, Attorney General Ferguson has listened to, learned from, and followed through on the advocacy of countless Native American leaders nationwide and Indigenous leaders globally who have defended the sovereignty and rights of their peoples," said Quinault Indian Nation president Fawn Sharp.[17]

BUILDING BRIDGES: THE TULALIPS AND MARYSVILLE

An example of how things can work is the Tulalip Tribes and the city of Marysville in Snohomish County. The twenty-two-thousand-acre Tulalip reservation is just west of Marysville. The tribe has 4,900 registered members, descended from the Skykomish, Snoqualmie, Snohomish, and other tribal groups who signed the Point Elliott Treaty in 1855. The Tulalips' historical range was more than half a million acres but was whittled down to 22,567 acres for the reservation, making it the fifth largest in the state. At one point the entire reservation was broken up for allotment until the Indian Reorganization Act of 1934 restored all tribes' right to self-government. The Tulalips wrote their first constitution in 1935 and elected their first board of directors in 1936.

The Tulalips have lived on the eastern shores of Puget Sound for thousands of years. Today they credit their ancestors' foresight and judgment for their current prosperity, which has seen them become an economic powerhouse in Snohomish County.[18]

The Tulalip Tribe has a seven-member board of directors, including a chair. They are elected by tribal members to serve three-year terms. Tribal government also includes managing directors for business operations, regulatory affairs, community enrichment, and health services. "Tribal governments are just another form of government," said John McCoy, state senator and former Tulalip tribal official. "They have the leg up of being mentioned in the U.S. Constitution. Consequently our sovereignty and all that is established, and because of treaties, treaties being the rule of law, that further solidifies their position as a government. Being a sovereign, they get to dictate how they operate.

"When you peel all of that back they're just like any other government," he said. "They've got social services, law enforcement, fisheries, and court systems, all that. They are what they are."

Marysville has been a city since 1891. Like a lot of cities in Washington State, it grew slowly over the next century until a spate of annexations increased the town's area and population. Now a city of more than sixty thousand, it has a mayor-council form of government.

As with many things that happen in government, it took one person with a vision for something to happen, and it was one of the city's mayors who worked to established positive relations with the tribe: the late Dennis Kendall, who served as mayor from 2003 to 2010. "As soon as he became mayor, he really turned around the relationship with the Tulalip Tribes. He figuratively built a bridge that exists to this day," said Bob Bolerjack, former editorial page editor for the *Everett Herald*.

"He understood our history and our future were inextricably bound together," said Mel Sheldon Jr., who was the Tulalip tribal chairman during part of Kendall's tenure. "We were able to develop a dialogue that was inclusive rather than exclusive. We all owe Mayor Kendall our gratitude."[19]

"There would be no relationship if it wasn't for Dennis," said Senator McCoy. "Him moving into the mayor's seat made a dramatic change in progress."

Kendall's successor agreed. "The relationship improved greatly under my predecessor," said Marysville's most recent mayor, Jon Nehring. "Prior to that things were a little rocky." Mayor Nehring said that now the city and the tribe meet regularly. "We meet with them at a government affairs committee level quarterly, staff and leaders from both cities," he said. "That's kind of the formal meeting. I'm in contact with somebody on the [tribal] board on a fairly regular basis. There's coordination on an informal level and on a formal level," he added. "This has been going on for quite some time."

This had led to joint efforts on salmon habitat restoration, transportation, public safety, and economic development. "They have their own priorities," Nehring said of the tribe. "We try to complement that. We've had a number of hotels pop up around our city. So we have a pretty robust hotel business here, same thing with restaurants, also retail development. So we kind of complement each other."

These businesses are driven by spillover from the Tulalips' substantial retail and casino development. The city does not get sales tax revenue from Tulalip businesses but doesn't see that as a problem. "We don't look at it as lost revenue," Nehring said. "We've tried to be very strategic about courting and recruiting the type of businesses that complement that. I think we've done a good job at that. Our sales tax base is very strong.

"The economic success [of the tribe] has really lifted them," the mayor said. "It's an overall positive story for the north [Snohomish] county here."

The tribe now employs 3,500 people, with two-thirds employed in tribal business enterprises. Those include the Tulalip Resort Casino, Quil Ceda Creek Casino, Tulalip Bingo, Leasing, Tulalip Broadband, Salish Networks, Tulalip Data Services, Tulalip Liquor & Smoke Shop, and Quil Ceda Village.[20] The village, the only federally chartered city outside of Washington DC, is one of the jewels of this collection, at least in terms of economic development. It hosts more than 150 businesses, including a Wal-Mart, a Cabela's, and a collection of premium outlet stores. It is one of the largest employers in Snohomish County. The tribe developed freeway interchanges for the site, along with water, wastewater, and telecommunications infrastructure.

"It began with me discussing with the attorneys on what type of structure should the Quil Ceda Village have," said McCoy, who was the manager of the development for several years from its inception. "If we were to function, we needed to provide the same services whether we're a municipality or not. We didn't want the limitations of being a political subdivision of the state. It was to maintain our sovereignty and be organized under the federal charter."

The Tulalips established Quil Ceda, the first tribal municipality in the country, in 2001. The village is governed by an elected three-member council, with a village manager, a village clerk, a village attorney, and fifteen administrative departments. The state imposes sales tax on activities in the village, leading the tribe to lobby for the right to collect its own share of local sales tax. Non-Indian state legislators responded that for that to happen, the village should become a regular Washington city and be subject to state law. The tribe has since sued the state over the tax issue.

McCoy said the key to having good relationships with other governments and businesses was "showing that Tulalip is a responsible citizen of the community and behaves in a way that they can understand what we're doing," he said. "We put a lot of transparency in. All the processes, they're all on the website. If someone wants to lease, the process is there to follow. Then people said, 'Oh, they're just like any other government.'"

McCoy said that the tribe also had the good fortune of a strong location near Interstate 5. "There's not many tribes can do a Quil Ceda Village," he said. "The reason the village is successful is it's rural abutting urban. The rest of the tribes are pretty remote. Or if they're like us, due to one-hundred-years-ago local jurisdictions already encompassing reservations in such a way that hinders them from growing. It depends on the circumstances," McCoy said. "I know a couple of tribes explored this. After they did their due diligence, they found they didn't have the same circumstance that we did."

TRIBAL GOVERNMENTS IN PRACTICE

Tribal governments aren't quite the same as nontribal governments. Historically, tribal government tended to be more deliberate and consensual. In some tribes it was traditional to elect separate chiefs for war and for peace, and typically a chief did not have autocratic or dictatorial powers. This presented challenges when negotiating treaties; a chief could have been a very influential person for a tribe, but not necessarily in a position to speak for the whole tribe.

Tribes today generally have elected councils and usually some form of elected chair. Some tribes, like other local governments, have appointed executive directors. Voting in tribal elections is limited to enrolled tribal members, which is not different from other governments in Washington State—a person doesn't get to vote for city council unless she or he lives in that city. Tribal governments may have special committees to oversee different parts of tribal operations. This points to a key difference from other local governments: tribes can start business enterprises, which local governments in Washington State generally can't do.

Overall, the form and practice of current governments appear to attempt to reclaim and preserve the earlier approaches of tribal governments, featuring efforts at being deliberative and seeking consensus in decision-making. "Ha!" was the response of one tribal leader when asked if that was true. Although, as with all governments in Washington, the great majority of people in tribal governments are ordinary citizens who are trying to make a difference for their communities, at the end of the day they're only human. Even good people sometimes disagree, and nobody's perfect.

YAKAMA NATION

The first example of tribal governments in Washington is the Yakama Nation. Formally, the Confederated Tribes and Bands of the Yakama Nation, the 1.4 million acres of the reservation stretches from Mt. Adams (Pahto) in the west to the Yakima River Valley in the east. It is 1.5 times the size of the state of Rhode Island and includes the cities of Toppenish, Wapato, and Union Gap.

The Yakama people suffered the usual horrors of being "civilized," including an allotment plan which sought to end common ownership of land and instead make every tribal member owner of a piece of land. Despite giving way 90 percent of their land to the United States, it wasn't enough. Governor Stevens, who had negotiated the Treaty of 1855 with the tribes, rapidly violated it. Yakama land was supposed to be off limits until the treaty was ratified, but Stevens basically declared it open season on Yakama land as soon as he could.[21]

Somehow, the Yakamas persevered. Although much land was lost to nontribal members, the Yakamas carefully used their resources to buy back land and generate revenue for the tribe. They generated funds from logging and timber sales, built their own steelhead hatchery, and invested in agriculture. Not every venture was a success; in the 1980s the tribe had a furniture factory and an aviation division, including aircraft leasing and pilot training. Only the timber operation survived.

To manage all this the nation has an elected tribal council, which sets policy and oversees the operation of the government. Their stated mission is to promote the general welfare, protect tribal property, and protect treaty rights. The council has fourteen members with eight standing committees, ranging from timber and economic development to budget and finance. There are also five special committees. Underneath this, tribal administration administers and plans tribal actions, and an operations level of government makes it all happen. Above all this is the general council, which includes every enrolled tribal member over the age of eighteen. They meet once a year.

Today the tribe has an impressive array of business enterprises, including its longstanding timber and forest products operation; an electric power company; a cultural center; a convenience store; a fruit and produce operation; a land development company; and a casino.

SNOQUALMIE TRIBE

The Snoqualmie Tribe are "the People of the Moon." In 1855 they became one of the treaty tribes with the stated rights of continuing to fish, hunt, and gather. At the time the tribe had four thousand members, making it one of the largest Puget Sound tribes. As with every other tribe in the state, the federal government did what it could to make the tribe go away; they lost federal recognition in 1953, not regaining it until 1999.

Today the tribe has around five hundred members, living in Snoqualmie, North Bend, Fall City, Carnation, Issaquah, Mercer Island, and Monroe. They built a casino in Snoqualmie, profits from which are used to support other tribal activities. In 2019 they were able to buy the Salish Lodge and Spa, an upscale hotel and restaurant overlooking Snoqualmie Falls, and the acreage around it from the Muckleshoot Tribe for $125 million. More than just a business enterprise, the falls are sacred to the Snoqualmie people, and with the purchase the tribe will be able to control development in the area. Later that same year the tribe purchased the Eighth Generation store in Pike Place Market, a maker of fine Native American wool blankets and other products. They also own and operate a market in Snoqualmie.

The tribe is governed by its constitution and by a nine-member, elected council, with an elected chair, vice chair, treasurer, secretary, honorary lifetime elder, two alternates, and two chiefs. But while the tribe is an economic force in the Snoqualmie area, its relations with the city that shares its name are somewhat uneven. For example, in 2017 the tribe held a forum at its casino for Snoqualmie city candidates, including the mayor and several council candidates. The mayor and all but one of four incumbents skipped the forum, expressing some displeasure at a separate local government holding a forum. (As one of the moderators of the forum, my comment was, "Had I been advising the mayor, I'd have said, 'Gambling is for casinos, not campaigns.'" Nonetheless, he was reelected.)

Still, some progress has been made. "The tribe and the city's relationship has improved somewhat, but there are still some major points of contention," said Jaime Martin, executive director of Governmental Affairs and Special Projects for the tribe. "One of the foundational breaks in vision and philosophy appears to center on the city's view of whether the land included in the city's jurisdiction is traditional Snoqualmie land and territory. Without this deeper understanding of the tribe's commitment and connection to this land, our ability to see eye-to-eye is very challenged," Martin said. "While the city does often ask about finding ways to establish partnership on various issues, it seems to be on a strictly monetary level, which is something we seek to break out of.

"The tribe's efforts on economic development this year in particular have been phenomenal," Martin said after the purchases were announced. "Snoqualmie is making values-based investments and utilizing the economic resources and structures (i.e., gaming) available to us to carry out the tribe's vision and priorities as a sovereign nation."

Part of the goal is to push beyond what people see as common tribal enterprises, she said. "While many associate tribes with gaming, cigarettes and liquor, and fireworks sales, Snoqualmie is providing a new vision for what tribal economic diversification can look like," Martin said. "Values and profits do not have to be separate."

CHAPTER EIGHTEEN

Jobs and Money

ECONOMIC DEVELOPMENT

Throughout our examination of Washington State government, we have talked a lot about how government is used by groups to get what they want. At the end of the day, what they most often want is money.

Everyone has her or his favorite issue, or at least an issue about which they care. It could be abortion, or it could be choice. It could be roads and transportation; it could be civil rights. It could be diversity, equity, and inclusion. It could be taxes, or it could be climate change (and no matter what you think, climate change ought to be pretty high on your list).

Whatever your issue, most of it all comes down to one thing: the economy. It's all about the jobs. State and local governments consider a lot of very important issues, ranging from crime to human rights to traffic and zoning. But in some ways those are all sideshows compared to jobs. If people have good jobs, other things tend to fall into place. People in the United States were okay with civil rights, for example, until their incomes stagnated and they began to worry about their jobs. And then everybody started blaming everybody else. Donald Trump played on this by demonizing immigrants, who contribute far more to the economy than they cost the country. Stagnant wages in this country are probably the biggest reason why the country has become so reactionary against immigrants and people of color. If enough people have good jobs, other things tend to work out: less crime, less racism, less poverty, less hunger, less homelessness, higher test scores, better civic participation. If people are doing well, they feel they have a stake in the system and they tend to support it.

Jobs matter. Spend any amount of time unemployed and you'll soon know why. If you have a job, your family eats, you have a roof over your head, your kids do better in school. No job is no fun. If enough people don't have jobs, that generally means that governments—especially in Washington—are getting less tax money precisely when the demands for government services are at their highest. And it's not just any jobs that we want—people want good jobs, "family wage" jobs, jobs with benefits and the occasional pay raise. Consequently, economic development is of paramount concern to state and local governments. More people working means more tax revenues and fewer demands on state services.

RANKING THE STATES

An annual rite of spring (or any season) is the ranking of the states. Publications, advocacy groups, and sundry other pundits regularly rank the states as to their business climates, tax ratings, and quality of life. The rankings are interesting and a point of departure for trying to assess what's going on with a state's economy. But by themselves they are largely devoid of context and rarely consider what's driving these rankings and what the consequences might be of having, say, the lowest business taxes in the country. As one scholar noted, the rankings don't generally reflect any real research, and they're generally done to promote a point of view, or to sell magazines.

Business climate rankings seem to hinge mostly on which states have which taxes. According to the Tax Foundation, a conservative, anti-tax group, Washington's state tax climate for businesses ranks twentieth in the county.[1] These numbers should always be suspect. For example, in the same analysis, New York and California, easily two of the wealthiest states in the country, rank forty-eighth and forty-ninth in business tax climate. But as we noted earlier, work by Seattle-area economist Dick Conway shows that there's no correlation between a state's tax system and its ability to produce jobs. Conway pointed out how constraints on Washington's tax system limited the ability to fund education so that before the McCleary decision, the state had slipped from above-average levels of school funding to forty-second in the country.[2] An educated workforce is generally regarded to be one of the keys to a healthy economy.[3]

On the other side of the state coin, *USA Today*, based on something called "economic climate," declared in 2018 that Massachusetts was the best state for business, given its high number of college graduates and high median family income. Massachusetts was twenty-ninth in the Tax Foundation's reckoning. In the *USA Today* ranking Washington was eighth.[4] CNBC had the state at number two by its measurements, just behind Texas.[5]

Probably the greatest value of these rankings is they tell us what people think matters in terms of economic development, a good starting point for trying to figure out what really does matter. States and localities have tried many different strategies to boost their economic fortunes, none with perfect success.

APPROACHES TO ECONOMIC DEVELOPMENT

The first thing we should understand is that state and local governments have a limited ability to affect economic outcomes. Unlike the federal government, they can't engage directly in trade or monetary policy, and they have limited and sometimes almost no ability to borrow money (deficit spend) to prime the pump by spending to increase overall economic activity. So what's happening with the economy is often about what the federal government is doing.

The second point we should keep in mind is state and local governments generally don't start businesses. They don't put up developments, they don't open offices or factories, they don't throw up strip malls or fast-food emporia. Investors, entrepreneurs, and established firms are the ones who take care of that part of the economy. But that doesn't mean governments don't have a role. They can create (or discourage) the conditions for economic growth. Public policy, in terms of taxes, regulations and infrastructure support, make it more or less likely that private efforts will soar or sink in trying to create jobs and wealth. It is sometimes overlooked that state and local governments help create the conditions for an organized society where markets can function, where people have the liberty to start businesses and create jobs and find that next big thing.

And even then, some of it is geography, and some of it is chance. Euro-Americans came to Puget Sound to cut and sell timber to San Francisco. William E. Boeing came to Seattle to manage his timber holdings. He happened to catch the airplane bug along the way. Puget Sound had a shipbuilding industry because it's connected to the ocean. The wealth of trees and fish and ships made the wealth of airplanes possible, which eventually made the wealth of software and coffee and e-business possible. Without the right geography and a little luck, none of this might have happened. Airplanes succeeded in part because they come with delivery included; theoretically, you could build them anywhere. Peter Kirk, a British-born steel tycoon, intended to make Kirkland the Pittsburgh of the west. That didn't happen, if only because Washington wasn't close enough to major markets to support a steel industry.

However, waiting for good luck—or hoping that your geography changes—won't get you very far. State and local governments therefore try to do things to generate jobs and wealth. Their toolboxes are smaller than the federal government's but not completely empty. Given their proximity to what's happening on the ground, they're sometimes better placed to seize on opportunities.

TAXES

As noted previously, taxes are often seen as a deciding factor in where businesses decide to go, especially among those folks who think taxes are just too high. The fact that the people who complain about taxes the most are also the wealthiest people ought to be the first clue that this might not be so. Moreover, as noted in economist Dick Conway's study of state taxes, state business climates (basically taxes) do not correlate with producing more jobs.

States and local governments can raise or lower taxes to encourage or discourage particular activities. States regularly give tax breaks to companies to move facilities to those states, but state constitutions such as Washington's may limit what can be done. For example, in Washington if the legislature offers a tax break to one business, it must be extended to every firm in that industry. This can put a strain on state and local budgets from lost revenue. Tax cuts tend to reduce revenues, which lead to less money available for public investment.

Nonetheless, in the early 1980s the much-criticized economist Arthur Laffer came up with what has since been called the Laffer Curve. Laffer's curve suggests that if taxes are too high, economic activity will be discouraged. If they are too low, economic activity will also fall since the public infrastructure that sustains markets would be missing. Laffer's idea was used as the underpinning of what has been called supply-side economics, which promised that cutting taxes would produce so much growth that budgets would be balanced despite tax cuts.

Despite the extent to which this idea is excoriated, it is not without merit. If taxes are too high, that will indeed discourage economic activity. Taxes left too low will achieve the same result. The flaw in supply-side economics appears to have been the assumption that taxes were currently so high that they were acting as a drag on the economy. This doesn't appear to have been true. The Reagan-era tax cuts of the early 1980s only managed to run up enormous budget deficits. The state of Kansas tried this in 2012 and 2013, slashing income tax rates. It failed to boost state finances or generate jobs or spur new business starts. In fact, Kansas's growth was lower than all its neighbors and less than half the national average. The state legislature was forced to cut spending on education and services, and the state's bond rating fell, costing taxpayers more money as the state had to pay higher interest rates on construction bonds. However you measure it, it did not work as advertised.[6] It's worth noting that the United States as a whole has the lowest effective business tax rates among developed economies, so it's not clear how our taxes are too high.

Tax cuts in general are supposed to stimulate the economy, but they never quite seem to work. The general idea is that by leaving more money in people's pockets, consumers will spend more and stimulate the economy. Part of the problem is that tax cuts are often instituted amid recessions when people are spending less to begin with. When they're worried about their jobs, people are more likely to either save the money from a tax cut or use it to pay down debt. Both of those are good things, but they won't stimulate the economy in the short term. The other issue with tax cuts is what we can now call the Kansas effect: especially for states, often tied to balanced budgets, cutting taxes also means cutting spending. This has the effect of decreasing overall demand, at best offsetting the stimulative effect of the tax cut, and at worst decreasing public investment in things that add to the productivity of the economy.

Business tax breaks are often doled out to keep existing firms or attract new ones; the record is mixed at best. Research finds that business tax cuts don't generate jobs, while closer to home a 2019 study by the Joint Legislative Audit and Review Committee also found mixed results for a few dozen tax breaks currently enjoyed by businesses in Washington State.[7]

One tax break was being utilized by out-of-state firms but was unavailable to their in-state competitors.[8]

REGULATION

Like taxes, regulation imposes costs and benefits on firms and consumers. For example, environmental regulation raises short-term costs but provides long-term benefits. Firms may have to spend more to comply with environmental regulations, but everybody tends to benefit from cleaner air and water—if only from smaller health care impacts. States have varying degrees of environmental regulation, though at least until recently federal regulations generally imposed the same restrictions on all the states. States sometimes relax regulations to encourage business activity, such as Delaware's remarkably loose incorporation laws, which has tempted more than half of all publicly traded U.S. companies to incorporate there.[9]

But regulation can come on a very small scale, and it can make a big difference. Consider the city of Des Moines, notable for having one of many confusing place names in Washington, and also an example of everything that can go wrong with a city. Although Native Americans and later Euro-Americans called the place home for centuries and decades, respectively, Des Moines wasn't incorporated until 1959. It was named after a development company, which was named after the city in Iowa. The name is pronounced without the S, by vote of the city council (although some residents insist it should have the S). Des Moines is not without its virtues. It has some lovely parks and trails; it has waterfront, including one of a relative handful of marinas on Puget Sound.

But from the 1970s onward, the city council decided that they liked the way Des Moines was—a "bedroom" community, without much business and hence no tax base. They actively made it difficult for businesses to locate there with requirements for things such as parking garages. Honestly the only parking problem in Des Moines is that there is no reason to park there. The city ended up with the worst per capita tax base for any city over ten thousand in the entire state and a reputation among investors as a difficult place to do business. Its four largest employers were all nonprofits and hence generated little in the way of taxes. Meanwhile, city leaders spent $5 million fighting expansion of nearby Sea-Tac Airport. In the end the airport expanded and the city had little show for its efforts.

City officials said they were able to get some environmental concessions from the Port of Seattle, but it isn't hard to imagine that they could have gotten the same thing by offering not to sue the port.

They could get away with this because of the sales tax equalization fund, which aimed to help cities with poor retail sales tax bases. It was funded by a tax on car tabs. Then in 1999 anti-tax initiative promoter Tim Eyman got a measure on the ballot to slash tab taxes. The car tab tax was very unpopular; the tax was high, and most of the money didn't go to roads. The measure passed, and although it was eventually declared unconstitutional, the legislature soon after enacted changes much like those in Eyman's initiative. Goodbye sales tax equalization fund.

Eventually city council turnover brought in new members who weren't so stridently anti-business. At that point, however, downtown redevelopment efforts were hamstrung by tiny Water District 54, which supplied water to the area. Water District 54's board long prided itself on never raising water rates for its eight hundred customers, which meant they never collected enough money to upgrade and maintain their system. As a consequence the fire marshal would not approve any permits for a building of any size unless it was entirely steel and concrete. The district's water mains to downtown were so small they could not supply adequate flow in case of a fire. Eventually the city worked with the district to address the situation and permit some redevelopment. Meanwhile, the Port of Seattle bought up an entire neighborhood that was so close to the flight path from Sea-Tac that homes could not be adequately insulated against noise. The homes were sold and moved, and the land was to become commercial development. For a brief moment the light at the end of the tunnel was not another jet taking off over the city. A developer proposed to put in a Target and a Costco, which would have greatly increased city sales tax revenues. But then the Great Recession hit in 2007–8, the financing dried up, and the project was shelved. The land did eventually get used for warehouses, manufacturing, and FAA regional headquarters, all of which provided good jobs but not as much in the way of taxes. The city was so short of funds it did not pave a road for ten years. It very nearly went bankrupt before the more aggressive city council took steps to drag the city out of the hole that it had basically dug for itself. The lesson of Des Moines is that if you want economic development, or at least a tax base, the first step is don't actively discourage it.

THE MINIMUM WAGE

One kind of regulation is the minimum wage, and this is an area where state and local governments can make a difference. Washington has already made a difference, with a minimum wage tied to the consumer price index, a standard measure of inflation. At $14.49 an hour in 2022, the state had the highest minimum wage in the country after the other Washington at $16.10. Seattle's minimum wage is $17.27 and the city of SeaTac's is $17.54.

The idea behind a minimum wage is to force business to share some of the wealth, and there is simply no evidence that high corporate profits will otherwise trickle down to the people who actually do the work. Conservatives and libertarians tend to oppose this idea, believing the market should sort out wages just like it sorts out prices. Liberals point to the apparent lack of limits to greed, noting that throughout history, when given the chance, too many employers are quite willing to pay their workers starvation wages.

There's a standard set of arguments against raising the minimum wage. First is that it will cause small businesses to fail. This one has a little logic behind it. If a firm can't afford to pay its workers more, it won't. If it is forced to, it may lay workers off or just go out of business. This puts some pressure on policymakers to craft minimum wage laws that exempt smaller firms and focus on large corporations who can afford to pay their workers more.

A second argument is that it will cause inflation, as workers who suddenly have more money will bid up the prices of goods. This would only be true if the economy was running at full capacity. However, the economy is almost never running at full capacity. Raising the minimum wage in the boomtimes of the late 1960s probably cost jobs and contributed to inflation but since then, not so much.

The third argument is that the minimum wage was never intended to be a family wage; it was intended for teenagers who are just starting out. Unfortunately, that's no longer true. While more than half of minimum-wage workers are under age twenty-five, the average age of minimum-wage workers is thirty-five: 88 percent are not teenagers, and 36 percent are forty or older. Fifty-six percent are women and 28 percent have children. Most tellingly, 55 percent work full-time. However much we might wish it, everyone is not going to go to college and get a great job, and it's not clear why we don't value all labor more than we do. Manufacturing employment, which normally pays better, is down worldwide. In the age of automation, it takes fewer people to wrangle a widget than it used to.

A 2018 University of Washington study found that Seattle's increase in the minimum wage did increase wages but also reduced hours, except in the restaurant industry, where it had no effect.[10] Conservative, pro-business groups had a field day with this. But a later study showed that what happened was that the number of jobs that paid below the new minimum wage was reduced, only to be replaced by new jobs that paid more. The difference between the two studies seems to be that the UW study only looked at Seattle, while the second study looked at the broader area, and that while Seattle's wage hike was 37 percent, in the second study wage hikes averaged about 10 percent.[11] The UW study also apparently left out large firms—chain stores, big box retailers—who typically pay low wages and whose workers presumably would have been major beneficiaries of the wage increase.[12]

Another study showed that raising the minimum wage helped small businesses by increasing the purchasing power of people who work there. It also showed that it encouraged more people to enter the labor force, boosting productivity as employers had a larger pool of workers to choose from. Further research showed no correlation between business failures and increasing the minimum wage.[13]

Most studies seem to show that raising the minimum wage can help everybody. Workers stay on the job longer, leading to gains in productivity (output per worker). Less turnover means less time and expense training new workers. Poverty and reliance on public assistance falls, meaning less demands for government services. People's health gets better.[14] And meanwhile, back in SeaTac, the first city in the country to adopt the $15 minimum wage, they're enjoying a boom in hotel construction. Developers say the increase does not bother them.[15] The real struggle has been getting everyone to pay it. Alaska Airlines, which spent a chunk of change unsuccessfully fighting the wage hike in court, still doesn't pay its baggage handlers the legal minimum wage. That's because of an exemption in the law for airlines since the baggage workers are unionized and can negotiate. The unionized workers get some benefits that other airport workers don't.

Even if it can be shown to make economic sense, a higher minimum wage won't fix everything. An estimated 2 percent of Americans earn the minimum wage, many more of them in the South and the Midwest than in the West or the Northeast. On the other hand, a 2019 change in state law changed the requirements for overtime pay, forcing more employers to pay overtime to workers who previously had been labeled as managerial and therefore exempt. This should also boost purchasing power for many workers, further increasing demand in the economy.

RECRUITMENT AND INCENTIVES

Recruitment is big business in a lot of states. States often maintain offices in places such as California, trying to encourage businesses to move elsewhere. Incentives can include lower taxes and less regulatory burdens; better living conditions; less traffic; cheap land. Every state has some sort of economic development office that works at getting firms to move. It's not clear how this pays off, but everybody does it. As noted earlier, Delaware targeted one industry—incorporations—and wrote the most liberal incorporation laws in the country. That's why so many large corporations, including Boeing, are incorporated in Delaware. It brings the state a lot of legal business and some cash flow from fees.

Common in a lot of states, but not Washington, are efforts to give businesses money, land, and buildings to relocate. This happens and it's not clear whether it truly pays off. The amount of money spent by states is remarkable. Illinois and Chicago spent $60 million to get Boeing's headquarters there—for only five hundred jobs, half of which were filled by existing Boeing employees. In theory this money could be spent somewhere else. Officials there said they hoped that Boeing would be encouraged to bring some manufacturing their way, but in twenty years, that didn't happen, and then Boeing announced it was moving its headquarters to Virginia.

Generous tax provisions might attract a firm, but that also means less revenue for the state or the city. At best, cities can make it easier for a business to locate within their borders. But studies have shown that businesses locate for perfectly sound reasons that are only marginally related to state and local government policy—proximity to markets, to suppliers, to communities where their need for skilled workers can be met.

For the most part large firms have realized that states and localities across the country will sell their first-born, their mothers, and their souls to attract high-paying jobs, particularly manufacturing jobs. Usually firms have already decided where they might go but don't tip their hands, knowing that making the location decision a "competition" will cause state and local governments to bid for those jobs by sweetening the pot with various incentives. Even if the business's executives have already picked a location, creating the competition means they'll get a better deal if governments think they are legitimately competing for a location decision.

For example, the state of Wisconsin agreed to incentives worth $3 billion to attract an electronics plant from the Taiwanese firm Foxconn, including $1.5 billion in wage subsidies and $1.35 billion to help them build the factory. All this for a factory that will employ three thousand to thirteen thousand people. If it's only three thousand jobs, that's $1 million per job; at best it works out to $230,000 per job. University of Georgia economist Jeffrey Dorfman, who can hardly be described as a liberal, said this kind of largesse does not pay out in terms of tax returns, and creates other costs as affected communities try to deal with the impacts.[16] The Wisconsin example is not isolated; states across the country have coughed up millions to attract manufacturing and other jobs. South Carolina offered Boeing $900 million in tax breaks to put a 787-production line there; meanwhile, their schools are chronically underfunded and underperforming.[17] Total South Carolina incentives eventually topped the $1 billion mark.[18] And as I predicted at the time, there weren't enough qualified workers in South Carolina to staff the plant; Boeing had to recruit at trade schools across the south to find an adequate workforce.

While Washington State doesn't just give money away, it has offered tax breaks to in-state firms (i.e., Boeing) with mixed results. One group's estimate of Washington tax breaks offered to Boeing is $12 billion.[19] It would be hard to argue that the sales tax exemption for aircraft sales, begun in 1949, hasn't penciled out. Boeing stayed here, grew, and helped build central Puget Sound into a thriving community, which arguably has benefitted the rest of the state.

But other tax breaks followed, with somewhat less tangible benefits. At the urging of Gov. Jay Inslee, the legislature met in a three-day special session in 2013 to push through an $8.7 billion tax break for Boeing in exchange for the company to produce the 777-x wings in Washington, along with final assembly of the jet. It was the largest tax break ever offered to one company in the history of the country. Boeing nonetheless moved thousands of other jobs out of state. By 2019, with Inslee running for president, he compared the experience of working with Boeing to being mugged.[20] In 2017 Boeing's tax breaks saved it $227 million in a year in which it cut six thousand jobs in the state. On the other hand, the company's overall economic contribution to the state is estimated at $95 billion.[21]

That last number underscores the dilemma faced by state and local governments when confronted by big employers seeking favors. It's one thing to simply not participate in a firm's shakedown of the states when it's looking to expand or relocate. But if the firm is already in your backyard, that's quite a different story. Politically and economically, it is difficult to ignore a good employer's request for tax breaks when they're already there. Boeing paid out $8 billion in wages in Washington in 2018, and pretty much nobody who worked there qualified for food stamps. If they leave, not only do you lose revenue, but your constituents lose their jobs. Boeing was apparently playing hardball with the state, and the current management of Boeing values short-term profit over the long-term health of the company (and the community). Inslee and the legislature were alone on the runway and Boeing was threatening, once again, to fly away.

The trade-offs are substantial. Boeing pays well and offers good benefits. These are the family wage jobs that most policy makers and people say they want. But when it comes to new jobs, small businesses and start-ups also play an important role, even though they may not pay as well as Boeing. While Boeing still employs eighty thousand workers in Washington State, 99 percent of the companies in the United States employ five hundred workers or less. Perhaps a third of workers are at firms that employ fifty people or less. And they account for a big chunk of job growth nationwide. So while it's good to have a Boeing in your back yard, chasing large firms might not be the only strategy for creating jobs.[22]

INFRASTRUCTURE

As previously noted, state and local government can help create the conditions for economic development. One of those ways is by creating and maintaining infrastructure. Infrastructure refers to things such as roads and bridges, schools, and other public facilities that may make it easier and better to do business somewhere. Increasingly, that also now includes items such as broadband internet capacity.

Infrastructure can make a difference. When the federal government started building dams on the Columbia River in the 1930s, it jumpstarted the aluminum industry in the Northwest. Aluminum takes huge amounts of electricity to produce, so that cheap electricity is important. As the aluminum industry has largely left the area, and the dams wiped out entire species of salmon, one might wonder how much better off we are with the dams. But for several decades aluminum smelting provided a lot of well-paid jobs around the state.

Infrastructure investment is widely regarded as a good way to spur economic development, but you must have the funds to invest. Local governments often rely on states, and state governments rely on the federal government to supply part of the funding necessary for large-scale projects. Most recent research concludes that the United States as a whole is not spending enough to maintain its transportation infrastructure, putting more pressure on states to pick up the slack.[23] One study showed that $1 billion in infrastructure investment would create eighteen thousand jobs, or 30 percent more than a cut in state income taxes (not a Washington study, obviously).[24] On a per-job basis this may seem a bit spendy, but unlike $1 billion spent to tempt Giant Megacorp to put its newest plant in your state, the infrastructure project won't shut down and leave in a few years when Megacorp's business plans change (which happens a lot).

Local governments might not want to wait for a bail-out from a federal white knight, especially in the age of Trump. In Whatcom County the government created its Economic Development Investment program after the state legislature allowed rural counties to keep a portion of state sales tax to finance construction of public facilities. Whatcom's program also invites local governments to make use of it for economic development initiatives.

"I believe the EDI program has overall been effective," said County Executive Jack Louws. "Infrastructure projects throughout the county have benefited from the use of the dollars, providing help overcoming the challenges of financing core storm water, sewer, road, and water facilities in the rural county, as well as within the municipalities. Other projects include dollars for workforce housing, tourism enhancement, and quite recently money for rural fiber availability has been approved."

The goal is to encourage private investment by creating the conditions that would make such investment worthwhile by providing transportation and utilities to support new or expanded operations by private firms. The money does not go directly to private firms. Applications are judged by a fourteen-member board, which includes both private and public sector representatives.

The program includes a revolving loan fund so that the money can be recycled into new initiatives. "That will give us multiple uses of the same money for years to come," Louws said. "I personally believe that if a community has good infrastructure, available land, reasonable codes, housing, [and] a track record of good public safety, economic development will happen organically. It's not a perfect program, but I think we can be quite proud of our accomplishments."

Sometimes infrastructure is about preserving what's already there, such as the Port of Pend Oreille's rescue and operation of the short-line railroad essential to businesses there, or the state Department of Transportation stepping in to rescue rural bus lines. The department participated in another rail rescue mission when it acquired the rights to a couple of short lines in southeast Washington, now known as the Palouse River and Coulee City Rail System, in 2004. Although it's a bit of an oxymoron, it's the longest short-line freight rail system in the state. DOT contracts with private operators to operate the line, which serves Grant, Lincoln, Spokane, Adams, and Whitman Counties. An intergovernmental agency, the PCC Rail Authority, oversees the business and development portions of the operation. In the heart of Washington's wheat country, the line plays a crucial role in helping farmers get their crops to market.

STADIA AND EVENTS CENTERS

Another kind of infrastructure is stadia and events centers. Usually built by some public entity, be it a city, a county, or a public facility district, the idea is that the facility will draw crowds and attract businesses. Sometimes it works, sometimes it doesn't. Studies generally show that large-scale professional sports stadia are a drag on local economies. They cost a lot of money; they don't tend to generate a lot of high-paying jobs; and they often displace firms that provided more jobs and paid better wages. Sports stadia just don't get used that much—eighty-one games a year for baseball; forty-odd games for basketball; ten to twelve games a year if your football team makes the playoffs. Stadium jobs are mostly part-time and seasonal;

the restaurants that spring up nearby, while very busy on game day, generally only make money for the people who own and manage them. And their seasonal nature limits how much tax revenue they may generate.

Stadia in Washington have long been subsidized by hotel/motel taxes, which have the virtue of taxing folks who don't live here, but also call out the eternal question of economic development: What else could you be doing with the money? Some argue that the sporting events and conventions are what drive the hotel/motel tax, since they draw people from out of town. There's some truth to that. Then again, building a stadium with public money means you're subsidizing a business, usually involving a game played by millionaires who work for billionaires. This doesn't mean they shouldn't be built; there's all kinds of civic value in having more entertainment options, especially for people who like to paint their faces and yell a lot. But they shouldn't be sold as engines of economic development because they're not.

A TALE OF THREE CITIES

Not every public events center caters to the billionaires et al. Washington State has at least two dozen public facilities districts, local special purpose districts created to build sports and events centers for their communities. Most of them are convention centers. The logic of such facilities is fairly simple and not different than the larger facilities in big cities: they hope to attract people from out of town who will come and spend money at local businesses, generating sales tax and hotel-motel tax revenues for local governments, plus a few jobs along the way.

There's some evidence that this can work. In 2016 a couple of scholars from Eastern Washington University surveyed nine events held at the Spokane Public Facilities District's venues (an arena, a convention center, and an arts center), and extrapolating from that survey, concluded that the facilities district had generated 1,100 jobs and $66.8 million in economic activity.[25] Most of the jobs were in service industries—retail, restaurants, and lodging.

The question remains, however, whether the taxes raised and the money spent are justified in terms of economic development. In the last few decades, three Washington cities—Kent, Wenatchee, and Federal Way— have built events centers. Each experience provides an example of the costs and benefits of pursuing this kind of public project.

SHOWARE CENTER

Construction of the city of Kent's Showare Center (formally the accesso Showare Center after the company that bought the company that bought the naming rights—after the first company that bought the naming rights never managed to write a check) began in September 2005 and was finished in January 2009 at a cost of $89 million. It hosts several minor league sports teams, and averages about 110 to 120 events a year. It seats 5,800 to 7,100 people depending on the configuration. The city got $3.175 million for the naming rights from a company that makes software for online ticket sales for ten years. They also got $21 million from the state, by virtue of being able to keep .033 percent of state sales tax (about 3.3 cents on a $100 purchase) collected in Kent. All this was done via a public facilities district, authorized by the state to collect taxes and build and operate a public venue.

By 2014 the city was spending $4.8 million a year to support the center, including $3.1 million to pay off the construction bonds. Showare lost $3.9 million in its first eight years of operation before turning a $16,000 profit in the first half of 2018, buoyed by a fistful of well-attended concerts. But in that same six months, it gave the city $260,000 in admissions tax, not a huge chunk of the city's budget but extra money nonetheless and up more than $200,000 from two years earlier. Sales tax and admissions tax together bring the city about $500,000 a year, offsetting operating losses of about the same amount.[26] A 2012 study estimated the facility's annual economic impact at $25 million, mostly in the restaurant and retail sectors.[27] Aside from entertainment, that's Showare Center's chief virtue. Its events generate lots of business for nearby Kent Station, although that appears to be true mostly for restaurants. The restaurants appear to have some staying power, whereas the retail establishments tend to come and go.

Kent Station is the key piece. The city spent $16 million to buy twenty acres of land in the late 1990s. Borden Chemical had closed its plant on that site in the 1990s, so the land was available. And while the Borden jobs had probably paid better than the retail jobs that replaced them, the new jobs would provide the city with more tax revenue. Kent found a willing developer to build the project and buy the land from the city. Kent Station opened for business in 2001. By 2005 the open-air mall had fifty shops and restaurants, a movie complex, and branch campuses for two colleges. And it's in easy walking distance of Showare.

"You can look at the number of businesses still open today because of Showare," then-mayor Suzette Cooke said. "We know specifically of businesses that kept their doors open because of people we brought into the city. Where would Kent be without Showare? There would be some missing businesses."[28]

"We look at it as a community asset," said her successor, Mayor Dana Ralph. "It infuses a ton of money in our economy. If you talk to the folks at Kent Station, they are 100 percent dependent on Showare."

By 2019 the city subsidy of the venue was averaging $500,000 a year which includes daily operation, building maintenance, and minor capital costs. Some years revenues from the center exceed operating costs and some years not. Nonetheless, Mayor Ralph said the city views it as one of the services it provides to citizens. "It's important to note the city exists to offer public services: we respond to 911 calls, build streets, inspect buildings, offer parks and recreation programs, etc. to enhance the lives of our residents—not to turn a profit or often even to break even," she said. "Much like the Kent Commons (our community center) or Kent Senior Activity Center, accesso Showare Center offers a community gathering space—for sports, concerts, community events, and college and high school graduations. Kent Station's full parking lots and busy restaurants prior to and after accesso Showare Center events are one measure of enhanced quality of life."

The city commissioned a 2015 study to measure primary and secondary impacts of Showare. That added up to $23 million a year, including ticket and concession sales, rental fees, event-related spending at local businesses, and employee and business-to-business spending.

TOWN TOYOTA CENTER

The Town Toyota Center got its start not in Wenatchee but in Olympia, with passage of a bill that allowed public facilities districts to impose a local sales tax to fund development of their projects. It passed the house and senate with only one no vote between them. Consequently, the cities of Wenatchee, East Wenatchee, Cashmere, Entiat, Waterville, Chelan, and Rock Island, plus Chelan and Douglas Counties, joined to create the Greater Wenatchee Regional Events Center Public Facilities District. Construction began that fall, and the facility opened in October 2008. The facility seats 4,300 to 5,800, depending on the event, and it cost $52.8 million to build. It got its name by selling naming rights to a local car dealership, recently renewed for $840,000 through 2023. It has been the home to several minor league sports franchises and has hosted a steady menu of concerts and other productions.

Building the facility didn't mean a hit to local jobs or tax rolls, fortunately. "This building did not displace another building as it was built on a vacant lot along our waterfront," said Wenatchee mayor Frank Kuntz. Although the center was busy, it wasn't busy enough to cover its costs. The firm hired to manage the facility had promised millions in revenue, but in most years the center lost money or broke even. The public facilities district took over management of the center in 2009. The facilities district had sold bonds to pay for its construction (standard practice), but on December 1, 2011, it missed a $42 million balloon payment. Default was one option, but it might mean bankruptcy for the governments involved, and it certainly would raise borrowing costs in the future. Municipal bonds are generally regarded as a safe option for investors because, in addition to the tax-free income they offer, they're theoretically backed by the full faith and credit of the issuing entity. But several municipalities across the country have defaulted in recent decades. Damaging your city or county's credit rating will cost everybody money going forward because of the higher interest rates that will be required to attract investors next time you want to build something. And forcing a city into bankruptcy would likely have serious long-term consequences.

With the default looming, Wenatchee-area legislators sought help from their colleagues in Olympia, whereupon the Town Center's troubles produced the tragicomic spectacle of anti-tax, anti-spending Republican legislators begging their colleagues to bail out the project back home. In November and December of 2011, amid a special session called to deal with the state's usual raft of budget problems, a bill that would have essentially borrowed existing state funds to make the bond payment passed a house committee but died in the full house when sponsors concluded they simply didn't have the votes to move the bill. A judge had ruled that Wenatchee couldn't issue new bonds to pay off the old bonds because to do so would exceed its statutory debt limit. Bondholders were threatening lawsuits, the federal Securities and Exchange Commission launched an investigation, and calamity beckoned.

Then, in December, East Wenatchee mayor Steve Lacey (also now on the facilities district board) proposed a small, districtwide sales tax increase to pay off the bonds. This kicked up some opposition, as only the city of Wenatchee had promised to guarantee the financing. The near disaster was one of the things that got Wenatchee mayor Frank Kuntz, now the president of the Public Facilities District Board (PFD), involved in politics in the first place. With help from the legislature, they managed to find the money to keep Toyota Town Center running on all cylinders. "We ended up raising sales tax by two-tenths in the city and one-tenth in the PFD region, which includes most of Chelan and Douglas Counties, and with that revenue source we floated new bonds and paid off the bonds that were defaulted," he said. Voters in the facilities district's service area approved the tax increase in 2012.

Since then the Town Center has survived and thrived. In 2016 center management said it had produced an impact of $6.5 million, and in 2018 they claimed a $64 million impact since its opening.[29] Town Center management says its economic impact rose to $8.1 million in 2018 based on its own research. Town Center officials would not say whether it's covering its operating costs, however. "As for if the ancillary revenue makes it worthwhile, I am not sure," Mayor Kuntz said. "What it does do is provide entertainment opportunities that never existed in our area. Buildings such as these never make money."

FEDERAL WAY PERFORMING ARTS AND EVENTS CENTER

Federal Way was named for a road. Military Road, once the main north-south thoroughfare in King and Pierce Counties connecting Ft. Lawton and Ft. Lewis, was often called "the federal way." People who settled around its midpoint, apparently incapable of thinking of something more melodious, started calling the area Federal Way. Inexplicably, after Federal Way became a city in 1990, the citizens voted to keep the name. Because Federal Way had such trouble convincing its residents to become a city, its central business district developed into something like the world's largest strip mall, then suffered as firms departed and big-box buildings were left vacant. As one city councilmember put it, "We have a location for downtown Federal Way, but there's nothing there."

"You don't want your downtown to die," said another. "You've got to get investment."

Among the suggestions for addressing Federal Way's retail blight was to build a performing arts center. The idea was that filling up an arts center with events and entertainment would attract other business and begin to resurrect the center of town. Understandably, people disagreed long and loudly over this idea. On the one hand, people had questions about the cost and whether it would pay for itself. On the other hand, as debate continued, the central business district seemed to get only more moribund, as trash and chain-link fences increasingly replaced retail emporia.

In the meantime, Weyerhaeuser left its epic corporate headquarters building in Federal Way for smaller digs in Seattle, motivated in part because it meant a much shorter commute for their new CEO. That punched another hole in the local economy—6,500 jobs just gone. Plans to use part of the more than four-hundred-acre campus for a fish-processing plant produced some civic uproar, and it's still basically vacant. The development firm that now owns most of the land hopes to reinvent it as the Woodbridge Corporate Park, but of course there's a citizens group that says it should be preserved as open space. Both ideas have their virtues, and once again there's a trade-off.

And then a city councilman, Jim Ferrell, led a fight to change the form of city government from council manager to strong mayor. "We weren't actually doing anything," under the old form of government, Ferrell said. "We had no strategic vision for the city." Ferrell, to his credit, made clear from the start that if the city decided it wanted an elected executive, he would be a candidate. The voters approved, and on his second try Ferrell was elected mayor. Ferrell had been opposed to the events center, but as mayor he convened a "blue-ribbon commission," a collection of business and civic leaders, to study the matter. No surprise: they approved. Ferrell then convinced the city council to provide the funds to buy up a bunch of the nearly vacant land in the city's core. It helped a lot that they got $5 million from the state. There was some logic to this; land prices were lower at the time, and a developer could easily have bought it and sat on it until prices and the economy rose again. The city cleaned up the land

and built a park, and it's hard to argue with that. Abandoned land and buildings have a magnetic attraction for trouble.

And then, led by Farrell, the city pushed ahead with building the performing arts center, despite not having all the financing in place. Expected tax credits didn't bring as much money as expected; and as of this writing the city still hadn't sold the naming rights. With everything put together, the city remained $7 to $8 million short of the cost of building the facility. Nonetheless, construction was started in 2016 and the 716-seat, $32 million facility was opened in August 2017.

"We need to turn this city around," Farrell said at the time, promising a "$32 million events center that will transform our downtown." It hosts events every weekend. In its first year it brought in $2.2 million in revenue with expenses of $2 million. It's a nice facility. It has brought a diverse range of entertainment to the community, and it has plenty of parking. Eventually Sound Transit's Light Rail project will have a station nearby, making it even easier to get to.

Meanwhile, although it's early in the process, nearby development has not yet happened. And that's the real test. While it passes the cultural test—is it bringing something to the community that people want to see?—will it also generate enough ancillary economic activity to do what city leaders hope it will do? The city is hoping for a hotel, restaurants, and ultimately mixed-use development to surround the center, but deals must be worked out with other nearby landowners and, most importantly, developers have to want to engage in these projects. In the end, if you build it, they will only come if it makes sense for their business to do so. On top of which, in buying the land for the hotel, city leaders somehow did not buy the development rights from the previous owner who wants another $3 million.

One city council member said the city could sell bonds to cover the remaining debt on the PAEC. "You have to move forward," rather than looking back at decisions you might not agree with, said the council member, who originally didn't support the project. "We're not where we need to be, but we're headed in the right direction."

And still, it could all work. A hotel plus a mixed-use development with ground-floor retail and upper floor apartments or condos could bring a lot of jobs and economic activity to the city, with further activity driven by the PAEC. Mixed-use development is an idea whose time has come. Previously cities tended to zone exclusively—retail goes here, manufacturing and so on goes there, and residential goes over there. The immediate problem with this pattern of development is that it leaves each part of the city vacant for one chunk of the day, and that's when crime happens. Residential neighborhoods have fewer people during the day, while retail and other business areas are emptier at night. Mixed-use development, on the other hand, means that by putting residential units in the same building, generally above retail and other business outlets, you have people around all the time. Presumably the businesses get the benefit of potential customers nearby, while residents have easy access to businesses close at hand. If Federal Way can pull that off, it could benefit the community greatly. Nearby Burien has created such a development, but its launch just before the Great Recession slowed the project for several years. Still, Burien's downtown core is lively, and the whole idea may yet pay off. "We're trying to create an urban village," Federal Way mayor Ferrell said. "The future of Federal Way is vertical."

OTHER PUBLIC ENTERPRISES

Another kind of state enterprise could be a state bank. Republican-dominated North Dakota has a state bank, a leftover from its farmer-populist roots. North Dakota's bank was founded in 1919, intended to provide financing for the state's farmers. But the fact that it would have competed with private banks produced a big business backlash, and the bank's activities were rapidly circumscribed. Today it has one branch, doesn't offer credit cards, and doesn't even have a drive-up teller window, though you can open an account there. It is the repository for North Dakota state funds, and it makes a little money for the state as well as offering loans to farmers, businesses, and college students.

In Washington the idea has been pushed by State Sen. Bob Hasegawa, an unrepentant liberal who has championed the idea for several years. "I believe in Keynesian economics and workers unions as the only real power that can challenge the powerful and bring equity for everyone," Hasegawa said. "I've been surprised by how so many people are so scared of doing anything to fix their circumstances, even when they know they're getting screwed by the status quo."

John Maynard Keynes, a British economist, concluded in the 1920s and '30s that the answer to long-term economic recessions was for government to prime the pump. Neo-libertarians notwithstanding, that has largely the been the economic response of the world ever since World War II.

Hasegawa, a South Seattle Democrat, argues that a state bank would keep Washington money in Washington, helping to finance state ventures as well as turning its profit over to state coffers. It could offer low-interest loans to students and entrepreneurs. Senator Hasegawa hasn't been able to push through a state bank bill yet, but he did get a study authorized in 2019.

GREEN INVESTMENT

Another possibility is doing something about climate change and also doing something for economic development. Understand first that 97 percent of scientists agree that climate change is real and largely caused by human activity. The other 3 percent are on the payroll of the energy industry. The oil industry has known about this for decades and had done what it could to keep a lid on the science.[30] Climate change means changing weather patterns, in particular greater extremes of temperature and more severe storms.

This is already being felt in Washington State. Climate change is destroying forests in the Pacific Northwest. The year 2014 saw a record number of forest fires and acres destroyed; but then in 2015 there were 3,800 wildfires and 1.7 million acres burned in Oregon and Washington, surpassing the old record by far. Lower precipitation means less snowpack in the mountains, leaving the trees drier and more vulnerable to pests and diseases and hence more susceptible to fire. Ironically the anti–forest fire efforts of the twentieth century, coupled with the preservation of acreage for other perfectly good environmental reasons (protecting salmon streams and watersheds), has helped build up the undergrowth in forests, literally adding fuel to the fire. Even removing downed timber for commercial purposes, which would remove potential fuel, was blocked for environmental reasons. As a result, the timber industry has taken a beating, again impacting rural communities. Fortunately, state forestry management is creeping back toward allowing some logging and using controlled burns to return forests to a less combustible condition. Moreover, the biomass collected can be used to produce energy.[31]

The key to addressing climate change is to reduce carbon emissions into the atmosphere. The two most commonly prescribed solutions are a carbon tax and cap-and-trade programs. Cap and trade works; you set a carbon emissions limit and tax firms that go over it and reward firms that go under, thus creating a market for carbon credits that can be bought and sold and encourage efficiency. This works best if everybody does it. But despite some apparent success in Europe, the secret to that success has been moving the most polluting facilities to China and India. So that's not really an answer.

Washington attempted to implement a carbon tax via Initiative 732 in 2016. It failed by nearly 60 percent of the vote, losing in every county but King where it barely passed. The measure didn't go far enough for many environmentalists, and it went too far for many others. Pitched as revenue neutral because it included a reduction in sales tax to offset the carbon tax (which would have raised a lot of prices), outside analysis showed that it would have punched a hole in the state budget, which is never a good thing. And in the end, "We couldn't spend as much as the oil industry," said a person who worked on the campaign.

A carbon tax makes economic sense: raise the price of something and people will generally consume less of it. However, a carbon tax is essentially a consumption tax, which will get passed on to consumers and hence fall most heavily on lower income and rural residents who have less resources to deal with the cost. Living in King County? There are alternatives to driving your car. Live in Okanogan or Pend Oreille or anywhere around the edges of the state? You're going to have to drive.

At some point we will have to collectively decide if we want to be right or if we want to do something about climate change. As logical as a carbon tax is, if it's not politically possible, perhaps we need to find alternatives. On a national scale it might make more sense to decide that oil and coal companies have a property right and buy it from them. If you think this isn't feasible, recall that King County bought development rights from farmers to ensure that not all the farms went under the bulldozer and the cement truck. This would be expensive, and it's probably beyond the ability of a single state to do.

But we probably can do something. Part of the challenge for Washington state is that 90 percent of its electricity already comes from renewable resources. But even there we find trade-offs, as the region's heavy reliance on hydropower tends to leave less water for farms, fish, and families. The state could invest in energy efficiency projects, such as more wind and solar power, through grants to local governments such as port and public utility districts, if not all kinds of local governments. People could be trained to install such systems; grants could be offered to universities to develop them.

Germany gets less sunlight than we do, and yet in 2018 they produced 7 percent of their energy from solar systems, fourth most in the world. Why don't we have solar panels on every roof? People say, in effect, "That won't fix everything." But it doesn't have to. It just has to make some difference. The answer is not planting more trees, erecting more windmills and solar facilities, or encouraging cleaner fuels—it's all of those things. If we can make those things also create healthier economies, especially for people outside of central Puget Sound, why not do that?

TOURISM

Every state also now pushes itself as a vacation destination since tourists bring in dollars from out of the area. The jobs are a mixed bag, however, containing a high percentage of seasonal, low-skilled, low-wage jobs. But because tourism brings in dollars from outside the state, it's generally regarded as a plus for the local economy. In recent decades, the state has attempted to brand and rebrand itself, with slogans such as "The Other Washington" and the mercifully short-lived "Say Wa." (Wa? Really?) The current version is "Washington, the state."

Whatever they call it, tourism has become a big industry in Washington, despite the state's rather sporadic support for it. (When budgets are tight, it's the kind of program most likely to be cut.) It employs more than 180,000 people, as visitors spent $18.4 billion in the state in 2017. That also generated $1.2 billion in state tax revenues and another $900 million in local taxes. King County is far and away the biggest beneficiary of this industry. But it's also very important to small counties including Chelan, Island, and San Juan, where it generates significant jobs, income, and taxes. Consider San Juan, with only eighteen thousand people. Visitors spent $233 million there in 2017, or $12,388 per person, making it on a per capita basis the most tourism-benefitted (and -dependent) county in the state.

It's no accident that many county residents celebrate in September at the end of tourist season, which gets at one of the costs of this industry. Too much tourism can mean environmental damage and general overcrowding; prime locations around the world have begun to limit the number of visitors so as not to wear out the natural and cultural icons that draw visitors and their money from far away.

One of Washington's great tourism success stories has been the cruise industry, built largely on the strength of having a deepwater port (Seattle) relatively close to a place lots of people want to go (Alaska). By the 1980s small-ship tours from Seattle to Alaska were becoming a regular thing. When Holland America Lines acquired Seattle-based Westours in 1983, they moved their combined headquarters to Seattle. But the cruise business was still some years from taking off.

In the 1990s Seattle was merely an occasional stopping point for West Coast cruises. The Port of Seattle opened the Bell Street cruise terminal in 1996, but by 1999 there were still only six ships and six thousand passengers sailing from Seattle. That all changed when cruise lines figured out how to make their ships a little bit faster. That allowed them to squeeze a round trip from Seattle to Alaska in only seven days, meaning you didn't have to sail from Vancouver, British Columbia (still a major cruise port, nonetheless).

And then the business took off. The cruise lines started showing up, homeporting vessels in Seattle for the summer season. The port opened the Pier 91 cruise terminal in 2009. In 2018 the passenger count had risen to 1.1 million people, with seven cruise lines and nineteen ships based in Seattle. This creates 5,500 jobs, mostly during the April–October cruise season, generating $260 million in income and $893 million in annual economic activity. The key here is that out-of-state visitors who come to Seattle to cruise spend an average of $1,547 before and after they cruise, so all their money doesn't just go to the cruise lines.[32] It's worth noting that the cruise industry succeeds because it is able to exploit global wage differentials. Most onboard cruise staff are paid a pittance by U.S. standards, but they generally do all right by the standards of the places where they come from. So you see very few Americans working on cruise ships, and you can usually tell whose currency is down relative to the dollar by who's working on the ship.

Tourism depends on having something somebody wants to see. A community can't just decide to become as scenic as the San Juans or as rustically splendid as Chelan County. Although once in a while somebody hits on a schtick that sticks. Leavenworth, nestled on the east side of Stevens Pass, was a boomtown in the early twentieth century, driven by gold and timber. For a brief period of time it was the headquarters of the Great Northern Railroad, but that moved to Wenatchee in 1920 and little Leavenworth settled into decades of decline.

In the 1960s city leaders decided they could capitalize on the surrounding alpine splendor by recasting the city as the Bavaria of the Cascades, borrowing the idea from a California town that had gone Danish. They were led by a couple of Seattle businessmen who had bought a failing diner on Highway 2.[33] Seriously, if you want to open a business in Leavenworth, it's going to look Bavarian, at least on the outside. Even the McDonald's looks Bavarian. To this they added year-round seasonal festivals and Leavenworth was reborn. Today it draws 2 million tourists a year who spend a lot of money while they're there. In 2017 the city took in $4 million in hotel-motel taxes and parking fees. Naturally, this doesn't please everyone, since that many tourists means a lot of traffic and a greatly altered civic and economic life. Leavenworth gets as many if not more tourists than Iceland. And like a lot of tourist towns, the boom has driven up real estate prices, making it harder for people who work in the tourist industry to live where they work.[34] Nor do the resulting jobs pay that well; the median annual income for Leavenworth is 25 percent less than the state average. Critics are now calling for some kind of management of the industry, understandably asking why the city is still spending nearly $1 million a year to promote tourism when the town is basically full.

Despite the mixed blessings of its success, Leavenworth's experience points to an important element of successful economic development: build on what you have. Like the Port of Seattle seizing on the cruise industry as a moneymaker, Leavenworth took advantage of its natural beauty to turn itself into a tourist attraction. Whatever you might think of its ersatz Bavarian splendor, it worked. But most tourism benefits are flowing to parts of the state that don't need the help; as usual, the farther reaches of the state are not necessarily sharing in the bounty.

INDIGENOUS BUSINESS SUPPORT

Based on what we've seen, it may be cheaper and more cost-effective to support existing businesses than it is to recruit new ones. Some of that support takes the shape of infrastructure development, but some support can be a little more direct. One sometimes overlooked opportunity is the arts. Seattle may be the only big city in the country that sells more arts tickets than sports tickets. Arts, like sports, can be a draw to tourists and travelers, and unlike with most sports teams, the profits don't all flow to Big Daddy Sportsbucks or whoever happens to own the team. Seattle-based ArtsFund's 2014 study on the economic impact of the arts found that arts and cultural organizations generate $2.4 billion a year in economic activity in the state, including thirty-five thousand jobs, $996 million in labor income, and $105 million in state and local taxes. They found that 58 percent of spending by patrons was "new money"—money spent by people coming in from out of the area.[35] It's worth noting that arts and culture organizations reported 13.4 million admissions to events that year, or more than all the local professional and college sports teams combined.

Despite that, arts organizations require subsidy. Nearly all are nonprofit, and ticket sales generally only pay for a part of the cost of productions and exhibits. ArtsFund's study found that, on average, arts and culture organizations got 57 percent of their revenue from ticket sales, with nearly all the rest from gifts, including 12 percent from government. Nearly every arts organization is constantly fundraising, but it also underscores the importance of public investment in the arts. As with sports, there's a cultural benefit, but the economic benefit tends to get spread around a bit more broadly. Moreover, arts organizations are, as one arts advocate group noted, not "outsourced, merged, or bought out."[36] Local governments can also help arts organizations with infrastructure, and cities around the country have gone so far as to create "arts districts" to encourage arts-related entrepreneurs. Arts and cultural organizations are also fairly adept at making use of otherwise abandoned spaces.

Education and training is another way in which state and local government can support business without mortgaging their souls. The concept is pretty simple: find out what skills local businesses need and develop programs to teach those skills. This typically happens through local colleges and trade schools. As the schools already exist, the upfront costs are not enormous. This isn't about producing career-ready high school graduates, which isn't always very realistic, but more about aligning vocational programs with the skills employers say they need. This has also already led to some over-emphasis on STEM fields—science, technology, engineering, and math—which are important but aren't the only skills employers are looking for.

Another interesting—and growing—approach is urban agriculture, taking unused urban and suburban land and turning it back into farmland. Globally urban agriculture accounts for 15–20 percent of world food production.[37] Local governments can support this by avoiding restrictive zoning (until recently, many large cities around the country effectively banned urban farming); providing land for "pea patch" programs that help people without land of their own to grow crops; provide incentives for organizations such as schools and hospitals to buy from local farms; and providing support by continuing to fund initiatives such as the WSU Extension Service, which helps farmers and gardeners all over the state. Several states have created urban agricultural incentive zones, allowing local governments to offer tax breaks for people who want to use land for urban farming.[38]

Many cities in western Washington have already found ways to designate space for and support farmers markets, which provide opportunities for local farmers to sell their produce and for consumers to buy it. This has environmental as well as economic benefits. The average bite of food you take has traveled 1,500 miles to reach your plate, so even if a farmer is driving a couple of hundred miles from eastern Washington (which they do), that's an improvement. Transporting goods is one of the leading sources of greenhouse gases.

Meanwhile, one study showed that direct sales of farm products produces twice as much economic activity as do sales of produce from those not involved in direct marketing. Furthermore, every $1 million in direct sales produces thirty-two jobs, versus ten and a half jobs for wholesale growers. Direct sales farmers are almost twice as likely to buy inputs from local businesses. Nationwide, farmers market sales topped $1.5 billion in 2015, nearly tripling in the last fifteen years.[39]

Another tool available for economic development is to buy local. Buying from local firms keeps income and profits at home, which echoes throughout the local economy. For Washington State that has meant buying new ferries from the state's few remaining shipyards. Before Boeing, ship building was the major industrial sector on Puget Sound, but after World War II the industry sailed away in search of cheaper labor. At one point, the ferry system bought ferries from a shipyard in Louisiana where wages were cheaper and environmental laws were not as restrictive.

But in 1993 the legislature finally became convinced that the cost of a ferry wasn't just its price tag, it's also how many jobs and how much tax revenue is generated by the contract and where that money goes. Since then state ferries have to be built in Washington shipyards, but with so few shipyards, the system may get only one or two bids on any given project. A recent study concluded that the state could save a bit of money by buying out of state, but also lose hundreds of jobs and $68 million in consumer spending, far more than the state would save in the actual cost of the ferry.[40]

Support for small business is yet another way state and local governments can spur economic development. A dozen or so states have programs aimed at boosting small businesses, mostly in the technology sector; it's not clear how well any of them work.[41] The goal is often to help a toddling business get up on its feet, after which it may attract private venture capital to take it to the next level.[42] Critics of these programs tend to look at the failure rate, but they're generally applying a standard not applied in private capital markets. Venture capitalists expect to hit one in ten bets—a 10 percent success rate. That shouldn't be an unreasonable standard for public support of start-ups.

In Washington no government except a port district could offer that kind of assistance to a private business, and port districts here aren't noted for that sort of largesse. It also puts the government in the position of picking winners and losers, which is a questionable thing. What could be done is to expand on local small business development programs, in which business veterans are hired to provide expertise to fledgling enterprises, giving them a much better chance of success. Although 80 percent of small businesses survive their first year, half are gone by year five. The biggest reason is that the business doesn't really fill a need, although lack of capital comes in at number two.[43] Still, solid advice can often steer someone in the right direction. Even in Washington, government could spend money to support that kind of program.

PEOPLE IN POLITICS: LISA BROWN

Lisa Brown was always drawn to help people. Appointed director of the state Department of Commerce in February 2019, that is her job. The department is as close as Washington gets to a statewide economic development agency, which means helping people do better.

Dr. Brown has been involved in politics for a while now. "I came to politics from the activist side. Early in my career I worked a lot on women's and family issues. For example, I helped organize the Women Take Back the Night March in Spokane; issues around low-income challenges, such as a coalition working for dental benefits (the 'Molar Majority')," she said.

Dr. Brown had earned a PhD in economics and taught at Eastern Washington University. "I started hearing 'Why don't you run for office?' I hadn't really thought about electoral politics before," she said. Her academic research took her around the state talking about women in the workforce. "Through that experience I became exposed to the whole state and saw similar issues of importance everywhere, such as access to childcare and pay equity," Dr. Brown said.

She was first elected to the state house of representatives in 1993, joining the state senate in 1996. There she rose to be Senate majority leader, serving until 2013. Along the way she taught at Gonzaga and was chancellor of WSU-Spokane.

As a state agency leader, all of that experience has proven to be helpful, Dr. Brown said. "Legislative experience is really important in this position," she said. "Being familiar with the environment in which policies get made gave me the lay of the land in terms of the issues. In twenty years in the legislature, I've come across most of the issues commerce is administering.

"It's also critical to understand how stakeholders fit into the process—lobbyists, advocates—all the entities that have an effect on public policy," Dr. Brown said. "My university administration experience—five years as chancellor at WSU—was really significant experience for this job. Leading an organization—I worked with a cabinet, leadership team; very similar functions. I was the leader of budget, communications, facilities and operations, IT, and so on."

When Gov. Jay Inslee called, she was ready to take on this new position. Dr. Brown said she was attracted by "the range of policy sectors that commerce has: economic development *and* housing *and* energy *and* infrastructure—no other agency has such broad impact in communities." As far as economic development, Dr. Brown tries to stick to basics. "The basic framework that happens at the state level is investing in education, and it's time to invest in early learning. We've expanded K–12 and higher ed, but the most important thing that needs to happen now is early learning," she said. "The earlier we engage in the early learning system—that means anyone who cares for young children—the better. . . . Another investment imperative for the state is infrastructure," Dr. Brown said. "We have a deficit in funding for transportation and broadband in some key areas." And regulation. "Clear, effective regulation is another state role-protecting water, public health; having sensible, smart rules in place for how we manage growth in a good way," she said.

The state needs more than a one-size-fits-all approach, Dr. Brown said. "One of the challenges is that all state agencies have different ways of looking at regions and their needs," she said. "What if we were to try to define our regions more, in a way that lets us look at data and talk with other state agencies more? At commerce we have three outreach people assigned by geographic area to do better regional analysis. Regional economies—not Washington State—that's where people live and work. Commerce plays an implementation role with local communities in that respect—we are in dialogue with legislators and we represent the administration."

The department has more than one thousand programs. "We do a lot more than most people are aware of," Dr. Brown said. "For example, we fund programs training nurse examiners to do sexual assault kits; our Office of Homeless Youth is working to ensure no young person exits a state institution or foster care into homelessness; our energy division is dealing with new energy efficiency standards for appliances and buildings, and investing in clean energy technology; we are helping expand broadband access in rural and underserved communities; we fund other public infrastructure investments for projects such as community facilities, water and sewer systems, roads, and bridges; our small business export assistance programs help companies grow through international trade; our Housing Trust Fund is helping to increase and preserve affordable housing units throughout the state; the Office of Economic Development and Competitiveness works with ADO partners and industry to attract and keep companies and jobs in the state and provides resources to startups and entrepreneurs... that's just a tiny sliver of the wide range of programs at commerce.

"They hope all that adds up to economies that work better for more people. Commerce's mission is to strengthen communities," Dr. Brown said.

THE DEVELOPMENT DICHOTOMY

Research shows that communities do better at economic development if they target certain industries.[44] For Washington State that seems less of an issue as we have a number of successful industries, making the challenge more about keeping them here and happy while finding ways to spread economic success to a broader swath of the population. But on the local level, counties and cities are often looking for something or someone that will produce jobs and wealth for the community. Federal Way, for example, became enamored of attracting a college or university to the city, despite the fact that three different colleges abandoned branch campuses there after failing to attract enough students.

Even if Federal Way succeeds, it raises the problem of the development dichotomy. The kinds of businesses that will bring good jobs are generally not the kinds of businesses that will generate lots of tax revenue.

For example, a 1989 study by a couple of Seattle-area economists found that every Boeing job created another 2.8 jobs elsewhere in the state's economy.[45] That's because Boeing jobs pay well. The people who have them also thereby have disposable income, which they use to buy cars and houses and all the things that go in them. Someone making a minimum wage job, who's working just as hard if not harder than the Boeing employee, doesn't have as much impact on the economy. The Boeing employee, on the other hand, doesn't directly generate that much tax revenue. Boeing doesn't pay sales tax on aircraft. The minimum wage worker's employer, on the other hand, is collecting lots of sales tax on the items that they sell, be it burgers or skateboards. So which kind of industry should a city pursue?

Cities thereby face what we might call the development dichotomy. Cities have two needs: jobs for their citizens and tax revenues to pay for the services citizens generally say they want. But there's the problem. The kinds of businesses that will generate revenues for cities are not the kinds of businesses that create family-wage jobs and vice versa. This is especially true in Washington, without an income tax. So manufacturing, warehouse, and research-related industries tend to offer higher paying jobs, but as they may produce little in the way of taxable sales, they don't generate much revenue for the city. On the other hand, retail and restaurant businesses tend to generate more in the way of sales tax, but they may not provide as many high paying jobs. None of these industries are bad, and none of these jobs are insignificant. But they create a dilemma for local governments that are pursuing economic development. Where do you start? What do you prioritize?

LOCATION, LOCATION, LOCATION

Businesses locate in states and communities for reasons that have everything to do with business and not as much to do with government policy. So Tukwila got Southcenter (or, if you prefer, Westfield Shopping Town, because putting your stamp on something is so much more important than hanging on to several decades of brand equity) in part because it's a good central location. Kent, meanwhile, got warehouses—lots of flat land with good road and rail connections, equidistant between the ports of Seattle and Tacoma, and close enough to Sea-Tac Airport. That was all good as long as sales tax was paid at the point of origin. Purchased goods shipped from warehouses in the city meant a lot of sales tax money for Kent. But then the state adopted streamlined sales tax, by which taxes are charged at the point of delivery. City officials expected this could cost the city $5 million a year. "We are the biggest loser in the state of Washington because of all those warehouses," said Kent mayor Dana Ralph in late 2018. The loss of some mitigation funds by 2020 could make the hole even bigger. "Kent is losing more money than any other city." The mayor and council responded by cutting $2 million from the city budget, while raising the B&O tax and trimming some other funds. A strong economy and revenue from building projects eased the city's burden heading into 2019, but that's not a permanent condition.

THE PARADOX OF GROWTH

Let's say your plans come to fruition. Your brilliant economic development initiatives succeed and you and your neighbors have good jobs, and your community gets enough tax revenues to pay the police, pave the roads, and keep the parks open. None of this is bad, but as with everything we've talked about, there are trade-offs.

I heard an economist once who, when people asked him where he'd most like to live, replied, "It's obvious: Los Angeles in the 1930s." California before it boomed was probably the nicest place in the country. And everybody figured that out, population soared, and the problems of growth became apparent: too much crime, traffic, and diminishing resources and quality of life; too many people! You are now living through that time in Seattle; California and New York have already been there. Boise is booming, but someday Idahoans will wake up and say, "Wait a minute! This used to be a great town! Where'd all these people come from?" In part from Idaho's efforts to recruit firms from California. This is the Paradox of Growth: communities try like heck to grow, do, and then face the challenges of growth. They try to manage them and often drive away the very growth they tried to so hard to get in the first place. And there's no easy answer.

Good jobs means growth—higher incomes, stronger communities, more civic amenities, less need to raise taxes. Which leads to the inevitable trade-off: if a community or a region grows enough, some things are lost, such as open space, farms, the familiar way of life. Traffic increases, housing prices go up, schools become overcrowded, and all of a sudden the problem switches from "How can we get jobs?" to "How can we control growth?"

The Paradox of Growth tends to produce a "last-person-over-the-bridge" response. In a presentation on this, I once was criticized by an audience member who didn't like all the development. "You're pro-growth!" he said, as though that were an obvious sin. The irony that he wasn't from Seattle—and had moved here for work—didn't seem to enter his thought process. Nonetheless, growth is a conundrum. What do you do when you've grown too much?

But first, a little history. The state's economy had and has a big impact on the state's politics. The first European residents were fur trappers who trapped species such as the sea otter and fisher into localized extinction. The first settlers in the state were farmers, but the first settlers in the Puget Sound area turned trees into lumber, sold to San Francisco. The need for trees was spurred by the California Gold Rush. There were lots of trees in Oregon, but Portland was difficult to get to thanks to the rough waters at the mouth of the Columbia River. Seattle had a natural deep-water harbor and trees right on the shoreline. Washington's destiny as a trade-dependent place had begun.

As much as the state's founders distrusted the railroads, they clamored to get them here. The completion of rail lines to Tacoma and Seattle in the 1880s led to big increases in population and commerce. Seattle's growth really took off in the 1890s with the discovery of gold in Alaska. Astute city leaders moved quickly to get the federal assay office located in the city, which meant you had to bring your claim through Seattle. Seattle's population grew from 42,000 in 1890 to 90,000 in 1900 and to 237,000 in 1910.

The next boom for the state was canned fish. When Euro-Americans got here, the rivers were stuffed with salmon. Canneries were built up and down Puget Sound, but as happens so often, overfishing and habitat destruction greatly reduced the fish population. The Puget Sound fishing fleet now goes to Alaska. Shipbuilding was a major industry up through World War II. Only a handful of shipyards remain on Puget Sound. The development of hydro-electric dams around the state aided irrigation in eastern Washington, though they negatively impacted the salmon population, including wiping out the "June hogs," eighty-pound Chinook nearly as big as a man.

For a time after the war, cheap electricity from the dams supported aluminum smelting operations in the state. Eventually cheaper electricity prices elsewhere greatly reduced the industry in Washington. When local electric rates began to rise in the 1980s, aluminum companies began to call for help as they struggled to remain competitive. Local media seized on the issue since the smelters paid much lower rates for electricity than did an average homeowner. What they missed, however, is that the smelters bought a lot more electricity and used it 24/7 to make aluminum, so they were getting a volume discount. (This is why deregulation of electricity has never worked anywhere—a typical homeowner doesn't use enough electricity to make it worth anyone's while to offer you a deal.) Moreover, it takes copious amounts of electricity to separate alumina from bauxite ore, so electricity is a much bigger expense for a smelter than it is for you and me. It's not clear that anything could have been done for the Northwest smelters, whose departure has cost the state a lot of high-paying jobs. If there's a lesson, it is that jobs are not a given. If you're serious about economic development, you don't want to chase them away.

The war also led to the development of the Hanford nuclear reservation, still an economic mainstay of the Tri-Cities area. Sadly, it also gave a lot of people cancer from radiation.

Boeing, still one of the state's major employers, came here largely by accident, but its story underscores a couple of things to keep in mind about economic development. First, wealth begets wealth. If you're going to lift yourself up by your own bootstraps, first you need boots. William E. Boeing came to Washington State to manage his timberlands near Aberdeen. No trees, no Boeing. And it's ridiculous to assume that something else would have taken its place (and I've heard people say that). Boeing saw an airshow and caught the flying bug, and eventually decided to get into the business. What became Boeing started in 1916, in a bankrupt shipyard that Boeing bought for a dollar. Mr. Boeing, already a successful businessman, had deep pockets, which kept his company going after the conclusion of World War I put 90 percent of the country's airplane makers out of business.

Mr. Boeing had left the company by the time World War II came around when Boeing prospered by building aircraft for the war. Afterward the company pioneered the first successful jetliner, the 707, and still builds jets in Renton and Everett. The company has had its ups and downs, from the boomtimes of the 1960s to the Boeing bust of 1969–71, when local company employment dropped from more than one hundred thousand to under forty thousand in a matter of months, and smaller cycles ever since. Although the local legend became that ex-Boeing workers started all kinds of businesses that diversified the economy, nobody is ever able to name more than a couple. Most of the spin-offs were parts suppliers for the aerospace industry.

What is true is that a healthy Boeing helped create a region with a strong middle class and lots of opportunities. In succeeding generations, people from here (or who came here) started Microsoft, Starbucks, and Amazon. Hate on them all you want, but these are successful firms that employ a lot of people, don't treat their employees too badly, and have generated a lot of wealth. And yet when New York decided against hosting Amazon's second headquarters project, a colleague of mine said, "Looks like New York dodged a bullet Seattle stepped in front of." How is having a firm in the community that provides jobs and pays people "stepping in front of a bullet"? That's the Paradox of Growth. Everybody wants economic development until they're caught in traffic.

Washington's other big problem, as noted previously, is that it doesn't have a tax structure that allows it to capture a consistent slice of all that wealth. Washington's tax revenues have lagged gains in income for several decades now, leaving state and local government with less revenue to try to address the costs of growth. Increases in sales and property taxes tend to hurt poor and middle-income citizens, while not tracking rising incomes.

The answers so far have been of a kind: building restrictions, impact fees, higher taxes to pay for the impacts of too much development. You may agree or disagree with this approach, but they all have one flaw: efforts to manage growth tend to affect the people who are already here as much as they affect the people you are trying to keep out. Washington State's 1990 Growth Management Act directed communities to plan for and pay the costs of growth, which are generally good things. On the other hand, it also led the cities of Renton and Everett to propose $50 million in fees when Boeing wanted to expand its production capacity at its plants in those cities. While the fees were eventually knocked down quite a bit, it still sent shockwaves through the region when then-CEO Frank Shrontz, generally a stand-up guy, soberly announced that if Boeing was to expand again, it might not be in Washington State.

The Paradox of Growth demands a degree of care and caution on the part of policymakers, especially given the challenges of getting jobs in the first place. The only certain thing is that it's easier to manage growth than it is to cope with contraction. One has only to look at communities where jobs are few and far between to recognize how that situation is much, much worse.

Epilogue

THE PEOPLE'S BUSINESS

We met many people in the pages of this book. Since it was written, many changes have happened. Hans Zeiger and John McCoy retired from the legislature. McCoy, seventy-nine, died in 2023. Kristine Reeves gave up her seat to run, unsuccessfully, for a seat in Congress, then ran to reclaim her old legislative seat in Federal Way (which she did) in 2022. Cyrus Habib did not seek reelection as lieutenant governor, and State Rep. Mike Pellicciotti defeated Duane Davidson for state treasurer in the 2020 election. Arch-conservative legislator Matt Shea did not seek reelection. In the 2022 election, radicals of the left and right tended to lose to candidates closer to the middle. Mary Kuney, who opposed changing Spokane County government to a five-member commission, was chosen as chair of the commission when it took effect in 2022. King County prosecutor Dan Satterberg also called it a day and retired. By the time you read this, many others from these pages will have moved on from their time in government. But the folks who replace them won't be that much different, for good and for bad.

Meanwhile, despite the COVID-19 pandemic, social and political unrest, and the many moods of Donald Trump, there are still free and fair elections in Washington State and government still generally works. My point in all of this is not that the state's governments are perfect. That would be absurd. But they do work all right, no matter how much we might disagree with any number of actions government takes. The state's response to the pandemic was better than many, unless you think masks and vaccines are a bad idea. Washington's cities, like many all over the country, do not always treat people of color fairly. As noted many times previously, the tax system hurts the poor and helps the rich. You may disagree with that, but that's what the numbers tell us. Liars can misuse numbers, but good numbers really don't lie. Meanwhile, my personal conclusion from decades of studying this is that if every person has a chance at a good job, other problems tend to become more manageable. People need less help from the government, which also gets more tax revenue as a result. People have a greater stake in the community, and they feel more valued. This doesn't mean life will be perfect, but it will be better.

Meanwhile, after the fall of The Firs (where we began our story), State Rep. Mia Gregerson was at a gathering where she happened upon a young man who had lived at the mobile home park. He was not happy about having had to move, but the experience convinced him that he could get involved and make something happen. So that's something.

We have the structures in place in Washington State for good things to happen. It is now up to you, as citizens, to pay a little attention, vote, and keep your government honest. It can be done, and it must.

NOTES

PREFACE

1. Valerie Strauss, "Many Americans Know Nothing about Their Government. Here's a Bold Way Schools Can Fix That," *Washington Post*, September 27, 2016, https://www.washingtonpost.com/news/answer-sheet/wp/2016/09/27/many-americans-know-nothing-about-their-government-heres-a-bold-way-schools-can-fix-that/.
2. "Americans' Views of Government: Low Trust, but Some Positive Performance Ratings," Pew Research Center, September 14, 2020, https://www.pewresearch.org/politics/2020/09/14/americans-views-of-government-low-trust-but-some-positive-performance-ratings/.
3. Jill Rosen, "Americans Don't Know Much about State Government, Survey Finds," HUB Johns Hopkins University, December 14, 2018, https://hub.jhu.edu/2018/12/14/americans-dont-understand-state-government/.

1. NOT-SO-MOBILE HOMES

1. Civil Rights & Judiciary Committee, House Bill Report, HB 1582, 2019.
2. Joel Moreno, "Settlement Announced for SeaTac Mobile Home Park, Tenants on Notice," KOMO News, April 10, 2019, https://komonews.com/news/local/settlement-announced-for-seatac-mobile-home-park-tenants-on-notice.
3. Rich Smith, "Just South of Seattle, a Fight to Flip a Conservative City Council and Their Trump-Loving Mayor," *The Stranger*, July 19, 2019, https://www.thestranger.com/slog/2019/07/19/40798970/just-south-of-seattle-a-slate-of-progressives-fights-to-flip-a-conservative-city-council-and-their-trump-loving-mayor.
4. Sell, "Politics and the Economy," 11. https://scholar.flatworldknowledge.com/books/30476/sell_1.0-ch01_s00/read.

2. OVERVIEW

1. European diseases, to which Native Americans had not been previously exposed, decimated the population of North and South America, greatly facilitating the European conquests of the continent.

2. Clayton and Alexander, "Washington's Constitution," 136.
3. Ficken and LeWarne, *Washington*, 31.
4. Ficken and LeWarne, *Washington*, 32.
5. "Briefing Report: 2022 How Washington Compares," Washington JLARC, July 2022, http://leg.wa.gov/jlarc/reports/WACompares/default.html.
6. Andy Kiersz, "Every US State Economy Ranked from Worst to Best," *Insider*, March 15, 2018, https://www.businessinsider.com/state-economy-ranking-ql-2018-2.
7. Clayton, Donovan, and Lovrich, *Governing the Evergreen State*, 2–3.
8. Chad Sokol, "Liberty State Supporters Raise Funds at Event After Tense 'Silent Protest' by ex–Matt Shea Backers," *Spokesman-Review*, May 24, 2019, https://www.spokesman.com/stories/2019/may/24/former-matt-shea-loyalists-escorted-out-of-51st-st/; Chad Sokol, "Washington State Lawmaker Matt Shea Defends Advocacy for 'Holy Army' as Spokane Sheriff Refers His Writings to FBI," *Seattle Times*, November 1, 2018, https://www.seattletimes.com/seattle-news/politics/state-lawmaker-matt-shea-defends-advocacy-for-holy-army-as-spokane-sheriff-refers-his-writings-to-fbi/.

3. FEDERALISM

1. Smith and Greenblatt, *Governing States and Localities*, 42–43.
2. Stehr, Hoard, and Sanders, "Continuity and Change in Public Policy," 211.

4. RULES OF THE ROAD

1. Bowman and Kearney, *State and Local Government*, 63.
2. Pall, "The Washington Constitution," 20–21.
3. Tsebelis, "The Time Inconsistency of Long Constitutions."
4. Pall, "The Washington Constitution," 28.
5. Pall, "The Washington Constitution," 35.
6. Avery, *Government of Washington State*, 17.
7. Avery, *Government of Washington State*, 20.
8. Clayton and Alexander, "Washington's Constitution," 137.
9. Clayton and Alexander, "Washington's Constitution," 141.
10. Clayton and Alexander, "Washington's Constitution," 139.

5. HOW WE CHOOSE

1. Pirch, "Political Parties in the Evergreen State," 47.
2. Pirch, "Political Parties in the Evergreen State," 51.
3. Pirch, "Political Parties in the Evergreen State," 52.
4. Donovan, "Elections in Washington," 26–27.

5. Chavez and Jacobson, "Progressive Federalism," 105.
6. "Voting and Voter Registration as a Share of the Voter Population, by Race/Ethnicity," KFF (website), November 2020, https://www.kff.org/other/state-indicator/voting-and-voter-registration-as-a-share-of-the-voter-population-by-raceethnicity/.
7. "Voting and Voter Registration."
8. "November 3, 2020, General Election Results," Elections & Voting, Washington Secretary of State (website), updated February 3, 2021, https://results.vote.wa.gov/results/20201103/turnout.html.
9. Donovan, "Elections in Washington," 32–33.

6. INITIATIVES AND REFERENDA

1. Chasan, "Ultimate Democracy," 192.
2. Chasan, "Ultimate Democracy," 191.
3. Chasan, "Ultimate Democracy," 194.
4. Chasan, "Ultimate Democracy," 210.

7. LET'S PARTY!

1. Pirch, "Political Parties in the Evergreen State," 60–61.
2. When I worked in the legislature, you could always tell when things weren't going well: they ordered the staff out of the caucus meeting room.
3. Long and Ammons, "The Governor and Other Statewide Executives," 172.
4. In fact, there have been only three Democrat secretaries of state in Washington's entire history, the last losing a reelection bid in 1964. At the same time, the great majority of Washington's other statewide officeholders have been Democrats.
5. "Our Party," King County Democrats, accessed February 23, 2023, https://www.kcdems.org/our-party/.
6. "Pierce County Republican Party 2016 Platform," Pierce County Republican Party, accessed February 23, 2023, https://piercegop.org/wp-content/docs/2016pcrpplatform.pdf.
7. "History of the Party," Washington State Republican Party, accessed February 23, 2023, https://wsrp.org/platform/.
8. "2020 WSDCC Platform," Washington State Democrats, June 13, 2020, https://www.wa-democrats.org/wp-content/uploads/2020/06/WSDCC-2020-Final-Platform.pdf.
9. "Constitution Party Platform," 2012 National Convention, https://www.constitutionparty.com/assets/National-Platform-Full-Version.pdf.
10. "Home," GPWA, accessed February 23, 2023, https://greenpartywashington.org/.
11. Emily Boerger, "Q&A with Ann Diamond, Independent Candidate for Representative of the 12th LD," *Washington State Wire*, June 4, 2018, https://

washingtonstatewire.com/qa-with-ann-diamond-independent-candidate-for-representative-of-the-12th-ld/.

12. Alan Greenblatt, "Moderates Are 'Politically Homeless.' Does Either Party Want Them?" *Governing*, March 26, 2019, https://www.governing.com/topics/politics/gov-moderate-voters-trump-centrists-2020.html.
13. David Frum, "There Is No Progressive Majority in America," *Atlantic*, November 14, 2018, https://www.theatlantic.com/ideas/archive/2018/11/what-midterms-showed-about-progressive-candidates/575899/.
14. Eric Levitz, "The Midterms Did Not Prove That Democrats Should Adopt Your Policy Preferences," *New York*, November 7, 2018, http://nymag.com/intelligencer/2018/11/the-2018-midterms-did-not-vindicate-your-policy-preferences.html.

8. INTEREST GROUPS

1. Thomas and Elgar, "Interest Groups in Washington," 68.
2. Thomas and Elgar, "Interest Groups in Washington," 69–70.
3. Thomas and Elgar, "Interest Groups in Washington," 77–78.

9. WHERE IT HAPPENS

1. Marjie High, "History of Redistricting in Washington State," *Washington State Wire*, February 4, 2019, https://washingtonstatewire.com/history-of-redistricting-in-washington-state/.
2. "About LEAP," State of Washington LEAP (Legislative Evaluation & Accountability Program Committee), accessed February 23, 2023, http://leap.leg.wa.gov/AboutLEAP.html.
3. "About JLARC: The Legislature's Auditor," Washington State Legislature, accessed February 23, 2023, http://leg.wa.gov/jlarc/Pages/aboutjlarc.aspx.
4. "House Housing Committee," Washington State Legislature, accessed February 23, 2023, http://leg.wa.gov/House/Committees/HOUS/Pages/default.aspx.
5. "House Labor & Workplace Standards Committee," Washington State Legislature, accessed February 23, 2023, http://leg.wa.gov/House/Committees/LAWS/Pages/default.aspx.
6. "House Agriculture & Natural Resources Committee," Washington State Legislature, accessed February 23, 2023, https://leg.wa.gov/House/Committees/AGNR/Pages/default.aspx.

10. THE GANG OF NINE

1. Laura McCallum, "The Political Legacy of Jesse Ventura," Minnesota Public Radio, December 17, 2002, http://news.minnesota.publicradio.org/features/200212/17_mccalluml_venturalegacy/.
2. Long and Ammons, "The Governor and Other Statewide Executives," 172–73.

3. "Washington Statewide Elected Officials," Washington State Legislature, accessed February 23, 2023, http://leg.wa.gov/legislature/Pages/ElectedOfficials.aspx.
4. "U.S. State and Local Government Outstanding Debt 2020, by State," Statista, October 21, 2022, https://www.statista.com/statistics/312660/us-state-and-local-government-debt-outstanding-by-state/.
5. "State Debt Rank," usgovernmentspending.com, accessed February 23, 2023, https://www.usgovernmentspending.com/state_spending_rank_2018pH0s.
6. Ben Steverman, "A Once Radical Idea to Close the Wealth Gap Is Actually Happening," *Bloomberg*, March 17, 2022, https://www.bloomberg.com/news/features/2022-03-17/baby-bonds-eyed-as-way-to-close-u-s-racial-wealth-gap#xj4y7vzkg.
7. Pat McCarthy, "About Performance Audits," Office of the Washington State Auditor, accessed February 23, 2023, https://www.sao.wa.gov/performance-audits/about-performance-audits/.
8. Mike Carter, "Former State Auditor Troy Kelley Convicted of 9 Felonies in Federal Retrial on Theft, Tax-Fraud Charges," *Seattle Times*, December 21, 2017, https://www.seattletimes.com/seattle-news/crime/former-state-auditor-troy-kelley-convicted-of-9-felonies-in-federal-retrial-on-theft-tax-fraud-charges/.
9. Pat McCarthy, "Holding Accountable Fiscally Rogue Local Governments," *Seattle Times*, June 6, 2019, https://www.seattletimes.com/opinion/holding-accountable-fiscally-rogue-local-governments/.
10. Chris Ingalls, "Small Governments Taxing Washington Residents Without Holding Elections," King 5, last updated May 2, 2019, https://www.king5.com/article/news/investigations/eyeteam-investigations/small-governments-taxing-washington-residents-without-holding-elections/281-e8cdf78d-fe30-4e5d-809b-c9eab9414849.
11. Joseph O'Sullivan, "Washington State Auditor and Lawmakers Target 'Unauditable' Local Government Districts," *Seattle Times*, August 23, 2020, https://www.seattletimes.com/seattle-news/politics/washington-state-auditor-and-lawmakers-target-unauditable-local-government-districts/.
12. O'Sullivan, "Washington State Auditor."
13. "Washington Statewide Elected Officials."
14. Ashley Gross, "Washington Charter Schools Are Supposed to Serve At-Risk Students, So, Are They?" KNKX, November 27, 2018, https://www.knkx.org/post/washington-charter-schools-are-supposed-serve-risk-students-so-are-they.
15. "Washington Statewide Elected Officials."

11. ALL RISE

1. Salamone and McCurley, "The Judicial System in the State of Washington," 199.
2. "IN RE: The Disciplinary Proceeding against Richard B. Sanders (1998)," FindLaw, April 28, 1998, https://caselaw.findlaw.com/wa-supreme-court/1087091.html.

3. Richard B. Sanders, "Justice Sanders Explains his Comments about Race and Criminality," *Seattle Times*, December 2, 2010, https://www.seattletimes.com/opinion/justice-sanders-explains-his-comments-about-race-and-criminality/.
4. Richard B. Sanders, "Judge-Election System Works Well," *Seattle Times*, August 9, 2005, https://www.seattletimes.com/opinion/judge-election-system-works-well/.
5. "The Court of Appeals," Washington Courts, accessed February 24, 2023, https://www.courts.wa.gov/newsinfo/resources/?fa=newsinfo_jury.display&altmenu=citi&folderid=jury_guide&fileid=appeals.
6. Salamone and McCurley, "The Judicial System in the State of Washington," 194.
7. Salamone and McCurley, "The Judicial System in the State of Washington," 194.
8. David Wilma, "Carroll, Charles Oliver 'Chuck' (1906–2003)," HistoryLink.org, July 8, 2003, https://www.historylink.org/File/4216.
9. Lewis Kamb, "Washington State Bar Association in Turmoil as Allegations, Lawsuits Mount against Governing Board," *Seattle Times*, April 9, 2019, https://www.seattletimes.com/seattle-news/washington-state-bar-association-in-turmoil-as-allegations-lawsuits-mount-against-governing-board/.

12. TURNING POLICY INTO PRACTICE

1. Brad Plumer, "Study: Privatizing Government Doesn't Actually Save Money," *Washington Post*, September 15, 2011, https://www.washingtonpost.com/blogs/ezra-klein/post/study-privatizing-government-doesnt-actually-save-money/2011/09/15/gIQA2rpZUK_blog.html.
2. Ron Haskins, "The Outcomes of 1996 Welfare Reform," Brookings, July 19, 2006, https://www.brookings.edu/testimonies/the-outcomes-of-1996-welfare-reform/.
3. Kathryn J. Edin and H. Luke Shaefer, "20 Years Since Welfare 'Reform,'" *Atlantic*, August 22, 2016, https://www.theatlantic.com/business/archive/2016/08/20-years-welfare-reform/496730/.
4. Drew Desilver, "For Most U.S. Workers, Real Wages Have Barely Budged in Decades," Pew Research Center, August 7, 2018, https://www.pewresearch.org/fact-tank/2018/08/07/for-most-us-workers-real-wages-have-barely-budged-for-decades/.
5. "10 Reasons to Oppose '3 Strikes, You're Out,'" ACLU, March 17, 2002, https://www.aclu.org/other/10-reasons-oppose-3-strikes-youre-out.
6. Michael Vitiello, "Three Strikes Laws: A Real or Imagined Deterrent to Crime," American Bar Association, April 2, 2002, https://www.americanbar.org/groups/crsj/publications/human_rights_magazine_home/human_rights_vol29_2002/spring2002/hr_spring02_vitiello/.
7. "Roles and Responsibilities," Washington State Transportation Commission, accessed April 17, 2023, https://wstc.wa.gov/roles-and-responsibilities/.
8. Alan J. Stein, "Turning Point 9: The Sound and the Ferry: The Birth of Washington State Ferries," HistoryLink.org, June 2, 2001, https://www.historylink.org/File/9309.

9. "About Labor and Industries," Washington State Department of Labor and Industries, accessed February 24, 2023, https://www.lni.wa.gov/Main/AboutLNI/.
10. "About Us," Department of Ecology State of Washington, accessed February 24, 2023, https://ecology.wa.gov/About-us.
11. "Spill Prevention, Preparedness, and Response Program," Department of Ecology State of Washington, accessed February 24, 2023, https://ecology.wa.gov/About-us/Get-to-know-us/Our-Programs/Spills-Prevention-Preparedness-Response.
12. "About WDFW," Washington Department of Fish and Wildlife, accessed February 24, 2023, https://wdfw.wa.gov/about.
13. "Economic Benefits of Parks," Washington State Parks, accessed February 24, 2023, https://parks.state.wa.us/971/Economic-benefits-of-parks.
14. "Study: State Park System a Strong Driver of Economic, Ecosystem Health," Washington State Parks, accessed February 24, 2023, https://parks.state.wa.us/DocumentCenter/View/6007/FS150-13-Study-concludes-state-parks-benefit-economy-and-ecosystems?bidId=.
15. "About Us," Washington State Department of Children, Youth & Families, accessed February 24, 2023, https://www.dcyf.wa.gov/about/about-us.
16. "Agency Overview," Washington State Department of Enterprise Services, accessed February 24, 2023, https://des.wa.gov/about/agency-overview.

13. WHERE IT COMES FROM AND WHERE IT GOES

1. "Total State Government Expenditures," Ballotpedia, accessed February 24, 2023, https://ballotpedia.org/Total_state_government_expenditures.
2. Oliver Wendell Holmes Jr., "Taxes Are What We Pay for Civilized Society," Quote Investigator, April 13, 2012, https://quoteinvestigator.com/2012/04/13/taxes-civilize/.
3. Stehr, Hoard, and Sanders, "Continuity and Change in Public Policy," 211.
4. Avery, *Government of Washington State*, 288.
5. Erica York and Jared Walczak, "State and Local Tax Burdens, Calendar Year 2022," Tax Foundation, April 7, 2022, https://taxfoundation.org/publications/state-local-tax-burden-rankings.
6. Burrows, "A Progressive State with Regressive Taxes," 105.
7. Burrows, "A Progressive State with Regressive Taxes," 97–100.
8. Burrows, "A Progressive State with Regressive Taxes," 103.
9. Burrows, "A Progressive State with Regressive Taxes," 96.
10. Stehr, Hoard, and Sanders, "Continuity and Change in Public Policy," 212.
11. "Washington: Who Pays? 6th Edition," Institute on Taxation and Economic Policy (TEP), October 17, 2018, https://itep.org/washington/.
12. Dick Conway, "Reform Our Tax System with a Flat-Rate Personal Income Tax," *Seattle Times*, April 9, 2015, https://www.seattletimes.com/opinion/reform-our-tax-system-with-a-flat-rate-personal-income-tax/.

13. "Capital Gains Tax Q&A (2019–21 Proposal)," Office of Financial Management, March 15, 2021, https://ofm.wa.gov/budget/state-budgets/gov-inslees-proposed-2019-21-budgets/proposed-2019-21-budget-and-policy-highlights/revenue-changes/capital-gains-tax-qa.
14. Sara Gentzler, "Where Senate Dems' Plan to 'Fix Our Tax Code' Stands Now," *Washington State Wire*, May 30, 2019, https://washingtonstatewire.com/where-senate-dems-plan-to-fix-our-tax-code-stands-now/?utm_source=Wire+News+Alerts&utm_campaign=afaab994c0-RSS_EMAIL_CAMPAIGN&utm_medium=email&utm_term=0_5c5dd551fd-afaab994c03-32762669.
15. Janelle Fritts, "To What Extent Does Your State Rely on Property Taxes?" Tax Foundation, May 1, 2019, https://taxfoundation.org/state-and-local-property-tax-reliance-2019/.
16. Katherine Loughead, "How Much Does Your State Collect in Property Taxes Per Capita," Tax Foundation, March 13, 2019, https://taxfoundation.org/property-taxes-per-capita-2019/.
17. Ann Boonn, "Raising Cigarette Taxes Reduces Smoking, Especially among Kids (and the Cigarette Companies Know It)," Campaign for Tobacco-Free Kids, July 28, 2021, https://www.tobaccofreekids.org/assets/factsheets/0146.pdf.
18. "Cigarette Smuggling Makes WA Tax Revenue Go Up in Smoke," *Seattle Business Magazine*, July 19, 2013, https://www.seattlebusinessmag.com/blog/cigarette-smuggling-makes-wa-tax-revenue-go-smoke.
19. Kim Justice and Andy Nicholas, "No Denying It: At Least $10 Billion Has Been Cut from the State Budget," Washington State Budget and Policy, http://budgetandpolicy.org/wp-content/uploads/2018/11/no-denying-it-at-least-10-billion-has-been-cut-from-the-state-budget.pdf.

14. COUNTY GOVERNMENT

1. Kit Oldham, "State Supreme Court Rejects Bid to Form Cedar County Out of Eastern King County on February 5, 1998," HistoryLink.com, August 14, 2006, https://www.historylink.org/File/7894.
2. Avery, *Government of Washington State*, 258.
3. Wire Service, "Editorial: 1 Percent Property Tax Cap Is Starving Counties," *HeraldNet*, April 9, 2017, https://www.heraldnet.com/opinion/editorial-1-percent-property-tax-cap-is-starving-counties/.
4. Emily Thornton, "Changes Eyed for Columbia County Sheriff's Office," *Union-Bulletin*, January 23, 2019, https://www.union-bulletin.com/news/local/changes-eyed-for-columbia-county-sheriff-s-office/article_56e4fff0-1f42-11e9-b278-47a9986835ec.html.
5. Anna Boiko-Weyrauch, "Rural Washington Counties Seek More State Money with Tax Revenue Hard to Come By," Northwest Public Broadcasting, January 2,

2018, https://www.nwpb.org/2018/01/02/rural-washington-counties-seek-more-state-money-with-tax-revenue-hard-to-come-by/; "Frustrated and Broke, Washington Counties Consider Suing State," KUOW, April 5, 2018, http://archive.kuow.org/post/frustrated-and-broke-washington-counties-consider-suing-state.

6. Chad Sokol, "Lawsuit Challenges State Law Expanding Spokane County Commission from Three to Five Members," *Spokesman-Review*, February 27, 2019, https://www.spokesman.com/stories/2019/feb/27/lawsuit-challenges-state-law-expanding-spokane-cou/.
7. "Clerk's Office," Grays Harbor County, accessed February 27, 2023, http://www.co.grays-harbor.wa.us/government/clerk/index.php.
8. "Clerk's Office."
9. "How My Business Property Is Valued," Department of Revenue Washington State, accessed February 27, 2023, https://dor.wa.gov/find-taxes-rates/property-tax/how-my-business-property-valued.
10. "Property Tax in Washington State," MRSC, accessed February 27, 2023, http://mrsc.org/Home/Explore-topics/Finance/Revenues/The-Property-Tax-in-Washington-State.aspx.
11. "Coroners and Medical Examiners," Washington Association of County Officials, accessed February 27, 2023, https://countyofficials.org/215/Coroners-and-Medical-Examiners.
12. "Washington State Sheriffs," Washington State Sheriff's Association, accessed February 27, 2023, http://www.washeriffs.org/.

16. SPECIAL PURPOSE DISTRICTS

1. Avery, *Government of Washington State*, 287.
2. "History of PUDs in Washington," Washington Public Utility Districts Association (WPUDA), accessed February 27, 2023, https://www.wpuda.org/pud-history.
3. Joe Smillie, "Irrigation, Central to Growth of Dungeness Valley, Now Changing for Farms with Recent Water Rule," *Peninsula Daily News*, May 11, 2014, http://www.peninsuladailynews.com/news/irrigation-central-to-growth-of-dungeness-valley-now-changing-for-farms-with-recent-water-rule/.
4. "History of KID," Kennewick Irrigation District, accessed February 27, 2023, https://www.kid.org/your-kid/history-of-kid/.
5. "Bill to Choose Potential Sites for Future Commercial Airports Moves to Governor," Washington State House Democrats, April 27, 2019, https://housedemocrats.wa.gov/blog/2019/04/27/bill-to-choose-potential-sites-for-future-commercial-airports-moves-to-governor/.
6. "About Us," Puget Sound Regional Council, accessed February 27, 2023, https://www.psrc.org/about/what-we-do.

17. TRIBAL GOVERNMENTS

1. See, for example, Mann, *1491*.
2. Morriset, "Boldt from the Blue," 122.
3. Ficken, *Washington*, 38.
4. Severn, *The State We're In*, 62.
5. Light and Rand, *Indian Gaming and Tribal Sovereignty*, 32.
6. Avery, *Government of Washington State*, 235.
7. Severn, *The State We're In*, 64.
8. Rosalie Murphy, "Indian Gaming Generated $29.9 Billion in 2015," *Desert Sun*, updated July 20, 2016, https://www.desertsun.com/story/money/business/2016/07/20/indian-gaming-commission-2016-stats/87294386/.
9. Jonathan B. Taylor, "The Economic and Fiscal Impacts of Indian Tribes in Washington," 2012, https://www.washingtonindiangaming.org/wp-content/uploads/2018/04/wigaeconseptupt3.pdf.
10. "The Economic and Community Benefits of Tribes in Washington," Washington Indian Gaming Association, 2022, https://www.washingtontribes.org/resources/.
11. "Washington Tribes: Contributing Now More Than Ever," Washington Indian Gaming Association (WIGA), 2012, https://www.washingtonindiangaming.org/wp-content/uploads/2018/04/FINAL-CIR-WEB-VERSION.pdf.
12. "Kalispel Natural Resources Department," Kalispel Tribe of Indians, accessed February 27, 2023, https://www.kalispeltribe.com/kalispel-natural-resources-department/northern-pike.
13. "The Economic and Community Benefits of Tribes in Washington."
14. Neah Bay Chamber of Commerce, http://www.neahbaywa.com/.
15. Lia Steakley Dicker, "The Tribe That Would Not Die," *Seattle Met*, February 11, 2009, https://www.seattlemet.com/articles/2009/2/11/0309-fea-duwamish.
16. "AG Ferguson Announces Historic Tribal Consent and Consultation Policy," Washington State Office of the Attorney General, May 10, 2019, https://www.atg.wa.gov/news/news-releases/ag-ferguson-announces-historic-tribal-consent-and-consultation-policy.
17. "AG Ferguson Announces Historic Tribal Consent and Consultation Policy."
18. Richard Arlin Walker, "10 Things You Should Know about the Tulalip Tribes," *ICT News*, updated September 13, 2018, https://newsmaven.io/indiancountrytoday/archive/10-things-you-should-know-about-the-tulalip-tribes-tftGlyAAX0y89F4xaPhrsQ/.
19. Chris Winters, "Dennis Kendall, Who Died Monday, Remembered as Great Mayor," *HeraldNet*, March 24, 2015, https://www.heraldnet.com/news/dennis-kendall-who-died-monday-remembered-as-great-mayor/.
20. "About Us," Tulalip Tribes, accessed February 27, 2023, https://www.tulaliptribes-nsn.gov/WhoWeAre/AboutUs.
21. O'Brien, *American Indian Tribal Governments*, 184–88.

18. JOBS AND MONEY

1. Janelle Fritts and Jared Walczak, "2023 State Business Tax Climate Index," Tax Foundation, October 25, 2022, https://taxfoundation.org/publications/state-business-tax-climate-index/.
2. Dick Conway, "It's Time for a State Income Tax," *Seattle Business Magazine*, March 29, 2017, https://seattlebusinessmag.com/economy/its-time-state-income-tax/.
3. Michael B. Sauter, Samuel Stebbins and Evan Comen, "The Best (and Worst) States for Business," *USA Today*, March 5, 2018, https://www.usatoday.com/story/money/business/2018/03/05/economic-climate-best-and-worst-states-business/376783002/.
4. "America's Top States for Business," CNBC, July 10, 2018, https://www.cnbc.com/2018/07/10/americas-top-states-for-business-2018.html.
5. Noah Berger and Peter Fisher, "A Well-Educated Workforce Is Key to State Prosperity," Economic Policy Institute, August 22, 2013, https://www.epi.org/publication/states-education-productivity-growth-foundations/.
6. Michael Mazerov, "Kansas Provides Compelling Evidence of Failure of 'Supply-Side' Tax Cuts," Center on Budget and Policy Priorities, January 22, 2018, https://www.cbpp.org/research/state-budget-and-tax/kansas-provides-compelling-evidence-of-failure-of-supply-side-tax-cuts.
7. John W. Schoen, "There's Little Evidence That Corporate Tax Cuts Create Jobs," CNBC, updated August 30, 2017, https://www.cnbc.com/2017/08/30/theres-little-evidence-that-cutting-corporate-taxes-creates-jobs.html.
8. "2019 Expedited Tax Preferences Reviews," State of Washington Joint Legislative Audit and Review Committee (JLARC), updated May 7, 2019, http://www.citizentaxpref.wa.gov/documents/reports/2019ExpeditedReport.pdf.
9. Suzanne Barlyn, "How Delaware Became a Hub of Corporate Secrecy," *Insider*, August 24, 2016, https://www.businessinsider.com/heres-why-corporations-are-flocking-to-delaware-to-conduct-business-2016-8. The firms don't even have offices there, just paperwork filed with the state and a contract lawyer to watch the paperwork.
10. Ekaterina Jardim et al., "Minimum Wage Increases, Wages, and Low-Wage Employment: Evidence from Seattle," NBER Working Paper Series, revised May 2018, https://www.nber.org/papers/w23532.pdf.
11. Christopher Ingraham, "The Effects of 137 Minimum Wage Hikes, in One Chart," *Washington Post*, February 5, 2018, https://www.washingtonpost.com/news/wonk/wp/2018/02/05/raising-the-minimum-wage-doesnt-cost-jobs-multiple-studies-suggest/?utm_term=.9daa25a8d074.
12. Josh Hoxie, "The Seattle Minimum Wage Study Is Uttee B.S.," *Fortune*, June 27, 2017, http://fortune.com/2017/06/27/seattle-minimum-wage-study-results-impact-15-dollar-uw/.

13. Owen E. Richardson IV, "The Economic Effects of Minimum Wage," *Chron*, accessed February 27, 2023, https://smallbusiness.chron.com/impact-raising-minimum-wage-4938.html.
14. Hoxie, "The Seattle Minimum Wage Study Is Uttee B.S."
15. Julie Weed, "Hotel Boom in SeaTac Is Unfettered by $15 Minimum Wage," *New York Times*, July 31, 2017, https://www.nytimes.com/2017/07/31/business/hotel-boom-seattle-15-dollar-minimum-wage.html.
16. Jeffrey Dorfman, "Government Incentives to Attract Jobs Are Terrible Deals for Taxpayers," *Forbes*, September 6, 2017, https://www.forbes.com/sites/jeffreydorfman/2017/09/06/government-incentives-to-attract-jobs-are-terrible-deals-for-taxpayers/#1dbed2f96eff.
17. Paul Bowers, "South Carolina Schools Lose $318 Million a Year to Corporate Subsidies, Report Says," *Post and Courier*, updated September 14, 2020, https://www.postandcourier.com/news/south-carolina-schools-lose-318-million-a-year-to-corporate-subsidies-report-says/article_84fb7678-f97f-11e8-9ad3-bfa71f9a0ec7.html.
18. Caroline Cournoyer, "The Company Getting the Most State and Local Tax Breaks," *Governing*, March 20, 2015, https://www.governing.com/topics/finance/tns-boeing-state-local-tax-incentives.html.
19. Cournoyer, "The Company Getting the Most State and Local Tax Breaks."
20. Melissa Santos, "Jay Inslee's About-Face on Boeing's Big Tax Break," *Crosscut*, March 25, 2019, https://crosscut.com/2019/03/jay-inslees-about-face-boeings-big-tax-break.
21. Dominic Gates, "Boeing Saved $227M from State Tax Incentives Last Year While It Cut 6,000 Jobs," *Seattle Times*, September 26, 2018, https://www.seattletimes.com/business/boeing-aerospace/last-year-boeing-saved-227m-from-state-tax-incentives-while-it-cut-6000-jobs/.
22. J. D. Harrison, "Who Actually Creates Jobs: Start-ups, Small Businesses or Big Corporations?" *Washington Post*, April 25, 2013, https://www.washingtonpost.com/business/on-small-business/who-actually-creates-jobs-start-ups-small-businesses-or-big-corporations/2013/04/24/d373ef08-ac2b-11e2-a8b9-2a63d75b5459_story.html.
23. Barry Sheff, "The Economic Benefits of Infrastructure Investment, Part I: Making the Case," Woodard & Curran, December 18, 2014, https://www.woodardcurran.com/blog/the-economic-benefits-of-infrastructure-investment-part-i-making-the-case.
24. Sheff, "The Economic Benefits of Infrastructure Investment, Part I."
25. Brian Kennedy and D. Patrick Jones, "The Economic Impact of the Spokane Public Facilities District in 2016," Institute for Public Policy and Economic Analysis, Eastern Washington University, April 2017, http://www.spokanepfd.org/documents/Final%20Report%204%2019%2017.pdf.

26. Steve Hunter, "Kent's ShoWare Center's Lofty Financial Losses Causes Debate among City Leaders," *Kent Reporter*, October 16, 2014, https://www.kentreporter.com/news/kents-showare-centers-lofty-financial-losses-causes-debate-among-city-leaders/.
27. Steve Hunter, "Kent's ShoWare Center Shows Profit for First Six Months for First Time," *Kent Reporter*, August 3, 2018, https://www.kentreporter.com/news/city-owned-arena-has-lost-money-each-year-since-opening-in-2009/.
28. Hunter, "Kent's ShoWare Canter's Lofty Financial Losses."
29. "Town Toyota Center: $6.5M Economic Impact," *Wenatchee Business Journal*, April 4, 2017, http://www.ncwbusiness.com/news/town-toyota-center-65m-economic-impact; Dave Bernstein, "Town Toyota and PFD Renew Naming Rights Agreement," 560KPQ, August 30, 2018, https://www.kpq.com/town-toyota-and-pfd-renew-naming-rights-agreement/.
30. Shannon Hall, "Exxon Knew about Climate Change Almost 40 Years Ago," *Scientific American*, October 26, 2015, https://www.scientificamerican.com/article/exxon-knew-about-climate-change-almost-40-years-ago/.
31. Weber and Rogers, "Environmental and Natural Resource Policy," 240–43.
32. Bill Conroy, "Cruise-Ship Industry Spending in Washington Is Approaching $1B," *Seattle Business Magazine*, November 20, 2019, https://seattlebusinessmag.com/tourismhospitality/cruise-ship-industry-spending-washington-approaching-1b/.
33. Laura Arksey, "Leavenworth—Thumbnail History," HistoryLink.com, July 5, 2010, https://www.historylink.org/File/9475.
34. Arksey, "Leavenworth—Thumbnail History."
35. "An Economic Impact Study of Arts, Cultural, and Scientific Organizations in King County: 2014 Executive Summary," ArtsFund, released November 18, 2015, https://www.artsfund.org/wp-content/uploads/2015/12/EIS_King_ExecutiveSummary_120115.pdf.
36. "Arts and Economic Development are Complementary," Useful Community Development, accessed February 27, 2023, https://www.useful-community-development.org/arts-and-economic-development.html.
37. Esther Ngumbi, "Growing Urban Agriculture," *Stanford Social Innovation Review*, October 23, 2017, https://ssir.org/articles/entry/growing_urban_agriculture.
38. "Research and Policy," National Conference of State Legislatures (NCSL), accessed February 27, 2023, http://www.ncsl.org/research/environment-and-natural-resources/growing-interest-in-urban-agriculture.aspx.
39. "Farmers Markets Stimulate Local Economies," Farmers Marker Coalition, accessed February 27, 2023, https://farmersmarketcoalition.org/education/stimulate-local-economies/.

40. Jerry Cornfield, "Study Mulls Costs of Building Ferries Out of State," *HeraldNet*, January 2, 2017, https://www.heraldnet.com/news/study-mulls-costs-of-building-ferries-out-of-state/.
41. Christopher Steiner, "States That Truly Bet on Small Business," *Forbes*, May 3, 2010, https://www.forbes.com/2010/05/03/state-small-business-funding-programs-entrepreneurs-finance-grants.html#1d912afb1ae2.
42. Christopher Steiner, "In Depth: 11 Serious State Small-Biz Funding Programs," *Forbes*, May 3, 2010, https://www.forbes.com/2010/05/03/state-small-business-funding-programs-entrepreneurs-finance-grants_slide.html#15957bf74bf9.
43. Chad Otar, "What Percentage of Small Businesses Fail—And How Can You Avoid Being One of Them," *Forbes*, October 25, 2018, https://www.forbes.com/sites/forbesfinancecouncil/2018/10/25/what-percentage-of-small-businesses-fail-and-how-can-you-avoid-being-one-of-them/#5e95dc43b5f8.
44. Ryan Donahue and Brad McDearman, "Making Economic Development Strategies More Strategic," Brookings, August 25, 2017, https://www.brookings.edu/blog/the-avenue/2017/08/24/making-economic-development-strategies-more-strategic/.
45. John Davies, "Study Says Washington Still Relies on Boeing State Official Rejects Finding," *Journal of Commerce*, February 20, 1990, https://www.joc.com/study-says-washington-still-relies-boeing-state-official-rejects-finding_19900220.html.

BIBLIOGRAPHY

Most quotes found in this book are from interviews conducted by the author, either in person, via phone, or via email.

Avery, Mary W. *Government of Washington State.* Seattle: University of Washington Press, 1973.

Bowman, Ann O'M., and Richard Kearney. *State and Local Government.* Boston: Cengage Learning, 2016.

Burrows, Donald R. "A Progressive State with Regressive Taxes." In *Turning Points in Washington's Public Life*, edited by George Scott, 95–120. Seattle: Civitas Press, 2011.

Chasan, Daniel Jack. "Ultimate Democracy: Initiatives and Referenda." In *Turning Points in Washington's Public Life*, 191–218. Seattle: Civitas Press, 2011.

Chavez, Maria, and Robin Dale Jacobson. "Progressive Federalism: Washington State as a Protector of Civil Rights Progress?" In *Governing the Evergreen State*, edited by Cornell W. Clayton, Todd Donovan, and Nicholas P. Lovrich, 89–110. Pullman: WSU Press, 2018.

Clayton, Cornell W., and Gerry Alexander. "Washington's Constitution: The Politics of State Constitutional Interpretation." In *Governing the Evergreen State*, edited by Cornell W. Clayton, Todd Donovan, and Nicholas P. Lovrich, 135–54. Pullman: WSU Press, 2018.

Clayton, Cornell W., Todd Donovan, and Nicholas P. Lovrich. *Governing the Evergreen State: Political Life in Washington.* Pullman: WSU Press, 2018.

Donovan, Todd. "Elections in Washington." In *Governing the Evergreen State*, edited by Cornell W. Clayton, Todd Donovan, and Nicholas P. Lovrich, 23–43. Pullman: WSU Press, 2018.

Ficken, Rober, and Charles LeWarne. *Washington: A Centennial History.* Seattle: University of Washington Press, 1986.

Light, Steven Andrew, and Kathryn R. L. Rand. *Indian Gaming and Tribal Sovereignty: The Casino Compromise.* Lawrence: University of Kansas Press, 2005.

Long, Carolyn N., and David Ammons. "The Governor and Other Statewide Executives." In *Governing the Evergreen State*, edited by Cornell W. Clayton, Todd Donovan, and Nicholas P. Lovrich, 171–89. Pullman: WSU Press, 2018.

Lovrich, Nicholas P., John C. Pierce, and H. Stuart Elway. "Two Washingtons? Political Culture in the Evergreen State." In *Governing the Evergreen State*, edited by Cornell W. Clayton, Todd Donovan, and Nicholas P. Lovrich, 1–22. Pullman: WSU Press, 2018.

Mann, Charles. *1491: New Revelations of the Americas Before Columbus*. New York: Knopf, 2005.

Morriset, Mason. "Boldt from the Blue: Struggles over Salmon." In *Turning Points*, edited by George Scott, 121–32. Seattle: Civitas Press, 2011.

Nice, David C., John C. Pierce, and Charles H. Sheldon. *Government and Politics in the Evergreen State*. Pullman: WSU Press, 1992.

O'Brien, Sharon. *American Indian Tribal Governments*. Norman: University of Oklahoma Press, 1989.

Pall, Linda Louise Blackwelder. "The Washington Constitution: Fundamental Law and Principles." In *Government and Politics in the Evergreen State*, edited by David C. Nice, John C. Pierce, and Charles H. Sheldon. Pullman: WSU Press, 1992.

Pirch, Kevin. "Political Parties in the Evergreen State." In *Governing the Evergreen State*, edited by Cornell W. Clayton, Todd Donovan, and Nicholas P. Lovrich, 45–66. Pullman: WSU Press, 2018.

Salamone, Michael F., and Carl McCurley. "The Judicial System in the State of Washington." In *Governing the Evergreen State*, edited by Cornell W. Clayton, Todd Donovan, and Nicholas P. Lovrich, 191–200. Pullman: WSU Press, 2018.

Sell, T. M. "Politics and the Economy." In *An Introduction to Politics*, 5–22. Boston: Flat World Knowledge, 2017.

Scott, George, ed. *Turning Points in Washington's Public Life*. Seattle: Civitas Press, 2011.

Severn, Jill. *The State We're In: Washington*. Seattle: League of Women Voters, 2018.

Smith, Kevin B., and Alan Greenblatt. *Governing States and Localities*. Los Angeles: CQ Press, 2014.

Stehr, Steven D., Season A. Hoard, and Christina M. Sanders. "Continuity and Change in Public Policy in Washington State." In *Governing the Evergreen State*, edited by Cornell W. Clayton, Todd Donovan, and Nicholas P. Lovrich, 211–33. Pullman: WSU Press, 2018.

Thomas, Clive S., and Richard Elgar. "Interest Groups in Washington." In *Governing the Evergreen State*, edited by Cornell W. Clayton, Todd Donovan, and Nicholas P. Lovrich, 67–87. Pullman: WSU Press, 2018.

Tsebelis, George. "The Time Inconsistency of Long Constitutions: Evidence from the World." *European Journal of Political Research* 52, no. 4 (April 3, 2017): 820–45.

Weber, Edward P., and Ellen Rogers. "Environmental and Natural Resource Policy in the Evergreen State." In *Governing the Evergreen State*, edited by Cornell W. Clayton, Todd Donovan, and Nicholas P. Lovrich, 235–54. Pullman: WSU Press, 2018.

INDEX

ABD (aged, blind, and disabled) program, 172
Abraham, Nick, 94
activists and activism, 80, 158, 328
Adams, Brock, 165–66
Adams, John, 37
Adams-Onis Treaty (1819), 20
ad hoc federalism, 31
AFDC (Aid to Families with Dependent Children), 171
Affordable Care Act (Obamacare), 82, 149, 152
aged, blind, and disabled program. *See* ABD (aged, blind, and disabled) program
agencies, state: about, 103, 169–70; for agriculture, 178–79; budgets of, 138–39, 186; for children's well-being, 181–83; coordination of, 183–84; for environmental issues, 178; for law enforcement, 172–73; legal representation for, 148–49; legislative oversight by, 116; for outdoor activities, 179–81; oversight of, 147, 185, 191; privatization compared to, 170; for public assistance, 170–72; for safety, 176–78; for transportation services, 173–76
agriculture, 92–93, 178–79, 266–67
agriculture, urban, 326

Aid to Families with Dependent Children. *See* AFDC (Aid to Families with Dependent Children)
airports, 174, 274, 275–77, 303
Alabama, constitution of, 38
Alaska, 323, 333
Alaska Airlines, 306
Alaskan Way Viaduct, 27–28
Alderwood Associates v. Washington Environmental Council, 44
Alicea-Galvan, Veronica. *See* Galvan, Veronica Alicea
Allen, Paul, 71
allotments of Native American lands, 283–84, 291, 295
aluminum industry, 310, 333
amendments: to bills, 10, 12–13, 15–16, 124, 130–31, 132, 188; to state constitutions, 38, 39, 45, 49–50, 108, 158, 166–67; to U.S. Constitution, 31–32, 38, 39–40, 43, 44
American Party, 86
Anglo-American Convention (1818), 20
appeals in court cases, 40–41, 158–59
Appelwick, Marlin, 159
Apple Health, 146
Appropriations Committee (House), 125, 186
Articles of Confederation, 32
arts in economic development, 317, 325

Asian American Affairs Commission, 191–92
Asian Americans, 23, 24, 60–61, 114
assessors, county, 211, 220–22
Association of Washington Businesses, 94–95
attorneys, 156–57, 167–68, 228–30
attorneys general, 148–49
auditors, 147–48, 191, 222–26
Avery, Mary W., 193–94
Aviation Division, 174
Avista, 260–61

Bagnariol, John, 165
Baird, Brian, 87
Baker v. Carr, 107
B&O (business and occupations) tax, 195, 198–99, 252
Bangs, Luisa, 248–49
banks as public enterprise, 319–20
Barclay, Jeremy, 172–73
base in politics, 80
Bellinghausen, Jeff, 264–65
BIA. *See* Bureau of Indian Affairs (BIA)
Bill, Craig A., 290
Bill, Willard, 287
Bill of Rights, 35
bills, legislative: about, 10–11; budget, 187, 188–89; checks and balances for, 154; influences on, 90, 94, 96–97; initiatives compared with, 72–73; for mobile home residents, 7–8, 11–17; negotiation over, 121–22; passage of, 119; planning for, 78–79; processes for, 119, 122–25, 128, 129–34; referendum, 73; vetoes of, 10–11, 45, 131–32, 133, 138, 189
Black Ball ferry line, 175–76
Blacks, 23, 24, 60–61, 75, 114, 146, 214–15
blanket primary elections, 56–57, 58

boards of directors, educational, 255–57, 288
Boeing, 97–98, 99, 141, 307, 308–9, 330, 334, 335
Boeing, William E., 300, 334
Boeing Field, 275, 276
Boldt, George, 284
Bolerjack, Bob, 292
bonds: about, 145; baby, 145–47; construction, 193, 260, 302; defaults on, 315–16; general obligation, 192; municipal, 315; projects financed by, 125; school, 254–55, 257
Bonneville Power Act (1937), 259
Borden Chemical, 313
Boston Gazette, 107
Boundary Review Board, 244, 248
Boyd, Mall, 265–66
Britain, 20–21
Brookings Institution, 171
Brown, Lisa, 328–30
budgets: about, 103; city, 241, 249–52; county, 210, 212–13, 223; local, 277–78, 279, 301; state-level, 301–2
budgets, Washington State: about, 185–86, 189–93, 200–201; development of, 187–89, 199–200; and governor, 136, 138–39; management of, 115, 125, 126, 128–29, 146; for park system, 180–81; tax cuts affecting, 301
Building Industry Association of Washington, 73
bureaucracies, 103, 169–70
Bureau of Indian Affairs (BIA), 284, 288
Burien WA, 230, 319
Burlington Northern, 204, 279
Burlington Northern Santa Fe, 270, 278
Bush, George H. W., 139
Bush, George W., 35, 288

business and occupations tax. *See* B&O (business and occupations) tax
businesses, support for, 94–98, 100–101, 192–93, 299–300, 303–4, 307–9, 313–14, 325–27
business taxes, 299–300
bus lines, 174–75, 278

California, 56–57, 141, 332
Callow, Keith, 156
campaigns for public office, 59, 62–67, 77–78, 84, 91
cannabis banking reform, 144
Canwell, Albert, and Canwell Committee, 164
cap-and-trade programs, 321
Cape Flattery, 286–87
capital budget, 186, 192
Capital Budget Committee (House), 125
capital gains taxes, 95, 197–98
Capital Investment Program Fund, 250–51
carbon taxes, 321
Carroll, Charles O. "Chuck," 164–65
car tab taxes, 304
case law, 158
caucuses, 78–79, 114, 130, 131
censuses, 19, 21, 107
Centennial Accord, 289–90
Century Link/Lumen Field, 199
CERB (Community Economic Revitalization Board), 271
Charles, Frances, 290–91
charter schools, 150
checks and balance system, 30, 103, 109–10, 154
Cherberg, John, 142
chief administrators, county, 214
Child Protective Services. *See* CPS (Child Protective Services)

children, 35, 48, 127, 146, 147, 150, 170–72, 181–83
Chinese Americans, 114
Choi, Nathan, 156–57
Chopp, Frank, 10, 12
Cichy, Ben, 165
cigarette taxes, 199
cities: about, 240–44, 246–48; annexations by, 209, 218, 247–48, 292; budgets of, 241, 249–52; incorporation by, 209, 218, 240, 244, 246–47, 251
Citizens Party, 84
city councils, 76, 120, 241–42, 243, 244–46, 248–49, 303–4
city managers, 233, 241–42, 243, 249
civil cases, 154–55, 160
Civil Rights & Judiciary Committee (House), 11, 126
Civil War, 21, 22, 23
Clarkston General Water Supply Company, 261
climate change, 94, 95, 151, 267, 280–81, 320–21
Clinton, Bill, 171, 288
code cities, 244
College & Workforce Development Committee (House), 126
Columbia River dam system, 35–36, 310
Commerce & Gaming Committee (House), 126
commissioners: city, 243; county, 208, 210, 214–18, 237; insurance, 152–53; public lands, 151; in scandals, 148; special purpose district, 253, 257, 258, 261–62, 263, 265, 266–67, 273, 274
Commission for Constitutional Alternatives, 50
committees, legislative, 10–11, 13, 115–16, 121, 123–29, 186–88
communists, 86, 164

Community Economic Revitalization Board. *See* CERB (Community Economic Revitalization Board)
compromise, 28, 105, 108, 132, 133, 134, 189
confederations, 32
Congress: about, 30; and budgets, 185; constitutional restrictions on, 39–40, 43; districts created by, 271; and federalism, 31–33; funding by, 35; and Native Americans, 284, 285; state government compared with, 206; and statehood process, 21, 37; and territorial laws, 22; welfare laws of, 171
Connor, Patrick, 95–97
conservatives and conservatism, 31, 80–81, 88, 171
Constitution, U.S., 31–33, 38–40, 43–44, 46, 47, 56, 150, 291
constitution, Washington State: about, 38–39; amendments to, 45, 49–50, 108, 158, 166–67; basis of, 46–48; beginnings of, 21, 44–45; importance of, 51; and initiatives, 69, 72; interpretations of, 40; and Native Americans, 284; and referenda, 69; requirements of, 106, 107, 136, 142–43, 190, 207, 208; specificity of, 48–49; and state courts, 41, 42–43; U.S. Constitution compared with, 43–44
constitutional conventions, 21, 44–45, 50
Constitution Party, 86
constitutions, state, 37–39, 43–44, 49–51
constitutions, tribal, 277–78, 291, 296
constructionism in U.S. Constitution, 39
consumer price index (CPI), 11, 214–15, 305
Consumer Protection Act, 149
Consumer Protection & Business Committee (House), 126

Consumer Protection Division, 152
Conway, Dick, 196, 299, 301
Cooke, Suzette, 314
coroners, 226–28, 229–30
corporations, distrust of, 45, 46–47, 48
Costco, 71, 99
council manager (weak mayor) governments, 241–42, 243
counties, 55, 159–60, 167, 204, 210–11, 269, 289. *See also* governments
county clerks, 211, 218–20
county councils, 9, 209, 211, 212–14
county executives, 211–14
court system, 30, 103, 154–60, 161–62, 167–68. *See also* Supreme Court, U.S.; Supreme Court, Washington State; supreme courts, state-level
COVID-19 pandemic, 139, 146, 195
Covington WA, 230, 251–52, 263
CPI. *See* consumer price index (CPI)
CPS (Child Protective Services), 182
criminal cases, 154, 160
Criminal Investigations service, 177
cruise industry, 323
Cutlar, Lyman, 20–21

Dave (film), 67–68
Davidson, Duane A., 144, 145, 336
debt, state, 145, 192
Delaware, 303, 307, 349n9
democracies, 29–30, 106
Democracy Vouchers, 64–65
Democratic Party: changes in, 79–80; elected officials from, 139–41, 219–20, 341n4; in elections, 56–58, 76–77, 83–84; and health care reform, 152–53; history of, 26, 75; as majority, 7–8, 13; minority groups in, 114; planning by, 78–79; Republicans at odds with, 74, 133–34, 189; Republi-

cans cooperating with, 188; and state constitution, 44; and statehood, 21; supporters of, 78, 99, 150; and taxes, 197–98, 200–201; and third parties, 84, 85–86, 87; values of, 76, 82–83
Democratic Socialists, 86
Dennis, Dean, 268
Dent, Tom, 111–12, 117, 118–19
dental industry, 99–100
Department of Agriculture, 178–79
Department of Children, Youth & Families, 181, 182
Department of Commerce, 15, 328–30
Department of Corrections, 172–73
Department of Early Learning, 182
Department of Ecology, 139, 178, 267
Department of Enterprise Services, 183–84
Department of Fish and Wildlife, 179–80, 286
Department of Labor & Industries, 177–78
Department of Natural Resources, 151
Department of Social and Health Services. See DSHS (Department of Social and Health Services)
Department of Transportation. See WSDOT (Department of Transportation)
Des Moines WA, 18, 248–49, 303–4
Diamond, Ann, 87
Dickens, Ishbel, 11
direct initiatives, 69–70
diseases, 19, 84, 237–38, 282, 339n1
dispute resolution, 163
district courts, 160
districts. See fire districts; hospital districts; legislative districts; port districts; public facilities districts; public utility districts; school districts; special purpose districts; water and sewer districts
diversity in legislatures, 114–15
Donovan, Todd, 208, 213, 289
Dorfman, Jeffrey, 308
drug addiction policy, 168, 232
DSHS (Department of Social and Health Services), 170–71, 182
Dungeness River Agricultural Water Users Association, 267
Duvall, Thad, 223–24
Duwamish River, 288
Duwamish Tribe, 283, 287–89

earthquakes, 27
Easton, David, 1
Economic and Revenue Forecast Council (ERFC), 187, 199–200
Economic Development Investment program (Whatcom County), 310–11
education. See school districts; schools
educational service districts, 257
Education Committee (House), 126
elections: about, 53, 67–68; local, 55, 76, 159–60, 210–11, 246, 255; national, 74, 88; tribal, 291, 293, 294. See also elections, state
elections, state: about, 106–7; electoral system in, 87; executive, 135; general, 58, 62, 77–78, 88; judicial, 42, 155–57, 159; and political parties, 79–80; primary, 55–58, 76–78, 88; special, 58
electric power, 258–61, 310, 333
elites, 17, 47, 74, 80, 89
Employee Disclosure program, 147
Enabling Act (1889), 19, 46
Energy Northwest, 260
enterprises, public, 81–82, 183–84, 250–52, 319–20

environmental issues, 92, 93–94, 126, 178, 180, 280–81, 303, 320–22
Environment & Energy Committee (House), 126
ERFC. *See* Economic and Revenue Forecast Council (ERFC)
Ericksen, Wayne, 84
Euro-Americans, 19–20, 282, 283, 284, 300–301, 332–33
Evans, Dan, 49–50, 139, 141
events centers in economic development, 311, 312–18
evictions, 4–5, 11, 14
executive branch, 116, 135–36, 169
executive sessions, legislative, 12, 124
experience in legislators, 116–17
Eyman, Tim, 72, 304

family issues, 127, 328
Farmer Labor Party, 84
FBI, 165, 166
federal investment, 35–36
federalism, 29, 31–36
federal republics, 30, 36
Federal Transit Administration, 174
Federal Way Performing Arts and Events Center, 316–19
Federal Way WA, 65, 247, 312, 317–18, 319, 330
Ferguson, Bob, 149, 290–91
Ferrell, Jim, 317–18, 319
Ferry, Elisha P., 22–23
ferry system, 175–76, 326–27
filing for office, 62–63
Finance Committee (House), 126
fire districts, 262–65
firefighters, 176–77, 262, 264–65
The Firs Mobile Home Park, 4–5, 7–8, 11, 16–17, 121, 337
fish and fishing, 179, 284, 286, 287, 333

Flight Plan group, 276
Foster, Kym, 218–20
Franz, Hilary, 151
freedom of speech, 39–40, 43–44
funding for campaigns, 63–65, 77–78, 91

Galvan, Veronica Alicea, 161–62, 168
gaming operations, 285, 286
GamScam, 165
Gardner, Booth, 139, 140
GDP (gross domestic product), 24, 25, 145
general fund budget, 186
General Waterworks Corporation, 260–61
geography, effect of, 25, 300–301
Georgia, constitution of, 38
Gerry, Elbridge, and gerrymandering, 107–8
ghost towns, 204–5
GMA. *See* Growth Management Act (1990) (GMA)
Goldmark, Charles, 164
Goldmark, John, 164
Gonzalez, Steven, 156–57
GOP (Grand Old Party), 57. *See also* Republican Party
Gorton, Slade, 149
government, federal: about, 1, 34–35; congressional style of, 30; economic power of, 300; and Native Americans, 282–85, 287–89; and states, 30–33, 35–36
governments: city, 240–52; council manager (weak mayor), 241–42, 243; county, 207–11, 213–14, 218, 220–21, 222–24, 226, 228–29, 230–31, 234–35; local, 1, 5–6, 29, 32, 203–5, 300–301; mayor council (strong mayor), 241, 242–43, 245–46, 317; parliamentary, 30; state, 1, 5–6, 31–33, 35–36, 45,

190–93, 300–301; super-regional, 17, 277–78; tribal, 284, 289–90, 291–92, 294–95, 296–97. *See also specific special purpose districts*
governors: about, 103; and budget, 186, 187, 189; in congressional systems, 30; and legislature, 16, 109–10, 131–33, 138–39; and Native Americans, 289–90; power limitations for, 46, 47, 105; protection for, 177; role of, 135–36, 141, 155; territorial, 21–23; third-party, 84; veto power of, 10–11, 45, 138
Governor's Office of Indian Affairs, 290
Grant, Ulysses S., 23
Gray, Robert, 20
Greater Wenatchee Irrigation District, 267
Greater Wenatchee Regional Events Center Public Facilities District, 314–15
Great Northern Railway, 23, 269, 324
Great Recession (2007–8), 4, 140, 171, 180, 190, 200, 286, 304
Greenbank Farm, 270, 271
green investment in economic development, 320–22
Green Party, 86
Green River Valley, 220–21
Gregerson, Mia, 7, 8–10, 11, 12–13, 15, 16, 337
Gregoire, Christine, 139, 140, 149
Greyhound, 174
Griffin, Charles, 20–21
Griswold, "Fast" Lucie, 87
gross domestic product. *See* GDP (gross domestic product)
growth, economic, 25, 301–2, 331–35
Growth Management Act (1990) (GMA), 97–98, 208, 248, 335
Gurol, Kamuron, 241–42

Habib, Cyrus, 143, 336
Hamilton, Darrick, 146
Hanford Nuclear Reservation, 35, 334
Hansen, Cecile, 287–89
Hartley, Roland, 181, 194
Hasegawa, Bob, 119, 319–20
Health Care & Wellness Committee (House), 126
health insurance, 152
hearings of bills, 123–25
Heck, Denny, 143
Hendersen, Nick, 226
Highline College, 18
Hill, James J., 269
Hill, Knute, 84, 85
Hirst decision, 189, 269
Hobbs, Steve, 143
Holmes, Oliver Wendell, Jr., 193
Homeland Security Division, 177
homelessness, 5, 8, 11, 13, 16, 172
homeowners associations, 4–5
home rule charters, 204, 207, 208, 211
hospital districts, 265–66
Housing, Community Development & Veterans Committee (House), 126–27
Housing Committee (House), 129
Housing Stability & Affordability Committee (Senate), 13
Hudson's Bay Company, 20–21
human services, 170–71, 182, 189–90
Human Services & Early Learning Committee (House), 127
Hunter, Ross, 182–83

immigrants, 75–76, 191–92, 246, 298
incentives, business, 307–9
income taxes, 194–95, 196–97
incumbents, 55–56, 77–78
Indian boarding schools, 283

Indian Citizenship Act (1924), 284
Indian Gaming Regulatory Act (1988), 285
Indian Reorganization Act (1934), 284, 291
Indian Self-Determination Act (1975), 284
indirect initiatives, 69–70
inflation, 145, 150, 192, 200, 305
infrastructure and economic development, 309–11
Inghram, Paul, 278
initiatives, 57, 69–73, 99–100, 310–11
Initiatives to the Legislature, 69–70
Initiatives to the People, 69–70
Innovation, Community & Economic Development & Veterans Committee (House), 129
Innovation, Technology & Economic Development Committee (House), 127
Inslee, Jay, 136–37, 139–40, 149, 153, 197, 308–9
insurance, 73, 146, 152–53
interest groups: about, 53, 77, 89–92, 98–99; for agriculture, 92–93; for business, 94–98; environmental, 93–94; initiatives used by, 71; for petrochemical industry, 93; for social justice, 94
internment of Japanese Americans, 167
Interurban (rail transit line), 3
irrigation districts, 266–69
Irwin, Morgan, 12

Jackson, John R., 181
Jamison, Sandy, 224–26
Japanese Americans, 167
JARRC (Joint Administrative Rules Review Committee), 115

Jinkins, Laurie, 8, 10, 117–18
JLARC (Joint Legislative Audit and Review Committee), 115
jobs: and events centers, 311–12, 313; and growth, 332, 335; impact of, 298–99; and infrastructure, 310; in local businesses, 326–27; in port districts, 274–75; and public assistance, 171; and public policy, 300–301; recruitment for, 307–9; and taxes, 301–3, 331–32; in tourism, 322; and wages, 305–6
John R. Jackson House, 181
Johnson, Charles, 156
Joint Administrative Rules Review Committee. *See* JARRC (Joint Administrative Rules Review Committee)
Joint Legislative Audit and Review Committee. *See* JLARC (Joint Legislative Audit and Review Committee)
Joint Transportation Committee. *See* JTC (Joint Transportation Committee)
Jouas, Jean-Marc, 271
JTC (Joint Transportation Committee), 115–16
judges: in checks and balance system, 154; organization of, 159–60; rights of, 155–56; role of, 40–43, 154–55, 158–59, 161–62, 163; in scandals, 166–67; selection of, 136, 155, 156–57
juries, 154–55, 162–63

Kalispel Tribe, 286
Kansas and Kansas Effect, 302
Keiser, Karen, 14, 15
Kelley, Troy, 148, 164
Kelly, Red, 87
Kendall, Dennis, 292
Kennedy, James, 228–29

Kennewick Irrigation District, 267–68
Kent Station, 313–14
Kent WA, 262–63, 312–14, 331
Keynes, John Maynard, and Keynesian economics, 319–20
King, Curtis, 92, 118, 134
King County International Airport. *See* Boeing Field
King County WA: districts in, 253–54; economy of, 274, 322; elections in, 55; environmental awareness in, 321; as home rule charter county, 208; impact of, 26; land use by, 220–21; officials in, 140, 211, 228–29; separatist movements in, 207–8; services of, 209, 241, 251, 264–65
Kirk, Peter, and Kirkland WA, 301
Kline, Kevin, 68
Kreidler, Mike, 152–53
Kuderer, Patty, 13–14, 15, 17
Kuney, Mary, 216–18, 336
Kuntz, Frank, 244–46, 315, 316

Labor & Commerce Committee (Senate), 128
Labor & Workplace Standards Committee (House), 127
labor issues, 92, 95, 177–78
Lacey, Steve, 316
Laffer, Arthur, and Laffer Curve, 301–2
land and Native Americans, 282–84, 288
landlords, 8, 13–14, 15–16
landlord-tenant rights, 5, 8
Larrabee State Park, 181
Latinx Americans, 4, 23–24, 60–61, 76, 246
Law Enforcement Assisted Diversion (LEAD), 168
law-making as legislative job, 109
lawyers. *See* attorneys

League of Women Voters, 108
LEAP (Legislative Evaluation and Accountability Program), 115
Leavenworth WA, 266, 324
Legislative Assemblies, 30
Legislative Budget Committee, 115
legislative districts, 9, 63, 76–77, 78, 106–9
Legislative Evaluation and Accountability Program. *See* LEAP (Legislative Evaluation and Accountability Program)
Legislative Joint Fact-Finding Committee on Un-American Activities, 164
legislators, 109–12, 114–15
legislature(s): about, 103, 105–6; citizen input to, 69–70, 72–73; and college funding, 6; committees of, 126–29; in congressional systems, 30; and constitutional conventions, 50; diversity in, 114–15; formation of, 45; oversight by, 115–16; political parties in, 76–77, 78–79; processes of, 10–11, 129–33; and public school funding, 48–49; redistricting by, 107–9; relationships in, 118–19; role of, 109–12; special sessions of, 133–34; territorial, 22
Leschi (Nisqually Indian man), 22
Lester WA, 204–5
levies, 221–22, 254–55
Levy, Chelsea, 280
Lewis and Clark Expedition, 20
liberals and liberalism, 80–81, 85–86
Libertarian Party, 58, 84–85
lieutenant governors, 129, 142–43
light rail transit, 3–4, 17–18, 278–81
Lincoln, Abraham, 23
Link Light Rail, 278
Little, Gary, 166–67
living constitution concept, 39, 40

Lloyd Corporation v. Tanner, 44
lobbyists and lobbying, 90–95, 96–97
Local Government Committee (House), 127
local support in economic development, 325–27
local taxes, 193–94, 196, 254, 264, 322
location in economic development, 331
Locke, Gary, 24, 57, 140, 141
Longview WA, 251
lottery, 199
Louisiana, primaries in, 57
Louws, Jack, 212–13, 289, 310–11
Lowry, Mike, 140
Luke, Wing, 24

Makah Tribe, 286–87
Maleng, Norm, 228
mandates, unfunded, 210, 215
Manufactured/Mobile Home Landlord-Tenant Act, 8, 13
Mardesich, August, 165
markets, economic, 81–82, 85, 300
Martin, Clarence, 181
Martin, Jaime, 296–97
Marysville WA, 291, 292
Massachusetts, constitution of, 37
mayor council (strong mayor) governments, 241, 242–43, 245–46, 317
mayors, 119–20, 166, 212, 241–43, 244–46, 292, 317
Mays, Christy, 11
McCarthy, Pat, 148
McCleary v. Washington, 48–49, 134, 188, 189, 190
McCloud, Sheryl Gordon, 40–43
McCoy, John, 79, 119, 291–92, 293–94, 336
McCrone, Donald, and McCrone's Rule, 124–25, 131

McEnderfer, Peter J., 221–22
McGill, Henry, 22
McKenna, Rob, 149
measures, referendum, 73
Medicaid, 146, 189–90
medical examiners. *See* coroners
Medic One, 264
Meise, Kayla, 235
mental illness, 84
Metro (Municipality of Metropolitan Seattle), 209, 213, 258
Meyers, Vic, 142
Michalopoulos, Chris, 270, 271
Microsoft, 182–83
Mike the Mover, 100–101
Military Road, 316
Millar, Roger, 175
Millennium Accord (1996), 290
Mishasek, John, 270–72
mixed-use development in economic development, 318–19
mobile homes and parks, 4–5, 7–8, 11, 13–14, 16–17, 121, 337
monopolies, natural, 258
Montana, primaries in, 57
Mosquito fleet, 175
moving business, deregulation of, 100–101
Mt. Rainier National Park, 181
Muckleshoot Tribe, 296
municipal courts, 160
municipality, tribal, 293–94
Munro, Ed, 253
Murray, Ed, 166–67
Museum of History and Industry, 175

National Federation of Independent Businesses. *See* NFIB (National Federation of Independent Businesses)
National Guard, 136

Native Americans: in cooperative agreements, 291–94; economic situation of, 285–87; government of, 289–91, 294–97; history of, 19, 22, 282–85, 295, 296, 339n1; population of, 23; proponents for, 287–89; and state committees, 128; voting rights for, 114
Natural Area Preserves, 151
Natural Law Party, 86
Natural Resource Conservation Areas, 151
Neah Bay Chamber of Commerce, 286–87
Nebraska, government of, 30
Nehring, Jon, 292–93
NFIB (National Federation of Independent Businesses), 95, 96–97
911 system, 264
Nisqually earthquake (2001), 27
No Child Left Behind (2001), 35, 150
North Dakota, banking system in, 319
Northern Pacific Railroad, 204
Northwest Seaport Alliance, 273. See also Port of Seattle; Port of Tacoma
Nowicki, Ron, 261–62
nuclear power, 260

Obamacare. See Affordable Care Act (Obamacare)
Office of Program Research (OPR), 116
Olympia WA, 22, 93
Open Public Meetings Act, 204
OPR. See Office of Program Research (OPR)
Optional Municipal Code, 244
Oregon, 19, 20, 195, 196
Oregon Treaty (1846), 20
originalism in U.S. Constitution, 39
Orwall, Tina, 12, 132–33

"Out With Logic, On With Lunacy" Party, 87
oversight as legislative job, 110, 115–16
overtime pay, 307
Owen, Brad, 142–43
OWL Party, 87

Pacific Highway South, 18
PAEC, 318–19
pages in legislative sessions, 130
Pall, Linda Louise Blackwelder, 40
Park, Jong Soo, 4–5, 7, 16
parks, 180–81, 240
parliamentary governments, 30
Patterson, Julia, 9, 84
PCOs (precinct committee officers), 78
PDC. See Public Disclosure Commission (PDC)
Pellicciotti, Mike, 144, 145–47, 336
Pend Oreille Valley Railroad, 270
pensions, 146, 191
People's Party, 84
Peterson, Lynn, 175
pick-a-party primary elections, 57
Pierce, Franklin, 22
Pig War (1859), 20–21
pluralism, 17, 28, 47
Point Elliott Treaty (1855), 288, 291
political parties, 53, 74–80, 82–88
Polk, James, 20
Populist Party, 84
populists, 141
port districts: airports in, 275–77; seaports in, 269–75
Port of Coupeville, 270–71
Port of Grays Harbor, 269
Port of Seattle, 269, 273–77, 304, 323
Port of Tacoma, 273, 275
Port of Tracyton, 272–73
Port of Walla Walla, 270

Prada, Stacie, 235–39
precinct committee officers. *See* PCOs (precinct committee officers)
precincts in legislative districts, 9, 78
prisons, 71, 156, 168, 172, 173
Pritchard, Joel, 142
private schools, 149–50
Problem Gambling Account, 199
Progressives: new, 80, 85–86; traditional, 76, 84, 85, 246, 269
property taxes, 48, 194, 198, 209–10, 214–15, 217, 220–22
public assistance, 171–72
Public Disclosure Commission (PDC), 64, 71
public facilities districts, 312–16
public lands, 151
Public Meetings Act, 120
Public Records Act, 120
Public Safety Committee (House), 127
public utility districts, 81–82, 257, 258–62
Puget Sound Clean Air Agency, 280
Puget Sound region, 3, 23, 25–26, 175–76, 178, 273, 276, 279
Puget Sound Regional Council, 277–78

Quil Ceda Village WA, 293–94

Rabel, Larry, 263
radicals, 80, 88, 336
railroad, 23, 47, 204, 269–70, 311, 333
Ralph, Dana, 314, 331
Ray, Dixie Lee, 56, 140–41
RCW (Revised Codes of Washington), 223
readings of bills, 12–13, 15, 123, 129, 130–31, 132, 188
Reagan, Ronald, 75
real estate taxes, 199
recalls of officials, 46, 166, 242

recognition for Indian tribes, 287–89, 290, 296
recounts of election results, 58
recruitment of business, 307–9
redistricting, 107–8
Reed, Sam, 49–50
Reeves, Kristine, 112–14, 336
referenda, 69–73
Regional Fire Authorities (RFAs), 251, 262, 263
registration for voting, 56, 59, 79
regressive taxes, 195–97
regulations in economic development, 303–4
Reid-Simons, Cheryl, 255–57
relationships in legislatures, 117–19
representation as legislative job, 110
representatives, federal, 107
representatives, state-level, 106–7
Republican Leadership Council, 78
Republican Party: and budget issues, 269; changes in, 79–80, 81; Democrats at odds with, 74, 133–34, 189; Democrats cooperating with, 188; and education, 150; elected officials from, 144; in elections, 56–58, 76–77; and health care reform, 149; history of, 26, 75; minority groups in, 114; planning by, 78–79; and sheriff's position, 211, 230, 233–34; and state constitution, 44; and statehood, 21; supporters of, 78, 99; and taxes, 197–98, 200–201; and third parties, 85–86, 87–88; and transportation issues, 175; values of, 76, 82–83
republics, 29–30, 36, 106, 111
reservations, Native American, 282–88, 291, 295
revenue: about, 103; for cities, 249–50, 252; for counties, 217–18; and jobs,

330–31; predicting, 187, 199–200; during recessions, 201; taxes as source of, 71–72, 194–95, 198, 199, 301, 335; for tribal governments, 285
Revised Codes of Washington. *See* RCW (Revised Codes of Washington)
Reykdal, Chris, 151
Reynolds v. Sims, 107
RFAS. *See* Regional Fire Authorities (RFAS)
Riccelli, Marcus, 217
Rice, Norm, 24
Rodriguez, Guadalupe, 16
Rogers, John, 84
Rolfes, Christine, 187–88
Roosevelt, Franklin, 67
Rossi, Dino, 140, 141
Rules Committee (House), 12, 125, 128, 188
Rules Committee (Senate), 15, 129, 188
Rural Communities Partnership Initiative, 151
Rural County Economic Development Fund, 271–72
Rural Development, Agriculture & Natural Resources Committee (House), 127
Russia, 20
Ryu, Cindy, 119–22

sales taxes, 195–96, 304
salmon, 282, 333
Sanders, Bernie, 86
Sanders, Richard B., 155–56
Satterberg, Dan, 167–68, 228–29, 336
Sawant, Kshama, 26, 86
scandals, 163–67, 219
Schinfeld, Eric, 273, 274
school districts, 35, 48, 71, 150, 204, 240, 254–57

schools: boards of directors for, 255–57, 288; charter, 150; funding for, 48–49, 71–72, 112–13, 136–37, 158, 190; Indian boarding, 283; oversight of, 149–51; private, 149–50; standardized testing in, 150–51; vocational, 325–26
Schwarzenegger, Arnold, 141
Sealth, Chief, 287
SeaTac WA, 4–5, 17, 230, 263–64, 306
Seattle Bridge accident, 28
Seattle School Board, 288
Seattle-Tacoma International Airport, 4, 274, 275–77
Seattle Times, 156
Seattle WA, 3–4, 24–25, 26–27, 64–65, 76, 246, 288, 323, 332–33
secretaries of state, 70, 143, 341n4
secretary of transportation, 175, 278
Sell's Second Law of Political Economy, 17
senators, state-level, 106–7, 128–29, 142
sentencing system, 163
sewer districts. *See* water and sewer districts
Shanks, Michael, 100–101
Shea, Matt, 26, 336
sheriffs, 210–11, 230–34
Shoreline WA, 120
Showare Center, 313–14
Shrontz, Frank, 335
signature gathering, 46, 50, 70, 71, 244
Silver Republicans, 84
Small Tribes of Western Washington, 288
SNAP (Supplemental Nutrition Assistance Program), 172, 189–90
Snaza, John, 231–34
Snaza, Robert, 231–34
Snoqualmie Tribe, 296–97
Snoqualmie WA, 296–97
socialism, 82
Socialist Party, 84, 86

Socialist Workers Party, 86
social media, 60, 66–67
Sohn, Chang-Mook, 200
Sounder Commuter Rail, 278
Sound Transit, 3–4, 17–18, 278–81
sovereignty, tribal, 285, 289–90, 291
Spain, 20
special purpose districts, 253–55.
  See also fire districts; hospital districts; irrigation districts; port districts; public utility districts; school districts; water and sewer districts
special sessions, 133
Spellman, John, 140–41
Spitzer, Hugh, 37, 39, 47, 253–54
Spokane County WA, 216–18
Spokane Public Facilities District, 312
Spokane Street Bridge, 28
Spokane WA, 250–51
sponsors and cosponsors of bills, 7–8, 122–23, 130
stadia in economic development, 311–12
staff, legislative, 116
stakeholders in bills, 13, 14, 15–16
State Fire Marshal and Fire Protection Bureau, 176–77
State Government & Tribal Relations Committee (House), 128
state insurance premium taxes, 199
State Need Grant Program, 190
State Patrol, 170, 176–77
State v. Arlene's Flowers, 41–42
Stevens, Isaac, 22, 283, 295
Stone, Corliss P., 163–64
Sun, Cy, 242
sunset laws, 115–16, 191–92
superintendents of public instruction, 149, 151, 255, 257
superior courts, 160–62

Supplemental Nutrition Assistance Program. *See* SNAP (Supplemental Nutrition Assistance Program)
Supreme Court, U.S., 35, 44, 56–57, 71, 107, 155, 284–85
Supreme Court, Washington State: cases of, 198; decisions of, 24, 44, 48–49, 67, 189, 194, 208, 269; elections for, 156–57; organizational position of, 155; role of, 41–42, 157–58, 168
supreme courts, state-level, 155, 158
Suquamish (ferry), 176

TANF (Temporary Assistance for Needy Families), 171–72
taxes: about, 6, 32, 103, 299–300; attitudes toward, 82, 279–80; and budget, 192, 200–201; in economic development, 299, 301–4, 308–9, 312–13, 314–16, 322, 330–31, 335; factors affecting, 71–72, 133; levels of, 209–10, 247, 250–52, 253–54; and Native Americans, 282, 284; purpose of, 193–99, 264, 271–72; regressive, 195–97; types of, 48, 95, 197–99, 214–15, 217, 220–22, 304, 321
Tax Foundation, 194, 299–300
Temporary Assistance for Needy Families. *See* TANF (Temporary Assistance for Needy Families)
tenants, 4–5, 7, 8, 14–16
term limits, 67
territories, pre-statehood, 19, 21–23
Thompson, Hayley, 226–28
three-strikes-and-you're-out laws, 14, 71, 156, 173
Tillicum (ferry), 176
tobacco industry, 149, 199
tobacco taxes, 199
top-two primary elections, 57–58, 76

tourism, 271, 286–87, 322–24
townships, 208
Town Toyota Center, 314–16
Toxicology Lab, 177
transit, 3–4, 17–18, 278–81
transportation budget, 186, 192–93
Transportation Commission, 175
Transportation Committee (House), 128
Travel Washington, 174–75
treasurers, 143–47, 234–39
treaties, 20–21, 22, 282–83, 284, 288, 291, 295
Treaty of 1855 (with the Yakama people), 295
Treaty of Washington (1871), 21
trial courts, 155, 160
Trump, Donald, 26, 81, 88, 298
tuition, 6, 190
Tulalip Tribe, 291–94
two-party systems, 74, 88

unions, 95, 306
University of Washington, 164, 306
USA Today, 299–300
utilities, 70, 81–82, 257–59
Utilities and Transportation Commission, 100, 258
utility taxes, 199

values, 1, 17, 83, 86, 297
Vance, Chris, 78, 80, 87
Ventura, Jesse "the Body," 141
vetoes, 10–11, 45, 109, 131–32, 133, 138, 189, 241
Virginia V (ship), 175
Vision 2040, 277–78
Voelker, Shelbea, 267–69
voir dire, 163
voters: contradictory decisions of, 71–72; demographics of, 60–61, 108–9;
distrust by, 70; likely, 66; misconceptions of, 67–68; Native American, 284, 294; party affiliation of, 79–80, 83–84, 87–88; political parties' misalignment with, 56–58; turnout of, 55, 59, 60, 255–56
voting, importance of, 60–61, 137
voucher systems, 64–65, 149–50

wages, 92, 177–78, 274, 298–99, 305–7, 309, 330
Walgren, Gordon, 165
Walla Walla Convention (1878), 44
Washington, about, 19–21, 23–28, 336–37
Washington as part of republic, 35–36, 106
Washington Association of Counties, 217
Washington Commission on Judicial Conduct, 155–56
Washington Conservation Voters, 93–94
Washington Environmental Council, 93
Washington Future Fund, 146–47
Washington Geologic Survey, 151
Washington Independents PAC, 87–88
Washington Public Ports Association. *See* WPPA (Washington Public Ports Association)
Washington Public Power Supply System. *See* WPPSS (Washington Public Power Supply System)
Washington State Bar Association, 168
Washington State Farm Bureau, 92–93
Washington State Ferries, 175–76
Washington State Grange, 57, 259
Washington State Labor Council, 95
Washington State Parks, 180–81
Washington State School Directors Association. *See* WSSDA (Washington State School Directors Association)
Washington Water Power, 260–61

water and sewer districts, 253, 254, 257, 261–62, 267–68, 304
Ways & Means Committee (Senate), 128–29, 186–88
Welfare Reform Act, 171
Wenatchee WA, 244–45, 267, 312, 314–16
West, Jim, 166
Weyerhaeuser, 317
Whatcom County v. Hirst, 189, 269
whips, legislative, 130
whites, 23, 60–61, 146, 167
Wolfe, Frank, 214–16
women's issues, 114, 156, 328
Woodbridge Corporate Park, 317
Woodland State Airport, 174
workers' compensation, 73, 177–78

WPPA (Washington Public Ports Association), 270–71
WPPSS (Washington Public Power Supply System), 259–60
Wright, Greg, 174
WSDOT (Department of Transportation), 170, 173–76
WSSDA (Washington State School Directors Association), 256
Wylie, Sharon, 12
Wyman, Kim, 61, 62, 143–44

Yakama Nation, 22, 283, 295–96
Yakima WA, 246
Yellowstone National Park, 181

Zeiger, Hans, 15–16, 106, 117, 134, 336

IN THE POLITICS AND GOVERNMENTS OF THE AMERICAN STATES SERIES

Alabama Government and Politics
By James D. Thomas and
William H. Stewart

Alaska Politics and Government
By Gerald A. McBeath and
Thomas A. Morehouse

*Arizona Politics and Government:
The Quest for Autonomy,
Democracy, and Development*
By David R. Berman

*Arkansas Politics and
Government*, second edition
By Diane D. Blair and Jay Barth

*Colorado Politics and Government:
Governing the Centennial State*
By Thomas E. Cronin and
Robert D. Loevy

*Colorado Politics and Policy:
Governing a Purple State*
By Thomas E. Cronin and
Robert D. Loevy

Delaware Politics and Government
By William W. Boyer and
Edward C. Ratledge

*Hawai'i Politics and Government: An
American State in a Pacific World*
By Richard C. Pratt with Zachary Smith

*Idaho Politics and Government:
Culture Clash and Conflicting
Values in the Gem State*
By Jasper M. LiCalzi

*Illinois Politics and Government: The
Expanding Metropolitan Frontier*
By Samuel K. Gove and
James D. Nowlan

*Kansas Politics and Government:
The Clash of Political Cultures*
By H. Edward Flentje and
Joseph A. Aistrup

*Kentucky Politics and Government:
Do We Stand United?*
By Penny M. Miller

Maine Politics and Government,
second edition
By Kenneth T. Palmer, G.
Thomas Taylor, Marcus A.
LiBrizzi, and Jean E. Lavigne

*Maryland Politics and Government:
Democratic Dominance*
By Herbert C. Smith and John T. Willis

*Michigan Politics and Government:
Facing Change in a Complex State*
By William P. Browne and
Kenneth VerBurg

Minnesota Politics and Government
By Daniel J. Elazar, Virginia
Gray, and Wyman Spano

*Mississippi Government and Politics:
Modernizers versus Traditionalists*
By Dale Krane and Stephen D. Shaffer

Nebraska Government and Politics
Edited by Robert D. Miewald

Nevada Politics and Government: Conservatism in an Open Society
By Don W. Driggs and
Leonard E. Goodall

New Jersey Politics and Government: Suburban Politics Comes of Age, second edition
By Barbara G. Salmore and
Stephen A. Salmore

New York Politics and Government: Competition and Compassion
By Sarah F. Liebschutz, with Robert W. Bailey, Jeffrey M. Stonecash, Jane Shapiro Zacek, and Joseph F. Zimmerman

North Carolina Government and Politics
By Jack D. Fleer

Oklahoma Politics and Policies: Governing the Sooner State
By David R. Morgan, Robert E. England, and George G. Humphreys

Oregon Politics and Government: Progressives versus Conservative Populists
By Richard A. Clucas, Mark Henkels, and Brent S. Steel

Rhode Island Politics and Government
By Maureen Moakley and
Elmer Cornwell

South Carolina Politics and Government
By Cole Blease Graham Jr.
and William V. Moore

Utah Politics and Government: American Democracy among a Unique Electorate
By Adam R. Brown

Washington State Politics and Government
By T. M. Sell

West Virginia Politics and Government
By Richard A. Brisbin Jr., Robert Jay Dilger, Allan S. Hammock, and Christopher Z. Mooney

West Virginia Politics and Government, second edition
By Richard A. Brisbin Jr., Robert Jay Dilger, Allan S. Hammock, and L. Christopher Plein

Wisconsin Politics and Government: America's Laboratory of Democracy
By James K. Conant

To order or obtain more information on these or other University of Nebraska Press titles, visit nebraskapress.unl.edu.

www.ingramcontent.com/pod-product-compliance
Lightning Source LLC
Chambersburg PA
CBHW030332240426
43661CB00052B/1605